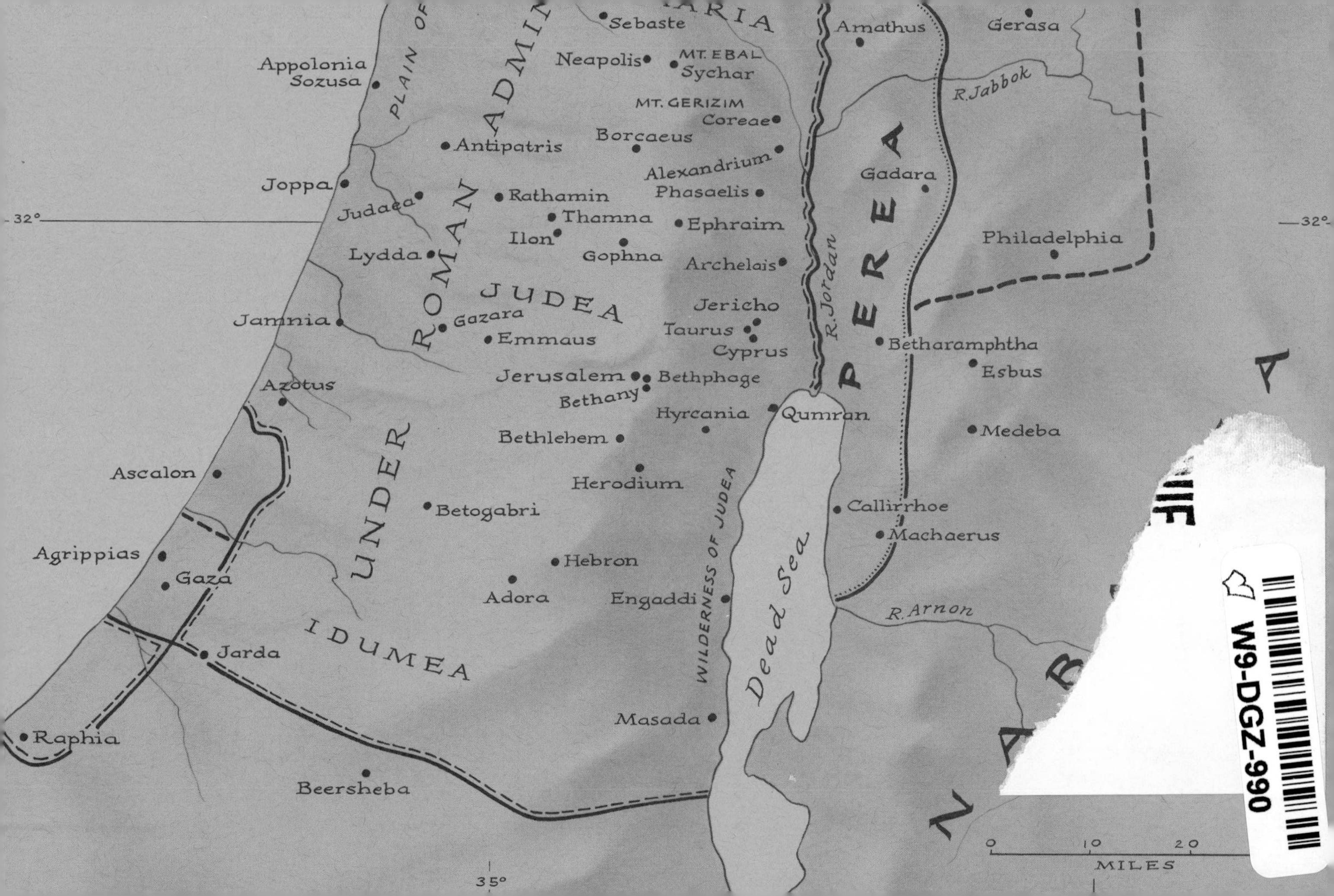

ROMAN ADMI
UNDER ROMAN
JUDEA
IDUMEA
PEREA
PLAIN OF
Sebaste
Neapolis
MT. EBAL
Sychar
MT. GERIZIM
Coreae
Borcaeus
Alexandrium
Phasaelis
Ephraim
Archelais
Appolonia
Sozusa
Antipatris
Joppa
Judaea
Rathamin
Thamna
Ilon
Gophna
Lydda
Jamnia
Gazara
Emmaus
Jericho
Taurus
Cyprus
Jerusalem
Bethphage
Bethany
Hyrcania
Qumran
Azotus
Bethlehem
Herodium
Ascalon
Betogabri
Hebron
Adora
Engaddi
Agrippias
Gaza
Jarda
Raphia
Beersheba
Masada
WILDERNESS OF JUDEA
Dead Sea
R. Jordan
Amathus
Gerasa
R. Jabbok
Gadara
Philadelphia
Betharamphtha
Esbus
Medeba
Callirrhoe
Machaerus
R. Arnon
32°
32°
35°
0 10 20
MILES

ERNEST W. SAUNDERS

JESUS IN THE GOSPELS

PRENTICE-HALL, INC.
Englewood Cliffs, N. J.

In honor of my father and in memory of my mother

Μακάριοι οἱ μὴ ἰδόντες καὶ πιστεύσαντες

Most of the scriptural quotations in this book are from the *Revised Standard Version of the Bible,* copyrighted 1946 and 1952 by the Division of Christian Education, National Council of Churches, and used by permission. The translation used in a few passages is *The New English Bible: New Testament,* copyrighted by The Delegates of the Oxford University Press and The Syndics of the Cambridge University Press, 1961, and is reprinted by permission. Qumran texts identified as Gaster, *Scriptures* are quoted from *The Dead Sea Scriptures,* translated by Theodor H. Gaster, copyright © 1956 by Theodor H. Gaster, reprinted by permission of Doubleday & Company, Inc. The *Gospel of Thomas* is cited from the English translation of *The Gospel According to Thomas,* edited by A. Guillaumont, H.-Ch. Puech, G. Quispel, W. Till, and Yassah 'Abd al-Masīḥ, copyright by E. J. Brill, Leiden and reprinted by permission.

Library of Congress Catalog Card Number: 67-10316
Printed in the United States of America

Current Printing (last digit):

10 9 8 7 6 5 4 3 2 1

PRENTICE-HALL INTERNATIONAL, INC., *London*
PRENTICE-HALL OF AUSTRALIA, PTY. LTD., *Sydney*
PRENTICE-HALL OF CANADA, LTD., *Toronto*
PRENTICE-HALL OF INDIA PRIVATE LTD., *New Delhi*
PRENTICE-HALL OF JAPAN, INC., *Tokyo*

PREFACE

No one will ever produce the single definitive study of Jesus of Nazareth, nor of any other decisive figure in human history. It is folly to try. Still it is necessary from time to time to gather the results of specialized studies in a fresh attempt at an interpretative presentation. This is just such a bold effort. It is designed principally for use in courses on the New Testament on the college level. The reading suggestions and documentation appearing in the notes are intended for the guidance of advanced students on the seminary level. Beyond that, I hope that the book will be of some interest to laymen and pastors.

The reader deserves to know something of the basic viewpoint that shapes this study. It seems clear to me that Jesus and his work can never be properly seen apart from the community that he brought to life and that preserved the memory of his words and deeds. This interpretation of his short career is therefore set within the preaching and teaching context of the early Church, which was the outcome of his mission. We may not possess the exact words of Jesus or know the precise circumstances of every action that occurred; but we do know what they meant at a very early date to those who knew him, and we have reason to believe that these associates had a faithful if sometimes faltering insight into their true meaning.

We accept the position of the "new quest of the historical Jesus" that through modern historical methods we can obtain valid insight into the actual happenings, the self-understanding, and the purposes of Jesus himself. To supplement the material in the Gospels, we have drawn upon the Dead Sea Scrolls from Qumran and the noncanonical sayings of Jesus in the apocryphal Gospels, especially the recently discovered *Gospel of Thomas*. To succeed at all, our quest must employ the disciplines of historical-critical study. But there must also be an openness and permissiveness on the reader's part to view these happenings "from the inside." Berdyaev's description of his search to understand Dostoevsky expresses our position:

> We are not going to imitate so many of our contemporaries, who are inclined always to suspect as it were a hidden disease in a writer whom they love and so treat of him scalpel in hand: we will come to [the Gospels] by the believer's road, plunging straightforwardly into the whirlpool of [their] dynamic ideas that we may attain the secret of [their] fundamental conception of the world." *

A word about the symbols. Q Matthew and Q Luke refer to the non-Marcan sayings and parables that appear in both these Gospels, with no argument about their derivation from one or more written sources. Similarly, M and L refer to collections of sayings and narratives that are reserved to the Gospels of Matthew and Luke respectively. The symbols used to identify the Dead Sea Scrolls follow the conventional form: 1QS, the *Manual of Discipline* or the *Rule of the Congregation;* 1QSa, the *Rule of the Future Congregation* or the *Two Column Fragment;* 1QSb, the *Blessings;* 1QM, the *War Scroll;* 1QH, the *Hymns of Thanksgiving;* CD, the *Damascus Document;* 1QpHab, the *Habakkuk Commentary;* 4Q Testimonia, the *Testimony Document*. Comprehensive discussions of certain texts have necessitated the duplicate use of some of the sayings and parables.

There remains the welcome task of saluting those persons who have given helpful guidance on particular matters. My teaching colleagues, Dr. Carl W. Christensen, M.D., and Dr. Tyler Thompson, gave me the benefit of their critical evaluation of the chapter on the miracles, where many a stronger ship than mine has foundered. Miss Margaret Rigg gave counsel on the interpretation of Jesus' mission in modern art. The Rev. Dr. Philip F. Whitmer gave many hours of service in checking references. The Reverend Adolf Hansen, doctoral candidate in New Testament studies at Garrett Theological Seminary, devoted painstaking care to the preparation

* Nicholas Berdyaev, *Dostoevsky* (New York: Sheed & Ward, Inc., 1957).

of the indexes. Bishop Dwight E. Loder, *amicus carus,* under whose seminary leadership this project was largely carried on, generously assisted at one critical point by arranging a term's leave of absence. These are all good friends to whom I am deeply indebted.

How is one to acknowledge the devotion and patience of a wife and family in the accomplishment of such a task? My wife has typed the manuscript several times and has helped on innumerable points of style and interpretation. These are labors of love, but a love gratefully requited.

E. W. S.
Garrett Theological Seminary

CONTENTS

LIST OF ILLUSTRATIONS

CHAPTER I

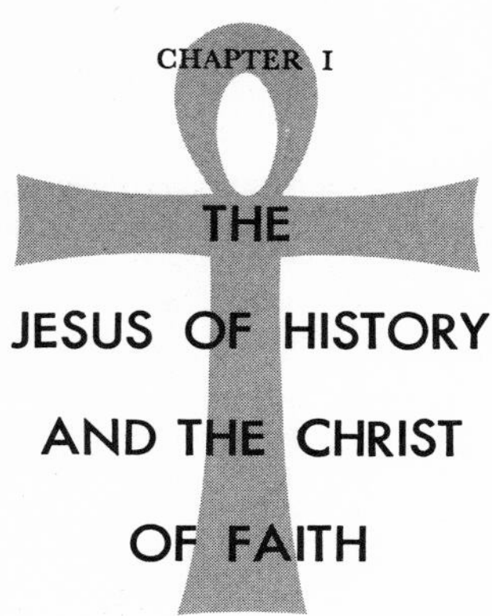

THE JESUS OF HISTORY AND THE CHRIST OF FAITH

> The fixed starting point of all our knowledge about him is that he is the crucified One whom the community, originating in his band of disciples, believed to be the risen Messiah.*

The religious movement that exploded out of Jerusalem into the world of Tiberius Claudius Nero Germanicus in the middle of the first century in the Christian era, eight hundred years after the founding of Rome, was destined to reshape the course of all subsequent history. At the outset this would have appeared preposterous to a citizen of the *Orbis Romanus*. To him, if he were aware of it at all, the Christian sect probably represented another of those exotic Oriental cults which in the later years of the Republic had been imported into the West and caught the popular fancy for guarantees of good fortune and eternal blessedness. He might have considered it a Jewish mystery sect, an Eastern dissentient movement in questionable relationship with the synagogues which spawned it. Other sacramental rites had claimed to impart divine grace to the believer from a risen lord who benevolently offered men deliverance from the rigid necessities of Fate or the caprice of Fortune. The Phrygian mother goddess Cybele and her son or consort Attis, Syrian-born Astarte and her consort Tammuz, the resurrected Egyptian god Osiris, or the bull-slayer Mithras—were not

* Nils Dahl in Carl E. Braaten and Roy A. Harrisville, eds., *Kerygma and History* (New York: Abingdon Press, 1962), p. 154.

their devotees equally noisy in their claims of a *soteria* (salvation) available to the initiate in their holy rites and ceremonies?

To others, this new cult may have exhibited more similarity to the popular philosophical societies of the day. Missionary philosopher-evangelists, representing the Stoic and Cynic schools, were a common sight in the streets and market places of Roman-Hellenistic cities. Like the Christian missionaries, they were itinerant preachers who exhorted all who would listen to renounce the sensual cares and fleeting pleasures of the world and to cultivate those basic virtues that were the hallmarks of the mature man.[1] Was this Christian philosophy, then, simply another program of living calculated to lead one to a new self-sufficiency to face with unruffled endurance the problems of ordinary existence?

To the orthodox Jew of the Dispersion, the new movement may well have appeared to be another abortive rebel force like that of the self-styled prophet Theudas.[2] It was no more than a gang of fanatical royalists or world upenders who made claims similar to those of the Covenanters of Qumran and other apocalyptic dreamers that the Davidic Kingdom was soon to be reinstated. Perhaps more sympathetic than their Palestinian kinsmen to the nonlegalistic aspect of the new message, Greek Jews nevertheless branded the sect heretical, a threat to the cherished faith of the fathers. It was notoriously lax toward the Law of Moses and openly blasphemous in its claim that the God who had promised to raise up a deliverer for his people Israel had actually fulfilled his word in a crucified Galilean peasant.

But the fellowship of those who held this belief in Jesus of Nazareth was for the most part unshaken by these contemptuous comments or hostile actions. In the opening sentences of what may be the earliest New Testament document, Paul expresses his deep gratitude for the faithful witnessing of a Greek society of Christians in the face of persecutions and afflictions (I Thess. 1:2–8; cf. II Thess. 1:3–12). Later there would be many confessors of the faith who would give testimony before tribunals and pay the penalty for it (Acts 22:20; Rev. 2:13; I Pet. 4:12–19). But neither the discipline of the syna-

[1] Some of the satires of Horace, Persius, and Juvenal are modeled on a literary form of these moral exhortations called a *diatribē*. Examples of the Stoic-Cynic popular addresses, together with other texts illustrative of life and thought in the Roman world of the first century, can be read in the excellent collection of C. K. Barrett, *The New Testament Background: Selected Documents* (New York: The Macmillan Company, 1957), pp. 75–79.

[2] Acts 5:36; Josephus, *Antiquities* XX.5.1.

gogues nor the repressive measures of imperial officers could subdue the rising voice of these preachers or control the expansion of new societies in the leading cities of the Eastern provinces. Their stubbornly held convictions and missionary zeal began slowly to exert a noticeable effect on the world-weary spirit of the empire.

The Messianic Faith of the Early Church's Message and Life

The last forty years in the study of the Gospels have witnessed an intensive investigation into the first two decades following the death of Jesus to determine how his memory was preserved in the period before the beginning of written records. This stage of oral transmission has been the object of a research method originating in Germany and employed subsequently by other biblical scholars. Termed form-history or form-criticism (*Formgeschichte*), this method calls for an analysis of the Gospel materials in the light of certain conclusions reached from a study of folk literature in general. Its professed aim is to study the oral tradition behind the Gospels, to discover the situations confronting the early Church that led to the selection of the individual stories and sayings we find in the Gospels, and to show how these reflections were used in the life and work of the Church. It is held that the form of a particular anecdote or parable is impressed upon it by the social-historical situation which prompted it. By relating single stories and sayings in the Gospels to specific situations in early Christian life, it is possible to recover a history of the development of the tradition and to distinguish the earliest and presumably most authentic accounts from the later and secondary material.[3]

Such studies have pointed up sharply the remarkably diverse activities of the early Jewish-Christian church. Of central significance was its mission into Jewish and, later, Roman society. Though often frightened, perplexed, and resistant, these first believers slowly realized

---

3 Pioneer works are those of Martin Dibelius, *From Tradition to Gospel*, trans. Bertram L. Woolf (New York: Charles Scribner's Sons, 1935), and *The Message of Jesus Christ*, trans. Frederick C. Grant (New York: Charles Scribner's Sons, 1939); and Rudolf Bultmann, *History of the Synoptic Tradition*, trans. John Marsh (New York: Harper & Row, Publishers, 1963). Other helpful studies are Vincent Taylor, *The Formation of the Gospel Tradition* (London: Macmillan & Co., Ltd., 1935); E. B. Redlich, *Form Criticism, Its Value and Limitations* (New York: Charles Scribner's Sons, 1939); and Rudolf Bultmann and Karl Kundsin, *Form Criticism*, trans. Frederick C. Grant (New York: Harper Torchbooks, 1962).

the full implications of Jesus' invitation to social outcasts and to non-Jews like a Roman officer or a Phoenician woman. When they were convinced, they went out to make disciples of all nations. Even before Paul, the great apostle to the Gentiles, the Jerusalem church had begun its mission to the Jews of the Dispersion, four million of them scattered in principal towns and cities of the empire. They carried the word of salvation also to those God-fearing Gentiles who were adherents though not full members of the synagogues of the Dispersion.[4]

By the middle of the century, a planned mission to the Gentiles was well established with the endorsement of the church leaders at Jerusalem. In friendly and unfriendly situations, in their own vicinity and farther afield, Christian partisans engaged in evangelical witness to the people of the empire, proclaiming Jesus as sole Lord, against the claims of Lord Mithras or Lord Caesar. They carried on debates with Jewish opponents, as Stephen and Paul had done,[5] endeavoring to prove by the Hebrew prophets and psalmists that Jesus was surely the Messiah and that John the Baptist was his forerunner. The converts they received, young and old, were given a graduated instruction on the practice of the new life "in the Messiah" and the nature of their faith in Christ as God's salvation for men.

For all who took their discipleship seriously, whether recent converts or more experienced followers, there were practical, everyday problems to be faced and solved in view of their growing understanding of the gospel. What about marriage and divorce in this new human situation before the Day of Judgment? Were Jewish dietary restrictions, fasts, and the observance of the Sabbath binding upon Gentile Christians? If believers were citizens of a new commonwealth, what about their obligations to the realm of Caesar? Did Christian scruples permit fraternizing with friends and neighbors in their cultic rituals? What was the total relationship of Church and culture? How were disciplinary problems within the fellowship to be dealt with and a responsible kind of leadership vouchsafed? For all these and similar questions, guidance had to be sought in prayer and a fresh inquiry about the way of the Master who called them to the same faith and obedience urged upon those who first heard the call of the earthly Jesus. The inner life of the community was nourished in acts of prayer,

---

[4] See Rom. 16:7 where two Jewish-Christian missionaries preceding the time of Paul's work are named. Acts 11:19–21 is the earliest mention of Greeks accepted into the Jewish-Christian fellowship.

[5] Acts 6:8–9; 9:22, 28–29.

preaching of the Word, singing of both Jewish and Christian psalms and hymns, and confession of faith in creedal formularies, and in observance of the Breaking of Bread or the Lord's Supper.[6]

Within the context of corporate worship, and certainly in relation to Baptism and the Eucharist, Christian preaching or *kērygma* declared the Word afresh to the concrete problems and relationships of the believers. But that word of preaching was always securely bound to the original event of Jesus' ministry, death, and resurrection which disclosed God's action for men. Hence it included a recital of some elements of Jesus' story or message which confirmed or illustrated the exhortation. Thus under the daily guidance of the Holy Spirit, whom they believed to be the risen Christ in their midst, brotherly relationships were formed, tested, and extended.

The stories and sayings that later found embodiment in the unique literary form known as the Gospels had their original formulation in the practical life situations of missionary preaching and apologetic, catechetical, disciplinary, and liturgical activity. Our Gospel records transmit a deliberate selection from a total memory of Jesus' works and words. Whatever was relevant to worship, problems of conduct, self-defense, and, above all, the experience of forgiveness and new life was told and retold. But it was a "bringing to remembrance," as John's Gospel stoutly affirms, and never a wholesale creation out of the community's collective unconscious.[7]

Preaching the Faith

What was the message the followers of Jesus brought to their fellow Jews and to the peoples of the empire? How did they challenge their hearers? A careful study of the Lucan summary of Peter's preaching to the household of the Roman officer Cornelius at Caesarea, recorded in Acts 10:36–43, might arrive at an outline similar to this:

> God has sent the Spirit-ordained Messiah to Israel in the person of Jesus of Nazareth whose ministry of preaching and healing is certified by Peter who was among the witnesses (vss. 36–39).

---

[6] See Acts 2:42; 4:31. Examples of the Christian hymns referred to in Eph. 5:19 may perhaps be seen in the Lucan nativity poems (Luke 1–2) and the hymns of Revelation. Confessional summaries may be identified in such passages as Rom. 10:9; I Cor. 12:3; I Pet. 3:22; I Tim. 3:16. An early tradition of the Lord's Supper that Paul probably received when he was in the church at Antioch (ca. A.D. 40) is to be found in I Cor. 11:23–25.

[7] Note the explicit function of the Holy Spirit in the life of the Church to bear witness to the historical Jesus (John 14:26, 16:13).

Rejected and done to death, he was raised to life by God and appeared to those who were to be his special witnesses (vss. 40–41).

They received a commission from him to announce that he has been appointed to exercise the divine judgment at the End (vs. 42).

All this is the fulfillment of the prophets' testimony; forgiveness of sin is available in his name to all who believe (vs. 43).

When we compare the references Paul makes to the message he brought into the cities of the empire[8] with these sermon digests in Acts, a summary can be drawn up as follows:

The prophecies have been fulfilled and the New Age has dawned.
The long expected Messiah, born of David's line, has come.
He is Jesus of Nazareth, who, after John's preaching of repentance,
  did mighty works by God's power,
  was spurned by the Jews and executed by the Roman governor,
  was raised from the dead,
  was exalted to the right hand of God,
  and will come again as judge at the End.
Therefore let all who hear repent, receive forgiveness of sins through his name, and be baptized and assured of salvation.[9]

If this represents a major form of the earliest Christian kerygma, it may be analyzed into an announcement, an argument, and an appeal.

1. The announcement. The message basically was a welcome report that deliverance from this present age of sin and enmity into the dawning Kingdom of God was now offered to men by God's own act in the Messiah Jesus. To characterize the announcement as a gospel or good news (*euaggelion*) would suggest to the Jewish hearer a fulfillment of promises heralded by the psalmists and the prophets of Israel. Centuries before, the unknown Prophet of the Exile, whose writings were bound with those of Isaiah, announced to the Jewish exiles in their Babylonian resettlement that God was about to perform a mighty act of deliverance on their behalf. He speaks of himself, or perhaps another, as a "herald of good tidings" (*b^e^sôrâh*; Isa. 40:9). The good tidings is a message of an anticipated deliverance by the hand of God, the advent of his saving help to an oppressed people,

---

[8] See especially the passages in I Thess. 1:9–10; I Cor. 15:3–7; Rom. 1:2–4, 16–17; Gal. 1:4.

[9] Compare the account of a modern Bartok missionary to Eban tribes in Sarawak, who reported that his message stressed these simple affirmations: Jesus Christ came. He suffered. He died. He was raised to life. He continues in power. These are the principal kerygmatic themes of the earliest preaching.

the proclamation of a new freedom, the bestowal of his favor and judgment in a particular historical situation.

Against this rich background of meaning, the Christian evangelists declared the new event that they believed to be of supreme significance for all men. We need to keep in mind that the word "gospel" in the New Testament does not refer to a printed book in the sense we use generally. It refers rather to the total message of salvation through the life, death, and resurrection of Jesus Christ. Thus it may be termed the "gospel of God"[10] or the "gospel of Jesus Christ"[11] or simply the "gospel."[12] The word may also be employed to signify the story of the whole ministry of Jesus, because both the earliest preachers and the later Evangelists or gospel writers were convinced that this message of salvation included not only the words Jesus spoke but also his curative skills and, in fact, his total person. He was both the bearer and the very embodiment of the good news. He taught about the nature and conditions of the Kingdom of God. But more: he himself *was* that Kingdom in living, concrete expression.

The announcement was presented as a message of salvation containing a twofold promise: (a) in the immediate present, the assurance of God's love which had forgiven the sinner and opened up prospects of a new kind of life for him; and (b) in the future, the judgment of all mankind and the believer's share in the new age of peace and blessing. That this had somehow been made possible in the life, death, and resurrection of Jesus was the determinative center of primitive theology and community life. God had certified the messiahship of Jesus by the fact of the resurrection (Acts 2:36) and given him that august name which is above every name, Lord (Phil. 2:9–11).[13] To them, Jesus had made himself known in all the magisterial authority of God himself and shared with him his glory and sovereignty over the whole world. In exercising his lordship he laid absolute claim to their obedience and devotion—an extraordinary claim.

2. The argument. The announcement was supported by an argu-

---

10 Matt. 4:23, 24:14; Mark 1:14; Acts 20:24; Rom. 1:1; I Pet. 4:17; etc.

11 Mark 1:1; Rom. 1:9; I Cor. 9:12; II Cor. 9:13; etc.

12 Matt. 26:13; Mark 1:15, 8:35; Acts 15:7; Rom. 1:16; Rev. 14:6; etc. The noun *euaggelion* alone or in combination is found seven times in Mark and four times in Matthew. Luke uses only the verb (twice). Both forms are lacking in John.

13 The Greek word for Lord, *kyrios,* was already a feature of the oriental Hellenistic religions of the empire as well as a divine title in the emperor cult. See the distinction Paul draws in I Cor. 8:5–6. For one of the earliest prayers addressed to Jesus as Lord see I Cor. 16:22 and compare Rev. 22:20.

ment designed to show that this ministry of life, death, and resurrection constituted the crisis and completion in a series of divine acts God had performed in the history of the Hebrew people. What had occurred was not an isolated event intruded into the course of history. Instead, Jesus' career represented the fulfillment of what had been spoken through prophet and psalmist of old. "We bring you the good news that what God promised to the fathers, this he has fulfilled to us their children by raising Jesus" (Acts 13:32f.; cf. John 1:45). In early Christian preaching this conviction is the outcome of a whole theology of history that recognized the continuity of a redemptive activity in the life of the people of God from their earliest days to the present hour.

It is often observed that the Gospel of Matthew in no less than a dozen instances correlates some experience in the ministry of Jesus with a prophetic testimony claimed to anticipate it. At least two are erroneously identified (Matt. 13:35 and 27:9–10), and others represent tortuous wresting of prophetic texts out of their original context to bear new meanings. Thus Jeremiah's graphic description of the heartbreaking division of families in the time of the Babylonian deportations of 597 and 586 B.C. is held to be fulfilled in the massacre of the infants of Bethlehem by the furious king. Though the modern reader may be unmoved by Matthew's effort to establish the continuities of prophecy and fulfillment, he may recognize that this is simply an extreme form of an insight which finds more sober and convincing expression by other New Testament writers. It is not simply that coming events cast their shadow before. There is also a divinely established pattern to history within which there are movements of God among men that are begun, continued, and brought to completion. For the early Christians the historical fact of Jesus Christ was a crucial act of God in which the hope of Israel was unexpectedly fulfilled and the true center and meaning of history were dramatically exposed. But they were sure that clues to what that interpretative event might be had already been given to the fathers and prophets of old, for as Amos had contended, "Surely the Lord God does nothing, without revealing his secret to his servants the prophets" (Amos 3:7).

These abundant scriptural quotations, together with the surprising number of manifest and subtle allusions to Old Testament sayings or events interspersed within the four Gospels, reveal the writers' intention to show the correlation of Jesus' ministry with earlier prophecies. There is a richly allusive language form, for example, in the prophecies of the sufferings Jesus will undergo in Jerusalem, which requires that we be well acquainted with the story of the Exodus from Egypt. The Passion Story was enriched by many details drawn from Psalms 22 and 60 as evidence of the fulfillment of scriptural promises. If we compare the prophecies of the Passion with the Servant Songs of the Second Isaiah, or the entry into Jerusalem with the prophecy of Zechariah, Chapter 9, it is strikingly evident that each of the Gospel writers is concerned to relate the total ministry of Jesus to the context of the Old Testament.

This argument bears witness to the conviction that there is a pattern of salvation history interwoven in a special way with the history of Israel. That process has its consequence and climax in the coming of Jesus Christ in whom all God's promises given through the prophets and psalmists of Israel find their *Yes* (II Cor. 1:20). Both Jewish and Greek converts to the new faith were encouraged to search the Scriptures (John 5:39; Acts 17:11) to discover that the prophetic witness to the Messiah had become an historical happening in Jesus of Nazareth.

3. The appeal. The message was brought to focus, finally, in an appeal to repent and to be baptized (Acts 2:38; 3:19, 26; 10:48). Men were even now confronted by God in judgment and were summoned to make a decision. They were earnestly exhorted to repent and believe the good news of God's act in Christ that they might receive forgiveness of sins and the gift of the Holy Spirit. Adopting the eschatological sign preached and enacted by John the Baptist, the early Christian communities accepted penitents by baptism in the name of Jesus. They offered the promise of the Spirit's entrance into their lives, filling them with all joy and peace in believing and supplying incontrovertible evidence that God's New Age was an assured reality. Jewish teaching had maintained that the power of the Spirit, singularly active in the time of the great prophets, would finally be bestowed upon all God's faithful at the beginning of that New Age which was the true destiny of history. In the reality of the Holy Spirit, the New Age was already realized for these believers. Through this divine power binding them into a community, the Messiah Jesus exercised his lordship. Even if allowance is made for some exaggeration in the figures reported in Acts, there was an impressively large response to the apostles' appeal, such that the Church experienced a rapid expansion in Jerusalem alone.

These, then, represent the chief themes of the primitive evangelical message. Yet it would be misleading to describe early Christian preaching simply as a kind of a pre-creedal summary or a series of confessional propositions. The message of salvation was never considered to be a moral discourse nor a theological exposition of cardinal tenets of the faith, let alone a recital of biographical information. In the witness of the word, the Son of God was proclaimed in such a way that he confronted the hearer in that immediate moment and called him to a decision that could lead him from slavery to freedom. Just as the word kerygma in common Greek of the time referred to both the message brought by a herald or crier and the act of proclaiming it, so in the New Testament, kerygma must be understood as both the recital of the historical facts of the gospel story and the presentation of an existential claim upon the hearer.[14]

Teaching and Defending the Faith

The proclamation of the gospel in the first generation of Christian believers was centered in the life, death, and resurrection of Jesus as the supreme redemptive event accomplished for man. But though the cross on the hill rather than the Sermon on the Mount determined the first form of the message, questions of an ethical and theological nature quickly arose for those who were initiated into the life of the community. Guidance and instruction in the faith and practices of Jesus' followers were needed for these beginners, for the gospel was preached both as an invitation and as a demand. Their distinctive personal and group behavior was to be a witness of salvation to the pagan world.[15]

Some scholars speak of this catechetical instruction, or *didachē,* exclusively in terms of ethical and disciplinary guidance, but it is more likely that the scope of Christian teaching embraced a full range of problems confronting the new converts. These included doctrinal, apologetic, and liturgical concerns as well as ethical considerations. There was probably a common body of such "disciple teaching," based upon the remembered words of Jesus, in use among the several Christian groups. Thus Paul praises some Corinthian friends because they "maintain the traditions even as I have delivered them to you"

---

[14] This aspect of the New Testament kerygma has been emphasized in the contemporary existentialist interpretation of the New Testament by Professor Bultmann and his followers, whereas Professor C. H. Dodd has called attention principally to its propositional or creedal character. For this two-fold meaning, compare I Cor. 1:21 and 2:4.

[15] Matt. 5:14–16; I Pet. 2:12. According to the Acts, one of the earliest descriptions of Christianity was the "Way," that is, a conduct and action: Acts 9:2; 16:17; 19:9, 23; 22:4; 24:14, 22.

(I Cor. 11:2), or exhorts the Thessalonians to "stand firm and hold to the traditions which you were taught by us, either by word of mouth or by letter" (II Thess. 2:15). When the catechetical portions of his epistles are compared with similar sections in non-Pauline epistles in the New Testament, a basic similarity is discovered, suggesting that these traditions and instructions are derived from a common body of teaching.[16] It is evident that these primitive Christian catechisms would include many of the sayings and parables of Jesus which described the nature of life in the Kingdom of God. Perhaps in just such practical life situations, the Church arranged and preserved many of Jesus' words before the gospel was written.

Unlike Stoic ethics, the moral guidance given the new convert was never understood as a self-contained way of life which led through rigorous discipline to a state of self-sufficiency independent of all outer circumstances. In the New Testament there is not the separation that modern man often makes between doctrine and ethics, religious faith and behavioral precepts. "In Christianity, as in Judaism, the *kerygma* announces the mighty acts in which God established His new covenant with His people, and the moral obligations set forth in the *didaché* arise within that covenant."[17] Failure to recognize this basic fact has often led to a distortion of the Jesus of the Gospels into the energetic religious reformer or humanitarian idealist of many liberal lives of Jesus, and to the popular summary of Christianity as an admonition to golden-rule living. But the New Testament witness is quite clear that Jesus' moral teaching is a theonomous ethic, a way of living which emerges out of a total way of looking at the world and man and their invisible origins.

Worship

As men and women met together for corporate worship within the fellowship, as well as in their evangelistic work, controversy and debate, and catechetical instruction, Jesus was affirmed Lord. In their services of baptism and general worship, summaries of the apostolic faith found expression in varied creedal forms. One of the earliest

---

16 Compare, for example, I Thess. 5:14–18 with Heb. 13:1–3 and I Pet. 3:8–9. Charles Harold Dodd, *Gospel and Law* (New York: Columbia University Press, 1951), Chap. i; also "The Primitive Catechism and the Sayings of Jesus," in A. J. B. Higgins, ed., *New Testament Essays* (Manchester: University of Manchester Press, 1959), pp. 106–18; Philip Carrington, *The Primitive Christian Catechism* (Cambridge: Cambridge University Press, 1940).

17 Dodd, *Gospel and Law*, p. 12.

may have been the brief phrase, "Jesus is Lord" (*kyrios*) (Rom. 10:9; I Cor. 12:3; cf. II Cor. 4:5; Phil. 2:11; Col. 2:6). These first forms of the later trinitarian confessions of faith, like the apostolic preaching, made the forthright claim that in the historical work of Jesus of Nazareth the reign of God in history had entered a new and final stage. A later creedal formulary, preserved in I Timothy, expresses it this way:

> Great indeed, we confess, is the mystery of our religion:
> He[18] was manifested in the flesh
> vindicated in the Spirit,
> seen by angels,
> preached among the nations,
> believed on in the world
> taken up in glory.

The psalter of the synagogue became the hymnal of the early Church, but from the beginning, Christian psalms and hymns were freely composed for use in worship (Eph. 5:19–20; Col. 3:16); fragments are found throughout the New Testament.[19] Paul believed that in the regular assemblies, for the purpose of giving thanks to God in worship, the life of the community was shaped into the form of the body of Christ. Early in the second century the Roman governor of the combined provinces of Bithynia and Pontus in Asia Minor described the practices of the Christians in his area as follows:

> They affirmed, however, the whole of their guilt, or their error, was, that they were in the habit of meeting on a certain fixed day before it was light, when they sang in alternate verses a hymn to Christ, as to a god, and bound themselves by a solemn oath, not to any wicked deeds, but never to commit any fraud, theft, or adultery, never to falsify their word, nor deny a trust when they should be called upon to deliver it up; after which it was their custom to separate, and then reassemble to partake of food—but food of an ordinary and innocent kind.[20]

In the expositions or sermons—"the ministry of the word" as Luke describes it (Acts 6:4)—which were a regular part of early Christian

---

[18] I Tim. 3:16. Most manuscripts read "God" for "he," and since in Greek the words are similar (*theos, hos*) it is not impossible that this was the original form.

[19] Rom. 1:3–4; I Cor. 15:3–5; Eph. 5:14; Phil. 2:5–11; Col. 1:15–20; II Tim. 2:11–13; I Pet. 3:18–22; the hymns of Luke 1–2 and the Revelation to John. See further, Oscar Cullmann, *The Earliest Christian Confessions* (London: Lutterworth, 1949); and J. N. D. Kelly, *Early Christian Creeds* (New York: Longmans Green & Co., Inc., 1950).

[20] Pliny the Younger, *Letters* X.96.

worship, opportunity was afforded for telling incidents from Jesus' life expressive of the total gospel message of salvation. The preacher elaborated these accounts in terms of the spiritual and ethical problems the community confronted daily. At the common meals, held at first daily and later on each "Lord's Day" or Sunday, the Passion Story was retold and the final messianic banquet anticipated. Some scholars even contend that the finished Gospels were originally written for use in services of worship. It is held, for instance, that the Gospel of Mark was a liturgical book framed on the basis of a primitive Jewish-Christian lectionary scheme. Others argue that the principal purpose of the writer of the fourth Gospel was to correlate the worship practices of the late first-century Church with their constitutive events in the ministry of Jesus.[21] In any event, it is important to recognize the intimate relationship of the Gospels to the worship life of the early Church. In them one finds the same convictional language voiced in the prayers and praises of early worship.

In these several ways the first members of the Christian societies of Palestine and the empire confessed their faith in Jesus as Lord and tried to win a similar response from others. But since the Messiah is never, in Judaism or Christianity, separated from his people, so these communities remembered and transmitted those teachings of the Messiah that marked out the path of the faithful follower. We have found no evidence of any identifiable interval between the historical ministry of Jesus and the budding faith of the Church where a view of a Jewish reformer was recast into a doctrine of a "Heavenly Redeemer." "The event was conceived of as a descending act of God, not as the ascending career of a man who was successful in the sphere of religion."[22] From the beginning of the Church's life, Jesus was acknowledged as the Messiah of Israel, the Lord of a new humanity, the coming Son of Man.

Jesus Beyond the Gospels

Evidence for the historical career of Jesus outside the four Gospels is admittedly scanty. Nonetheless it is important to remind ourselves

---

[21] For further discussion of these views see, e.g., Frederick C. Grant, *The Gospels: Their Origin and Their Growth* (New York: Harper & Row, Publishers, 1957); and James L. Price, *Interpreting the New Testament* (New York: Holt, Rinehart & Winston, Inc., 1961).

[22] Edwyn Hoskyns and Noel Davey, *The Riddle of the New Testament* (New York: Harcourt, Brace & World, Inc., 1931), p. 176.

that it is by no means wholly lacking. Jewish, Roman, and Christian documents testify to the reality of this life and the movement which found in it its origin and direction.

Years ago, the French historian Renan argued that a brief life of Jesus could be constructed from passages in the letters of Paul.[23] We learn that Jesus was born a Jew of the line of David (Gal. 4:4; Rom. 1:3; 9:5) and that he had a brother named James (Gal. 1:19). He observed a special meal with his disciples just before his death, signifying that they would share in the benefit of this ratification of a new covenant (I Cor. 11:23–25). He was crucified and buried (Gal. 3:1; I Cor. 2:2, *et passim;* 15:4). His own disciples are witnesses to the reality of his resurrection from the dead (I Cor. 15:5–7). Words of Jesus are quoted in the discussions of marriage in I Corinthians 7:10; ministerial support, I Corinthians 9:14; the Lord's Supper, I Corinthians 11:23–25; and perhaps in the teaching concerning the coming end of the age, I Thessalonians 4:15–16. Anyone familiar with the Sermon on the Mount cannot fail to catch its echoes in chapters 12–14 of the letter to the Romans. Renan sadly exaggerated the case; nonetheless some knowledge of the life and teaching of Jesus is presupposed by these fragmentary references.

This is true of other New Testament writings. The Caesarean speech of Peter in Acts 10 and the sermon of Paul in Antioch of Pisidia (Acts 13:23–31) show familiarity with some of the leading events in Jesus' career. It is well known that the famous dictum of Jesus, "It is more blessed to give than to receive," is not to be found anywhere in the Gospels, but rather in Paul's farewell address to the Ephesian elders (Acts 20:35). The Epistle of James may preserve a more original form of Jesus' plea for honesty in speech (5:12) than the more familiar wording of Matthew (5:37). The most graphic account of the agony of Jesus in Gethsemane is found in the Epistle to the Hebrews (5:7–8), which also specifies that the site of Jesus' execution was outside the city walls (13:12).

Of more debatable worth are the numerous stories and sayings ascribed to Jesus found outside the New Testament, scattered in the writings of early Church fathers, apocryphal gospels, marginal notes in early manuscripts of the canonical Gospels, and stray fragments of

---

[23] Cf. Maurice Goguel, *Life of Jesus,* trans. Olive Wyon (New York: The Macmillan Company, 1949), p. 119. Such an attempt, based on fifty passages, has been made by Giuseppe Ricciotti in his *Life of Christ,* trans. Alba I. Zizzamia (Milwaukee: Bruce Publishing Co., 1947), p. 91.

papyrus leaves.[24] In most instances they reflect the tradition incorporated in the New Testament Gospels, but there is a substantial residue of noncanonical sayings (*agrapha*) that claim to be authentic yet are unrepresented in the New Testament. However, many of these quickly reveal the sectarian interests of the groups in which they gained currency. One scholar sifts a hundred or more sayings and finds a maximum of twenty-one which are coherent with the teaching and attitudes of Jesus in the Gospels or which carry convincing attestation by reliable early leaders. We have no proof of their authenticity, but they lay a claim to historical value that merits consideration.[25] That number may well be extended in the light of the recently published collection of one hundred and fourteen sayings of Jesus collected in the Coptic *Gospel of Thomas.*

Reading the story of the baptism of Jesus in the *Gospel of the Hebrews,* a second-century Jewish-Christian Gospel which may have been used by the Jewish Christians at Alexandria,[26] one detects the apologetic concern to defend the sinlessness of Jesus in the face of his submission to baptism. This is even clearer in the account found in the *Gospel of the Ebionites* where the baptism becomes the moment when the heavenly Christ descends upon the human Jesus, forming a composite personality, as certain heretical teachers maintained.[27] Their position finds striking expression in the revised form of Jesus' words from the cross in the Gnostic *Gospel of Peter.* Other sayings involving free composition or modifications of canonical words may

---

24 The witness of early Christian inscriptions to the story of Jesus falls outside the scope of our inquiry. However, it is worth mentioning here that a Swedish scholar assigns two graffiti containing the name of Jesus to a date before A.D. 50. They appear on two ossuaries found near Jerusalem. See B. Gustafsson, "The Oldest Graffiti in the History of the Church?" *New Testament Studies,* III (1956–57), 65–69; cf. E. L. Sukenik, "The Earliest Records of Christianity," *American Journal of Archaeology,* LI (1947), 351–65.

25 Joachim Jeremias, *Unknown Sayings of Jesus,* trans. Reginald H. Fuller (London: SPCK, 1957), p. 30.

26 A detailed study of the Synoptic Gospels (a term signifying the similarity among the first three Gospels) necessitates the use of a synopsis or harmony. One of the most useful is the revised edition of *Gospel Parallels,* 2nd ed. (New York: Thomas Nelson & Sons, 1957), which employs the text of the Revised Standard Version supplemented with alternative readings from the manuscripts and the extra-canonical parallels. See pp. 10, 11.

27 Extant fragments of these Jewish-Christian Gospels and other apocryphal writings can be read in M. R. James, *The Apocryphal New Testament* (Oxford, Clarendon Press, 1953), or E. Schneemelcher, ed., *New Testament Apocrypha,* I, *The Gospels,* trans. ed. R. McL. Wilson (Philadelphia: The Westminster Press, 1963).

represent sanctions for the distinctive rules and ascetic practices of sectarian groups of heretical leanings.

Considerable excitement has recently been aroused over the discovery of a fourth-century Coptic manuscript near the little southern Egyptian hamlet of Es-Sayyâd (the ancient Chenoboskion), which contains no less than one hundred and fourteen sayings and parables ascribed to Jesus. The library of Chenoboskion was accidentally discovered in 1945, but the first of the writings was not made available until 1956; and the *Gospel of Thomas,* not until 1959.[28] There is no

Fig. 1. Ossuary with the name "Jesus" in Greek letters scratched in charcoal on the back was discovered in 1945 in a suburb of Jerusalem. In translation the graffito reads "Jesus, woe," which possibly is to be interpreted as a prayer of invocation meaning "Jesus, help." The ossuary (no. 7) dates from the early forties of the first century. See Chapter I, note 24. *From Plate LXXX, American Journal of Archaeology, Vol. 51 (1947), by courtesy of The Department of Archaeology, The Hebrew University of Jerusalem.*

28 The English translation of the Coptic text, made by an international committee of scholars, has been published as *The Gospel According to Thomas,* ed. Antoine Guillaumont *et al.* (New York: Harper & Row, Publishers, 1959). A popular account of the discovery of the codex and its significance, with a commentary on the text, is offered by R. M. Grant and D. N. Freedman, *The Secret Sayings of Jesus* (Garden City, N.Y.: Doubleday & Co., Inc., 1960). Interpretative studies may be consulted in Bertil Gaertner, *The Theology of the Gospel of Thomas,* trans. Eric J. Sharpe (New York: Harper & Row, Publishers, 1961); H. Montefiore and H. E. W. Turner, *Thomas and the Evangelists* (Naperville, Ill.: Alec R. Allenson, Inc., 1962).

doubt that the Gospel provides new evidence of the process involved in transmitting Jesus' teachings in the early Church and how they were understood in certain Egyptian circles. Some of the sayings offer minor variations to the more familiar forms of Jesus' teachings, explainable as stylistic improvement rather than doctrinal distortion. Others are known to us from the writings of the Church fathers. Mark's reference to the parables of Jesus (4:2) suggests that he is giving single examples of Jesus' teaching taken from a larger collection of parables than he intends to report. John disclaims any exhaustive comprehensiveness to his narrative account (20:30, 21:25).

Sweeping judgments on this bewildering variety of traditional material in the *Gospel of Thomas* are out of order. Each story and saying must be critically examined and evaluated by the criteria developed for determining levels of historical value. As we proceed with this present study, reference will be made from time to time to the Thomas collection of sayings. After such excursions, however, one returns to the New Testament Gospels with a new appreciation of their worth as sources for the understanding of the mission of Jesus.

There remains only to take account of the brief notices of the life of Jesus found in non-Christian sources. Rabbinic sources of the earliest period made sparse reference to Jesus, although the later period became bolder with defamatory stories contesting the Christian claims. The Jewish scholar Joseph Klausner has sifted the references to Jesus by the *Tannaim*,[29] identifying eight of those that may claim some historic value. The testimony may be summarized as: Jesus (Yeshua), they allege, was the offspring of an illicit union between a Roman soldier and a Jewish girl,[30] practised magic, ridiculed the teachings of the Jewish sages, led the people astray, asserted that he had not come to supplement, nor supplant, Torah, and expounded Scripture after the Pharisaic manner. On the eve of Passover he was hanged as a false teacher and a rabble-rouser. His five disciples were effective in curing some sick people in his name.[31] It seems as though these references are dependent upon Christian tradition; hence they offer little help

[29] Rabbis of the first two centuries of our era.

[30] A story known to Origen of Alexandria, who takes pains to refute it. *Contra Celsum* I.28, 32, 33.

[31] Joseph Klausner, *Jesus of Nazareth,* trans. Herbert Danby (New York: The Macmillan Company, 1925), pp. 18–54. Three allusions in the Mishnah are often identified as referring to Jesus (*Yebamoth* iv.13, *Aboth* v.19, *Sanhedrin* x.1f). Morris Goldstein, *Jesus in the Jewish Tradition* (New York: The Macmillan Company, 1950) counts 5 authentic references and 14 indirect allusions by the Tannaim; 7 authentic references and 15 indirect allusions by the Amoraim (third to the fifth centuries).

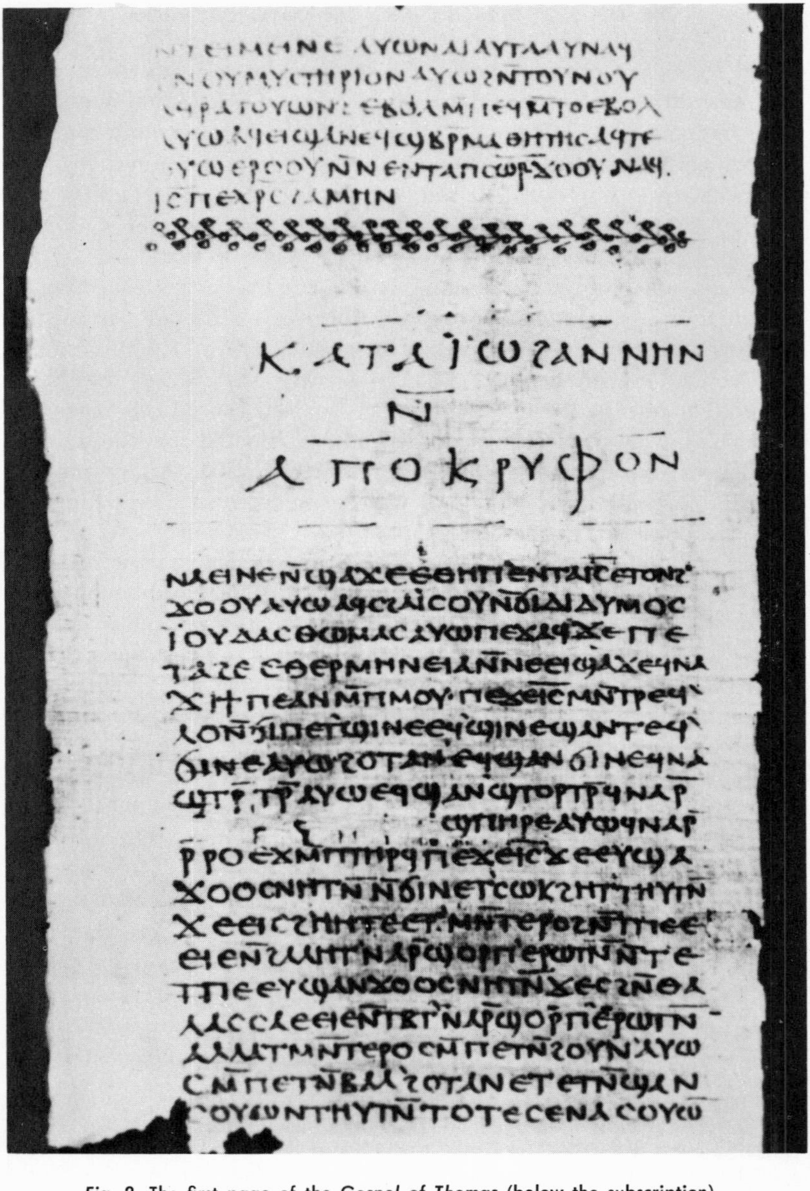

Fig. 2. The first page of the *Gospel of Thomas* (below the subscription), one of a collection of forty-nine Coptic writings unearthed about 1945 in a cemetery near the ancient town of Chenoboskion in Upper Egypt. The original Greek work was probably composed about A.D. 140. *Courtesy of Dr. Martin Krause.*

in our study. They do, however, confirm indirectly the basic witness of the Gospels and enable us to see how Jesus and the Christian movement were understood by the authorities of Judaism in the first two hundred years of Christianity.

Two passages referring to Jesus in the voluminous writings of the Jewish historian Flavius Josephus, a contemporary of the Evangelists (ca. A.D. 37–100), are frequently cited and variously assayed. In the *Antiquities* XVIII.3.3, a brief description of Jesus is given as a miracle worker and teacher who perished under the rule of the Roman governor Pilate. Coloration by a Christian editor of Josephus is patent, but it is possible that the passage has been adapted from a briefer reference to Jesus as one of those who instigated unrest among the Jews.[32] The second passage in Book XX.9.1, which records the violent death of James, "the brother of Jesus who was called the Christ," is more generally accepted as genuine.

The Samaritan chronicler Thallus, who may have written his now lost three-volume history about A.D. 50, refers to the darkness at the crucifixion as due to an eclipse. The most significant thing about this reference is that it would establish a knowledge of the Passion Story in non-Christian circles at Rome as early as the middle of the century, but the date of Thallus is uncertain.[33] In a letter addressed to the emperor Trajan about A.D. 110, Pliny the Younger, Roman governor of Bithynia-Pontus in Asia Minor, asks for advice about the handling of members of a "crude superstition" who, he says, assemble themselves together regularly on an appointed day and sing a hymn to a god they call Christ.[34] A few years later, ca. A.D. 115–117, the Roman historian Tacitus similarly associated a "mischievous superstition" during Nero's time with a certain Christus who was crucified during the administration of Pontius Pilate under the rule of Tiberius.[35]

---

32 This passage and the following may be read in Barrett, *Background,* pp. 196–200. So careful a scholar as Maurice Goguel is disposed to recognize the essential authenticity of both notices (*Life of Jesus,* pp. 75–82). The claim of Robert Eisler that a genuine historical reference to Jesus appears in two passages in a thirteenth-century Slavonic version of the *Jewish War* (*Halôsis*) is dismissed by most scholars, who regard them as pieces of late Jewish apologetic interpolated into the text. They may be read in Barrett, *Background,* pp. 205–7.

33 "Thallus, in the third book of his history, calls this darkness an eclipse of the sun, but in my opinion he is wrong." Julius Africanus, quoted by the Byzantine historian George the Syncellus.

34 Pliny the Younger, *Letters* X.96.

35 "Exitiabilis superstitio," Tacitus, *Annals* XV. 44 (ca. A.D. 115).

Finally, in his studies on the *Lives of the Caesars,* written in the first quarter of the second century, the historian Suetonius (A.D. 65–135) refers to disturbances within the Jewish community in Rome in the time of Claudius, which he indirectly attributes to the influences of an agitator named Chrestus.[36] The information gleaned from these pagan writers adds nothing to the witness of Josephus.

Were we limited to these Jewish, Latin, and Greek sources, we should know little of consequence about the mission and message of Jesus. Nevertheless, they bring testimony to the existence of a Jewish leader who lived in Judea and was called the "Anointed One" by his followers. He was supposed to have performed miracles and taught the people. He was executed by a Roman civil governor named Pontius Pilate. Twenty years later a sect of his followers instigated riots among the Jews at Rome which resulted in the expulsion of the Jewish community. And finally, the sect continued to flourish after Nero's time in the face of considerable adversity and persecution. Now we must turn to the Gospels to fill in this outline.

The Continuing Search for the Historical Jesus

It is indubitable that the four Gospels and the complexes of earlier oral tradition which underlie them afford primary knowledge of what first-century Christians believed about Jesus and how they understood his mission. But the serious student is not content to consider only the beliefs and practices of the early Church. He wants to know whether this presentation of the life and teachings of Jesus is the product of a devotional imagination, the imitation of other cult figures in Hellenistic religions, or whether there is an essential reliability to these Gospel records for an understanding of Jesus *as he actually was.* The contemporary search for Jesus is cognizant of the paucity of biographical-chronological data and the peril of a psychological analysis of his personality. It finds more significance in an existential rather than a positivistic approach to the history. It asks what the Gospels can tell us about Jesus' understanding of his purpose and mission and about his engagement with the concrete issues of his own time. It

36 "Since the Jews constantly made disturbances at the instigation of Chrestus (*impulsore Chresto*), he expelled them from Rome" (*The Life of Claudius* xxv). "Punishment was inflicted on the Christians, a class of men given to a new and mischievous superstition" (*The Life of Nero* xvi).

inquires after the basic meaning behind the stories and sayings embedded in these books.[37]

However, it is important to understand certain presuppositions of this new phase of a centuries-old task to confront the Jesus of history. The truth of Adolf Harnack's dictum, *"Vita Christi scribi nequit,"* is no longer open to question; it is quite impossible to write a story-book biography of Jesus from the materials at our disposal. Furthermore it must be recognized that the history of Jesus has survived largely as kerygma; that is to say, the Jesus who is available to us is the Jesus experienced and interpreted as the living Christ of early Christian devotion. It is manifestly impossible to discover a Jesus who can be wholly separated from the Christ-centered faith of these early followers. But it does not follow that we cannot or need not push an inquiry behind their preaching to determine what substantiation, if any, there was for the bold claim they made. It must not be forgotten that apostolic preaching itself is at once both *martyrion* and kerygma, a *report* of determinate events and a *preaching for decision* on the basis of their significance for salvation and judgment. The very fact of the Gospel accounts of Jesus' ministry represents the concern of the early Church not to regard the message of redemption as a cultic myth or an abstract proposition, but to anchor it in an actual historical event. If we are not to ignore the claim of these early partisans of Christ that the Word did not become simply word but a genuine person, we cannot default on our search for the real Jesus.

---

[37] Good surveys and critiques of the "new quest" can be found in James M. Robinson, *A New Quest of the Historical Jesus* (Naperville, Ill.: Alec R. Allenson, Inc., 1959); Paul Althaus, *The So-called Kerygma and the Historical Jesus,* trans. David Cairns (Edinburgh: Oliver & Boyd, 1959); Reginald H. Fuller, *The New Testament in Current Study* (New York: Charles Scribner's Sons, 1962), Chap. iii; Heinz Zahrnt, *The Historical Jesus,* trans. J. S. Bowden (New York: Harper & Row Publishers, 1963); Hugh Anderson, *Jesus and Christian Origins* (New York: Oxford University Press, 1964); Joachim Jeremias, *The Problem of the Historical Jesus,* trans. Norman Perrin (Philadelphia: Fortress Press, 1964). An example of studies on the lines of the "new quest" is Günther Bornkamm, *Jesus of Nazareth,* trans. Irene and Fraser McLuskey with James M. Robinson (London: Hodder and Stoughton, 1960). The older historical approach is represented in such a book as Ethelbert Stauffer, *Jesus and His Story,* trans. Richard and Clara Winston (New York: Alfred A. Knopf, Inc., 1960), and from a liberal standpoint, Morton S. Enslin, *The Prophet from Nazareth* (New York: McGraw-Hill Book Company, 1961). An eclectic approach is advocated by C. Milo Connick, *Jesus, the Man, the Mission, and the Message* (Englewood Cliffs, N.J.: Prentice-Hall, Inc., 1963).

Still we must ask the proper and important questions of these records. It will not do to try to fix precise points of chronology or geography, to determine the causal relationship between separate incidents, much less to probe the inner consciousness of Jesus to decide how his conceptions developed or to gauge his emotional responses. Far more important is the effort to determine the meaning of the events in his ministry, the characteristic features of his message of the Kingdom, his basic view of the realities and possibilities of human existence, the impression that he made upon friend and foe, the understanding of his own self implicit in his deeds and words.

What is the relationship between the preaching of the first community and the preaching of Jesus, between the kerygmatic Christ and the historical Jesus? To give a negative answer is to deny the relevance of Jesus for Christian history, to make of him an utterly solitary figure, misunderstood and ineffective, and to regard the kerygma as the groundless creation of a community activated by its own devotional imaginings. Our efforts to trace Jesus' history in the community's kerygma and his kerygma in the community's history hopefully will bear a better result. It is the position of this study that the Church expressed, extended, and to some extent, reoriented the claim inherent in Jesus' own kerygma. It neither simply repeated nor presumptuously invented that claim. There is a discernible continuity between the Jesus-tradition that is the oldest material in the Synoptic Gospels and the Christ-kerygma of the first believers.

What shall be the procedure to follow in this analysis of Gospel material? How are we to penetrate this "kerygmatized history" and determine for ourselves the genuine historical tradition about Jesus? Every historical inquiry is based upon hidden presuppositions and embodies a methodology that ought to be made available to the critical scrutiny of its readers. Three conclusions and procedural steps for the present study may be suggested.

1. We need to study carefully the individual units mounted in their later framework to distinguish the primary from the secondary material. We must recognize the elaboration of the earliest recollections of Jesus' deeds and words in their use by the early Church. Dogmatic, apologetic, even legendary elements have accreted to these memories as they have been told and retold in varying situations of congregational life, modifying and, in some instances, transforming them. Tendencies toward increasing orderliness and precision and the omission of unimportant, offensive, or erroneous details may be recognized

in the development of the tradition. A heightening of miraculous and apocalyptic features, the magnification of the divine character of Christ, and the underlining of the mission to the Gentiles—these adaptations and interpretations are an understandable part of any records in which faith and fact interact.[38]

Although this may be generally recognized, it is another matter to establish such distinctions for specific sayings and episodes. Certain sayings of Jesus, however, are recognized as out of character with the faith of the early community. Their appearance is not likely to be explained in terms of a life-setting in the Church that produced them. Thus to admit that the Lord himself submitted to the sin-baptism of John (Mark 1:9 ff., par.) or was frustrated in his healing work by unbelief (Mark 6:5) or did not know the complete details of the calendar of God's work in history (Mark 13:32) testifies to the integrity of these reporters. The Church preserved radical utterances of Jesus which it neither understood nor practiced, proof that its picture of Jesus was not simply a wish-fulfillment nor satisfaction of practical needs. This is only a relative guide, however, for we cannot conclude that there were no points of agreement between the attitudes and actions of Jesus and those of the post-Easter group of followers.

Similarly it may be argued that sayings alien to the faith and practice of Judaism may be accepted as genuine, since the incontestable fact of the hostile reaction is evidence that Jesus' mission at many points ran at cross-purposes to contemporary Judaism. But here again the opposite cannot be concluded; for Jesus by no means repudiated the whole morality, piety, and cultic system of his fathers. Sometimes, therefore, a saying or story may be best attributed in origin to a life-setting in the Church; sometimes to a life-setting in the Jewish environment of Jesus' work. In most instances, we believe, Christian and Jewish influences may have shaped the form, but not created the substance, of a pericope, so that it cannot be claimed to be wholly unmodified Jesus-tradition nor simply the formation of the community. The resultant is a mixture that invites, if it does not perfectly submit to, separation into components. As we shall see later, the recognition of distinctively Aramaic features and the characteristic structure of Aramaic poetry beneath the Greek form of a saying of Jesus is a signal to the alert observer that this must either be assigned

---

[38] See the ten laws of transformation of the tradition distinguished by Joachim Jeremias, *The Parables of Jesus,* 6th ed., trans. S. H. Hooke (New York: Charles Scribner's Sons, 1963), pp. 113–14.

to the Aramaic speech of Jesus himself or else to the primitive pre-Hellenistic community of his followers. So the language patterns as well as the content provide some clue to the original teaching material.

2. Secondly, we must relate the single saying or story to the layer of tradition in which it is located, and then appraise the historical worth of this larger collection. Here the analysis of the several literary collections that have grown from small complexes into larger written sources will prove helpful. Wherever a saying is found in the collection common to Matthew and Luke (termed Q) or wherever a story can be read in its Marcan form, we may presume to possess older material. If there is a corroboration in a Marcan parallel of a Q saying, we have good grounds for pronouncing this to represent an early and reliable stratum of tradition.[39]

3. Finally, it is necessary to determine the theological position of the individual Gospel writers. They are neither newspaper reporters nor rewrite men, but committed Christian authors who have impressed the material they have collected with their own distinctive beliefs and understandings. Establishing inductively the theological position of each author may help us distinguish redactional activity from the earlier form of a pericope.

Through these procedures it is possible to trace the formation and development of the tradition of Jesus within the Church. Despite the modification and elaboration of the earliest material, a comparison of the several layers yields a self-consistent, recognizable picture of a single person and the characteristic features of his message. Both primary and secondary traditions have been imprinted with his person and point of view. A critical comparison of the individual units and the layers of tradition in which they are embedded enables us to gain a clear impression about Jesus' message of the coming Kingdom, his position toward the Torah and the tradition of Judaism, the reaction to him of both adherents and adversaries, and what he believed about his own relationship to the judgment and salvation he announced.

Historical inquiry of this sort can only correct or corroborate; it cannot create faith in Jesus as God's word spoken to men. It can establish what were the convictions and claims of his first followers, and it can come to certain conclusions about whether they rest on

[39] Along with *Gospel Parallels,* the student will find a helpful, correlated discussion of literary-historical aspects of the Gospel materials in Francis W. Beare, *The Earliest Records of Jesus* (New York: Abingdon Press, 1962). On a more advanced and critical level, he may consult Bultmann, *History of the Synoptic Tradition.*

Jesus' own convictions and claims. But retrospective historical investigation cannot tell us whether in fact Jesus of Nazareth was the revelation and act of God. Such a faith-claim could never be verified by historical research. That question can only be settled by a decision and commitment in faith by the one who has heard and accepted the claim.[40] Historical inquiry alone can not give the certainty of faith, but it can prepare the way for it.

---

40 Søren Kierkegaard undervalued the importance of an historical knowledge of Jesus; nevertheless, he reminds every believer that true faith cannot be dependent upon the results of historical research. "If the contemporary generation had left nothing behind them but these words: 'we have believed that in such and such a year God appeared among us in the humble figure of a servant, that he lived and taught in our community, and finally died,' it would have been more than enough. The contemporary generation would have done all that was necessary; for this little advertisement, this *nota bene* on a page of universal history, would be sufficient to afford an occasion for a successor, and the most voluminous account can in all eternity do nothing more." Søren Kierkegaard, *Philosophical Fragments,* trans. David F. Swenson (Princeton, N.J.: Princeton University Press, 1946), p. 87. Cf. his *Training in Christianity,* trans. Walter Lowrie (London: Oxford University Press, 1941), p. 28, where he concludes, "All historical communication is communication of 'knowledge,' hence from history one can learn nothing about Christ" (since he is properly not an object of "knowledge," but of "faith").

CHAPTER II

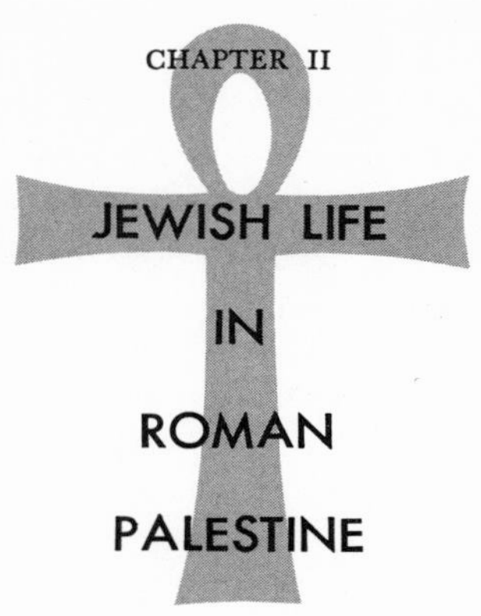

JEWISH LIFE IN ROMAN PALESTINE

Journey to the Holy Land

But even if you go you are not there.
For too much rubble has defaced the land,
For too much gunsmoke has obscured the air,
And wire and walls impede. On every hand
Pretentious buildings do but give the lie—
Signposts thrown down, their lettering all awry.

Open the Book and learn the ancient Greek,
See, as it were for the first time, the land.
Follow and let the changeless pages speak.
Here at the lakeside walk. Here on the mountain stand.
Now once again the field flowers are in bloom.
Here is the street, here is the upper room.*

To the writers of the New Testament, surveying the exciting and eventful years since the beginning of the Church in Jerusalem, the coming of Jesus represented the climax of the whole divinely guided history of Israel. This was truly the end for which the first was made. Paul gave expression to the conviction of the centrality of the Christ-event when he wrote, "But when the time had fully come, God sent forth his Son, born of woman, born under the law, to redeem those

* From "Journey to the Holy Land" by Edith Lovejoy Pierce, copyright, The Christian Century Foundation, 1962.

who were under the law" (Gal. 4:4). Indeed, Jesus himself recognized the decisive hour when he commenced his public work with the solemn words, "The time is fulfilled; the kingdom of God is at hand" (Mark 1:14). A pivotal point in history had been reached.

Within the Roman world, the universal relief and gratitude for the termination of the destructive Republican civil wars and the establishment of a new peace under the leadership of Octavian led to enthusiastic predictions of an imminent Golden Age. When the Roman Senate in 27 B.C. conferred upon Octavian, the *Princeps Senatus,* or First Citizen of the Senate, a new title, *Augustus* (the Worshipful or Worthy-to-be-Adored), the poet Virgil sang exultingly,

> This, this is he, whom thou so oft hearest promised to thee, Augustus Caesar, son of a god, who shall again set up the Golden Age in Latium amid the fields where Saturn once reigned and shall spread his empire past Garamant and Indian, to a land that lies beyond the stars, beyond the paths of the year and the sun, where heaven-bearing Atlas turns on his shoulders the sphere, inset with gleaming stars.[1]

Here was the divine fulfillment of the earlier expectation voiced in his Fourth Eclogue:

> Now the last age by Cumae's Sibyl sung
> Has come and gone, and the majestic roll
> Of circling centuries begins anew:
> Justice returns, returns old Saturn's reign,
> With a new breed of men sent down from heaven:
> Only do thou, at the boy's birth in whom
> The iron shall cease, the golden age arise,
> Befriend him, chaste Lucina; 'tis thine own
> Apollo reigns.[2]

On the eastern border of the empire, in the vassal state of Herodian Palestine, some priests and laymen living in the rocky barrenness of the Dead Sea area prepared for the final battle of the present evil age which would issue in the beginning of God's Era of Favor.[3] Men were

---

[1] Virgil, *Aeneid* VI 791–97.

[2] This evidence of a pagan messianic hope may be read in full in C. K. Barrett, *The New Testament Background: Selected Documents* (New York: The Macmillan Company, 1957), pp. 8–10. The passage is quoted from J. Rhoades, *The Poems of Virgil,* published in the World's Classics series No. 227 (London: Oxford University Press, 1921). For an account of the Roman advent hope in the Augustan era, see Ethelbert Stauffer, *Christ and the Caesars,* trans. K. and R. Gregor Smith (London: SCM Press, 1955), Chap. vi.

[3] See the *War Scroll* in the Qumran library (1QM), Theodor Herzl Gaster, *The Dead Sea Scriptures* (Garden City, N.Y.: Doubleday & Co., Inc., 1956), pp. 281–306.

found in various stages of preparation. The messianic hope of both Jew and Roman was destined to be fulfilled, but in a fashion neither would recognize nor accept. The curt report of the Roman historian Tacitus registers their combined judgments upon the one hailed by his followers as Messiah and Lord: "Christ suffered the penalty when Tiberius was emperor through the procurator Pontius Pilate."[4]

On a small strip of the eastern corridor of the vast Roman provincial empire, the drama of Jesus' life was acted out. Let us look more closely at this local scene and see what life was like in the small district attached to the Roman province of Syria in Jesus' day.

The National Crisis and Response

The Augustan Age, whose glories were heralded in the poetry of Horace and Virgil, had brought a new and blessed relief to the strife-torn peoples of Italy and diffused its benefits across the sea to the provinces. *Pax Romana,* it was wonderful! Dreaded slave rebellions, decimating civil wars, the struggle of rival contenders for the leadership of the state—these were ugly memories that the people were grateful to relegate to the past. The willingness to pay divine honors to the First Citizen of the Roman Empire was in no small measure expressive of their gratitude to the one who had made this political stability possible.

But in Palestine there was no happy acceptance of the Roman intervention that began with Pompey's occupation of the Holy City in 63 B.C. The ministry of John the Baptist and the work of Jesus of Nazareth were carried out in a period of violent political turbulence and tension. An insight is found in the *Habakkuk Commentary,* written at Qumran in Judea, which speaks with venomous antagonism of the hated Roman who rules the land:

> This [Hab. 1:8–9] refers to the Kittaeans [Romans] who thresh the earth with their horses and their beasts. Like a vulture they come from afar, from the isles of the sea, to devour all the nations; and they are insatiable. In the heat of fury, in searing rage, in scorching anger and with tempestuous mien they speak with all the peoples.[5]

---

4 *Annals* XV. 44; Barrett, *Background,* pp. 15f.

5 1QpHab iv.10–14 (Gaster, *Scriptures,* p. 250). After previous uncertainty, scholars are now generally agreed that the mysterious Kittim in the Qumran literature refers to the Seleucid kings and/or the Romans. See J. T. Milik, *Ten Years of Discovery in the Wilderness of Judea* (Naperville, Ill.: Alec R. Allenson, Inc., 1959), pp. 64–65, 123.

The more carefully we study the Gospels against the background of our enlarging understanding of the maelstrom of events in first-century Palestine, the more we are forced to recognize the agony of the times in which the gospel drama was enacted.

The Political Situation

The rule of Herod the Great (37–4 B.C.) brought to new intensity the anguished longing for that "consolation of Israel" which would liberate the Jewish people from Roman control and establish the New Age of peace and righteousness. A man capable of brilliant achievements and frightful crimes, Herod had engineered an incredible building program throughout his own land and in foreign cities, yet at the same time he had ordered the death penalty for his beloved wife Mariamne and three of his sons. The last, his eldest son Antipater, was ordered to be slain for his plot to seize the throne only four days before death brought to an end the horrible sufferings that marked Herod's last years. It was this final act of the wretched king that lead his friend and patron Caesar Augustus to quip in a Greek pun, "It is better to be Herod's swine (*hŷs*) than his son (*hyiós*)."[6]

Known to his Roman overlords as *rex amicus Caesaris et socius Romani populi* (a friendly king of Caesar's and an ally of the Roman people), this Idumean ruler had cleverly won the support in turn of Julius Caesar, Antony, and Octavian. He had secured Palestine in the status of a vassal kingdom exempt from imperial taxation and military service. He used his skills with the influential minister of Augustus, Marcus Vipsanius Agrippa, who supervised the affairs of the eastern provinces, to secure extraterritorial rights for Jews living in the cities of the empire. Nevertheless, his collaboration with the Romans and the hollowness of his alleged ardor for the religion of Judaism, despite his gift of the magnificent Temple in Jerusalem,[7] resulted in the stubborn refusal of his subjects to hold him in respect and pay him loyalty. Particularly offensive was the celebration in Jerusalem of games in honor of Augustus. About the year Jesus was born some six thousand Pharisees refused to take the oath of allegiance to Caesar and Herod and predicted that at God's decree Herod's government

---

6 Macrobius, *Saturnalia* II.4.11.

7 See the description of Herod's Temple in Jos., *Antiq.* XV.11; *War* V.5, and the tractate *Middoth* of the Mishnah: Herbert Danby, trans., *The Mishnah* (London: Oxford University Press, 1958).

was to be destroyed. They escaped without reprisal only because the sick king feared an open breach with these influential leaders.[8]

The situation worsened after his fatal illness and death in the seven hundred and fiftieth year of Rome (4 B.C.). According to the last of the four wills he had drawn up, and subsequently confirmed by Augustus, his kingdom was to be divided among three of his sons, the eldest only eighteen years of age. To Philip was assigned the northeastern lands: Trachonitis, Paneas, Gaulonitis (Luke 3:1), and several other smaller districts. It was through the tetrarchy of Philip that Jesus traveled with his disciples after their withdrawal from Galilee. In the vicinity of Philip's residence at Caesarea Philippi, Peter made his declaration of faith that Jesus was in fact the long-expected Messiah, and a few days later that strange and pivotal experience of the Transfiguration took place (Mark 8:27–9:8). Philip held office until his death in A.D. 34, at which time his tetrarchy was assigned to Syria, and in A.D. 37, incorporated by Caligula into the newly established kingdom of Herod Agrippa I.

In the Gospels the ruler of Galilee and Transjordan is referred to as Herod, although he ought to be distinguished from his father by the use of his full name, Herod Antipas. He and his brother, the nefarious Archelaus, were Herod's sons by his Samaritan wife Malthake; both were beneficiaries named in their father's last testament. In Luke 13:32 Jesus refers contemptuously to the Galilean tetrarch, his own provincial ruler, as "that fox." In A.D. 18 Herod Antipas transferred his capital from Sepphoris near Nazareth to the port city of Tiberias, newly built on the site of a former Jewish cemetery and hence a flagrant offense to Jewish concerns for ritual purity. He found himself at war in A.D. 36 with his Nabatean father-in-law Aretas IV as a result of his divorce of Aretas' daughter to marry his half-brother Herod's wife,[9] an alliance bitterly denounced by the wilderness prophet John the Baptist. His tyrannical rule was brought to a close in A.D. 39 when Caligula had him deposed through a rival's scheming and banished to Lugudunum in Gaul.

---

8 Stewart Perowne has given a vivid account of this colorful figure in his *The Life and Times of Herod the Great* (New York: Abingdon Press, n.d. but pub. 1959). Passages from Josephus are given in Barrett, *Background,* pp. 118–22.

9 Erroneously identified in the Gospel accounts (Matt. 14:3–12; Mark 6:17–29) as the wife of Philip, who, in fact, actually married Herodias' daughter, Salome. Herodias was the former wife of another Herod (Jos., *Antiq.* XVIII.5.1), an older half-brother of Antipas.

The deep resentment of Jewish citizens to Roman intervention in their national life was only matched by their hatred of the whole Herodian family. The Roman ratification of Herod's will instated the cruel and incompetent oldest son Archelaus as ethnarch over the heartland of Herod's realm: Samaria, Judea, and Idumaea, *Palestinia Prima* as it was to be known in Roman administration. It is possible that the additions found in Luke's version of the parable of the Talents-Pounds reflect an independent parable based on Archelaus' journey to Rome to have his inheritance confirmed (19:12–27).

Only a few weeks after the death of his seventy-year-old father, Archelaus dealt with riots that broke out as pilgrims were crowding into Jerusalem for the Passover celebration by ordering an attack by his police guard. Three thousand of the rioters were trapped and killed. A few months later, at the feast of Pentecost, two thousand resistance fighters were crucified—to crush the rebellion they had aroused—by the order of the Roman legate L. Quintilius Varus, who marched from Syria at the head of two legions. After ten years of tyrannical administration, this unpopular son of Herod was removed from office by Augustus' order and banished to Vienne in Gaul in A.D. 6.

Judea now became an official province of the Roman Empire, no longer a vassal kingdom. As a smaller and restless possession, it was to be governed by imperial governors or procurators, drawn from the equestrian order of Roman society and civil service. Of the fourteen who represented the *imperium* in Judea from A.D. 6 until the outbreak of the revolt against the Romans in A.D. 66, the fifth was destined for dubious recognition in the annals of history because, during his undistinguished administration from A.D. 26–36, a Nazarene prophet, hailed by some of his followers as messianic king, was brought to trial for high treason and executed. With his keen interest in historical details, Luke opens his account of the summons to repentance by John the Baptist with this notice:

> In the fifteenth year of the reign of Tiberius Caesar [A.D. 14–37], Pontius Pilate being governor of Judea and Herod [Antipas, 4 B.C.–A.D. 39] being tetrarch of Galilee, and his brother Philip [4 B.C.–A.D. 34] tetrarch of the region of Ituraea and Trachonitis. . . [Luke 3:1].

The Jewish historian Josephus' account of the administration of Pontius Pilate supports the general picture of these functionaries as bored exiles from the colorful life of the capital city, often indifferent

Fig. 3. Head of the deified Augustus (27 B. C.–A. D. 14) on a bronze coin dating from the principate of Caligula (A. D. 37–41). The inscription reads *divus augustus s. c.*, that is, the Deified Augustus by the decree of the Senate. *Courtesy of The British Museum.*

Fig. 4. Jewish coins from the two revolts. *Top, obverse :* First Revolt (A. D. 68–69), cup (of salvation ?); *reverse :* branch (of David?). *Center, obverse :* Second Revolt (A. D. 133), sanctuary surmounted by Star (of Jacob?) ; *reverse :* jar with vegetation (Branch of David?). *Bottom, obverse:* grape cluster (messianic banquet or grapes of wrath?) ; *reverse :* jug (of messianic oil of anointing?). *Courtesy of Cecil Roth.*

to the peculiar sensibilities of their Jewish subjects.[10] We read, for example, of Pilate's appropriation of monies belonging to the temple treasury in order to accomplish necessary repairs to a Jerusalem aqueduct. At the beginning of his rule, he precipitated a massive street demonstration at his Caesarean headquarters by announcing his decision to allow his soldiers to carry into the city of Jerusalem troop standards which bore the effigy of the emperor Tiberius. This was contrary to the policy of previous procurators. The Jews had been forced to suffer this violation of the second commandment in the Roman coins that circulated through the land, but this flagrant insult they found intolerable. When we hear further of Pilate's slaughter of some Samaritan fanatics at Mount Gerizim, an act that brought about his recall and banishment, we are the more ready to believe the reference in Luke to a similar outrage against some Galileans "whose blood Pilate had mingled with their sacrifices" (Luke 13:1).[11]

The Anatomy of Rebellion

Jewish resistance to the rule of the Herods and the Caesars resulted from several causes deeply rooted in the national life. We may distinguish economic, cultural, and religious factors.

To begin with, the burden of taxation had become unbearable. Once Judea passed directly into Roman hands, with the banishment of Archelaus, the citizenry felt the additional weight of Roman taxes compounded upon their annual half-shekel tax to the temple and the Mosaic prescriptions about the tithe. Preliminary to the actual assessment was a thorough census by Roman surveyors of all the public and private lands and a registration of all taxable persons. It was the official edict calling for this census in A.D. 6 that touched off the ill-fated rebellion of Judas the Galilean and his Pharisee associate Saddok, and led to the organization of the party known later as the Zealots or *Kanna'im*.[12]

Land and poll taxes were payable to finance officers or procurators in the official Roman coin known as the *denarius,* the "tribute money." A silver coin worth about eighteen cents, the *denarius* bore a bust relief of the emperor and an inscription containing such titles as *divus,* divine, and *augustus,* worthy of worship (Mark 12:13–17). In addi-

---

10 See Barrett, *Background,* pp. 123–24.

11 For Josephus' account of this administrator, see *Antiq.* XVIII.3.1–2; 4.1–2; *War* II.9.2–4. Cf. also Philo, *Embassy to Gaius* II.589f. and 1QpHab vi.4. See Fig. 8.

12 Jos., *Antiq.* XVIII.1.6, XX.5.2; *War* II.8.1; Acts 5:37.

tion to the tribute levied on all provincial subjects, there were collections for the support of the Roman constabulary, sales taxes, customs taxes, salt taxes, fees on the freeing of slaves, and so forth, which were collected by the *publicani*. Their quisling Jewish subordinates regularly extorted their own profits above the stipulated fees. To be called a "friend of tax collectors and sinners," as Jesus was, was to be judged unfit for the company of both God and the devout Jew. There is little doubt that the economic malaise of Roman Judea contributed heavily to the agitation and unrest widespread in Jesus' day. One scholar has estimated that the double taxation program took as much as thirty to forty per cent from the average family income.[13] The problem was vastly complicated by the need to support a dense population of a million Jews together with thousands of foreigners in a relatively primitive agrarian economy.

The most galling thing was not the economic privation, however. The poor were always with them, as Jesus observed. What ate into the soul of the Jew was the realization that a foreign culture threatened his way of life, and an alien ruler denied the conviction that they were a free people under divine sovereignty alone. Pagan cities established across the land from Hasmonean times and, more recently, encouraged by the Herods, were centers of propaganda for Western culture and bitter reminders to the Jew of the defilement of the holy land.

In the Gospel of Mark, mention is made of Jesus traveling with his disciples through the region of the Decapolis (Mark 7:31). In Jesus' day, this federation of ten cities was independent of the reigning tetrarchs, Herod Antipas and his brother Philip, and was attached to the Roman province of Syria. From either Tiberias or Capernaum, one could look across the lake to see the proud city of Hippos on a high hill, a symbol of the penetration of Greek culture into Jewish Palestine. In fact all about Galilee there were urban centers of Hellenism: cities like Tyre and Sidon, Damascus, Ptolemais, Sebaste, and Caesarea, without the borders, and Sepphoris and Tiberias within. Intended to be models and mission stations of an alien culture, they were feared and despised by every loyal Jew. Had not the apocalyptic tract embedded in Zechariah's prophecy predicted the clash of the cultures?

---

13 See the article by F. C. Grant, "The Economic Background of the New Testament," in the collection edited by W. D. Davies and D. Daube, *The Background of the New Testament and Its Eschatology* (Cambridge: Cambridge University Press, 1956).

I have bent Judah as my bow;
  I have made Ephraim its arrow.
I will brandish your sons, O Zion,
  over your sons, O Greece,
and wield you like a warrior's sword.
[Zech. 9:13]

The sons of Israel were under bondage to no one but Yahweh and his way of righteousness defined by the Torah. The theocracy was now imperiled. Throughout the land from "Galilee of the nations" in the north to the garrison of Bethlehem in the south the age-old supplication was raised:

O God, why dost thou cast us off for ever?
Why does thy anger smoke against the
  sheep of thy pasture?

. . . .

Have regard for thy covenant;
  for the dark places of the land are full of
    the habitations of violence.
Let not the downtrodden be put to shame;
  let the poor and needy praise thy name.
[Ps. 74:1, 20–21]

The Freedom Fighters

The reaction to the Jewish national crisis of the first century was multiform. To Judas the Galilean and his followers, as we have seen, the only answer was armed revolt.[14] Most patriotic Jews believed that a holy war was inevitable. It was largely a matter of discovering the opportune hour when God's wrath would strike through them upon their adversaries. Like their Maccabean predecessors, they believed that God would support their cause by sending legions of angels to deliver his oppressed people. The *War Scroll* from Qumran describes the intervention of these angelic swordsmen for the Almighty.[15] Without such assistance, they knew they would be no match against the superior might of powerful Rome. During the procuratorship of Antonius Felix in A.D. 52–60, an Egyptian Jew led a suicidal march of

---

[14] See William Reuben Farmer, *Maccabees, Zealots, and Josephus* (New York: Columbia University Press, 1956), Chap. viii; Oscar Cullmann, *The State in the New Testament* (New York: Charles Scribner's Sons, 1956), Chap. i. Cf. M. Hengel, *Die Zeloten: Untersuchungen zur jüdischen Freiheitsbewegung in der Zeit von Herodes* (Leiden: E. J. Brill, 1962).

[15] 1QM xii.8–10.

four thousand *Sicarii* (Assassins) from the Judean desert against the Roman legionaries stationed in Jerusalem.[16]

Against the background of these leather-lunged cries of religious nationalism, the words of Jesus gain in pathos and urgency: "Love your enemies and pray for those who persecute you" (Matt. 5:44); "All who take the sword will perish by the sword" (Matt. 26:52). However, one of his own disciples, Simon the Canaanean, may have been a former revolutionist (Mark 3:18). In view of Rome's demand for loyal obedience in the provinces, it is ironical that Jesus, who counseled nonresistance, perished in the place of a Jew named Barabbas who had been arrested for his part in a recent insurrectionist plot (Mark 15:6 ff.).

Unceasing vigilance on Rome's part was always necessary. A desperate people finally chose the way of the sword and moved toward the disaster of the Jewish-Roman War (A.D. 66–73) that resulted in the fall of Jerusalem in A.D. 70 and the temporary collapse of the nationalistic hope.[17] The decisive defeat of these fervent messianic hopes came in the tragic Second Jewish Revolt under Bar Kosebah in A.D. 132. Mute testimony of the desperate longing for freedom is read in coins struck in the first month of the rebellion and inscribed "of Jerusalem's liberation."[18]

The Essenes

Our knowledge of another form of the resistance movement has been considerably increased in recent years as a result of the many manuscripts discovered in remote caves in the limestone cliffs of Khirbet Qumran.[19] Fragments of almost six hundred writings from

---

16 Acts 21:38; Jos., *Antiq.* XX.8.6; *War* II.13.5; perhaps the Ben Stada of the Talmud and Midrash.

17 V. G. Simkhovitch presents a vivid description of the national resistance movement in his essay, *Toward the Understanding of Jesus* (New York: The Macmillan Company, 1925).

18 Two letters sent by this Jewish rebel leader were found in 1951 in caves in the Wâdī Murabbaʿât, about fifteen miles southeast of Jerusalem. See Milik, *Ten Years of Discovery,* pp. 136f.

19 The first of the scrolls was discovered in the spring of 1947 and publicly announced in 1948. Good introductions to the community and its library are available in J. M. Allegro, *The Dead Sea Scrolls* (Baltimore: Penguin Books, Inc., 1956); Frank M. Cross, Jr., *The Ancient Library of Qumran and Modern Biblical Studies,* rev. ed. (New York: Doubleday & Co., Inc., 1961); R. K. Harrison, *The Dead Sea Scrolls* (New York: Harper & Row, Publishers, 1961; and Menahem Mansoor, *The Dead Sea Scrolls* (Grand Rapids, Mich.: Eerdman's Pub. Co., 1964). Convenient English translations are available in Gaster, *Scriptures;* G. Vermes, *The Dead Sea Scrolls in English* (Baltimore: Penguin Books, Inc., 1962); and J. Dupont-Sommer, *The Essene Writings from Qumran,* trans. G. Vermes (Oxford: Basil Blackwell, 1961).

the century before Christ and contemporary with his mission have been identified. They were evidently sealed in these caves at the outbreak of the revolt in A.D. 66 as the Essene community fled before the advance of the Romans or joined the ranks of the Sicarii and Zealots in the struggle against them.

Originating with the resistance of the *Ḥasîdīm* or "Pious Ones" to the Seleucid rulers of Palestine in the second century B.C., the Qumran community seems to have consisted of a small group of priests and laymen under the leadership of a "true exponent of the law," usually called the Teacher of Righteousness. Horrified at the appointment of an irregular priest to the high priesthood and incensed at the increasing compromises of the Hasmonean rulers with Syrian politics and Greek culture, they withdrew from Jerusalem about 150 B.C. for a voluntary exile to this wilderness settlement above the shores of the Dead Sea. In Jesus' day the Essene movement numbered more than four thousand, with a principal center at Engedi and smaller settlements like Qumran scattered about in both urban and rural areas.

Like the Pharisees with whom they shared many concerns and practices, the Essene community at Qumran was fanatically devoted to the practice of ritual purity in accordance with the prescriptions of the Torah. From the outset the brotherhood was ruled by a messianic hope that stirred them to make suitable preparation for the coming Age of Favor. Unlike the advocates of revolt, however, they abstained from direct involvement with the political affairs of the nation and trained themselves to become the militia of God for that day of the holy war when all the enemies of God would be defeated. New light on the historical references in the *War Scroll* indicate that in the final stage of their history, they identified the demonic foe with the Romans and became increasingly sympathetic with the Zealot conviction that the life-and-death battle must be joined immediately. During the national uprising, those who had not already fled were massacred or captured by the Tenth Roman Legion Fretensis in the summer of A.D. 68.

The Pharisees

The third and best known sectarian movement is that of the Pharisees.[20] Like the Essenes, the Pharisees emerged out of the conservative Jewish protest to the Hellenizing program of the Seleucid rulers of the early second century B.C. Scandalized by the rapid Jewish

---

20 For Josephus' account of these Jewish sects, see Barrett, *Background*, pp. 124–27.

Fig. 5. Cave 4 at Khirbet Qumran. The entrance may be seen below and slightly to the left of the man standing on the top of the terrace. Explored in September 1952, this cave yielded an enormous number of fragments, representing more than three hundred books. *Courtesy of The Palestine Archaeological Museum.*

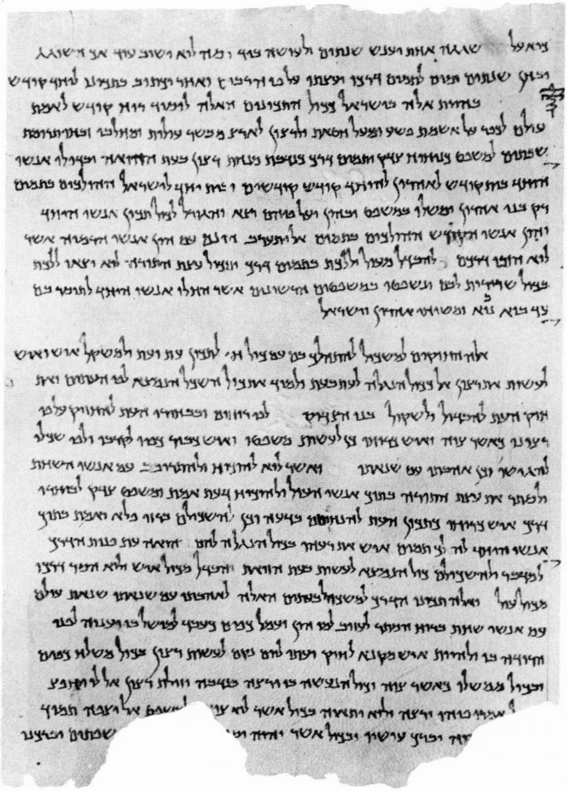

Fig. 6. The *Manual of Discipline* (*Rule of the Congregation*, 1QS) from Cave 1 at Qumran, column ix. For the translation, see Gaster, *Scriptures*, pp. 57-60. Courtesy of *The American Schools of Oriental Research.*

assimilation of Greek ways—a contemporary Jewish writing describes young priests even joining in athletic contests[21]—a reactionary movement developed known as the *Ḥasîdīm* or "Pious Ones." They counseled strict separation from this alien way of life and from all wicked and apostate Jews. The nickname Pharisee or *Pĕrûshîm,* the Separatists, probably was applied to a group of the Pious who broke from the Maccabean revolutionists about 162 B.C., after religious independence had been secured.[22]

Although the Gospels refer to these studious and devoted practitioners of the Torah as Pharisees, they themselves preferred to be known as the Associates, *Ḥabĕrîm.* They were organized into societies called Brotherhoods, *Ḥabûrôth,* that were pledged to maintain strict ritual purity according to the teaching of the Torah and to keep apart from anyone who would not take similar vows. On occasion they had suffered for their stubborn devotion to the ancestral faith and customs, even at the hands of Jewish rulers who favored a more friendly attitude toward Western culture. It may be that a number of them fled for refuge to the community at Qumran to escape persecution in the latter part of the reign of John Hyrcanus (134–104 B.C.). About the time of Jesus' birth a group of six thousand refused to take the oath of allegiance to Augustus and Herod and were heavily fined. Basically a lay movement, their religious fraternities in Jesus' day were making a persuasive appeal to the new Jewish population in Galilee, which was considered to be too lax in its obedience to the Torah commandments.

Against the encroachments of a strange culture which induced the Jew to relapse from his traditional beliefs and practices, the Pharisees urged absolute devotion to the Torah and the tradition to keep Israel a holy people unto God. The intent of their hair-splitting definitions and refinements of the law was, on the one hand, to eliminate any confusion or uncertainty about the divine prescriptions, and on the other, to humanize the stringent requirements and bring them within range of practice. Thus their specifications of the thirty-nine inter-

---

21 II Macc. 4:10–15; cf. I Macc. 1:13f.

22 See Barrett, *Background,* pp. 163–64. The origin of the name Pharisee, which first appears about 150 B.C., is not certain. Some derive the word from a Hebrew verb meaning to define accurately, and translate it "Precisionists," referring to their interpretation of Scripture. It has also been proposed that the name originally meant "Persianizers" because of certain affinities of their thought with Iranian religion.

dictions against work on the Sabbath, drawn from Exodus 35,[23] represent a casuistical attempt to safeguard the day honored by all Jewry in the ancient world. To keep from conscious or unwitting violations of God's revealed way to men, the Pharisees and scribes thought their task was to "make a fence around the Torah" (*Aboth* 1.1). Theologically progressive, they stressed the value of prayer and works of love and mercy. They taught a doctrine of resurrection from the dead and of angels as divine messengers, and they maintained God's gracious but determined governance of history. Although they longed with others for the end of Roman rule in Palestine, they believed that deliverance was wholly in God's hands. Hence they abstained from active participation in politics, without the complete withdrawal from society that the stricter Essenes advocated. No one was more conscious than the Pharisee of the threat posed by the presence of the foreigners in the land. But the pattern of this nonviolent resistance featured devotion to the divinely ordained way and complete confidence in God's management of the human situation.

Most of the professional teachers of the civil and canon law were members of the Pharisaic societies. Note the recurrence of the expression "scribes and Pharisees" in the Gospels. Known variously in the Gospels as scribes, rabbis, teachers, or lawyers, these men were the jurists, moralists, and theologians of their day. They gathered schools of disciples about them for the study of the law and the deduction of legal precepts or *halakôth* from the written Scripture. "The scribes and Pharisees sit on Moses' seat"—that is, they are the official interpreters of the law in the synagogues (Matt. 23:1). In Jesus' day there were two principal scribal schools, one led by the more conservative teacher, Shammai, whose followers dominated the Pharisaic societies in Galilee; the other, taught by the learned Babylonian Jew, Hillel.[24]

Pharisaic attitudes of spiritual superiority and of condescension toward all who were not enrolled in their societies find pointed expression in rabbinical writings. We might question John's report of the Pharisees' sneering comment, "This crowd, who do not know the law, are accursed" (John 7:49). But the wise and gentle Rabbi Hillel once observed, "An ignorant fellow (*bor*) dreads not sin, a member

---

23 Such discussions as to whether one could eat an egg that had been laid on the Sabbath, the definition of a Sabbath day's burden exceeding the weight of a fig, etc.

24 See the portrait of the scribe drawn in the Wisdom of Sirach 39:1–11.

of the *'am ha'arets* cannot be saintly" (*Aboth* 2.6; cf. 3.1; *Berakoth* 43b). Rabbi Akiba recalls the bitter dislike he had for these haughty holy men, the intelligentsia of Jewish society, when he was still a member of the common people (*Pesaḥim* 49b). Zealous missionaries that they were (Matt. 23:15), they still abstained from contaminating relationships with the outcast and the sinful whom Jesus put first in his ministry (Mark 2:17).

The Sadducees

The response of the Sadducees to the national crisis was to urge a peaceful coexistence between the Roman overlords and the Jewish people. Unlike their puritanical brothers, this bourgeois religious movement, whose economic and ecclesiastical status depended on Roman patronage, minimized the points of friction between the two societies. It was this small patrician party, made up of wealthy priestly families, especially the hierarchy, in league with the bankers, merchants, and landed aristocracy, which dominated the Sanhedrin or High Court in Jesus' time. The Sadducees were probably descendants of the Hellenizing factions and Hasmonean supporters of the Maccabean period (143–63 B.C.).[25] Theologically, as well as politically, they were conservative, accepting the sole authority of the Torah as the revealed word of God and denying belief in angelic spirits and any deterministic view of history. Jesus once engaged some Sadducees in theological discussion in Jerusalem when they ridiculed belief in the resurrection. In reply, he sided with the Pharisaic position without, however, wholly identifying himself with it (Mark 12:18–27 par.).

Violent resistance, strict abstention from the political-cultural struggle, strengthening of the ancient landmarks, restricted collaboration—these were the ways first-century Judaism responded to annexation and cultural unification. The common people, who constituted more than ninety per cent of the total population, reflected all these varying courses of action as resolutions of the national distress. Jesus was to present still another way.

The Synagogues

The faith of the Jew in a blessed future and his devotion to the divine law found expression and confirmation through the synagogue,

---

25 The name may originally have designated an adherent or partisan of the priestly aristocracy of Zadok's lineage. The priests of Qumran, by contrast, claimed that they were true sons of Zadok (*bene Zadok*).

school, and temple. Although the origins of the synagogue are obscure, these Jewish societies were certainly well established two hundred years before the birth of Christ. Consisting of a minimum of ten adult males, the congregation gathered during the week and especially on the Sabbath for religious services of prayer and praise. The men of the Great Assembly in the time of Ezra and his successors were said to have developed the liturgy (*Aboth* 1.1). Several special prayers were included in the simple ritual that shaped the pattern for early Christian worship. A confession of faith, the *Shema'*, "Hear, O Israel" (Deut. 6:4–9, 11:13–21; Num. 15:37–41), was followed by the solemn *Shemoneh 'Esreh* or Prayer of Eighteen Benedictions and a benediction pronounced by a priest if one happened to be present. Lessons were read from the Torah lectionary and some briefer texts freely chosen from the prophets, followed by a translation into the vernacular and an exposition on the meaning and relevance of the passages for daily living. After the sermon, the service concluded with a prayer called the *Kaddish* that begins "May his great name be magnified and hallowed in the world which he has created according to his pleasure."

A didactic emphasis pervaded these services of prayer. The congregation was instructed by any qualified person whom the *ḥazzan* or attendant invited to speak on the truths and duties of life under the Torah. So, once upon invitation, Jesus selected a passage from the prophet Isaiah and, assuming the seated posture of a teacher, began to unfold to his Nazareth neighbors the relevance of that scriptural text to his own work (Luke 4:16ff.). In the earliest phase of his ministry, Jesus was often found teaching in synagogues on the Sabbath. Often in the smaller towns and villages the meeting house served also as the center for more formal study of the Scriptures. That synagogue life had become central in the devotional activities of the Jew both in Palestine and the Diaspora (Acts 15:21) is evidenced by the unbroken continuation of corporate worship following the destruction of the temple in A.D. 70. The lay and democratic character of these Jewish congregations made effective instruments for the Pharisaic brotherhoods to exert their influence upon the common life.

The Schools

As a lad in Nazareth Jesus may have attended the local elementary school for Jewish boys, the *Beth ha-Sefer*. Since the time of Shimeon ben Shetach (ca. 75 B.C.) and his disciple Joshua ben Gamla, many villages had established reading and writing schools. They usually met in the synagogue building under the tutelage of the synagogue reader or *ḥazzan*. Here a boy would have first learned to read the Torah, beginning with Leviticus. Later, there would be instruction in the canon of the prophets. In a sing-song recitation by the teacher, repeated by the class, passages of Scripture of astonishing length, to our way of thinking, were committed to memory. Rabbi Joḥanan ben Zakkai (ca. A.D. 1–80) once described a favorite pupil thus: "He is a plastered cistern which loses not a drop" (*Aboth* 2.8f.). It is an apt commentary on the Jewish educational system of Jesus' day.

The synagogue, or an adjacent building, was also a center for adult education. In the *Beth ha-Midrash,* to which the Jewish boy graduated after he had been initiated as a Son of Torah, instruction was given in both the Scripture and the Tradition of the Elders.[26] On sabbath afternoons this advanced school was a favorite gathering place of the men of the village for the study of the Torah and the rules of the unwritten law. "If a man has gained a good name he has gained [somewhat] for himself," observed Rabbi Hillel; "If he has gained for himself words of the Torah he has gained for himself life in the world to come" (*Aboth* 2.7).

But beyond the hearing of the biblical scrolls read weekly in the synagogue service and the possibility of any formal instruction, Jesus must have been a serious student of the Bible by himself. His teaching reflects a broad knowledge of canonical literature and familiarity with some of the apocryphal writings of his people. Some fourteen Old Testament books are quoted by him in the Synoptic Gospels. Half of the texts are drawn from the Prophets; the remainder distributed evenly between the Law and the Psalms. Apart from that, many of his sayings are deeply colored with scriptural imagery and allusions.

The Temple

Officially the temple continued to serve as the center of Jewish religion. Here alone, in the dwelling place of Israel's God on Mt. Zion, could sacrifices be offered in gratitude for a recovery from illness or deliverance from national distress, or in contrition for a sinful action. On the high altars outside the magnificent marble building that had been Herod's gift to his unhappy subjects, the smoke of incense and the savor of roasted meat mingled daily with the prayers of the devout in public and private sacrifices.

---

[26] *Aboth* 5.21.

According to John's Gospel, which shows a special interest in the Jewish festivals, Jesus visited Jerusalem during the ceremonies of *Sukkoth* (Booths or Tabernacles), a popular vintage feast that lasted for a week and commemorated the march through the Sinai wilderness by the Hebrews lately escaped from Egyptian slavery.[27] This Gospel also mentions *Ḥanukkah,* the festival of Dedication or Lights, an eight-day celebration commemorating the reconsecration of the temple in 165 B.C. after its desecration by the Seleucid king Antiochus Epiphanes. All four Gospels, of course, associate the arrest, trial, and death of Jesus with the joyous springtime rites of *Pesach* or Passover, the festival of freedom memorializing the flight of the Hebrew fathers across the Sea of Reeds before the pursuing armies of the Egyptians. In the Acts of the Apostles, furthermore, the confirmatory event of the infant Church's summons to mission occurs on the festival of *Sheḇūʿôt* or Pentecost, which recalls the historic giving of the law to Moses on Mt. Sinai. These celebrations, of a joyful as well as solemn character, dramatically re-enacted the constitutive events of the Jewish community and enabled the Jew to relive and repossess his whole tradition.

The priesthood in Judaism was an hereditary office. In the first century those who were qualified to officiate at the national sanctuary were so numerous that a village priest like Zechariah, father of John the Baptizer, was on duty with his class one week every six months. At other times he may have joined with the Levitical assistants and laymen to compose a congregation for the responses at the public services. One of the bitter protests of the Covenanters of Qumran was over the appointment of the high priest, who also served as head of the supreme court, by the Roman governor who thus exercised control over the powerful families of the chief priests. Other Jewish literature of the time invokes the sharpest criticism of the corrupt priesthood—a kept hierarchy bent on placating the procurators.[28]

Jesus' collision with the temple authorities during his Jerusalem ministry and his accusation of their malfeasance must be seen in terms of the function of the temple as the principal banking center in his day. Besides the annual tax of one-half shekel levied upon all Jews in the empire, additional revenues flowed into the treasury from properties, tithes, quit-monies, and voluntary contributions.

---

27 Barrett, *Background,* pp. 157–59.

28 Cf. *I Enoch* 89:73f.; CD iv.19ff., vi.11f., viii.12, ix.47; 1QpHab viii.8–13, xii. 7–9; *Test. Levi* 14–16; *Pss. Sol.* 1:8, 2:3, 8:12f., 26; *Asmp. Moses* 4:8, 5:1–6:1, 7:5, 7. Cf. Chapter XI, note 47. These Jewish apocryphal writings can be read in R. H. Charles, *The Apocrypha and Pseudepigrapha of the Old Testament,* 2 vols. (Oxford: The Clarendon Press, 1913).

It was a testing time for Israel. Greek and Samaritan auxiliaries in Rome's employ kept an uneasy peace in the land. Fiscal and administrative agents from the capital along with local magistrates gingerly held the reins of government. An orientalized, syncretistic Greek culture permeated the traditional way of life and made an indelible imprint upon the architecture, fashions, government, and religious thought of the sons of Moses. But in synagogue, school, and temple, in Torah and tradition—vigilant guardians of Judaism—the ancient folkways and beliefs were redefined and confirmed, the stubborn convictions of a responsible relationship to the God of the Sinai covenant were strengthened. Israel would survive this latest threat to her existence as she had the others, but the scars of the conflict would be ineffaceable.[29]

The Christmas Gospel

To the first followers of Jesus, his whole career beginning with his birth and culminating in his resurrection-exaltation was explainable only in terms of a mighty miracle of God's action in a human life. From the vantage point of their Easter faith they looked back upon Jesus' earthly ministry and declared that he had come originally from the side of God and had "emptied himself, taking the form of a servant, being born in the likeness of men" (Phil. 2:7). The writer of John's Gospel puts it still more strongly: the divine Word actually became flesh. Thus he ruled out any speculations about the particular moment in his ministry when the man Jesus was invested by the descending heavenly Christ, as certain teachers were debating. On the other hand, replying to Jewish charges about Jesus' legitimacy, these early Christians vigorously proclaimed divine paternity for Jesus and a legal relationship to the royal lineage. The infancy stories recorded by the Evangelists Matthew and Luke reflect the bitter argument between the Church and the synagogue and the persuasion that Jesus' total earthly work was veritably Immanuel, "God with us."

Each writer in his own way utilizes the basic birth tradition. Matthew develops it into an apologetic story confirmed by the history of the exodus and by the prophets. Luke interlaces a highly dramatic

---

29 For further study consult such works as Henri Daniel-Rops, *Daily Life in the Time of Jesus* (New York: Hawthorn Books, Inc., 1962); Frederick C. Grant, *Ancient Judaism and the New Testament,* rev. ed. (New York: The Macmillan Company, 1960); George F. Moore, *Judaism,* 2 vols. (Cambridge, Mass.: Harvard University Press, 1944); William Foerster, *Palestinian Judaism in New Testament Times* (Edinburgh: Oliver and Boyd, 1964).

and imaginative account with the matchless poetry of the nativity hymns. Whatever historical details are embedded here are subordinated to the conviction of the early Palestinian church about the divine character of Jesus. The historian cannot pass upon the accuracy of that claim, but he is bound to present carefully and sympathetically, with critical comparison, the stories expressive of that faith. Through the birth stories we may hear early Christian communities confessing their faith that Jesus truly is the Son of God in whose coming men are met by God and offered pardon and new life.

The Birth-Stories

The significance of Jesus' birth in Bethlehem, claimed in Matthew 2:1ff. and Luke 1:4, is that this was the ancestral home of the royal family (I Sam. 16:4). Furthermore, one of several prophetic speculations connected the birthplace of the Messiah with this important southern garrison outpost (Mic. 5:2; cf. John 7:42). The Evangelists Matthew, Luke, and perhaps John assume that Bethlehem was the scene of the birth, but John indicates that the crowds who heard Jesus believed he was a native Galilean (John 7:27, 41, 52; cf. 1:45–46; Acts 4:10). It may well be that, in fact, Nazareth was Jesus' birthplace as well as his residence, and Bethlehem was introduced into the tradition later for apologetic reasons. John refers to Judea as Jesus' own country (John 4:44), but Mark relates the saying to Galilee (Mark 6:4), and Luke explicitly identifies Nazareth as his *patria* or native town (Luke 4:16, 23f.). If the Roman law of census followed in Egypt obtained also for Palestine, then Bethlehem would be the city to which Joseph as a descendant of David would travel to declare his share in the family holdings.[30] Had Joseph been a resident of Bethlehem, the return from Nazareth would be explainable, but there is no basis for this in Luke's story. Matthew, however, makes no mention of Nazareth before the birth and assumes a permanent residence in Bethlehem (Matt. 2:11).

Here in a stable-cave, according to Luke 2:7 and an early Christian tradition, Mary bore her first child and laid him in the straw of a rock-cut manger, tightly bound in swaddling clothes, according to the custom of the Near East. The small guest-house just outside the city where Mary and Joseph stopped would not have offered the necessary

30 See Stauffer, *Jesus and His Story,* pp. 27–35; E. F. F. Bishop, *Jesus of Palestine* (London: Lutterworth Press, 1955), pp. 39–40.

privacy for a woman in labor, and this animal shelter was the best that could be quickly found.[31]

According to Luke 2:1 (cf. Acts 5:37) Joseph and his wife had traveled from Nazareth to Bethlehem because of an imperial decree for a census during the administration of Quirinius, legate of the province of Syria. We know of an official census taken under Quirinius' administration in A.D. 6,[32] and some suppose that Luke has erroneously dated that enrollment ten years too early. An early Church father corrected Luke's notice by reminding his readers that the census occurred during the governorship of C. Sentius Saturninus, 9–6 B.C.[33] Recently, it has been contended that the consul P. Sulpicius Quirinius served as a commander-in-chief in the East from 12 B.C. to A.D. 16 and that an official registration of taxable objects and persons was commenced in 7 B.C., which was not completed until fourteen years later.[34] This would satisfy the claims of both Luke and Josephus, but the evidence is not conclusive.

The Gospels and the New Testament as a whole assert the Davidic lineage of Jesus. Our earliest witness, Paul of Tarsus, refers to him as born "under the law" (Gal. 4:4) and "descended from David according to the flesh" (Rom. 1:3; cf. Acts 2:30; II Tim. 2:8). Of course, the purpose of reciting the genealogical lists in Matthew 1:1–17 and Luke 3:23–34 is similarly to assert that Jesus fulfills the prophetic hope of Israel for an anointed king who would re-establish the glorious days of the earlier kingdom of David (*Pss. Sol.* 17:23).[35] Matthew does it by tracing the royal line from Abraham in a triad of fourteen names, probably an acrostic for the Hebrew spelling of the name David. In

---

31 The text of Luke used by Epiphanius in the fifth century read "cave" for the word "stable" (or "manger") in Luke 2:7, corroborated by Justin Martyr (ca. A.D. 150, *Dial.* 78), some apocryphal Gospels, and early Christian art. "Houses in places on both sides of the Jordan were and still are built out from caves, especially on the sides of hills" (Bishop, *Jesus of Palestine,* p. 42).

32 Jos., *Antiq.* XVII.13.5, XVIII.1.1; *War* VII.8.1.

33 Tertullian, *Adv. Marc.* IV.19.

34 Stauffer, *Jesus and His Story,* pp. 27–36. He cites evidence for a similar census in Gaul which extended over more than forty years (p. 167, n. 23). Sir William Ramsey earlier interpreted certain Asia Minor inscriptions to mean that Quirinius was nominally governor of Syria from 11–10 to 8–7 B.C., but there is no record of any imperial enrollment during those years. See the article on Census in A. R. C. Leaney, *The Gospel According to St. Luke* (New York: Harper & Row, Publishers, 1958), pp. 44–47.

35 Mark 12:35–37a does not deny a royal lineage; it questions its significance for a doctrine of messiahship.

an independent list, Luke carries the ancestral line of Joseph behind Abraham, the father of the Hebrews, to Adam, the universal parent of the human race. We may believe that the test of any genealogy is not in its length but in its product, but we must reckon with Jewish pride in ancestral lineage and the widespread use in Judaism of genealogical registers for legal purposes related to family relationships, property claims, and priestly offices.

Since both Matthew and Luke believed that the birth of the Messiah was a special act of God, it follows that they understood the lineage of Jesus in legal rather than literal terms. To be sure, he is several times referred to as the son of Joseph (Luke 3:23, 4:22; John 1:45, 6:42), but these are views of men who are held to be mistakenly confident that they understand who he is and where he comes from. In the early Church, some Jewish Christians evidently believed that Joseph was the natural father of Jesus.[36] The Gospel of John (8:41) hints of the early Jewish accusation that Jesus was an illegitimate child, protesting the pagan claim by his devotees that he was miraculously born of the Spirit of God.[37] Appealing to Isaiah's prophecy of the divine child who would bear the titles of Wonderful Counselor, Mighty God, Everlasting Father, Prince of Peace (Isa. 8:6), Matthew describes the promised child of Mary as one whose name is "God is Salvation," signifying that he will bring salvation to his people (1:21).[38]

Jesus was born not long before the death of Herod the Great in 4 B.C., probably 7–6 B.C. In the third century, January 6th was identified as the natal day, and that date still marks the Christmas feast in Eastern Orthodoxy. A Latin monk in the following century

---

36 Cf. Justin, *Dial.* 48; Irenaeus, *Adv. Haer.* I.26.1. The Sinaitic Syriac version of Matt. 1:16, which is ambiguous but permits the translation: "Joseph...was the father of Jesus who is called Christ," has been held by some to reflect the earliest form of the original Greek. Even so, it is likely that the translator understood legal not literal parentage.

37 What may be the earliest reference to Jesus in the Talmud reports Rabbi Shimeon ben 'Azzai saying: "I have found a genealogical roll in Jerusalem wherein was recorded, 'Such-an-one is a bastard of an adulteress' " (*Yebamoth* IV.3, 49a). In the latter part of the first century, Jewish gossip had invented a story of Mary's illicit relationship with a Roman soldier named Pandera or Pantere. See Joseph Klausner, *Jesus of Nazareth*, trans. Herbert Danby (New York: The Macmillan Company, 1925), pp. 23ff.

38 The Hebrew-Aramaic name Joshua, which was Grecianized into the form *Iēsous* or Jesus, was a fairly common name among the Jews. In the New Testament three others bearing the name are mentioned: Matt. 27:16–17; Acts 13:6; Col. 4:11. Syriac-speaking Christianity calls Jesus Yeshu'.

confirmed the Western tradition of December 25th and erroneously calculated the year as the 754th from Rome's founding. But Herod died in the year 750 (4 B.C.). As a consequence we are forced into the anachronism of fixing the correct date before the traditional beginning of the Christian era.[39]

In Matthew's birth-legend the messianic sign is the appearance of a strangely luminous star in the sky that guides Eastern astrologers to the new-born babe. Johannes Kepler in 1606 concluded that in the latter half of the year 7 B.C. several conjunctions of the planets Jupiter and Saturn occurred. Certainly the popularity of astral cults in a day anticipating the advent of a world deliverer makes credible the story of the speculations and search by Babylonian sorcerers. An Egyptian inscription dating from 7 B.C. speaks of Augustus as the star of the whole Greek world. In Nero's time, some Parthian astrologers led by the Armenian king Tiridates I visited Rome in their search for the "Wonder-Child."[40]

"We have seen his star at its rising," the magi announced to Herod. To the Jew, this could certainly be a divine portent. Did not the Torah teach, "A star shall come forth out of Jacob and a scepter shall rise out of Israel?" (Num. 24:17). According to the *Testament of Levi* 18:3, "His star shall arise in heaven as of a king, lighting up the light of knowledge as the sun the day" (cf. *Test. of Judah* 24:1). More than a century later an ill-fated messianic rebellion broke out, led by a Jew named Simon bar Kosebah, dubbed enthusiastically Simon bar Kokheba (Son of the Star) by his rabbinic mentor Akiba.[41] To the Matthean church, the story of the magi signified the witness of God among heathen peoples and the recognition of Christ as the Savior of all men.

Into the stories of the birth of John and Jesus, Luke has inserted five poetic pieces that may have been early Christian hymns, derived, perhaps, from Jewish messianic canticles of the sort represented in the Qumran *Thanksgiving Hymns* and the *Psalms of Solomon*. Each has come to be known in Christian worship by the opening words of its Latin form: the *Ave Maria*, Gabriel's announcement (1:28–33);

---

39 Dionysius Exiguus, in the sixth century, calculated the Era of the Incarnation beginning in March 25, 754, of Rome. Thus 754 became the year 1 *anno domini.*

40 A.D. 66. Cf. Pliny, *Nat. Hist.* XXX.1.6 (16); Dio Cassius, *Roman History* IX.1–7; Suetonius, *Lives of the Caesars: Nero* xiii.30.

41 See note 18. The star as a messianic portent is referred to in the Qumran literature, e.g., CD vii.19ff.; 1QM xi.6; 4Q Test. 4.

the *Magnificat,* or song of Mary (1:46–55); the *Benedictus,* Zechariah's hymn (1:68–79); the *Gloria in Excelsis,* or angels' chorus (2:14); and the *Nunc Dimittis,* Simeon's prayer of benediction when the young child was presented by his parents in the temple (2:29–32). Like peals of bells they ring out the polyphonic sound of a community's faith in Christ as God's own act. Matthew hails him as the Star, the Branch, Salvation, and Immanuel. Luke names him by other titles: Son of the Most High, the Horn of Salvation, the Dawn, the Sign who will provoke a crisis among men, resulting in either deliverance or condemnation.

The historical worth of the birth-stories has been, and certainly will continue to be, variously judged. Scholars find evidence of two traditions behind the accounts in Matthew and Luke, one assuming a natural, the other a supernatural, birth. The evidence of miraculous births associated with Babylonian and Egyptian king worship or Hellenistic philosophers and rulers is to be noted and critically compared. But such parallels cannot decide the accuracy of the biblical account, which presents significant differences. Furthermore, there are sound linguistic reasons for believing that some elements of the miraculous birth-story rest upon Hebrew originals, showing that the belief may have been current in Jewish-Christian circles before the gospel was heard in the Roman world. This is the more surprising when we realize that a virginal conception was never an element in Jewish messianic prophecies.[42]

We mistake the character of the Gospels and misunderstand the intention of the Evangelists when we insist on treating these stories as sober historical-biological descriptions of the manner of Jesus' entrance into the world. They are primarily confessional and apologetic. They express one form of the kerygma's bold assertion that Jesus Christ is the appearance and act of God within human history to inaugurate a new phase of his reign on earth. By declaring that he is at once by nature and function the Son of God, conceived by the Holy Spirit (Luke 1:35), and the Son of David, born of woman (Matt. 1:18), these writers express in their own terms their persuasion that the Anointed One had come in the flesh (I John 4:3). In sharp

42 Pagan parallels may be read in Robert M. Grant, *Miracle and Natural Law in Graeco-Roman Thought* (Amsterdam: North Holland Publishing Co., 1952), pp. 173ff. Alexandrian Judaism seems to have recognized divine conception: Philo, *De Cher.* 45–50; *Leg. All.* ii.49–51. For a recent study see Thomas D. Boslooper, *The Virgin Birth* (Philadelphia: Westminster Press, 1962).

refutation of any understanding that regarded his physical life as apparitional, they affirm that God had truly and genuinely entered into manhood. Nor was there some point in this history when a heavenly Christ merged with a human Jesus to form a composite personality. From the very beginning he was fully and truly the divine-human Son.

It was this affirmation, not the manner of his coming, that was the cardinal statement of early faith. We have no mention of the precise form of his coming in the oldest apostolic preaching, nor do such principal interpreters of the gospel as John or Paul ever suggest that belief in the miraculous birth is essential to discipleship. For the New Testament the crucial issue is not *how* one describes his appearance in history, but whether one recognizes and receives him for *who* he is and *why* he has come.

The birth-stories are an attempt to explain in narrative form the divine authority of Jesus that is disclosed in his whole ministry. They do not establish his identity; that is given in the nature of the ministry he performs. Mark makes no such attempt to explain Jesus' sonship and divine authority; rather he believes that this relationship to God is a secret that cannot be explored by men, only believed. There is a secret about the Messiah as there is a mystery about the Kingdom he brings. But it is John in the prologue to his Gospel who gives that relationship matchless hymnic expression. The God who revealed himself in the primordial acts of creation had now communicated himself in an act of salvation by invading a particular moment of history in a single truly human life. A new genesis had occurred; a new humanity begun. "The Word became flesh and dwelt among us, full of grace and truth" (John 1:14a).

The Hidden Years

Growing up in the frontier Galilean village of Nazareth,[43] a name unknown in Jewish literature earlier than the Gospels, Jesus was part of a large household which included at least six other children (Mark 6:3; cf. Luke 8:19).[44] From the height of neighboring Neby Sa'in he may have surveyed historic landmarks of his people; watched the caravans of commerce, the Roman militia, and imperial couriers; and begun those long watches in prayer that were decisive in his later

43 *Natserath,* "it guards."

44 Luke 2:7 speaks of Jesus as Mary's "first-born son." The brothers' names are James, who became the leader of the Jerusalem Christian community until his martyrdom in A.D. 62, Joses or Joseph, Judas, and Simon.

ministry. Besides his native Galilean Aramaic tongue, he learned to speak a form of neo-Hebrew that may have been the dialect of the southern district of Judea and was the language, at least, of rabbinic discussion. Perhaps he acquired enough Greek to converse with the many Gentiles who lived in Galilee. Joseph, his father, is described as a carpenter, in Aramaic a *naggar,* a craftsman who worked both in stone and wood. Justin Martyr tells us that Jesus himself fashioned yokes and plows in his father's shop.[45] He may have known from first-hand experience what it meant to stand all day in the broiling heat of a market place, perhaps in neighboring Sepphoris or Japhia, waiting for a day's employment. Such an experience is described in the parable of the laborers in the vineyard (Matt. 20:1–16).

The early Church that is reflected in the Gospels and the whole New Testament had little interest in the personal, pre-public life of Jesus. Apart from the stories of the birth, there is recorded only one incident that offers a glimpse of the so-called "hidden years." Luke singles out one item of interest at the time when, according to Jewish law, the adolescent boy was formally recognized as an adult member of the community, a *ben Torah,* or son of the law. In the fashion of ancient biographical literature, the precociousness and sensitivity of the Nazareth boy are revealed in his eager questioning of learned teachers as they taught in the temple precinct during the festival of Passover (Luke 2:41–52).

It is clear that early Christians saw in the story of Jesus' understanding of the subjects discussed by the rabbis an indication of the one who was to bring the revelation in the law and temple to its fulfillment. Even more significant are the questions the boy addresses to his distraught parents: "How is it that you sought me? Did you not know that I must be in my Father's house?" In legend form the incident reflects Luke's conviction that the true identity and vocation of Jesus were grasped from his boyhood days. He was conscious of a special relationship with the Father whom he called *Abba,* and he sensed the significance of the house as a symbol of the family of God. Here in prospect is his mission as the Evangelist sees it. As the Father's eldest Son, Jesus will call the scattered children of men back home to the Father's house.

---

[45] Justin, *Dial.* 88. Cf. the infancy *Gospel of Thomas* 13.1. But the oldest form of the text of Mark 6:3 reads, "the son of the carpenter (and of Mary)," leaving the occupation of Jesus unmentioned: P[45], 13, 33, 69, Origen, *Contra Celsum* VI.36.

From the standpoint of basic historical evidence, this pre-history of Jesus yields little information beyond the fact that he was born into the home of a craftsman and grew to manhood in the unimportant garrison town of Nazareth in Galilee. Beyond this, these stories must be read as Christological statements testifying to the reality of the Incarnation: God meeting men in this man. With this, the Gospel narratives begin the account of the vocational commission that drew him out of the obscurity of this Galilean hill village and thrust him into an exciting and hazardous mission to the nation. This will be the historical warrant for their bold claim that he is the truly crucial figure in all history.

CHAPTER III

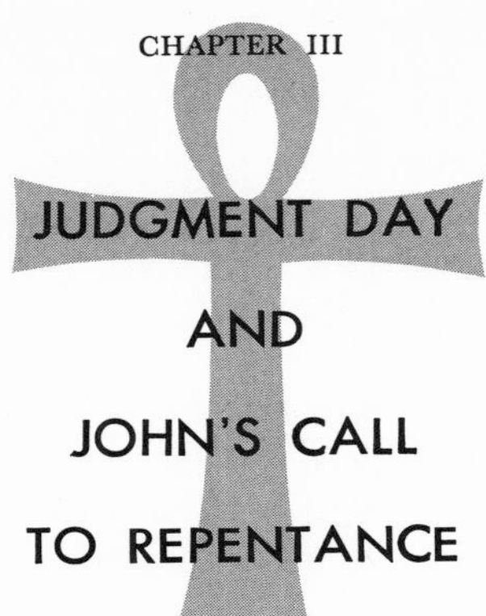

JUDGMENT DAY AND JOHN'S CALL TO REPENTANCE

> He was a good man and commanded the Jews to practice virtue, by exercising justice toward one another and piety toward God, and to come together to baptism [Jos., *Antiq.* XVIII.5.2].

> I tell you this: never has there appeared on earth a mother's son greater than John the Baptist [Matt. 11:11 NEB].

The rebel priest who was dubbed "the Baptizer" by the Jewish crowds in first century Palestine is one of the most intriguing figures in the gospel drama. Mark begins his Gospel with a description of the fire-and-brimstone preaching of this hermit who had emerged out of seclusion to conduct a religious revival on the banks of the Jordan in the Judean desert. In the Synoptic Gospels, John the Baptist is presented as the herald of the Messiah Jesus, the second Elijah who preaches a demand for repentance before the coming Day of Judgment and seals it by the act of baptism. John is convinced that God is ringing down the curtain on the present age of man's rebellious history and making ready for his new and final act in the coming of Israel's Deliverer.

The Mission of John ben Zechariah

The birth and infancy of John the Baptist are described in Luke 1:5–25, 57–80 which, with Chapter 3, may be based upon a Jewish

Baptist source, adapted by the Evangelist to his purposes. John is born of parents who are of the lineage of Aaron and thus members of the ancestral tribe of priests in Israel. The promise of his birth is divinely given to the aged priest Zechariah as he officiates in his turn at the altar in the temple at Jerusalem. Couched in the solemn words of Malachi's prophecy, the angelic announcement declares the priest's child will be empowered by the Holy Spirit. Like the expected prophet Elijah, he will prepare his people for the coming of the dreadful day of the Lord. Bearing a nonfamily name, "God is gracious" or "God gives grace," he will be the prophet of the Most High (*'Elyôn*), in whose name he will extend the assurance of salvation to the truly penitent.

According to the birth-legend, Zechariah and his wife Elizabeth retired to a Judean town in the hill-country near Jerusalem that has been identified since the sixth century with the valley village of 'Ain Karim, about three and a half miles west of Jerusalem. It lies cupped in a rugged region well suited to offer the seclusion they sought (Luke 1:24).[1] It may have been near here that the child was brought up, but it is possible that the wilderness mentioned by Luke (1:80) may refer to the Judean desert to the east of the Holy City, the scene of the Essene community of Qumran and the rallying point for numerous rebel bands. In Jewish thought, the desert had become a symbol of the historical deliverance from Egypt and the forthcoming messianic redemption. That Luke may have had this in mind is indicated by his mention of the locale.[2] Then the record drops away into silence. It might be imagined that John was befriended and brought up as a child in the care of these Jewish monks who were known to receive children, but evidence is lacking.[3]

No more is heard of John until suddenly he appears as a man in the south Jordan valley, addressing the wayward nation with the exultant cry of an earlier prophet: prepare, prepare...for the salva-

---

1 The Jewish poet E ha-Kalir (ninth century), however, identified the Abijah order to which Zechariah belonged with Kephar Uzziel, a little village north of Nazareth in Galilee.

2 See T. F. Glasson, *Moses in the Fourth Gospel* (Naperville, Ill.: Alec R. Allenson, Inc., 1963), Chap. i; Ulrich W. Mauser, *Christ in the Wilderness* (Naperville, Ill.: Alec R. Allenson, Inc., 1963); R. W. Funk, "The Wilderness," *Journal of Biblical Literature*, LXXVIII (1959), 205–14.

3 Cf. Jos., *War* II.8.2. A. S. Geyser proposes that Luke's source had a parallel to 2:41–52 for John that was suppressed. It told of how John was adopted and brought up by Essenes: "The Youth of John the Baptist," *Novum Testamentum,* I (1956), 70–74.

tion of God is soon to become manifested (Isa. 40:3–5).[4] Luke provides a valuable chronological note, locating John's summons to national repentance in the fifteenth year of the principate of Tiberius Caesar, that is to say in the year A.D. October 1, 27–28, or October 1, 28–29.[5] But John has forsaken the family vocation. He is a rebel priest who has fled into the desert as did the Essenes who denounced the corrupt Sadducean hierarchy controlling the temple. His rude attire and meagre diet signify the abject penitence he calls for.[6] He warns all who come to hear him of the imminent intervention of the heavenly Ruler and Judge to destroy evil and rescue the people of God.

The crackling of the fires of judgment can be heard in his impassioned warnings to flee from the approaching wrath that would utterly consume the unrighteous. The "Mightier One" who was to follow him would bring a baptism of fire by the Holy Spirit. Or perhaps John was not speaking of the Spirit at all, but of the storm wind; the word he used can mean either.[7] The imagery was familiar. In one of his nocturnal visions Daniel had vividly described the fiery stream that flowed from before the "Ancient of Days" on his heavenly throne and consumed the latest heathen world-power in divine judgment (Dan. 7:10–11).[8] In the Jewish apocalypse of Ezra, both apocalyptic images appear: "All these were mingled together, the stream of fire and the flaming breath and the great storm, and fell on the onrushing multitude" (IV Ezra 13:11). John's "Coming One" who would

---

4 This is the view of John's Gospel (1:23). The Synoptic writers use the Isaiah passage as their interpretation of John's role. Mark, in his conviction that John was none other than the predicted Elijah-prophet, introduces and identifies the unknown voice of the Isaiah passage as the messenger of Mal. 3:2 and Exod. 23:20.

5 A similar date is reached if we read John 2:20 in the light of Josephus' statement that the reconstruction of the temple was begun in the eighteenth year of Herod (20–19 B.C.). See G. Ogg, *Chronology of the Public Ministry of Jesus* (Cambridge: Cambridge University Press, 1940), pp. 151–67.

6 His attire may simply be that of a desert dweller. But perhaps the Evangelist understood it as a mark of the ancient prophetic order (II Kings 1:8; Zech. 13:4).

7 On the wind as a symbol of judgment see IV Ezra 13:10, 27; Isa. 11:4, 29:6, 30:28; Ezek. 1:4; II Thess. 2:8. See E. Best, "Spirit Baptism," *Novum Testamentum,* IV (1960), 236–43.

8 The Qumran Teacher of Righteousness related the consuming fire to the work of Belial, the Evil One: "The torrents of Belial overflowed all banks/ Devouring like fire all those who draw from them" (1QH iii.29). Cf. vi.18; 1QS ii.8, 15; iv.13. For other references to the fire of judgment see Mal. 3:2f., 4:1; Isa. 56:15f.; *Pss. Sol.* 15:4; IV Ezra 13:4, 10; Luke 12:49; *Gospel of Thomas,* Sayings 10, 82; II Thess. 2:8; Rev. 20:9.

baptize with wind and fire is like the "Righteous Ruler" of the *Psalms of Solomon* who was to purge Jerusalem of aliens and judge the nations.

"Even now the axe is laid to the root of the trees; every tree therefore that does not bear good fruit is cut down and thrown into the fire" (Q Luke 3:9). This apocalyptic evangelist meant "every tree" to be taken with deadly seriousness. No preferential treatment was to be accorded anyone or any group. With the Essenes, he hurled strictures of criticism at the religious leadership of the nation. To haughty lay teachers of the Torah and proud members of the priestly hierarchy, his warning was merciless: "You brood of vipers! Who warned you to flee from the wrath to come? Bear fruit that befits repentance" (Matt. 3:7–8). As Jesus was later to insist,[9] descent from Father Abraham conveyed no special privilege. Only those, whether Jew or Gentile, who had reoriented their lives toward God and been purified from their sins by divine forgiveness could endure the day of his coming. A change of heart was required that found practiced expression in a radical amendment of personal and national behavior.

The response to this stern warning of divine recompense came chiefly from the common people who seemed to be more concerned about their souls than about religious niceties. Prostitutes believed; the respectable ridiculed (Matt. 21:32). Tax collectors and members of the Roman garrison troops, convicted in conscience by his preaching, were given some directive counseling about their future and advised to desist from their grafting practices in accepting *bakshish* to supplement their wages. It was the voice of the messenger Malachi castigating a faithless people who had profaned the covenant, threatening that God would smite the land with a curse in his great and terrible day unless his people returned to him.

John does not bid them accept the monastic ideal and retreat to the desert. Nor does he condemn their occupations, questionable by Torah standards and hence repugnant to Essene and Pharisee alike. Instead he pleads for an inner purity and a social righteousness within their daily work. While representatives of official Judaism watched with disdain, those who heard these searing words and repented in fear and sorrow were banded together in a "confraternity of penitents," as M. Goguel terms it. They constituted a messianic militia, sealed by the act of baptism and confident of their salvation in the final hour.

---

9 John 8:33, 37, 39; Luke 13:6–9, 22–30.

The Baptism of Repentance

In this ceremonial use of water there was nothing unusual. The Pharisees practiced daily ablutions far beyond the requirements of the law to remove the defilements of the market place. It now appears that there were numerous baptizing sects, Jewish and later Jewish-Christian, in first-century Palestine. One of the oldest was certainly the Essene movement which had an important monastic center at Qumran. The Jewish historian Josephus gives the fullest account of the ritual lustrations regularly practiced by the Essenes,[10] and hints of these ceremonial baths are found in some of the Qumran writings.[11] The seven large cisterns discovered at the Khirbet may actually have served as baptistries. However, the baptism of John offered some striking differences. Whereas daily ablutions were a feature of these Jewish groups and signified primarily a ritual purification, it is clear that John's was a single, unrepeatable act charged with ethical and eschatological meaning. It was an act of repentant submission to the divine judgment, already anticipated, and it carried the assurance of God's invitation to be saved from doom and to share in the coming Kingdom.[12]

The Jewish practice of receiving converts from Gentile society by a ritual act of baptism furnishes only a partial parallel, for John was summoning his own people to a decision in the face of the approaching world revolution confronting Jew and Gentile alike. Proselyte baptism received foreigners into the historical reality of Israel. John believed he was sent "to prepare a people that shall be fit for the Lord" (Luke 1:17 NEB). It may be that he intended the act to rebuke Jewish pride in a special status before God by requiring a purification of them that they were accustomed to demand of Gentiles!

John and Qumran

Our new knowledge of the Essene brotherhood of Qumran has suggested the attractive hypothesis that John had been trained in this Essene community. Like him, the brotherhood believed that it was preparing a way in the desert.

---

10 Jos., *Antiq.* XVIII.1.5; *War* II.5.

11 Notably 1QS v.13f.; cf. iii.3–6, iv.20f.; 1QM xiv.2–3; CD x.10ff.

12 Josephus' account of John represents a view of baptism more akin to that held by the Essenes: "For the baptism would be acceptable to God if they used it, not for the putting away of certain sins, but for the purification of the body, the soul having previously been cleansed by righteousness" (Jos., *Antiq.* XVIII.5.2).

> When these men exist in Israel, these are the provisions whereby they are to be kept apart from any consort with froward men, to the end that they may indeed "go into the wilderness to prepare the way," i.e., do what Scripture enjoins when it says, "Prepare in the wilderness the way...make straight in the desert a highway for our God" [1QS viii. 12–13; cf. ix. 16–21; Gaster, *Scriptures,* pp. 56, 59].

Had John broken away from the group, convinced that their work was inadequate in the face of the expected crisis, boldly identifying the wilderness voice of Isaiah 40:3 with himself? Or was he preaching the spirit of the Essene ethic adapted to meet the situation of the ordinary man, thus creating a sort of "Third Order"? The questions are tantalizing but as yet unanswerable. However, this much seems clear: John divides sharply with the Qumran brotherhood on the nature of the preparation and range of the invitation. He believes that men avert the wrath of the approaching judgment by heartfelt repentance and amendment of their lives. To the "sons of light" at Qumran, preparation focused upon the study and discussion of the law, as their comment on the Isaiah passage makes clear. Furthermore, they were to abstain from any discussion with men of ill repute. "They must needs keep apart from all other men" (1QS ix. 21). Only those of the Essene movement constituted the holy remnant of Israel. John, conversely, addressed his appeal to the whole nation. Despite the increasing confidence among scholars that John was at one time identified with the movement, there is no firm evidence that suggests anything more than that he emerged out of a religious background that was influenced by such sectarian views and practices.

The Martyr

A careful reading of the brief notices in the Gospels shows that John's preaching won considerable attention and a devoted following. Mark describes the interest aroused throughout the province of Judea (Mark 1:5). The Evangelist John speaks of John the Baptist's work in Perea, across the Jordan (Wady el-Kharrar?), and in Samaria at Aenon (ed-Der?) in the domain of Scythopolis, some thirty miles north of Jerusalem (John 1:28, 3:22). Perhaps Jesus referred to the earlier work of John and his disciples in Samaria when he spoke of his own disciples' future activity in this territory as a confirmation of previous work: "I sent you to reap that for which you did not labor; others [John?] have labored, and you have entered into their labor" (John 4:38). John and his disciples were rigorously faithful to the law of Moses, impressing others by their acts of piety in regular prayer (Luke 11:1) and fasting (Mark 2:18). John's Gospel observes that at least two of Jesus' disciples had belonged earlier to John's movement (John 1:35–37).

It was no doubt John the Baptist's uncompromising stand on the normative authority of the revealed Torah that finally brought about his death. The matrimonial scandal of the Galilean tetrarch Herod Antipas must have excited whispering and gossiping in the homes and market places throughout the district. Antipas had brazenly divorced his Nabatean wife in order to marry the wife of his half-brother Herod, and John had publicly denounced him for it.[13] To the New Testament writers, this daring accusation of adultery brought John to prison in the royal capital of Tiberias and cost him his life when the tetrarch's step-daughter demanded his head (Mark 6:17–29). Josephus gives another reason. In fear of the growing popularity of the apocalyptic preacher and alarm at the prospect of a rebellion, the tetrarch had John imprisoned and executed at the hill-fortress of Machaerus, a southern frontier post facing the Nabatean border.[14]

Perhaps both explanations are compatible. Both personal and political criticism of this intransigent priest may have contributed to his death. To the masses, however, John became an honored Jewish martyr. Months later in answer to Jesus' question, "Who do men say that I am?" his disciples reported the popular speculation that he might be John the Baptist risen from the dead (Mark 8:27–28). At the very least this must indicate their hope that Jesus would carry out the incomplete program of John. The authority and power operative in John's life were recognized again in Jesus' work. The Pharisees were reduced to fuming silence by Jesus' question about the authority of John's baptism, for fear of popular reprisals if they doubted its divine sanction (Mark 12:32). Several years later (A.D. 36), when Herod's Nabatean father-in-law Aretas IV inflicted a serious defeat upon Herod's troops, the Galilean commoners whispered to one another that this was an act of divine retribution for his execution of John the Baptist. Small wonder that he was called a prophet by the common people.

After his death some of his followers may have allied themselves to

---

13 See Chapter II, note 9.

14 Jos., *Antiq.* XVIII.5.2 (C. K. Barrett, *The New Testament Background: Selected Documents* [New York: The Macmillan Company, 1957], p. 197); and see the description of John in the Slavonic version of Josephus (Barrett, *Background,* pp. 205–6) where the explanation in the Gospels is confirmed.

Jesus' following. But it is likely that the majority of his disciples continued as a distinct sect, ultimately merging with the Mandaeans or one of the many other baptist groups of the time. They may even have strongly contested the witness of Jesus' followers, arguing that their own leader was destined to be the future redeemer whose coming would be marked by heavenly signs and wonders far greater than the healing miracles performed by Jesus. Evidently they enjoyed recognition among the people of Palestine and engaged in widespread missionary activity. Members of the Baptist sect are found in the middle of the century as far apart as Alexandria (Acts 18:24ff.) and Ephesus (Acts 19:1ff.). A Jewish-Christian writing called the *Homilies* of Clement identifies Simon the Magician of Samaria, who was converted by Philip, as a disciple of John (Ps. Clem. *Hom.* II. 22–24; cf. Acts 8:9).

Contemporary Views of John

What was the significance of John's work? How did his followers regard him? Who did he think he was? The answers to these questions are not so readily given, for we must recognize that the New Testament firmly subordinates John's role to the larger work of Jesus whom John was believed to herald. The early Church identified Jesus as the Messiah of John's preaching and vigorously denied any claim of John's independent and superior role. So intimate is the relationship between the two that Luke speaks of John preaching the gospel (3:18), and Matthew puts on John's lips Jesus' own message of urgent repentance before the coming Kingdom (cf. Matt. 3:2 and 4:17).

Nowhere is this subservience more evident than in the Gospel of John. Here the Baptist insists again and again that the normal relationship of teacher and pupil is reversed, for the one who comes after him is greater than he and is destined to increase while he decreases (John 3:30). In this Gospel it is John the Baptist who first speaks the Church's confession of faith in Christ: "Behold the Lamb of God who takes away the sin of the world" (John 1:29, 36). On the other hand, it is this same Gospel that intimates that John the Baptist was thought by some to be the messiah (John 1:20, 3:28; cf. Luke 3:15).

Among his own sympathizers John may have been regarded as the eschatological prophet whose appearance signaled the beginning of God's New Order. They doubtless looked upon him as the herald preparing the way for God's direct intervention in the earthly situation. That, at any rate, is what is clearly meant by the line in Zechariah's hymn: "And thou, child, shalt be called the prophet of the Most High [*'Elyôn*]; for thou shalt go before the Lord [that is, God] to prepare his ways" (Luke 1:76, cf. 14–17). It was only a further refinement of this estimate in John the Baptist's circle to regard him as *both* the prophet and the messiah who acted in God's stead.[15] Among the Mandaeans, whose origins probably go back to the pre-Christian period, Jesus is regarded to be a fake messiah and John appears as the true prophet in Jerusalem, in the sense of a messianic figure. Indeed the so-called Clementine *Recognitions*, an early Jewish-Christian writing, charges that the disciples of John argue falsely (Matt. 11:9, 11) that John is the messiah![16] But the common people generally regarded him as a prophet of God, uttering God's word in their midst (Q Luke 7:26; Mark 11:32 par.). That no little excitement was stirred up by this desert preacher of repentance is indicated by Jesus' words, "He was a kindled and shining lamp, and you were willing to rejoice for a while in his light" (John 5:35).

Even to speak of him as a real prophet, however, was to make a significant appraisal. There was a common belief, shared by the populace and the rabbinic authorities alike, that the voice of prophecy had been silent since Ezra and would reawaken only in the eschatological hour (Joel 2:28ff.).[17] Jesus refers to this popular estimate on one occasion in a tribute to John. He asks the crowds if indeed they had not recognized a prophetic figure in this man now languishing in Herod's jail. Certainly such a fearless preacher was the very opposite of an appeaser bending like a wind-blown reed or a collaborationist enjoying state patronage (Q Luke 7:24–25).

What follows is a most important clue to Jesus' own understanding of the meaning of John's ministry. A prophet, he has been called. Yes, is Jesus' reply and more than any prophet, greater than any member of the ancient prophetic order (Q Luke 7:26).[18] But in what sense? This becomes apparent only when we understand the popular belief in Judaism that in the last hour God would raise up a great priest-

---

15 As in the *Test. Levi* 8:15, 16, where both roles are merged, but this may be a Christian redaction. Cf. M. deJonge, *The Testaments of the Twelve Patriarchs* (Assen, 1953), p. 90.

16 Ps. Clem., *Recog.* I.60. Cf. Ephraem Syrus, *Evangelii Expositio,* ed. Mösinger (1876), p. 288. In turn John is denounced as a false prophet (*Hom.* II.16f.).

17 Cf. Ps. 74:9; I Macc. 4:46, 9:27, 14:41; Jos., *Against Apion* I.8.

18 The version of this saying in the *Gospel of Thomas* makes John the greatest of all mankind! (Saying 46).

prophet who would prepare the way for the Almighty to destroy evil and establish righteousness to the ends of the earth. Alternately, Jewish expectation associated the returning prophet with the messiah either as forerunner or companion, the High Priest of the messianic era.[19] Indeed the two roles were merged at times. The messiah was thought of as one who would accomplish the work of the prophet at the same time. Sometimes the prophet was identified as the second Moses,[20] more commonly as the second Elijah,[21] and even as the second Enoch. "Israel will not fulfil the great repentance before Elijah comes," said Rabbi Eliezer. It was natural enough, therefore, for bystanders to misunderstand Jesus' cry from the cross as a prayer for miraculous rescue by *Mar Elias,* who in Jewish folk piety is still thought of as one who aids people in distress.[22]

When Jesus spoke of John as more than a prophet, those who heard would understand that in the Baptizer the prophet of the end-time had already appeared. Yet, Jesus observes, John had been ridiculed by some as a queer ascetic and put to death as had been predicted (Mark 9:13; cf. Sirach 48:10). But "If you are willing to accept it, he is Elijah who is to come" (Matt. 11:14).[23] Jesus declares that John is the reappearance of Elijah in the world, the prophet who is to come before the Day of the Lord.[24]

Even so, John's greatness cannot obscure his preparatory relationship to the Kingdom of God, signified in Jesus' mission. "I tell you, among those born of women none is greater than John; yet he who is least in the kingdom of God is greater than he" (Luke 7:28). In a real

---

19 At Qumran, three eschatological figures are anticipated: the prophet, the lay messiah, and the priestly messiah (1QS ix.11). But see Matthew Black, *The Scrolls and Christian Origins* (New York: Charles Scribner's Sons, 1961), pp. 145–57.

20 Deut. 18:15, 18; 34:10; 1QS ix.11; 4Q Test. 1; Ps. Clem., *Recog.* I.43. See Howard M. Teeple, *The Mosaic Eschatological Prophet,* Journal of Biblical Literature Monograph Series (Philadelphia: Society of Biblical Literature, 1957), X.

21 Mal. 4:5; Sirach 48:10f.; Justin, *Dial.* 8.4, 49.1.

22 L. Ginzberg, *Legends of the Jews* (Philadelphia: The Jewish Publication Society of America, 1913), IV, 195–235.

23 Cf. Mark 9:13; Luke 1:16–17, 7:27; Matt. 17:10–13. John A. T. Robinson has suggested that John 5:35 may be the equivalent in the fourth Gospel to the identification of John as Elijah in the Synoptics. See "Elijah, John and Jesus," in *Twelve New Testament Studies* (Naperville, Ill.: Alec R. Allenson, Inc., 1962), pp. 39–40.

24 So, essentially, Carl H. Kraeling, *John the Baptist* (New York: Charles Scribner's Sons, 1951), pp. 141–45; G. S. Duncan, *Jesus, Son of Man* (New York: The Macmillan Company, 1949), pp. 99–103.

sense the *"beginning* of the gospel" occurred in the antecedent ministry of John; yet Mark recognizes that the *preaching* of the gospel begins by Jesus only after the arrest of John. In one of the most difficult sayings in the Gospels, Jesus asserts that John marks the dividing point between two periods of history. The old, represented in the work of Moses and the prophets, has come to its transitional point in John's ministry. Now the balance has shifted. *"Since then"* the Kingdom of God exercises its power in Jesus' action, and men of violence try to obstruct it in every possible way (Q Luke 16:16).[25] Everything that had gone before, the law given through Moses and the preaching of the prophets of Israel, had risen to its zenith in the work of John. The time of preparation—warning and repentance—had given way to the new time of the Kingdom's coming—deliverance. Something greater than John had begun.

John's View of Jesus

It is far less certain what John thought about Jesus and of his own relationship to the Nazarene. Despite the confident testimony of John at the time of Jesus' baptism, reported by Matthew and John, one must consider carefully the troubled note in the Baptist's blunt query of Jesus later: "Are you he who is to come, or shall we look for another?" (Q Luke 7:9). Even if there had been some earlier surmise that Jesus would fufill the work of the final prophet, the messenger of the end-time (John 6:14, 7:40), the nature of Jesus' activity and the character of his message were in sufficient contrast to John's understanding to make any such identification most improbable. John looked for a righteous judge and king who would requite the evil and punish the lawless. "His winnowing fork is in his hand, to clear his threshing floor, and to gather the wheat into his granary, but the chaff he will burn with unquenchable fire" (Q Luke 3:17). Now John is bewildered and disillusioned. Jesus does not act like the messenger of the covenant of Malachi's prediction, and certainly one would never recognize messianic traits in him. His preaching about the approaching end was in a new key, and he seemed to accomplish little beyond healing a few sick and gathering about him some simple peasants for instruction. Here was no new Elijah to call down heaven's fire upon the enemies of God!

---

25 Even the alternate translation that interprets the latter clause actively—"men of violence, i.e., enthusiasts, who make every effort to press into it"—does not alter the saying's emphasis on the division of the New from the Old.

Jesus' own reply, concluding with the poignant words, "Blessed is he who takes no offense in me" (Q Luke 7:23), has about it a sense of pathos that this prophet should fail to identify the one who marked the onset of God's reign among men. The rich allusions to Isaiah's prophecy in Jesus' words would suggest that Jesus was identifying himself with the Servant figure of Isaiah rather than the messenger whom Malachi spoke of as the divine precursor.[26] So he is *not* the kind of leader John is looking for. Furthermore, the continuation of John's movement as a separatist group after his death indicates that the leader and his followers rejected any messianic claim in Jesus' program of action. Indeed as we have seen, the later sect of John's followers believed that he himself was both the messenger of the covenant and the messiah.

John, the prophet of righteousness, exposed the sickness of society and warned of the consequences of evil so that men would prepare themselves to meet their God. Jesus freed men who were prisoners of the age, bringing pardon and power for a new life lived with God. The hour was later and other than this ascetic desert prophet himself supposed. The prophet had come, but it was not yet the great and terrible Day of the Lord that John expected. Instead, it was the hour of forgiveness and judgment, the time of God's call to fellowship which was the prelude to his reign.

The Baptism of Jesus

The year A.D. 27 was marked by the coming of a new Roman governor to Palestine. In that year Pontius Pilate succeeded Valerius Gratus as procurator. About the time the new official was getting himself embroiled with the crown's subjects over his order concerning the use of imperial ensigns in Jerusalem,[27] a man about thirty-four years old was drawn with the crowds to listen to John's shrill warnings of onrushing disaster. Leaving the humdrum village life of Nazareth in Galilee, Jesus came down into the Jordan Valley near an out-of-the-way Perean village called Bethany where John was preaching and baptizing (John 1:28). The significance of that experience is already interpreted in the early apostolic preaching. In his Caesarea sermon

[26] Whether Jesus interpreted his mission as a realization of the Suffering Servant continues to be vigorously debated among scholars. See *infra,* Chapter X, pp. 239–43.

[27] Jos., *Antiq.* XVIII.3.1; *War* II.9.2–3; Barrett, *Background,* pp. 123–24.

Peter observes, "God anointed Jesus of Nazareth with the Holy Spirit and with power" (Acts 10:38), and this is put into relationship with the baptism of John (Acts 10:37; cf. 1:22) as the beginning of Jesus' proclamation of good news of peace.

The Baptism as Jesus' Experience

The report of that commissioning experience in the Synoptics has been judged by a number of scholars to represent a faith-legend developed from some inaugural event of Jesus' ministry intended to validate the Christian conviction that Jesus is the Messiah. Hence they argue that the baptismal and temptation stories can tell us nothing about Jesus' own experience and the decisions he reached here. But it is by no means unlikely that these stories represent the substance of a pivotal inner experience which Jesus later shared with his disciples. In any event, the assertion that Jesus was baptized by John was certainly not invented by the early Church. There was perplexity and embarrassment enough in trying to explain how the one they claimed as Messiah could have submitted to a washing signifying repentance and the forgiveness of personal sinfulness.[28] Only Mark is untroubled by the act. John's Gospel omits any description of the event; Luke reduces the notation to a single participle in his Greek text (*baptisthentos,* "being baptized," 3:21); and Matthew inserts an obscure explanation plainly intended to guard against any charge that Jesus came with other sinners to acknowledge his own need for the divine mercy.

What seems quite clear is that the early Christian Church interpreted the difficult story of the baptism as an authentication and confirmation of Jesus' vocation as the Servant-Son. In the heavenly words addressed to Jesus,[29] "Thou art my beloved Son; with thee I am well pleased,"[30] there is to be found a variant form of the opening lines of the first Servant Song.

---

28 This is strikingly illustrated in the account of the baptism in the Jewish-Christian apocryphal *Gospel According to the Nazarenes* (*Hebrews*), (*Gospel Parallels,* 2nd ed. [New York: Thomas Nelson & Sons, 1957], p. 10), and Ignatius' explanation: "He was baptized, that by himself submitting he might purify the water" (*Eph.* 18:2; cf. *Smyr.* 1:2; Tert., *Adv. Jud.* 8).

29 So Mark 1:11 and Luke 3:22, although Matthew 3:17, by his use of the third person, understands a wider audience.

30 The rabbis taught that since the time of the prophets the heavens were parted occasionally and men could hear the echo of the divine Voice (*bath qôl,* lit. "daughter of the voice").

> Behold my servant, whom I uphold,
> my chosen, in whom my soul delights;
> I have put my spirit upon him,
> he will bring forth justice to the nations.
> [Isa. 42:1][31]

It may be that this same prophetic foundation of the Suffering Servant lies beneath the witness of John the Baptist to Jesus in the fourth Gospel when he hails Jesus as the Lamb of God.[32]

Who is this Servant pictured by Isaiah? The prophet seems to have conceived him as the embodiment of all the faithful in Israel, endowed with the Spirit of God to establish the divine justice within Israel and among all the nations of mankind. In the mysterious and rapturous climax to these Servant Songs (Isa. 52:13–53:12), the Servant takes upon himself the burden of human guilt and willingly goes to death as a vicarious sacrifice who will make at-one-ment between God and man. It is of vital significance, therefore, to understand that in the Church's earliest tradition Jesus had consciously identified himself with this representative suffering figure. It happens that subsequent development of the doctrine of Christ made little use of this figure. That it is so prominent a feature of the portrait of Jesus in the Gospels —without explicit mention of the name—supports the conclusion that it was a model chosen by Jesus himself.

The association of the baptismal experience with a mission leading to suffering and death, suggested by the account in the Gospels, finds an echo in a saying of Jesus. Luke preserves a haunting cry of a later moment in the ministry when Jesus recognizes the disturbing and divisive effect of his appearance among men. "I came to cast fire upon the earth; and would that it were already kindled! I have a baptism to be baptized with; and how I am constrained until it is

---

31 The Western text of Luke 3:22 combines Isa. 42:1 and Ps. 2:7, followed also by the apocryphal *Gospel of the Ebionites* (*Gospel Parallels,* p. 11), but this reading is clearly secondary. Cf. Reginald H. Fuller, *The Mission and Achievement of Jesus* (Naperville, Ill.: Alec R. Allenson, Inc., 1954), p. 87, though others share with Bultmann the view that this reading and even Mark 1:11 express an adoption formula.

32 See Isa. 53:7, 12. C. F. Burney and J. Jeremias have suggested that the "Lamb of God" in 1:29, 36, could represent an alternative translation of the Aramaic term "servant of God." C. H. Dodd argues that the lamb is a reference to the messianic king, represented often in Jewish apocalyptic writing as a ram. See *The Interpretation of the Fourth Gospel* (Cambridge: Cambridge University Press, 1953), pp. 230–38.

accomplished!" (Luke 12:49; cf. Mark 10:38–39).[33] This baptism of suffering and death is crucial to his task from first to last. Whether or not Jesus understood himself as the embodiment of the Servant figure, he viewed his prospective death as climacteric in God's plan.

The compelling God-consciousness of Jesus in the Gospels, that magnificent obsession with the immediate presence of the Holy in human life, finds expression in this inaugural event in the prophetic language of address. Jesus is called the Beloved Son; he is the Chosen One. It is this realization that he is bound in complete concord of will with the Father, entrusted with the true knowledge of God and his purpose, that is fundamental to the baptismal experience. He is the Beloved, the Son of God in a unique, unshared sense. He will give authentic declaration to the Father's will and enact the events through which his reign will be established among men. We are not to imagine that this consciousness of special filial relationship had its origin at the baptism. It is rather given fresh assurance and confirmation in this luminous moment.

The meaning of that sonship is already determined by the Servant language in which it is set. As Israel of old is called Son and Servant by God in the context of a summons to service, so for Jesus sonship is to be demonstrated not by self-conscious claims but by a devoted obedience to the Father's will. "Although he was a Son, he *learned obedience* through what he suffered" (Heb. 5:8). This is quite a different conception from the messianic Son-King of the second Psalm who executes the wrath of God by breaking proud nations with a rod of iron. Thus these simple and profound words in which the baptismal experience is couched, when grasped in terms of their traditional Old Testament association, open impressive dimensions of insight into Jesus' conception of his vocation. He will represent faithful Israel to faithless Israel. That task was the expression in action of a deep consciousness that the Father recognized him as the Beloved through whom the Kingdom of God and his righteousness would be disclosed to men.

The Church and the Baptism of Jesus

This is not to deny that this epiphany story of the baptism is indelibly imprinted with the faith-witness of the resurrection com-

33 Compare Paul's expression "baptism into death," Rom. 6:3–4; Col. 2:12; and note the Old Testament prototype in Pss. 42:7, 69:2, 15; Isa. 43:2. The corresponding saying in the Thomas Gospel omits the reference to baptism (Saying 10).

munity. Interpreting this initial event of the redemptive work of Jesus, the early Church joyfully proclaimed the *rapprochement* between heaven and earth. Doubtless the early preachers recalled the words of a Jewish apocryphal writing describing the consecration of the messianic high priest:

> The heavens shall be opened, and from the temple of glory shall come upon him sanctification, with the Father's voice as from Abraham to Isaac. And the glory of the Most High shall be uttered over him, and the spirit of understanding and sanctification shall rest upon him.[34]

It is the view of the earliest Gospel that from the time of his empowerment by the Spirit coming upon him at his baptism Jesus was confirmed as the unique Son of God, commissioned to perform the sacrificial work of Isaiah's righteous sufferer and consecrated as the perfect High Priest.

This account of the gift of the Spirit at the baptism was a clarification and deepening of the older Christian view that Jesus entered into his messianic office in and through his death and resurrection. Rabbinic teaching maintained that the Spirit which had departed earlier from Israel would return with the messiah and through him bless and empower his people.[35] It was just this experience the early Church knew in its encounters with the risen Lord that brought the strange, new power of the Spirit into their lives and gave promise of their final salvation. But in identifying that manifestation of God's Spirit with the *beginning* of Jesus' ministry, Mark and Matthew emphasize that his messiahship was the cause, not the consequence, of his mission on earth. They testify, in effect, that in Jesus the Spirit of God had invaded the earthly realm of Satan and joined the battle that would finally issue in the victory of God. Here, to them, was the beginning point of that cosmic struggle wherein the sovereign Lord would reclaim and renew his creation. The dawn of a new day had broken upon the darkness of this world in the messianic mission

---

34 *Test. Levi* 18:6–7 (a Christian insertion?). Note the central significance of the priestly office to interpret Christ for the writer of Hebrews (4:14–10:18); cf. Rev. 1:13 and the sacerdotal overtones of John 17. Further, the emphasis in Hebrews upon Jesus as both High Priest and mediator of a new covenant (9:15, 12:24) shows a close relationship between the concept of the High Priest and the Servant whose function is to re-establish the covenant with God (Isa. 49:8). The Isaiah scroll from Qumran (1QISa) contains a striking reading at 52:14–15a in which the Servant is said to make an expiation (lit. covering) for many nations, i.e., a cultic act.

35 Cf. *Pss. Sol.* 17:42, 18:8; *I Enoch* 49:3, 62:3; *Test. Judah* 24:1. The *Targum* on Isa. 42:1–4 reads, "I will make my Holy Spirit rest upon him."

of Jesus, and these Gospel writers and their circles bore witness to it. Basically this was their own experience of a new existence seeking rationalization in their interpretation of Jesus' mission.

The Messianic Trials

For the Evangelists, recounting and interpreting the story of Jesus, the double event of the baptism and the temptations signifies the onset of the new and final stage in God's purposive action in history. As they see it, this is the point in history where God's lost creation, fallen under the power of Satan, hears the word of deliverance as Jesus, the obedient Son of God, confronts humanity's jailer and defeats him. In the vain effort of the Evil One to gain control over Jesus, there is signaled a turning point in the relation of men to God. Centuries before, Israel had undergone trials in the wilderness and suffered defeat. In Christ, Israel faced anew the ancient challenge to choose whom it would serve. The early Church saw in his victory over God's arch rival the promise of man's own choice of the true God over all rival demi-gods. The dialogues at the Jordan and in the desert thus mark a decisive event in the whole salvation history.

In such a parable as the Strong Man (Satan) who is bound by an invader and his possessions plundered, Jesus himself interprets the hour of his healing action as a conflict of cosmic dimension that will result in the Evil One's defeat (Q Luke 11:21–23; Mark 3:27).[36] The binding of Satan by the messiah is vividly described in a Jewish apocalyptic tract of the times:

> In his priesthood shall sin come to an end, and the lawless shall cease to do evil. And he shall open up the gates of paradise, and shall remove the threatening sword against Adam. And he shall give to the saints to eat from the tree of life, and the spirit of holiness shall be on them. And Beliar shall be bound by him, and he shall give power to his children to tread upon the evil spirits [*Test. Levi* 18:9–12].

The ecstatic cry of triumph which echoes the enthusiastic reports of the seventy missioners at a later point in the story, "I saw Satan fall like lightning from heaven" (Luke 10:18; cf. Isa. 14:12; Rev. 12:8f.), and what may be its Johannine form, "Now is the judgment of the

[36] Cf. Rev. 12:10; Thomas, Saying 35. Jeremias suggests that the parable is an allusion to this same experience of temptation and victory (*The Parables of Jesus,* 6th ed. trans. S. H. Hooke [New York: Charles Scribner's Sons, 1963], pp. 122f.). Cf. James M. Robinson, *The Problem of History in Mark* (Naperville, Ill.: Alec R. Allenson, Inc., 1957), p. 31.

world, now shall the ruler of this world be cast out" (John 12:31)—confirms the conclusion that Jesus believed himself to be God's own champion in the mortal combat between the Kingdom of God and the Kingdom of Satan. It is in the light of the battle now joined and the initial victory won over the power that seduces men from God that Jesus confidently proclaims, "The time is fulfilled, and the kingdom of God is at hand; repent, and believe in the gospel" (Mark 1:15).

The threefold crisis-decision found in the major Sayings-Source Q contains certain stylized features. Yet it is a superfine criticism which dismisses the story simply as a Hellenistic-Christian legend dealing with the problem of miracle[37] or an apology for the Church as the true Israel of tested faithfulness.[38] Nor is it any more certain that it represents in legendary form simply an epitome of all the doubts and temptations Jesus faced throughout his eventful mission. There are echoes of the forty-day desert fast of Moses when the covenant law was received (Exod. 34:27f.) and the tryst of Elijah with Yahweh at the end of the forty-day fast in the wilderness of Horeb (I Kings 19:8ff.). But it is entirely plausible that the first reaction to the Servant task would take the form of a prayerful wrestling with the alternatives to action, and the firm rejection of every popular conception of messianic leadership which ran counter to the Father's will. Here in the solitude of a wilderness retreat, traditionally identified with the slopes of Quarantana, the recesses of Jesus' inner self furnished the ground on which the cosmic strife between God and not-God was waged: "And the angels ministered to him" (Mark 1:13b).

The trials may be viewed as three parabolic signs of the nature of God's New Order and, accordingly, the essential function of messianic leadership. Two begin with the insinuation that Jesus is misguided in the conviction that he is the Beloved, the elect one of God: "If you are the Son of God. . . ."[39] Surely one who believed himself to be God's

---

37 Rudolf Bultmann, *History of the Synoptic Tradition,* trans. John Marsh (New York: Harper & Row, Publishers, 1963), pp. 255f.

38 J. A. T. Robinson, *Twelve New Testament Studies,* p. 60.

39 Though not a common designation for the messiah in Judaism, there are a few instances of the title Son of God: viz. *I Enoch* 105:2 (interpolation?); IV Ezra 7:28f., 13:32, 37, 52; 14:9. In the Gospels the title suggests that Jesus is at once the representative of faithful Israel (Son of God is a common title in the Old Testament for the nation or its anointed leader, the king) and the one who stood in unique relationship with the Father.

Son must exercise miraculous power and display the authority of a righteous ruler. But since the concept of the chosen leader in Judaism cannot be separated from the concept of the community, these testings also involve considerations of what the nature of ransomed Israel will be, an imperialist nation or a servant people.

1. *The bread sign.* For a people living for the most part amid dire poverty, it is quite understandable that the messianic age was often construed as a time of unparalleled material prosperity where hunger was no longer a principal enemy of humanity. In the related form of a ministry centering in physical relief to situations of starvation and sickness, Jesus was to face continuously the decision of determining the inclusive and interior character of the divine salvation. Was it restricted to the outward circumstances and exterior forms of human life? "To provide the hungry man with bread is to prepare the way for the coming of grace."[40] Surely the bread problem was implicated in the whole predicament of man, but it was an illusion to believe that solving the bread problem automatically solved the manhood problem. The bread of the village ovens was God's gift now; but eaten ungratefully it became simply man's bread and nothing more. An economic interpretation which defines the three central questions of life as What shall we eat? What shall we drink? and What shall we wear? is the mark of pagan man who is still insensitive to the basic hunger of the soul (Matt. 6:31–32). The Torah itself declared: "Man does not live by bread alone, but man lives by everything that proceeds out of the mouth of the Lord" (Deut. 8:3b). Had not the God of Moses fed the Hebrew refugees in the wilderness with both manna and his word?

The context of the Deuteronomic passage makes clear that men are to live in humble dependence and faithful obedience upon God, who alone satisfies their hungers and preserves their lives. Keeping his commandments, walking in his ways, fearing him—this is the course of the true people of God. For Jesus, to lead and live in the Kingdom is to seek first the righteousness of God and to have implicit confidence in his power to supply all man's needs. Even the Son is to manifest humble, trustful obedience, rather than dazzling men with displays of miraculous power. Jesus' word to his disciples on one occasion when they were traveling through Samaria to Galilee expressed his firm conviction about man's proper regimen: "My food is to do the

40 Dietrich Bonhoeffer, *Ethics,* ed. Eberhard Bethge, trans. Neville Horton Smith (New York: The Macmillan Company, 1955), p. 95.

will of him who sent me and to accomplish his work" (John 4:34). Like Amos of old, he believed the greater famine among men was for the authentic word of God.

2. *The political sign.* The principal messianic temptation is second in the Lucan order. National longing for release from Roman oppression shaped the popular politico-national definition of the New Age God would usher in. It was this conception of secular power and political ascendancy that informed the popular understanding of the office denoted by the titles Messiah or Christ and Son of David. In the present text, the Adversary, whom John's Gospel calls "the ruler of this world," offers to confer his authority upon God's Son in exchange for homage and service.[41] The Gospel of John also records a very illuminating detail in connection with the feeding of the multitude that gives substance to the reality of this temptation. "Perceiving then that they were about to come and take him by force to make him king, Jesus withdrew again to the hills by himself" (John 6:15). Here was the re-emergence of the Maccabean ideal in the revised apocalyptic editions of the Zealots and the Qumran Essenes. Can this have been the meaning of Jesus' cryptic reference in the tribute to John the Baptist, "Until now the kingdom of heaven has suffered violence, and men of violence take it by force" (Matt. 11:12)?[42]

But Jesus, after careful deliberation on his life's mission, thrusts the political ideal aside as satanic. The depth of that decision is forcefully illustrated in the retort to Peter's shocked reaction at the first prediction of a suffering that must be faced: "Out of my way, Satan! You are a stumbling-block to me; for you are more concerned for a human empire than for the kingdom of God!"[43] Jesus' role as God's Son is not jealously to usurp his power but in humble and reverent obedience to submit to the divine will. The words of the Torah summed it up: "You shall fear the Lord your God; you shall serve him and swear by his name" (Deut. 6:13).

---

[41] Compare the account in Rev. 13 where the political power represented in the empire does, in fact, become the agency by which the Adversary continues to exercise control over the world. Stephen Vincent Benét's play, "The Devil and Daniel Webster," portrays the story of a man miraculously freed from such fateful bargaining with the supreme pretender.

[42] Note the interesting reference to the "men of violence who rebelled against God" in the *Habakkuk Commentary* of Qumran (1QpHab viii. 11; G. Vermes, *The Dead Sea Scrolls* [Baltimore: Penguin Books, Inc., 1962], p. 237) and the allusion to coercion in John 6:15.

[43] Matt. 16:23, in the translation of Thomas Walter Manson, *The Servant-Messiah* (Cambridge: Cambridge University Press, 1956), p. 36.

3. *The miracle sign.* Such was the penetration of Greek culture into Jewish Palestine that Jesus and his people were likely aware of the Hellenistic belief in "divine men" (*theioi andres*) who exercised wonderful powers and claimed to be sons of God. Might there not be a spectacular demonstration of power that would authenticate Jesus' work and persuade men that he had truly been sent from the Father? The Gospels provide numerous instances of such situations marked always by his firm refusal to legitimate his ministry in any such way. "Then some of the scribes and Pharisees said to him, 'Teacher, we wish to see a sign from you.' But he answered them, 'An evil and adulterous generation seeks a sign; but no sign shall be given to it except the sign of the prophet Jonah," (Q Matt. 12:38–39; cf. 16:1–4; Mark 8:11–12; Luke 23:8; John 2:18–21, 6:30). Cheap wonder-working was not the way of God, but the prompting of Satan. The Torah maintained that the real test of a prophet was not signs or wonders but the stimulation of a passion for God (Deut. 13:2–6).

Here, in this final vision of a miraculous rescue from death in an imaginary fall from the dizzy height of the royal cloister of the temple overlooking a deep chasm,[44] the prospect of a riskless, guaranteed victory is faced and rejected as satanic. Quoting Scripture, Shakespeare's Antonio observes,[45] Satan reminds Jesus of the scriptural promise of angelic protection given the Chosen One against every pitfall or danger (Ps. 91:11f.). In reply Jesus recalls the peevish attempts of the Israelites to force God's hand once and the rebuke of Moses, "You shall not put the Lord your God to the test, as you tested him at Massah" (Deut. 6:16). The best commentary on this trial of Jesus is furnished by the perceptive words in the Epistle to the Hebrews: "Although he was a Son, he learned obedience through what he suffered; and being made perfect he became the source of eternal salvation to all who obey him" (Heb. 5:8f.). The way of salvation led directly into and through suffering and death, not around it.

Clearly the Evangelists have localized in this narrative the victories that in fact were not wholly won short of Easter. Nevertheless we may believe that from the outset of his ministry Jesus was keenly aware

---

44 See the description of the southeast cloister of the temple area in Jos., *Antiq.* XV.11.5. Cf. *Pesikta Rabba* 162a on the manifestation of the king messiah on the temple roof.

45 *The Merchant of Venice,* Act I, scene 3, line 99.

of the threats to the full accomplishment of the challenge that came to him at the Jordan. His was something more than a personal ethical problem centering in human desires for security and popularity. The ordeals both anticipate and summarize the struggles of this whole mission conceived as a frontal attack on the dominion of darkness. As Professor Jeremias has proposed, one may actually view the three temptations as three parabolic versions of a single experience centering in the role of the Davidic warrior prince, the folk messiah of the time. To Jesus, this was not God's messiah at all, but the Devil's messiah who must be defeated if God is to hold sway.[46] To oppose him was to spurn those marks of his deceitful power that attract his victims: material security, imperialist authority, and safety first at any price. Continually, Satan was to be engaged and subdued; and this initial defeat was the harbinger that man's ancient foe was destined for destruction. The Gospel stories of Jesus' victory over the demons of disease plaguing human life were but further evidence of the power of the Spirit manifest in this New Age.

The Early Ministry of Jesus

According to Luke's chronological notation, Jesus was about thirty years old when he began his public ministry in A.D. 27–28 (Luke 3:23). Both Matthew and Mark date the beginning of his work from the time of the arrest and perhaps the execution of the desert prophet by Herod's police. On the face of it, this comes into collision with the report in John's Gospel that for some time Jesus and John carried on parallel but independent missions in Judea (John 3:22–4:2). Are we forced to decide between these two accounts? A fuller realization that symbolic and theological interests have determined the arrangement of the events in the Synoptic Gospels as well as in John's will induce some caution at this point. Actually it is worthy of note that Mark does not *exclude* an earlier Judean and Samaritan ministry; he merely observes that the preaching of the Gospel of God in *Galilee* did not begin until John's arrest. Perhaps he did not know of any earlier work. Or perhaps he believes, as we shall suggest, that the distinctive proclamation of Jesus that the Kingdom of God was at hand, the fulfillment of John's eschatological preaching, coincided with the end of John's work. It may be that Mark thinks of Galilee

46 Jeremias, *Parables*, pp. 122f.

as the proper scene for the Messiah's revelation, whereas John holds that Jerusalem is the appointed place for his work and death.

It is not primarily the localization of Jesus' work to Galilee, but the new note in his preaching that the Evangelists want to relate to John's arrest. Matthew emphasizes this still more strongly by establishing a causal relationship between the two events. The arrest was the occasion of Jesus' withdrawal into Galilee and the call to repent in the conviction that the sovereign intervention of God was even then upon them. In one passage, at least, Luke is at pains to correct the Marcan picture of a ministry confined to Galilee, for he makes mention of Jesus preaching in the synagogues of Judea, though Mark and Matthew read "Galilee" (Luke 4:44 and par.).

It is the Gospel of John that offers some description of these concurrent ministries. We are told that two of Jesus' first disciples were originally members of John the Baptist's circle: Andrew and, presumably, John, the son of Zebedee (John 1:37–40). We learn that Jesus and his disciples carried on a ministry of baptism in Judea after John and his followers had moved into Samaria to a watering place called Aenon ("Springs" the modern ed-Der). Here, in a dispute with a Jew[47] about the meaning of purification, the piqued disciples of John report the increasing popularity of Jesus and his group. Refusing the role of a rival, Jesus is said to have departed from Judea to return to Galilee.

This close association of Jesus with the preaching and baptizing of John finds confirmation in two interesting stories Luke reports in the Acts. One refers to an Alexandrian Jew named Apollos who is curiously said to have spoken and "taught accurately the things concerning Jesus, though he knew only the baptism of John" (Acts 18:25). Subsequently Paul instructs some Ephesians who, though called disciples, had only received the baptism of John (Acts 19:1–7). Evidently the tradition of a close relationship between John and Jesus related to baptism persisted beyond the midpoint of the century.

From the time of the Church fathers it has been speculated that Jesus began his public activity as a disciple of the Baptist who, like his teacher, preached the baptism of repentance for the forgiveness of sins. Professor Dodd interprets the Baptist's word in John 1:30 to mean, "There is one among my disciples who has gained precedence over me, for he is my superior." Furthermore, the expression "He who comes after me" is a common designation for the pupil of a rabbi,

---

47 Reading *John* 3:25 with P^{75}, S^{3}, B, and W. An attractive conjecture is that the original text read "Jesus" here, but there is no manuscript support.

and therefore his inferior.[48] But though this is an interesting possibility, our evidence permits only the conclusion of parallel activity in Judea and Samaria on the part of the two men and their associates, followed by a separation.[49]

Despite the insistence on an earlier ministry concurrent with John the Baptist, even John's Gospel recognizes that the principal period of Jesus' work followed temporally on John's. Was this simply rescuing the mission of John from failure now that political forces had conspired to reduce him to silence? This cannot be the explanation, since John's witness continued to be made by his followers even after his death. More significantly, it is evident that Jesus' message and his activity differ appreciably from the former work of John. No mention is made again that either Jesus or his disciples practiced the ritual of baptismal sealing of repentance. There are differences between the two groups of disciples with respect to fasting (Mark 2:18) and fixed prayers (Luke 5:33, 11:1). Beyond this, Jesus is a traveling preacher bringing his message of God's new day to town and city throughout the province. John is a desert recluse summoning people to come to him. John's austere way of life, redolent of the fiery Elijah of old, stands in sharp contrast to Jesus' acceptance of the normal life of the Palestinian peasant.

But the basic difference is not to be found in conflicting ideas about the significance of baptism nor even in their attitude toward the Torah, as some have suggested. The crisis details are unknown, but they probably center in Jesus' conviction that the day of Elijah had already occurred in the ministry of John; the time was now ripe for the dawn of the New Age of God's rule. In the arrest and death of John, Jesus recognized an event of eschatological fulfillment. John's work was now over. "I tell you that Elijah has come, and they did to him whatsoever they pleased, as it is written of him" (Mark 9:13). A new hour had struck. The time of the proclamation and the manifest signs of the Kingdom of God had arrived.[50]

---

48 Compare Cullmann's suggestion that Matt. 11:11 refers to Jesus, who though least as a disciple of John is nevertheless greater than John in the Kingdom of Heaven. Oscar Cullmann, *The Early Church,* ed. A. J. B. Higgins (Philadelphia: The Westminster Press, 1956), pp. 180ff.

49 See also Maurice Goguel, *Life of Jesus,* trans. Olive Wyon (New York: The Macmillan Company, 1949), Chap. x. Goguel believes that Matt. 2:23 originally referred to Jesus' membership in the Nasareans, the sect associated with John (p. 197). Cf. Ethelbert Stauffer, *Jesus and His Story,* trans. Richard and Clara Winston (New York: Alfred A. Knopf, Inc., 1960), Chap. iv.

50 Kraeling, *John the Baptist,* pp. 152f. Cf. Goguel's more sharply pointed account of the differences, *Life of Jesus,* pp. 310–16.

For a time Jesus had labored beside John in an appeal for a national conversion, perhaps believing that by moral amendment man could stay God's wrath and induce him to give the Kingdom as reward. But now a turning point was reached with the termination of John's work. What lay behind it we do not and cannot know. But in the principal period of Jesus' ministry there is a sharp criticism of Pharisaic moralism and ultralegalistic piety, on the one hand, and an insistence on the divine pardon and the immediacy of God's reign on the other. True preparation demanded not so much rededication to the law of God as an entire submission of will to the God of the law. That rule signified blessing, not cursing. God sought to reconcile men out of a father-love rather than to condemn them out of a dispassionate justice. Men were to rejoice in the forgiveness God now freely extended; this was their only hope to find a place in the Father's house and to share in the joy of a restored family fellowship. Not terror in the prospect of the coming wrath pronounced by a righteous judge, but gratitude before the presence of a forgiving father, marked the appropriate response. It is this new announcement of promises now beginning to be realized in a surprising way that divides the time of Jesus from the time of John.

CHAPTER IV

THE CRISIS HOUR OF GOD'S COMING

> He has allotted them [[the spirits of truth and falsehood]] to the children of men that they may know good [and evil, and] that the destiny of all the living may be according to the spirit within [them at the time] of the visitation.*

> The time has come; the kingdom of God is upon you; repent, and believe the Gospel [Mark 1:15 NEB].

Cry, the Beloved Country

From the time of his return to Galilee after John the Baptist had been captured by Herod's police, Jesus was engrossed in the task of alerting his people to the imminent ingression of the Kingdom, the new world of glory. Mark's summary of this "good news" of God's sovereign action clearly demonstrates Jesus' controlling conviction that God's rule, long delayed, was now about to upset the confused and contradictory history of the age of man: "The time is fulfilled, and the Kingdom of God is at hand; repent and believe in the gospel" (Mark 1:15).

In the Gospels the Kingdom is a symbol for God's sovereign rule over the earth and its peoples. As such, men can pray for its coming (Matt. 6:10), rise to meet and accept it (Mark 10:15), seek it (Luke 12:31), enter into it by anticipation (Matt. 5:20), or inherit it

* 1QS iv.20; G. Vermes, *The Dead Sea Scrolls in English* (Baltimore: Penguin Books, Inc., 1962), p. 78.

(Matt. 25:34). But its coming is not determined by human willingness nor readiness to receive it, let alone men's creative skills to fashion it! If its full power has not yet been manifest it is because the divine patience permits an opportunity of repentance and life to men who would otherwise be doomed in the hour of reckoning (Luke 13:6–9). But the Kingdom is God's to give and to withhold. Nevertheless it is his good pleasure to give men the Kingdom, such is his outreaching, unrestricted, incautious mercy and love (Luke 12:32). Men are to prepare for its coming by renouncing all lesser claims upon them: in some cases family obligations and property rights, and manifesting a self-forgetting love in all their dealings with others and with God.

Images of the Kingdom

Nowhere in the Gospels does Jesus offer a definition of the Kingdom. He never constructs a formula that begins: "The Kingdom of God can best be described as. . . ." Nevertheless we gain insight into its meaning by examining the terminologies he employs, as well as by the comparisons he delineates in the parables. A study of the Semitic expression *malkûth* that underlies the Greek word *basileia* in the Gospels reveals that the principal emphasis falls upon kingship, the activity of God as ruler.[1] Thus we may more accurately translate the familiar expression, the rule or reign of God. The Kingdom is not some *thing;* it is God himself who in a powerful love repossesses his own creation and transforms it until it becomes plastic to his intention. Nevertheless the Greek concept already embraces the resultant effect of sovereign action in the establishment of a new realm, a citizenry that embodies the peace and the righteousness of its ruler.

Whereas the recurrent term "Kingdom of God" outnumbers all others, other word pictures are borrowed from the rich vocabulary of Jewish eschatology which the Evangelists utilize in their reports of Jesus' proclamation. Thus Matthew speaks in terms suggestive of Jewish liturgy and piety about the Kingdom of Heaven, where Heaven is to be understood as a reverential substitute, like Place and Name, for the unutterably sacred name of God. Once (Matt. 13:43) it is called the Kingdom of the Father.[2] This new world of divine engineering is

---

[1] Cf. K. L. Schmidt *et al., Basileia* in *Bible Key Words,* VII, trans. H. P. Kingdon (London: Adam and Charles Black, Ltd., 1957), 12, 16; similarly the Greek equivalent, p. 32.

[2] Several times the expression Kingdom of Christ or Kingdom of the Son of Man is employed (Matt. 13:41, 16:28; Luke 22:30, 23:42). These are probably secondary formulations originating in the distinction the early Church

sometimes described figuratively as a wedding feast or banquet celebrated by the messianic bridegroom, as in the parable of the ten maidens (Matt. 25:1–13). The imagery of a family table fellowship in the Father's house finds frequent representation. "I tell you," says Jesus, "Many will come from east and west and sit at table with Abraham, Isaac, and Jacob in the kingdom of heaven" (Q Matt. 8:11, recalling Isa. 25:6ff.).

Jesus' references to the destruction of the earthly temple and the creation of a new, spiritual house of prayer for all people of the earth are to be understood in terms of the biblical and extracanonical image of the new temple on Mount Zion which would mark the New Age.[3] This is, of course, nothing other than the Father's house in which the messianic banquet is to be celebrated (John 14:2; cf. 2:16; Luke 2:49).[4] As the chosen of the Father, Jesus speaks of himself in the same familial language as "the master of the house" (Matt. 10:24f.). It has been proposed that the saying about the city set on a hill pictures the New Age as the City of God located on the world-mountain of Zion (Matt. 5:14).[5] Surely early Christian writers, like the author of the Epistle to the Hebrews and John of Patmos, found rich meaning in this symbol of the New Jerusalem.[6]

Finally we may note two other descriptive phrases taken over in the Gospels from a Jewish background. The favorite rabbinic designation "Age (World) to Come (*olam ha-ba*)" appears a number of times.[7] Judaism's description of the life of that New Age as a participation in the very life of God himself becomes the favorite term for the Kingdom in the Gospel of John: eternal life (*chayai ʿolam*). But it is worth noticing that the same eschatological image is found in the Synoptics also. In Mark 10:30 Jesus promises eternal life in the age to come to those who have paid the expensive price of discipleship (cf. Mark 9:45, 47). Other terms like Sabbath, wine, clothing, and harvest also serve as eschatological metaphors in the Gospels.

Thus a portfolio of pictures pointing toward a new order under

---

drew between the present period of Christ's rule and the final Kingdom of God. See Charles Harold Dodd, "Matthew and Paul," in his *New Testament Studies* (Manchester: Manchester University Press, 1953); and Schmidt, *Basileia,* pp. 36–37.

3 Mark 14:58 par.; John 2:19ff.; cf. Isa. 56:7; Ps. 96:8; *Test. Ben.* 9:2; etc.

4 Cf. the "house of his kingdom," Thomas, Saying 21.

5 See the expanded form of this saying in the *Gospel of Thomas,* Saying 32; cf. Isa. 2:2–4; Mic. 4:1–3.

6 Heb. 11:10, 16; 12:22; 13:14; Rev. 21–22.

7 Matt. 12:32; Luke 20:35; Mark 10:20 par.; etc.

God's direction is exhibited in the message of Jesus, but they are sketches redrawn from their Jewish originals. Indeed it is only in terms of Jesus' total message about God and the view he holds of his own role in the unfolding divine plan that the real meaning of these several eschatological terms can be understood. We must continually ask to what extent Jesus' interpretations coincide with, fulfill, extend beyond, or even contradict the views that his contemporaries associated with these same or analogous symbols. The single term "democracy" marks out variant horizons of understandings to Soviet, South African, and

Fig. 7. Head of Christ from a twelfth-century crucifix. *Courtesy Foto Marburg.*

United States citizens. Linguistic analysis, which must be practiced upon contemporary political vocabularies, is no less necessary in any attempt to probe the meaning of such a cardinal conception as the Kingdom of God in Jesus' teaching.[8]

Form and Function in Jesus' Message

While it is conventional to speak of Jesus' message as teaching and to describe his work as a teacher, it is important to recognize that the image of teacher is inadequate to describe him. He is rather presented in the Gospels as a provocative evangelist, a messenger of critically important news, a passionate prophet of God's word to a callous generation. As Goguel put it, "He [Jesus] never said: 'I am come to teach,' but 'I am come to kindle a fire upon earth...I have a baptism to be baptized with.' "[9] To be sure he was addressed by his disciples and others as Teacher, my Great One, or Master (*rabbi* or *mari*), and one can identify certain similarities in the form of his teaching with the practical moral counsels of the scribes. Like them, he made extensive use of figurative sayings and parables drawn from the common life of farming and fishing, the household, business management, and politics. But the rabbinical schools were preoccupied with the correct exegesis of Scripture and the derivation and justification of formal rules (*halakoth*) to regulate the everyday life of the Jew. Jesus' sayings and stories are centered in the message of the approaching Kingdom of God and the imperative need to recognize the eschatological character of the present hour as the time for decision. His "teaching" is the heraldic proclamation of this blessed event and the character of human life which is fitted to participate in it. Even those sayings which most resemble the wisdom teaching of the scribes are qualified by that approaching New Order and gain their meaning from it. His use and interpretation of Scripture cut through the literalism of scribal exegesis to lay bare the fundamentals of the divine will (Matt. 5:17–48) and

---

8 For a historical account of the interpretation of this concept from the late nineteenth century to the present, see Gösta Lundström, *The Kingdom of God in the Teaching of Jesus,* trans. Joan Bulman (Richmond, Va.: John Knox Press, 1963); and under the same title the book by Norman Perrin (Philadelphia: Westminster Press, 1963).

9 Maurice Goguel, *Life of Jesus,* trans. Olive Wyon (New York: The Macmillan Company, 1949), p. 280.

to define that higher righteousness that is the condition of entry into the Kingdom.

The Speech Mode of Jesus

Those who listened to Jesus speak were often amazed and offended at his words, yet they were unable to deny the sense of unmediated authority that was imprinted on his message. "He taught them like a sovereign and not as the Rabbis," is E. G. Selwyn's paraphrase of Mark 1:22.[10] The speech mode of Jesus in the Gospels is marked by an immediacy, a piercing directness, and a spontaneity both impressive and distinctive. There was no wearisome citation of precedents for his interpretations, as scribal argument required. The authority of the individual prophetic conscience stamped his sayings, and the claims inherent in them transcended any heretofore made by prophet, wise man, or rabbi. Nor was he content to restrict his teaching activity to a small group of pupils like those who listened and respectfully questioned the pundits of rabbinical circles. Although the Gospels represent Jesus at times as giving private instruction to his immediate associates, it is clear that synagogue desks, market places, bazaars, fishing caiques, friendly homes, open fields, and waysides served as meeting places for Jesus and the commoners who listened to him eagerly and gladly. Here were the sick of body, mind, and soul to whom he came to offer God's forgiveness and salvation.

Sayings and Parables

The message of Jesus in the Gospels finds expression through two principal literary types: (1) short sayings, in the form of brief statements, questions, or commands, such as proverbs and aphorisms; and (2) parables, short narratives centering usually in a single theme. The former are often found as the climax to stories about Jesus' encounters with people, as well as in collections of detached sayings virtually independent of any historical setting in the ministry.[11] Such

10 "The Authority of Christ in the New Testament," *New Testament Studies* (Cambridge: Cambridge University Press), III (1956/57), 86.

11 On the form of Jesus' teaching, see Thomas Walter Manson, *The Sayings of Jesus* (London: SCM Press, Ltd., 1961), pp. 28–35; Goguel, *Life of Jesus*, Chap. xi; Bennett Harvie Branscomb, *The Teachings of Jesus* (Nashville, Tenn.: Cokesbury Press, 1931), Chap. vii; Charles Fox Burney, *The Poetry of Our Lord* (Oxford: The Clarendon Press, 1925); J. M. Robinson, "The Formal Structure of Jesus' Message," in William Klassen and Graydon F. Snyder, eds., *Current Issues in New Testament Interpretation* (New York: Harper & Row, Publishers, 1962), pp. 91–110.

brief appeals as "Let your light so shine before men, that they may see your good works and give glory to your Father who is in heaven" (Matt. 5:16); or an aphorism like "A disciple is not above his teacher, but everyone when he is fully taught will be like his teacher" (Luke 6:40); or a warning such as "Woe to you that are rich, for you have received your consolation" (Luke 6:24) are examples of pithy comments which may originally have served as the core of a longer discourse.[12] That many of these sayings were not originally part of the specific situations in which they are now preserved is shown by a comparison of the varying contexts and applications in the Synoptics for sayings like the blind guide (Matt. 15:14 = Luke 6:39), the salt (Matt 5:13 =Luke 14:34f.), the lamp (Matt. 5:15 = Luke 11:33), and the grapes and thistles (Matt. 7:16 = Luke 6:44).[13] One can easily understand how many sayings and parables were remembered and repeated by the early Christians long after time had dimmed the recollection of the original situation in Jesus' ministry which had called them forth.

We have also to recognize that the vigorous dogmatic, hortatory, apologetic and catechetical activities of the early Church definitely shaped the form and the order of these sayings and stories. Collections grouped about a common theme, for example, the attitude toward the Jewish law, were developed very early for teaching purposes. In some instances, the words of Jesus may have been repointed to speak more directly to the practical problems of everyday Christian living concerning fasting, marriage and divorce, state taxes, persecution, or the problems of leadership and back-sliding in the Christian congregations. New concerns about the Church's mission to the Gentile world, the delay of the final coming of the Son of Man, and the signs of the End may have led to some of the applications now found connected to both sayings and parables in the Gospels. Thus we may doubt that the sayings about the patch and the wineskins originally contributed to the dispute about fasting (Mark 2:18–20 par.; Thomas, Saying 47b)[14] or that the interpretation of the parable of the weeds and the wheat

---

12 "Short and concise are the words that have come from Him, for He was no Sophist, but His speech was God's power" (Justin, *Apol.* I.14).

13 For another example, compare the Matthean settings of Q sayings in 7:16–21 and 12:33–35 with Luke 6:43–46.

14 B. T. D. Smith, *The Parables of the Synoptic Gospels* (Cambridge: Cambridge University Press, 1937), p. 45; Joachim Jeremias, *The Parables of Jesus*, 6th ed., trans. S. H. Hooke (New York: Charles Scribner's Sons, 1963), pp. 117f.

(Matt. 13:36–43) correctly grasps the point of Jesus' story in stressing the fate of the good and the bad at the Last Judgment. This leads us to a very important principle of interpretation with respect to these figurative sayings. The discerning student of the Gospel records will recognize that these secondary expansions, additions, and situations in which the words of Jesus appear afford no certain clue as to the primary meaning of the passage in question. The Church's use of the parables in the guidance of its community life led to changes of emphasis and often of meaning through allegorical interpretation and the tendency to append moralizing conclusions. *Each saying and parable must first be examined in itself, apart from its context and application, and against the background of what is concluded to be the dominant nature of Jesus' work and words.*

The sayings of Jesus abound in the rich imagery and symbolism which are still commonplace in Oriental speech and a marvel compared to the more pedestrian Western speech. Hired laborers, tenant farmers, wealthy land owners, fishermen, children, housewives, merchants, slaves, and kings are the *dramatis personae* of Jesus' stories. Similes like "Be wise as serpents," metaphors like "Beware of the leaven of the Pharisees," and hyperboles like "If any one comes to me and does not hate his own father and mother"—tumble out in rich profusion. His speech is colored by the exaggerations which delight the Oriental mind. He speaks of specks and planks obstructing one's vision, of mountains uprooted by faith and tossed into the sea, of camels slipping through the eye of a needle, or again of camels swallowed whole while gnats are delicately strained out. Debts as colossal as ten million dollars are canceled, while others as trivial as twenty dollars are retained. A woman kneads yeast into some fifty pounds of flour, enough bread to serve one hundred and fifty persons!

It is, however, the parable that becomes the distinctive literary form and teaching method employed by Jesus. These short stories, describing some recurring or particular human situation, were frequently employed by the rabbis as a means of elucidating the meaning of a scriptural text. Actually the Hebrew *mashal*[15] describes a wide range of figurative sayings, including the proverb, allegory, oracular or predictive saying, and riddle as well as a more detailed description in narrative illustration, example story, or similitude. Note that Mark refers to the brief saying of the two kingdoms as a parable (Mark 3:23).

---

15 Aramaic, *mathla;* Greek, *parabolē:* a likeness or comparison; lit. to throw alongside.

Luke speaks of the sayings about the patch and the wineskins as parables (Luke 5:36); and the proverb about the physician is actually called a parable (Luke 4:23). One of the forms of a *mashal* in the Old Testament is *hidah,* that is, a riddle or dark saying. Such metaphors as "Beware of the leaven of the Pharisees and the leaven of Herod" or "Can the wedding guests fast while the bridegroom is with them?" illustrate these cryptic utterances whose meaning is not immediately apparent. The "parable" in Mark 7:15 on what really defiles a man has all the characteristics of a dark saying.

But it is the narrative-parable that is of particular interest to us at this point. Some fifty to sixty-five are to be found in the Synoptic Gospels,[16] and an understanding of their form and function in relation to allegory and the allegorical interpretations which sometimes are attached to them is necessary to discern Jesus' own message. It is doubtful that we can assume, as do some scholars, that Jesus taught only in parables and never used allegory;[17] nevertheless it is probable that, like the rabbinical teachers, he characteristically employed the former.

Stated in simplest form, the parable is an extended simile; the allegory is an expanded metaphor. In terms of an anatomy of form, the parable describes a familiar and representative or a special life situation, which is identified as having one principal point of likeness to another more abstruse situation being defined. Thus the parable of the good Samaritan (Luke 10:25–27) is a particular, realistic story of human compassion designed to establish a single point, which is, to a son of the Kingdom, responsibility for others is not dependent upon legal definitions of a neighbor but solely on the impulsion of unreserved love. By eliciting a judgment on an obvious situation in the realm of everyday experience, the hearer is led to recognize the parable's application to a higher, more spiritual but related level. Such a story dramatically exhibits the characteristic of a parable to center upon a single point of comparison. Occasionally a double emphasis is made, as in the story of the prodigal son, where the reaction of both the father and the elder son have special significance.

Conversely, the allegory is a story not necessarily descriptive of a

---

16 Estimates of their number range from forty to one hundred, depending on how narrowly or broadly one identifies a genuine parable.

17 A position taken emphatically by the German scholar A. Jülicher, whose pioneer study of the parables, *Die Gleichnisreden,* published in Tübingen in 1866, has set the tone of all subsequent research on the parables.

realistic situation which, like the metaphor, actually substitutes one item or set of items for another. Its message is disclosed in the interpretation of each of its symbolic details, point by point. A clear example of allegorical exegesis is furnished in the interpretation that Mark appends to the parable of the sower (4:13–20). Here the various soil types are interpreted as symbolic of different kinds of responses to the preaching of the gospel. In this instance, we may recognize a secondary comment by the Church or the Evangelist for preaching purposes. The point of the original story (4:3–8 par.; Thomas, Saying 9) seems to be, not the gradations of response to the preaching, but rather the certainty of God's activity in the world despite failure and opposition.[18] The symbolic discourses of the good shepherd and the vine in the Gospel of John (10:1–39, 15:1–10) represent parabolic forms that have moved toward allegory.[19] Of the Gospel writers Matthew is most prone to the use of allegory; Luke most chary. But it is the author of the non-canonical *Gospel of Thomas* who is most reserved in the allegorical treatment of the fifteen parables he preserves.

The Purpose of Parabolic Teaching

Contrary to popular belief, the parables of Jesus were intended to do more than illuminate heavenly truths in earthly forms. Not betraying any studied composition preparatory to address, the parables often appear to be spontaneous *extempore* responses inspired by the vigorous give and take of disputation with friend and foe.[20] They certainly are not the dainty little samplers of the God-is-love variety that they are often represented to be. C. W. F. Smith puts it bluntly but convincingly: "No one would crucify a teacher who told pleasant stories to enforce prudential morality."[21] We shall soon see how the radicalism of Jesus finds expression in these strategic weapons, which thrust a dagger into the inflated national pride and snobbish exclusivism of his day. These stories were designed to arrest attention, excite the imagina-

---

18 Jeremias, *Parables,* pp. 150–51. I acknowledge here gladly and gratefully my indebtedness to Jeremias' interpretation of many of these parables.

19 Other allegorical interpretations may be read in the parables of the wicked husbandmen (Mark 12:1–11 par.), the two sons (Matt. 21:28–32), the pounds (Luke 19:11–27), and the appendices to the parables of the tares (Matt. 13:36–43) and the net (Matt. 13:49f.).

20 See especially C. W. F. Smith, *The Jesus of the Parables* (Philadelphia: The Westminster Press, 1948), p. 19 *et passim.*

21 *Ibid.,* p. 17.

tion, and impell their hearers to decide to give up their old ways and henceforth live responsibly before God. Their success or failure was not to be measured in terms of the light they shed upon spiritual principles but the kind of choice men made before the fact of God's reign.

A special problem arises here which must be faced honestly. Mark's report of Jesus' parabolic teaching contains an explanation that has created acute difficulties for his readers from that day to this (Mark 4:10–12 par.). On the face of it, the Evangelist evidently understood a distinction in Jesus' teaching methods depending on his audience. To his followers and sympathizers he spoke directly and forcefully of the mystery of the Kingdom of God. But to the general public he spoke in a veiled and obscure manner through parables with the avowed intent of concealing the truth and preventing repentance (4:11–12).[22]

Perhaps the original form of Jesus' explanation, which now can only be conjectured, was not so restricted to his parabolic teaching method or to be construed so literally. It may have been a comment upon the divided reaction to his whole ministry of preaching, teaching, and service to the sick. Reflecting with wonder and anguish on the sharply divided response to his whole ministry (John 7:43, 9:16, 10:19) and believing that it still must be ascribed to God's inscrutable will, he may have recalled ironic words of Isaiah spoken in a similar situation. Isaiah assigned to God's intention what in fact was the result of his own prophetic ministry; those who heard him refused to understand and pay heed to this words (Isa. 6:9–10; cf. Deut. 29:4).

In such a case Jesus was referring, not only to the parables by which he challenged his critics or sounded the alarm of danger, but also to the meaning of his whole mission which continued to be so misunderstood by the people. The disciples had the secret of the Kingdom of God[23] revealed to them. The outsiders persisted in their confusion and insensitivity, just as the prophet had warned that they would

---

22 Mark and the Roman church evidently conceived Jesus' intention through the cryptic form of the parables to conceal an esoteric teaching from the uninitiated. Similarly the Judean covenanters of Qumran withheld their *Book of Secrets* (1Q 27) from the laymen lest they, by misunderstanding, fall into apostasy. Cf. 1QS viii.11- 12, ix.17–19; Jos., *War* II.8.7. Note the Gnostic position in Thomas, Saying 62.

23 "Secret" or "mystery" (*rāz*) characteristically referred to the self-revelation of the hidden God. Cf. Dan. 2:28f., 47; Tobit 12:7, and extensively in the Dead Sea Scrolls.

"see and yet not see; hear and yet not understand, unless (or perhaps) they turn and God forgives them."[24]

We turn next to a special study of Jesus' declaration that the Kingdom of God had moved out of a nonrelevant and remote future into an oppressive nearness, and the crisis this declaration posed for men.

A Matter of Life or Death

The Imminence of God's Future

Like John the Baptist, Jesus' preaching orbits about the central conviction that God's future is imminent. The day is at hand, he believes, when God will be exalted among the nations and will re-establish supremacy over his entire creation.[25] So near had it come that it stared them in the face, if they but looked up. The signs of the new season were everywhere to be seen, like the bursting buds of the fig tree heralding the end of winter's death and the beginning of summer's life (Mark 13:28f. par.).

In the difficult saying of Mark 9:1, Jesus evidently predicts the establishment of the Kingdom within the lifetime of the generations now listening to his words: "Truly, I say to you, there are some standing here who will not taste death before they see the kingdom of God come with power." Attempts have been made frequently to soften the shock of that unfulfilled prophecy by urging that Jesus referred to some unbelievers who would finally acknowledge that the Kingdom had *already* come.[26] Others interpret the saying as a prediction of the Transfiguration or the fall of Jerusalem or Jesus' death and resurrection[27] or the coming of the Spirit marking the advent of the New Age.[28] It has also been regarded as a prophetic saying originat-

---

24 So Jeremias, *Parables,* p. 17.

25 The verb *eggizein* in Mark 1:15 and Q Luke 10:9 cannot be translated "has come" as C. H. Dodd and the advocates of "realized eschatology" propose. It means "to come near"; hence properly "at hand" or "drawn near." See Reginald H. Fuller, *The Mission and Achievement of Jesus* (Naperville, Ill.: Alec R. Allenson, Inc., 1954), pp. 20ff.; Werner G. Kümmel, *Promise and Fulfilment,* trans. Dorothea M. Barton (Naperville, Ill.: Alec R. Allenson, Inc., 1957), pp. 19–25.

26 Charles Harold Dodd, *The Parables of the Kingdom,* rev. ed. (New York: Charles Scribner's Sons, 1961), pp. 28, 37f.

27 E.g., Archibald M. Hunter, *The Work and Words of Jesus* (Philadelphia: Westminster Press, 1950), p. 75.

28 Alan Richardson, *An Introduction to the Theology of the New Testament* (New York: Harper & Row, Publishers, 1959), pp. 63f.; Thomas Francis Glasson, *The Second Advent,* 2nd. ed. (London: Epworth Press, 1947), p.112.

ing in the early Church under the inspiration of the Spirit of Christ. But its authenticity as a word of Jesus referring to the appearance of the Kingdom of God in the immediate future is confirmed by his warning that "This generation will not pass away before all these things take place" (Mark 13:30 par.). This interpretation is supported also by the equally perplexing counsel in the mission charge Jesus gives his disciples: "When they persecute you in one town, flee to the next, for truly, I say to you, you will not have gone through all the towns of Israel, before the Son of man comes" (Matt. 10:23). It can hardly be imagined that such a prediction emerged out of the apocalyptic forecasting of the early Church, for as soon as the mission was extended from Palestine into the Gentile world, the validity of the prediction would have been thrown into question. Whatever else is signified, this counsel to an activity without rest or leisure points to an early manifestation of the Kingdom, since in the Gospels the coming of the Son of Man and the coming of the Kingdom cannot be separated.[29]

Besides these passages there are many other sayings that reflect the expectation of the Kingdom as a future event. Jesus bids his disciples pray for the coming of the Kingdom (Matt. 6:10; Luke 11:2; cf. 17:20f., 22:18). Indeed he solemnly affirms that the attitude men take now toward him, and that "something greater than Solomon" that has now appeared, will determine their situation before God in the final assize (Mark 8:38; cf. Q Luke 12:8f.). He speaks of a Day of Judgment in which the people of such nefarious cities as Sodom and Gomorrah, Tyre and Sidon, will fare better than the Galilean towns that refuse to hear the gospel (Q Luke 10:12–15). Even Sheba's queen and the heathen Assyrians will put to shame the unrepentant Jews on the Day of Judgment (Q Luke 11:31f.), for they heard the word of God and took it to heart. A vivid description of that final assessment of men's words and conduct appears in the court scene presided over by the Son of Man (Matt. 25:31–46).[30] The complete responsibility of men before God is nowhere more sharply put than in the sober words, "I tell you, on the day of judgment men will render account for every careless word they utter, for

---

29 Kümmel, *Promise,* pp. 25–28.

30 Cf. on the Judgment: Mark 12:40 par.; Q Luke 6:37; Matt. 5:21f., 23:33; John 5:28f., 6:40, 12:48; and see the Qumran description in 1QS iii.18; iv.18–20, 26; ix. 23; x.16–18.

by your words you will be justified, and by your words you will be condemned" (Matt. 12:36).

On the Edge of the Abyss

The last hour, Jesus warns, is rapidly approaching. The refining fire of judgment is about to be kindled (Luke 12:49; cf. Thomas, Saying 10); the watery deluge is about to flood the earth (Luke 12:50; Q Matt. 7:24–27, 24:37–39). The heavenly axe is just about to strike lethal blows against the diseased tree (Q Matt. 7:19; Luke 13:6–9). The *Gospel of Thomas* preserves a corresponding apocryphal saying found elsewhere in early Christian literature. "Jesus said: Whoever is near to me is near to the fire, and whoever is far from me is far from the Kingdom" (Saying 82). Jesus warns of the strife and hardship that will signal the days of the Son of Man of the messianic period (Mark 3:9, 11, 13; Luke 23:28–31). Significantly enough, however, there is an absence of apocalyptic calculations that would try to anticipate the exact time and circumstances under which God would usher in the final events.[31] Like the prophets, apocalyptists, and rabbis,[32] Jesus warned of the internal strife that would decimate family life in the closing days of the old order, and the unpredictable separations of the righteous from the unrighteous in the hour of judgment, without regard to the distinctions recognized in society.[33] He parts company with the apocalyptists by refraining from their fanciful descriptions of eschatological conditions, only briefly mentioning the resurrection life of the blessed in Paradise[34] and the torments of the wicked in Gehenna.[35]

We may recognize further evidence of the imminent crisis confront-

---

31 Mark 13:32, 35 par.; cf. Q Luke 12:40, 17:24; Matt. 25:13. It is true that much of Mark 13 seems to contradict this, for earthly and cosmic signs are adduced that point to the end of time. There are grounds for believing that verses 7, 8, 12, 14–20, 24–27 reflect Jewish or early Christian apocalyptic views that have been merged with these sayings of Jesus. On this chapter, which constitutes a thorny problem in determining the eschatological preaching of Jesus, see George Raymond Beasely-Murray, *A Commentary on Mark Thirteen* (New York: The Macmillan Company, 1957).

32 Mic. 7:6; Isa. 19:2; Ezek. 38:21; *I Enoch* 100:1f.; *II Baruch* 70:3–7; IV Ezra 5–6; *Jub.* 20:11–15; 23:16, 19. The rabbis described these tribulations as the birth pangs of the messiah. Cf. 1QH iii.3–36; Mark 13:8; Matt. 24:8; Rom. 8:18, 22f.

33 Q Luke 12:52f. (Thomas, Saying 16b); Q Luke 14:26, 17:34f. (Thomas, Saying 61).

34 Mark 12:25 par.; Luke 16:22, 23:43.

35 Mark 9:43ff.; Luke 12:5 (cf. 16:23); but seven times in Matthew.

ing the nation in Jesus' urgent call to repentance and threat of disaster which find utterance in a number of his parables. "Let your loins be girded and your lamps burning," he beseeches his critics, as he tells a parable of watchful servants who are prepared for the sudden return of the master of the house. The implication of what a reversal of this situation would mean for them does not need to be spelled out (Luke 12:35).[36] The story of the barren fig tree and the owner's reluctant decision to grant only one additional year before the tree is cut up for firewood (Luke 13:6–9);[37] or the anecdote of a village wedding in which the bridegroom appears tardily to claim his bride, to the embarrassment of some of her attendants (Matt. 25:1–13); or the story of the thief who was able to break into a house only because the owner was unprepared for the emergency (Matt. 24:43f. = Luke 12:39f.)[38]—all these testify to the vivid consciousness that a crisis confronted the men of this world who were tragically oblivious to the impending judgment.

When that hour of God's consummate action came, it would be with lightning swiftness, thorough and complete. A study of the Q passage on the day of the Son of Man makes this self-evident (Luke 17:22–37). The appearance of that day will be unpredictable, though false alarms would often be raised and false messiahs clamor for support. "As the lightning flashes and lights up the sky from one side to the other, so will the Son of man be in his day" (vs. 24), or like the vulture who sweeps upon his prey with terrifying speed (vs. 37). A tragic-comic domestic situation highlights the divisive abruptness of that hour: "In that night there will be two men in one bed; one will be taken and the other left" (vss. 34f.).[39] As in ancient times, so also now, men refused to take seriously the crisis of the present moment that might prove to be their last (vss. 26–30).

The securities in which men put their trust are demolished by the God who suddenly confronts men and requires a reckoning in this zero hour. The rich fool (Luke 12:16–20; Thomas, Saying 63) and

---

[36] Found in Mark 13:33–37 as the parable of the doorkeeper. The same point is made in the counterpart parables of the servant promoted (Q Matt. 24:45–51) and the talents (Matt. 25:14–30; Luke 19:12–27).

[37] Is this the basis for the strange incident of the actual cursing of a fruitless tree by Jesus, according to Mark 11:12–14, 20–21?

[38] An instructive example of how early Gnostic Christians adapted this eschatological parable to a counsel of world-renunciation may be seen in Saying 21b of the *Gospel of Thomas.* A variant free form is found in Saying 103.

[39] A de-eschatologized form of this saying is found in Thomas, Saying 61.

the servants entrusted with sums of twenty dollars each (Luke 19:12–27; cf. Matt. 25:14–30) are examples of men who are content to move along comfortably with the ways of the world, only to be brought up short with the frightening realization that all their business fundamentally involves the God whom they had ignored. By the same token, house servants may be chagrined by the unexpected return of their householder who is angrily impatient with the way they have kicked over the traces in his absence.[40] But these common emergencies are mild compared to the peril that now confronts mankind. God is marching on Israel and the world. There is nowhere to hide from him. Like death at midnight or a house-breaker or a tardy bridegroom or the unannounced return of a traveler—so the hour of crisis overtakes man's familiar routines. So in parable after parable Jesus cried out his warnings to a people who preferred to carry on their business as usual and quieted their consciences with the narcotic assurance that they enjoyed the divine endorsement in all their ways.

The Offer of Amnesty

The Baptist's call to the Kingdom carries the same ominous note of Amos' doleful prediction of the Day of the Lord as a thick darkness upon the people (Amos 5:18–20). Even Pharisees and Sadducees joined in the procession of penitents who came streaming to him, terrified by his unrelieved harping on the wrath to come (Matt. 3:7). Jesus' call to the Kingdom is a contrapuntal word in which the variant melodic line is forgiveness and salvation, and multitudes listened hopefully to his declaration of the divine amnesty. For the judge of all the earth is shown to be a father of forgiving love who does not desire the death of one of these little ones (Matt. 18:14). As the messenger of the Father, Jesus announces that the door is open to the Father's House. The invitation is extended to all strangers and sons to enter and share in that happy reunion. "Strive to enter by the narrow door; for many, I tell you, will seek to enter and will not be able" (Q Luke 13:24). Now is the hour of the invitation and the open door.[41] As at Qumran, the meals with the disciples had deep spiritual significance, anticipating the joyous fellowship of the heavenly banquet. The invitation of the servant in the parable of the great

---

[40] The servant with authority, Q Matt. 24:45–51; cf. the doorkeeper, Mark 13:34–36 par.

[41] Q Matt. 7:7f. On the language of entrance: Mark 10:15 par., 23–25 par.; 9:43–47 par.; Matt. 5:20, 7:21, 19:17, 23:13, 25:46; Q Luke 11:52.

supper is the host-Father's own bidding "Come; for all is now ready" (Luke 14:17b).[42]

But the time for repentance is limited. The door will not always be open to receive the guests of God's high table. Popular pride that the people of the covenant were guaranteed places at that heavenly banquet was to suffer a rude jolt in the discovery that repentant Gentiles would be seated with the patriarchs and the prophets and the door closed to those who waited too long to seek admission (Q Luke 13:24–30, the parable of the closed door).[43] The same emphasis is made in the parable of the great supper (Q Luke 14:16–24).[44] The first respondents to the banquet invitation, the upper level of the city's society, pleaded the feeble excuses of business transactions and marital responsibilities and declined the hospitality. Accordingly the host offered dinner to passers-by, definitely from the lower classes, who must have presented a strange spectacle with their rags and rude manners as guests at this formal meal.

The emphasis that it is God's will to restore the outcast gains in significance when we notice that the story was actually told at a dinner where one of the guests indulged in a pious platitude about the blessedness of the man who would eat bread in the Kingdom of God. In reply, Jesus intimates that he and others like him who claimed inalienable rights would not really want the Kingdom of God if they had the chance, despite their pious chatter about it. "Truly, I say to you, the tax collectors and the harlots go into the kingdom of God before you" (Matt. 21:31).

There is no denying the fact that the first invitation may be rescinded and the banquet finally begun with every place filled by others. But it is worth noting as a clue to Jesus' attitude toward the Judgment that those who were excluded made their own choice, just as the five foolish maidens found themselves finally shut out from the wedding feast by their own neglect.

---

42 On table fellowship: Mark 6:30–44 par., 8:1–10 par.; Q Luke 13:26; Luke 24:30f. On the messianic feast: Q Matt. 8:11; Q Luke 14:24; Mark 14:25 par.

43 Cf. the parable of the woman and the jar, Thomas, Saying 97.

44 The Matthean form (Matt. 22:1–10) is generally recognized to be composite, fusing the Q parable with another story similar to Mark's parable of the tenants in the vineyard and appending still another in vss. 11–13. See Thomas Walter Manson, *The Teaching of Jesus* (Cambridge: Cambridge University Press, 1931), pp. 83–86. A slightly expanded form of this Q parable is to be found as Saying 64 in the *Gospel of Thomas*.

> The two essential points in His teaching are that no man can enter the Kingdom without the invitation of God, and that no man can remain outside it but by his own deliberate choice. Man cannot save himself; but he can damn himself.[45]

The real tragedy of human sin is the misuse of the Father's bequest (Luke 15:12b) and the rejection of his greatest gifts of love and fellowship.

The offer of forgiveness finds no clearer expression than in the three companion parables gathered by Luke or his source in the fifteenth chapter of his Gospel. Most scholars prefer the simpler and shorter form of the parable of the lost sheep found in Matthew 18:12–14 as the more original. Both versions, together with the twin parable of the lost coin (Luke 15:8–10), accent the active, seeking love of God, which searches for even the one per cent of his possessions and rejoices over the recovery. It is this emphasis in Jesus' teaching on the seeking and waiting Father that has been acknowledged as unique by some Jewish scholars, who otherwise point out that there are parallels to almost everything he said in the Jewish literature of the period.[46]

Though the element of search is not highlighted in the story of the prodigal son—it would be better to call it the forgiving father—it is impossible to understand the "turning" of the young delinquent apart from the prior experience of accepting love.[47] This loving pursuit, no less than the eventual reinstatement in the family life after his return, depends entirely upon the father's forgiveness. Describing the sense of corporate man in Hebrew society, J. D. Pederson writes, "Wherever a man goes, he takes his 'house' with him."[48] So did the younger son. Jesus' word is that man is not an orphan but a runaway. If man admits that, he has already begun the trip home to the waiting Father.

---

[45] Manson, *The Sayings of Jesus,* p. 130. Cf. Jean-Paul Sartre's play *No Exit* for a modern portrayal of the self-initiated doom of the damned (*No Exit and Three Other Plays* [New York: Vintage Books, 1959]).

[46] C. J. G. Montefiore, *Rabbinic Literature and Gospel Teaching* (London: Macmillan & Co., Ltd., 1930), p. 269; cf. Joseph Klausner, *Jesus of Nazareth,* trans. Herbert Danby (New York: The Macmillan Company, 1925), pp. 361ff.; and see the more recent work of a Gentile scholar, Morton Smith, *Tannaitic Parallels to the Gospels* (Philadelphia: Society of Biblical Literature, 1951).

[47] That is why repentance can be described as a gift of God in the early Church: Acts 5:31; Rom. 2:4; II Tim. 2:25.

[48] Johannes Pederson, *Israel, Its Life and Culture,* 2 vols., trans. Annie I. Fausbøll (London: Oxford University Press, 1926, 1940), I (1926), 51.

Grace and Forgiveness

It was only by the mercy of God that men long since had not been brought to book by him who judges the secrets of human hearts. So the parable of the barren fig tree (Luke 13:6–9) warns of the inevitable judgment of God upon an unproductive people, yet testifies to the mercy that postpones the final hour: "Let it alone, sir, this year also." Were it not for this amazing patience of God, the final act of Judgment would have occurred long ago. In part, at least, both the parables of the weeds in the wheatfield (Matt. 13:24–30) and the net (Matt. 13:47f.) are reproaches to presumptuous persons who would anticipate the final Judgment, urging God to draw up the lists of the saved and the damned at once. Jesus may have been thinking of sectarian groups like the separatist Pharisees when he reproached judgmental attitudes and assigned to God alone the right to make the separations among men. The delay may not be long, but the last opportunity for a realignment of man's relationship to his Maker has not yet been passed. "And if it is madness to fly in the face of His justice, it is desperate wickedness to flout his mercy."[49]

Thus the offer to fellowship with the Father is wholly the gracious invitation of the host. The Kingdom is an act of grace rather than a reward bestowed upon the deserving. Jesus is the foe of all human pretensions to gain advantage before God or to put God at human disposal. These are distorted understandings of man's life before God, whose legitimate expectations outrun every human effort at fulfillment. Thus in the parable, the Pharisee recited pridefully in his temple prayer his own accomplishments in extrareligious activities, assured of divine reward. "I fast twice a week, I give to others of all that I get beyond the legal requirement of the law" (Luke 18:12). His fellow worshiper, a revenue agent employed by Rome, assumes the posture of utter humility and beseeches God for an ill-deserved forgiveness. The shocking conclusion to the story is that it was not the learned theologian but the grafting petty official who went back to his home acquitted of his sins. It is not difficult to imagine the reactions of any Pharisee who might have been (or be) in the audience. In Pauline terms, this justification by grace through faith, which Jesus sanctions, is the very antithesis of an acceptance based upon the works of the law. Humility and thankful love, not an arrogant sanctity, honored the Giver in accepting his great gift.

---

49 Manson, *The Sayings of Jesus,* p. 275; cf. Rom. 11:25f.; II Peter 3:9; Rev. 6:11.

The same claim that men misunderstood or denied the true nature of God's attitude toward them is disclosed in additional parables and sayings spoken against the critics of his gospel. In the story of the slave who, while serving faithfully, received no special commendation, Jesus' hearers are told to admit, "We are unworthy servants; we have only done what is our duty" (Luke 17:10). For men are in no position to put God under obligation to them. They are tenants in this world, though they try to play the part of proprietors. They are more ready to question God and require that he defend his ways to them rather than to be questioned and exposed.

Similarly those day laborers who were paid the same as others who had worked in the vineyard since daybreak, remind us of the lavish expenditure of God's love upon the weak and the poor (Matt. 20:1–15). That the last are first and the first last is a terse summary of the way God's Kingdom upsets all human calculations and status scales, reversing the human situation. The point of the parable of the beneficent employer is not to sanction economic injustice. In fact there was no injustice, for the men who had worked all day received the full day's wage they had contracted for. But the basis for God's action toward men, Jesus maintains, is not to be measured by the categories of strict justice and retribution, but rather of grace and goodness beyond all deserts. It is the Father's good pleasure to give his friendship as he chooses, moved rather by his concern for human need than by any obligations imposed by human achievement.[50] Such is the goodness of God, Jesus teaches, that he is moved to infinite pity by our poverty, and out of his goodness gives generously to those who are in need and know it. It was not an academic circle nor the sanctimonious elite, but rather those who all but despaired of being recognized, let alone blessed, by God to whom Jesus addressed his assurance. "Fear not little flock, it is your Father's good pleasure [will] to *give you* the kingdom" (Luke 12:32; cf. Q Luke 11:11–13, 22:28–30).

For the joy of sharing in the life of that New Age men ought to be willing to make every sacrifice, however costly, for this was the "chief end of man." Better to enter that life maimed than to miss the opportunity by shrinking from the surgical act of self-discipline

---

[50] Joḥanan ben Zakkai (ca. A.D. 80) counseled, "If thou hast practiced Torah much, claim not to thyself, for thereunto wast thou created" (*Pirke Aboth* 2.8; Herbert Danby, trans., *The Mishnah* [London: Oxford University Press, 1958], p. 448).

(Mark 9:43–50 par.). Truly valued, the reign of God will induce men to part with other possessions for the consummate joy it makes possible, just as the jeweler will part with his whole gem collection in order to obtain a flawless pearl (Matt. 13:45f.; cf. Thomas, Saying 76) or a poor ploughman might go to the same lengths to acquire a parcel of property with buried treasure (Matt. 13:44; cf. Thomas, Saying 109).

Repentance and Conversion

The practical outcome of picturing the ultimate Judgment in the starkest language is to enliven the consciences and stir the lethargic wills of men to decision and action, which involves accepting the reality of one's actual life (repentance) and taking a lease upon authentic life (faith). In the vignette of the dishonest steward (Luke 16:1–8), Jesus draws a quick sketch of a clever estate manager who, after twice defrauding his employer, nevertheless was able to secure his own future against disaster by writing off his master's debtors. The point of the story is certainly not to be found in the connection Luke makes to the proper use of money.[51] The actual meaning is to be read in verse 8a in the admiration won by the ingenious and knavish precaution this fellow took in order not to be plunged into ruin. As a man of the world, he was smart enough to take any and every means to stave off personal disaster and get a fresh start. It is not his chicanery that is approved, but his readiness to grasp the gravity of his situation and to act with prudence. So, too, a life-or-death decision is called for in the present eschatological situation. Action must be taken immediately to ensure a new life for oneself.

No one is exempt from the plea to turn and be turned toward God.[52] Jesus speaks ironically of having come not to call the righteous but sinners (Mark 2:17), but it is quite clear that he assumes the universality of sin and man's need to be forgiven: "If you, then, being evil..." (Luke 11:13). That some misfortune had not befallen all of them, comparable to the public disaster when the Siloam tower in Jerusalem fell or to the slaughter of some rebel Galileans

---

[51] The primitive hurch reinterpreted this parable to illustrate the proper use of possessions (vss. 9, 10–12, 13), as it did the parable of the rich fool (Luke 12:21).

[52] The Greek word *metanoein* may signify simply "to change one's mind"; more often it carries the meaning of a turning which affects the whole complex of personal life. Compare the rabbinic understanding of turning to God, *teshubhah*.

by Pilate's police, must not be interpreted to mean that God's hand had spared them because they were guiltless (Luke 13:1–5). "I tell you, No; but unless you repent you will all likewise perish." Jesus often speaks of man's sinfulness as the misappropriation of what is rightfully the Father's own substance. With wasteful prodigality, men use the good things they receive from God, their time, their possessions, their very lives, and pervert them to their own selfish ends. Sin is seen as a condition of indebtedness to God (Matt. 5:25f.; Luke 15:11–13, 16:1–8).

A sign as certificate of his authority to speak for God is called for, but Jesus' reply is to offer the inquiring Pharisees only the sign of Jonah. "For as Jonah became a sign to the men of Nineveh, so will the Son of man be to this generation" (Q Luke 11:30). The ensuing elaboration of this cryptic allusion suggests that the appearance of Jonah as a preacher of repentance was the truly effective sign of God's demand to the people of that pagan city. So to those requiring some authentication that Jesus is truly God's messenger, the reply is, You will hear within my words the imperious summons of God that you be turned from your own profligate ways and come home, or you will hear nothing!

The rabbis, too, put a premium on repentance. According to Rabbi Abbahu (ca. A.D. 300), the penitent would occupy a higher place than the completely righteous in the world to come.[53] But "All that God does is only in the way of warning and reminding man that there is an eye watching him, and that he will be responsible for his choice."[54] To Jesus this eschatological repentance is God's *gift.* It comes by means of his grace which has already accepted the sinner before he has come to any conscious decision. God is not the prying Eye but the seeking Father.

The Promise of New Life

To repent is to become like a little child (Matt. 18:3), or in the language of John's Gospel, to be newly born of the Spirit (3:3–8).[55] God makes himself known less to the confident adult than to the questioning, childlike mind (Q Luke 10:21). The little ones in

[53] Quoted by B. T. D. Smith, *The Parables of the Synoptic Gospels,* p. 190, from C. J. G. Montefiore, *Rabbinic Literature,* pp. 260f.

[54] Solomon Schechter, *Some Aspects of Rabbinic Theology* (New York: The Macmillan Company, 1923), p. 185.

[55] Cf. also I Pet. 1:3, 23; I John 2:29; 3:9; 4:7; 5:1, 4, 18; Titus 3:5.

Matthew's story of the lost sheep are clearly repentant sinners (Matt. 18:14). In the child, Jesus identified the model of that life fitted for the Kingdom.[56] The figure was not without precedent in Jewish teaching. The Talmud likens the baptized convert to Judaism to a new-born child, declaring that "all his previous sins are forgiven."[57] What is the force of such a symbol in the Gospels? In our study of discipleship we shall have occasion to investigate this more thoroughly.[58] Here it will suffice to emphasize its relationship to the confession of guilt, that is, the renunciation of previous self-images and claims to recognition. The littleness and the helplessness of the small child is the precondition for receiving or entering the Kingdom. For in the willingness to be reoriented radically and to accept a new kind of life from God, there is a fresh start, a new beginning, analogous to birth into this world. To become as small children is to accept God's reign as his good gift to us, and to know that the Giver is no tyrant but one whom men can address as *Abba,* or Father.

As a life-or-death matter, the choice now laid before men is irrevocable. The Kingdom's claims are totalitarian, demanding utter and complete commitment. To one who pleads the priority of filial duty, Jesus' reply was brusque; leave to others such cares; your call is to proclaim God's reign (Q Luke 9:59f.). There can be no return to the old life, as though discipleship involved only some new duties added to the daily agenda: "No one who puts his hand to the plow and looks back is fit for the kingdom of God" (Luke 9:62). It is a "turning" not a "twisting." The present crisis looming up before men summons them to a full halt and a march begun in a new direction.

Jesus called men into a new kind of existence "between the times," oriented less to the revelatory moments of God's action in Israel's past as to the shape of his completed act of salvation that awaited them. To be ready for the Kingdom was to recognize the eschatological character of the present moment as the scene of God's action, to permit it to qualify one's life, and to walk now in the way of love.

Jesus and the Kingdom

Had Jesus spoken only of the forthcoming reign of God, his message could have been adequately described as a revised standard version of the popular Jewish hope. What constituted the scandalizing newness

---

56 Mark 10:15 = Matt. 18:2–4; cf. Mark 9:37 par., 9:41f. par.

57 *Yebamoth* 4a, 22a, 48b, 62a.

58 See *infra,* Chapter VIII.

of his message is the claim implicit in his acts and explicit in his words that God's reign is already effective in his mission. This is what divides the time of John from the time of Jesus. The former was the time of fasting and repentance; the latter is the time of joy and salvation. "Blessed are your eyes, for they see, and your ears, for they hear. Truly, I say to you, many prophets and righteous men longed to see what you see, and did not see it [that is, the work Jesus performs], and to hear, and did not hear it [that is, the message of the Kingdom]" (Matt. 13:16f.; Thomas, Saying 38). To those who criticised his disciples for failing to practice the voluntary fasts observed by Pharisees and John the Baptist's group, he replied, "Can the wedding guests fast while the bridegroom is with them? As long as they have the bridegroom with them, they cannot fast. The days will come when the bridegroom is taken away from them, and then they will fast on that day" (Mark 2:19f. par.). A time of separation is coming that will interrupt the companionship they now enjoy, but the present is a festal hour, a time of nuptial joy which is a harbinger of the blessedness of the Kingdom to come.[59] The Gospel of John incisively interprets the meaning of this saying as, "These things I have spoken to you, that my joy may be in you, and that your joy may be full" (John 15:11; cf. 16:24, 17:13).

Such is the immediacy of the hour of salvation that it shapes the present situation of men whether they will or no. Any kind of temporal calculation that would enable them to postpone a decision and continue in their accustomed way is really impossible. This is the most probable meaning of the well-known and frequently misunderstood saying in Luke 17:20f. As W. Kümmel paraphrases it, "The Kingdom of God will not come according to calculations made in advance, nor will a search have to be made for it; for lo, the Kingdom of God is present in our midst."[60] Indeed the "Yes" or "No" of the hearer of Jesus' words, the decision that Jesus' presence forces from him, anticipates the verdict that will be delivered upon him on the Day of Requital (Mark 8:38; Q Luke 12:8f.). For the fate of

---

59 On the joy of the messianic age see further Matt. 25:21, 23; Luke 15:7, 10; John 4:36. There is no warrant for dismissing the authenticity of the Marcan saying, though it may be that 2:19b–20 resulted from the shaping force of the tradition.

60 Kümmel, *Promise and Fulfilment,* p. 35. *The Gospel of Thomas* conflates the two possible meanings of the preposition *entos* here by reading "The Kingdom is within you and it is without you" (Saying 3; cf. 113).

a man depended upon what he did about this call to discipleship, Jesus insisted.

This recognition of God's sovereign activity disclosed in Jesus is probably the meaning of the much disputed phrase in Mark 4:11, "To you [disciples] has been given the secret of the kingdom of God." Elsewhere in the New Testament, the term *mysterion* is used in the sense of God's total plan of redemption for all mankind. In the present passage, too, the *mysterion* is no longer a private secret, but rather a public announcement, disclosed to everyone who has ears to hear and eyes to see. The mystery of the Kingdom is the astonishing realization that the impending event of God's future is already occurring in their midst in the person, activities, and words of the one who stands before them! In him the final stage of the eternal plan to gather together God's scattered people was actually materializing.

Thus the mystery of the Kingdom is inseparable from the mystery of Jesus himself. Some might see only a carpenter turned teacher or a prophetic leader or a skillful healer. "Blessed is he who takes no offense at me" (Q Luke 7:23). With deep discernment, the Church father, Origen of Alexandria, once remarked: "In the Gospel Jesus is *autobasileia,* the kingdom himself."[61] The true light which the prophets had promised would shine in the new creation of the last days was now shining in Jesus and bringing light into the lives of men.[62] The metaphor of the lamp calls the follower to fulfill his proper function by serving as a light bearer in a darkened world, but the implication is that the true light has already come into the world.[63]

In the healing ministry of Jesus further evidence is provided that the powers of the New Age are already operative. A detailed investigation must await a future chapter,[64] but here attention may be called to several highly interesting words of Jesus that reveal his own evaluation of this work. Far from being simple acts of charity or credentials to validate his divine sonship, as has often been supposed, Jesus' own words show that he believed the healings were a direct expression of God's kingly power overcoming the demons of darkness. As such they were an integral part of his proclamation of the gospel. Accused of

---

61 *Comm. on Matt.* XIV.7.

62 Isaiah 60:19; Zech. 14:6f.

63 Mark 4:21; Matt. 5:15; Luke 8:16, 11:33; Thomas, Saying 33b. A study of the contexts shows that the saying was subject to several interpretations in the primitive Church.

64 *Infra,* Chapter VII.

being a conspirator with Satan to deceive men, Jesus cleverly draws the conclusion that if true this would actually signify civil war in Satan's realm which would certainly spell the collapse of his rule. Alas, it is not so simple for the prisoners of the age to gain their freedom. Then he continues, "If it is by the finger of God[65] that I cast out demons, then the kingdom of God has come upon you" (Q Luke 11:20).

More dramatically still, the inauguration of eschatological history is set forth in the parable of the strong man bound. It was the Prince of Demons who held men captive in his cruel bonds (cf. Luke 13:10–17). But now in Jesus' ministry Satan himself was under attack. The battle was now joined and initial victories already won, which presage the total defeat of God's Adversary. The strong man is none other than Satan, who now finds his domain invaded by one who is stronger than he and who is already despoiling him of his ill-gotten gain (Mark 3:27; Q Luke 11:21f.).[66]

The Promise Fulfilled

We turn to a final group of parables which, properly understood, testify to the reality of the reign of God and the certainty of its full establishment. Three parables preserved in Mark and Q are often termed "growth parables." But the primary purpose of the stories of the patient farmer (Mark 4:26–29), the mustard seed (Mark 4:30–32; Q Luke 13:18–21; Thomas, Saying 20), and the leaven (Q Luke 13:20f.; Thomas, Saying 96) is to highlight quite another aspect of the Kingdom. Growth and productivity to the ancients were never understood as a natural, but as a miraculous, process. We might better term them parables of contrast, for their purpose is not to call attention to the process of development but to the striking contrast between an inauspicious beginning and an impressive and inescapable conclusion.

In the story of the sower (Mark 4:1–9 par.), the misleading allegorical interpretation of verses 13–20 must be set aside as second-

65 A figure for the power of God in action. Cf. Exod. 8:19.

66 Cf. Luke 10:18; John 12:31, 14:30, 16:11. A close parallel to the Marcan form is given in Saying 35 of the *Gospel of Thomas* where, however, the meaning is shifted to the assault of evil powers upon the body (cf. also Saying 98). See Bertil Gaertner, *The Theology of the Gospel of Thomas*, trans. Eric J. Sharpe (New York: Harper & Row, Publishers, 1961), p. 183. On the eschatological binding of Satan see *Asmp. Moses* 10:1; *I Enoch, passim; Test. Simeon* 6:6; *Test. Zeb.* 9:8; and cf. Isa. 24:22f.; Rev. 20:2.

ary in order to discover the original purpose. A farmer starts out to seed his fields preparatory to plowing, according to Palestinian custom. In the free broadcast of the seed as the farmer strides across the fields, some of the seed is wasted, for it falls on infertile places, rocky or sandy spots, or on paths which the villagers have beaten through the stubble for a shortcut to town. But despite these losses there is a harvest, a miraculous harvest, thirty to a hundred times greater than the original planting.[67] The stress falls on the marvelous fulfillment of the Kingdom, now veiled in the work of this obscure Galilean teacher, not on the analysis of the soils nor the discouraging fact of waste. Failure there may be, but God continues to sow seed in the assurance of a result to his labors. It may be that the epigrammatic saying appended to the parable of the children in the market place—"Yet wisdom is justified by all her children" (Q Luke 7:35)—in the context of the scribes' curt dismissal of both John the Baptist and Jesus, likewise calls attention to the response. However limited, there are those who hear John's call to repentance and Jesus' proclamation of the Kingdom. God's eschatological hour arrives in his own time, and it cannot be hastened or detained by human agency.

The Call to Hope

The present time is no ordinary moment. To those who could only cry "How long?" shake their fists against the sky or complain about the absence of any evidence that God is alive and active in the world, these words of Jesus bring reproach. To those oppressed but faithful souls who seemed to beat upon the doors of heaven to no avail, Jesus told the story of a poor widow. She besought an unfriendly court for an injunction against her oppressor (Luke 18:2–8); and eventually her petition was granted because of her intolerable annoyance.[68] If that can happen in a civil court where justice is frequently a plaything in the hands of the privileged classes, can anyone imagine that God will go heedless to the plight of the pious? "Will not God

---

67 An exceedingly bountiful but by no means impossible yield in the rich Galilean soil. G. Dalman estimated a yield at seven and a half as average. Sherman E. Johnson points out that by contrast the average yield of wheat for the United States is 20 to 30 times the sowing (*A Commentary on the Gospel According to St. Mark* [New York: Harper & Row, Publishers, 1960], p. 89). According to the parallel in the *Gospel of Thomas* (Saying 9) the percentage yield varied from 60 to 120! (Note the more accurate detail in Thomas, "Some [seeds] fell *on* the road.")

68 The vivid Greek verb describes her naggings as beating him black and blue.

vindicate his elect, who cry to him day and night? Will he delay long over them? I tell you he will vindicate them speedily" (Luke 18:2–8).[69]

A similar emphasis is made in the closely related parable of the helpful neighbor (Luke 11:5–8). Roused out of sound sleep in the middle of the night by a friend who had nothing in his larder to refresh an exhausted traveler, this man, all yawns and grumblings, nevertheless gets up to help his embarrassed neighbor. In the face of this response to human need by worldlings not especially distinguished for their charity and thoughtfulness, can it be supposed that God in his perfect goodness overlooks the poor or fails them in their distress? Men in all their selfishness and cruelty still are wondrously tender in their treatment of their own children, anxiously concerned to satisfy their needs (Q Luke 11:11–13). Is it imaginable that God can be any less considerate? He can be counted on to keep watch above his own. They must not give way to doubt or despair. "God's hour is coming: nay more, it has already begun."[70]

The God who will meet men at the end of history is uttering his word of salvation even now in the mission of Jesus. The present hour is pregnant with eternity. Heeding that, there can be no doubt about the outcome, for that salvation cannot be stayed permanently from encompassing the whole world. The very fact of Jesus' presence, therefore, introduces an eschatological character into man's present, bringing him under judgment and extending to him the offer of forgiveness. In his mission men were confronted with the telic issues of life and death. The call to discipleship was an invitation to share now in the reality of the new Kingdom life.

---

69 The explanation of the parable in Luke 18:1 shows how easily other meanings were read into the parables. The point of this parable is surely not persistence in prayer.

70 Jeremias, *Parables,* p. 153.

CHAPTER V

THE FATHER AND HIS SONS

> The first step in conversion and the new life is learning how to call God *Abba* with child-like confidence, safe under his protection, and conscious of his boundless love.*

> Every life of Jesus remains therefore a reconstruction on the basis of a more or less accurate insight into the nature of the dynamic self-consciousness of Jesus which created the history.†

Abba, Father

A summary of Jesus' teaching still widely entertained is that he taught a doctrine of the fatherhood of God and the brotherhood of man. As generally understood, however, this risks a distortion of Jesus' understanding of the proper relationship between God and man. He countenanced no optimistic nor shallow universalism that signified an "I'm all right, Jack" attitude. The popular slogan is misleading in both its propositions: the conception of divine fatherhood, and the nature of sonship involved in the message and mission of Jesus. Neither the indulgent grandfather nor the spoiled children figures of popular fancy are adequate equivalents to the language Jesus employs about God and man.

---

* Joachim Jeremias, *The Parables of Jesus,* 6th ed. trans. S. H. Hooke (New York: Charles Scribner's Sons, 1963), p. 191.

† Albert Schweitzer, *The Quest of the Historical Jesus,* trans. W. Montgomery (London: A. & C. Black, 1954), p. 395.

The King Who Is a Father

To begin with, we may note that we face a nettlesome linguistic difficulty in referring to God as Father. Jesus employed a name for God in his discussions with his disciples and in his own prayers that must have sounded strange to the ear of any devout Jew. In the rabbinic discussions and Jewish liturgical prayers, it was not uncommon to speak of God as "Father in Heaven," or "our Father," and, rarely, "my Father," but in all these cases a formal Hebrew word was used: *Ab* or *Abinu* or *Abi.* Thus, an ancient Jewish prayer recited before returning the Torah scroll to the Ark begins with the introductory formula, four times repeated, "May it be thy will, O our Father which art in Heaven."[1] But always these Hebrew words were used. When Jesus speaks of God, however, he daringly employs an Aramic vernacular word, *'ăbbā,'* which, as the early Church fathers recognized, meant "father" or "my father" or "our father" in the intimate everyday language of younger children in the home. The referent, of course, was the human paternal parent. To the sensitive ear of Jewish piety, therefore, this word *abba* would be shockingly familiar and presumptuous, as though one were to substitute the word "Dad" or "Papa" for "Father" in the model prayer Jesus taught his disciples. To use another analogy, it was as if a Roman Catholic were to replace the formal Latin salutation *Pater noster* with the "Our Father" of vernacular speech.[2]

It may be surprising to discover that Jesus spoke of God as Father far more sparingly than it is popularly supposed.[3] Primarily this name is reserved for texts in which Jesus is speaking of his own relationship to God. Thus, in three passages where the divine fatherhood is certainly referred to in the Gospel of Mark, the context of each makes it clear that it is the origin of Jesus' own life and authority in God that is meant.[4] But in the material common to Matthew and Luke, the so-called Quelle or Q source, we find the term "Father" also used in a context that includes those who share with Jesus the experience of God's immediacy and intimacy. The disciples by their good

[1] Quoted by Joseph Klausner, *Jesus of Nazareth,* trans. Herbert Danby (New York: The Macmillan Company, 1925), p. 387.

[2] Walter Grundmann, *Die Geschichte Jesu Christi* (Berlin: Evangelische Verlaganstalt, 1961), p. 66. (The use of vernacular speech in the liturgy has become much more common since the Second Vatican Council concluded in 1965.)

[3] Forty-one times in the Synoptics; 107 in John.

[4] Mark 8:38, 13:32; and implicitly in Mark 14:36. Mark 11:25f. is textually uncertain.

works are "to give glory to your Father who is in heaven" (Matt. 5:16). They are to address him as *Abba* (Matt. 6:9) and to be assured that he will provide them with the best gifts (Q Matt. 7:11).

Matthew's Gospel makes the most extensive use among the Synoptists of the name Father, where we may suppose that the Aramaic *'ăbbā'* is denoted.[5] But it is in the Gospel of John that it finds most frequent occurrence (120), usually in conversations with Jesus' colleagues.[6] Evidently this distinctive name for God was rarely used in Jesus' public teaching, which suggests that this understanding of the divine nature, and the concomitant in man's self-understanding, applies first of all to Jesus himself and, as a corollary, to those who receive his revelation and become his disciples.

It is this special meaning of God as *Abba* which is probably presupposed in the bold claim that follows the thanksgiving prayer Jesus offers:

> All things have been delivered to me by my Father; and no one knows the Son except the Father, and no one knows the Father except the Son and any one to whom the Son chooses to reveal him [Q Matt. 11:27; cf. Thomas, Saying 61].

If this is a genuine saying, it speaks of more than the special relationship of Jesus to the Father. The understanding that men stand before God as children in the presence of their *Abba* is the special secret now disclosed to those who will receive it. It is on the strength of this revealed knowledge that Christians from early times were moved to say, "We make bold to call God our Father." An early liturgy introduces the recitation of the Lord's Prayer with the words: "Render us, O Master, worthy, that we may boldly without condemnation dare to call upon Thee, the Heavenly God, as Father, and to say. . . ."[7]

---

[5] Forty-four references of which 20 are unique to this Gospel.

[6] Q, 5 and possibly 7 other references; Luke, 17, of which 6 are unique to this Gospel; John, 120. See Thomas Walter Manson, *The Teaching of Jesus* (Cambridge: Cambridge University Press, 1931), Chap. iv.; and H. F. D. Sparks, "The Doctrine of the Divine Fatherhood in the Gospels," in D. E. Nineham, ed., *Studies in the Gospels* (Oxford: Basil Blackwell, 1953), pp. 241–62; rebutted by H. W. Montefiore, "God as Father in the Synoptic Gospels," *New Testament Studies,* II (1956), 31–46.

[7] From the Liturgy of St. Chrysostom. The prayer is found in both Eastern and Western liturgies from the earliest times. Cf. Origen, *Treatise on Prayer* xxii.1; *Comm. on John* xix.1; Cyril of Jerusalem, *Cat. Myst.* V.11. Professor W. C. van Unnik calls my attention to a similar passage in the *Catechetical Homilies* of Theodore of Mopsuestia, (Alphonse Mingana, ed., *Woodebrooke Studies* [Cambridge: W. Heffer and Sons, Ltd., 1933], VI, 6, 131). Cf. I Pet. 1:17.

A striking instance of this way of addressing God is to be found in Matthew 23:9 where the context shows that Jesus is commenting on the custom of rabbinic pupils affectionately calling their teacher *Abba,* a title otherwise restricted to the family circle. "Call no man your father [*abba*] on earth, for you have one Father [*Abba*], who is in heaven." That this was a distinctive title in Jesus' vocabulary and the early Church's language of faith is shown by its preservation in the original Aramaic in three places within the Greek New Testament: the Gethsemane prayer (Mark 14:36) and two instances in the letters of Paul.[8] It is reported that the Ta'amri Bedouins who found the caves containing the Dead Sea scrolls prefer to speak of God as the *Abu' Isa* (Father of Jesus) rather than their customary *Allah.*[9]

A charming story is told in the Talmud of a certain Rabbi Choni ha-Me'aggel (late first century B.C.) who had a reputation for success in his prayers for rain.

> If the earth needed rain, the rabbis used to send children to him who touched the hem of his garment and said to him, "*Abba, Abba* give us rain!" He spoke to him [God]: Master of the world, do this for the sake of these who cannot yet distinguish between an *abba* who can give rain and an *abba* who cannot give rain [B. *Ta'anit* 23a].

Now as Professor Jeremias has observed, if the famous rabbi actually addresses the Holy One of Israel by the wholly nonliturgical *Abba,* he does so by imitating the speech of little children who look to him trustingly to fulfill their requests.[10] But had Jesus not searchingly observed, "Unless you turn and become like children, you will never enter the kingdom of heaven" (Matt. 18:3)?

This unadorned name *Abba,* however, is not some new cult name, but a disclosure of the essential nature of God in his relationship to men.[11] Just as men may say "Lord, Lord" but do not mean it (Matt.

---

[8] Rom. 8:15; Gal. 4:6. It is found also in the Old Syriac version in Matt. 10:32, 15:13; Luke 2:49; and John 6:32. See Matthew Black, *An Aramaic Approach to the Gospels and Acts* (Oxford: The Clarendon Press, 1946), p. 217.

[9] E. F. F. Bishop, *Jesus of Palestine* (London: Lutterworth Press, 1955), p.26.

[10] "Kennzeichen der *ipsissima vox Jesu,*" in *Synoptische Studien,* A. Wikenhauser zum 70 Geburtstag (München: K. Zink, 1953), pp. 88f. See his essay on *abba* in *The Central Message of the New Testament* (New York: Charles Scribner's Sons, 1965).

[11] In this section I am especially indebted to the penetrating interpretations of the East German scholar Walter Grundmann, *Die Geschichte Jesu Christi,* pp. 72ff.

7:21; Luke 6:46), it is quite possible to recite "Father, Father" but behave in ways that betray no real comprehension of that secret name. It is clear from the mention of the heavenly Father in the conclusion of the story of the unmerciful servant (Matt. 18:23–35) that he who has learned to address God as *Abba* cannot talk of repayment of what he has misused of God's trust, but can only pray, "Forgive us our debts, as we also have forgiven our debtors." But the parable reveals that the heavenly Father is at once more just and more merciful than men.[12] He is *Abba,* dear Father. He does not deal with them in terms of a calculating economics. There is no way of establishing ourselves vis-à-vis the Father as though we could put him under obligation to us. That means that human pride must be broken by the realization that men live, if they live at all, out of the goodness and forgiveness of God, who as *Abba* gives himself and his Kingdom to them. Professor Grundmann is quite right: "The revelation of the name of God as *Abba* is an eschatological and universal event."[13]

What does it mean to look to God as *Abba* in the trustful faith of a little child? It means to possess and to be possessed by the Kingdom as one's own true inheritance (Mark 10:14f.). It is to be driven out of one's previous mode of existence by this new reality and to enter into a new kind of existence lived from and to God. It is to know him as *Emmanuel,* God with us, and *Abba,* God for us. These little ones will avoid thoughts or acts of vengeance upon their enemies; rather they will intercede with the Father on their behalf, for as *Abba,* "He makes his sun to rise on the evil and on the good, and sends rain on the just and on the unjust" (Matt. 5:45). It is to pray to the Father in the full confidence that he knows man's needs and will give him those things which are most necessary (Matt. 6:25–33; Q Luke 11:9–13). Even the very hairs of his head are all numbered! (Q Matt. 10:29f.). If Jesus as their Master knew each of them by name and prayed for them, what question could be raised of the Father's concern (John 10:3, 17:9–26)? Though God is King of the universe, his throne is established upon a Father's love. It is the *Father's* Kingdom (Matt. 26:29).

---

12 E. Fuchs, "The Parable of the Unmerciful Servant," in K. Aland *et al.*, eds., *Studia Evangelica* (Berlin: Akademie-Verlag, 1959), p. 493.

13 Grundmann, *Die Geschichte Jesu Christi,* p. 74. Cf. T. W. Manson, "The Lord's Prayer," *Bulletin of the John Rylands Library,* XXXVIII (1955), 436–48.

The God-Man Relationship

At the outset of this chapter we took issue with one part of a popular slogan of culture-Christianity. Now we look at the corollary proposition, the brotherhood of men as common sons of God. Whereas the relationship of men to God as children to a Father is well known in the Hellenistic and Oriental worlds, there was a significant difference between their thought and the faith of Israel. Primitive Greek thought emphasized the physical parentage of the gods, who were responsible for the origin and protection of the human race. But it is otherwise for Judaism and Jesus. Natural sonship of men as the progeny of divine procreation plays no part in biblical thinking, except as the views of heathen cults are questioned. To the Old Testament writers, the sonship of Israel signified the miracle of God's gracious choice of this people to be his people and to represent him before the nations of mankind.[14] Sonship meant selection for protection and service, on the one hand, and filial love and obedience, on the other. It was an event of grace, not an occurrence of physical generation. In the Exodus, God had adopted Israel to be his own people, pledged his constant care, and in turn, laid upon them the obligation of loving obedience. To break that covenantal relationship was to be called "Not my people" rather than "sons of the living God" (Hos. 1:9f.). The Qumran community, it is interesting to note, sometimes referred to itself as "the sons of his good pleasure," an expression that brings to mind the frequently misunderstood phrase in the *Gloria in Excelsis,* "men with whom he is pleased," that is, his chosen ones.[15]

It is this biblical understanding of sonship as divine choice and obedient response, God's call to a special mission and man's loyal reply, that is presupposed in Jesus' message. Only two passages in the Gospels expressly use the term "sons" to refer to those who hear and respond to the preaching of Jesus.[16] The summons to love one's enemies involves the inviting promise that in so doing "you may be sons of your Father who is in heaven" (Matt. 5:45). The second is an M passage in the same great sermon which likewise enshrines a demand and a promise. Those who stand as makers of peace in the breach torn open by human enmities seek to bring about the recon-

---

14 Exod. 4:22f.; Hos. 11:1; Isa. 1:2, 30:1; Jer. 31:9.

15 *Bene resono* 1QH iv.32f., xi.9.

16 Matt. 5:9, 45, addressed apparently to both the disciples and the crowd. A third, Luke 20:36, is omitted because of certain textual uncertainties that are involved.

cilitation that Jesus manifests as the act of God towards men. "They shall be called sons of God" (Matt. 5:9).

Elsewhere the term children is more freely employed but always with the same implication. Such a relationship to God is not an inherited privilege or a natural right of man; it is a miracle of divine grace that must elicit an appropriate response of devotion. To know God as *Abba* means to receive the divine forgiveness and to actualize it in all one's relationships with other people. It is not that the Father withholds himself from those who are not forgiving. It is rather that only those who know themselves forgiven, and are forgiving in turn, are open to receive the glad truth that God is *Abba*. Otherwise God comes, but there is no encounter. Again it is the Gospel of John that puts the whole truth in succinct terms:

> To all who received him, who believed in his name [that is, the Son of God who reveals the true nature of the Father], he gave power to become children of God; who were born not of blood nor of the will of the flesh nor of the will of man [that is, by natural procreation] but of God [John 1:12f.].

In the light of all this, the party cry of people's-choice-Christianity is shown to be deficient on two counts. As popularly understood, its God as the Father of all men suggests one who is controllable rather than one who controls. It cannot be forgotten that the Father-God of biblical faith is not to be confused with the role of the male parent in contemporary society, the American Daddy apotheosized, as it were. The corollary proposition about the brotherhood of men as sons of God, whether expressed in naive or sophisticated form, is centered on matters of human origins and status before God by virtue of his act of creation. Jesus is preoccupied with the more existential issue concerning whether men hear and heed the Father's voice, whether they are led out of isolation into relationship with him and the whole family in Heaven and earth that owns his name. The test of the relationship is as simple as it is exacting: "He who is of God [that is, claims God as his Father] hears the words of God; the reason why you do not hear them is that you are not of God" (John 8:47).

Prayer, Worship, and Acts of Piety

In Jesus' message, the Father and his children were drawn together in mutual love which found expression, in part, in the life of prayer and worship. Prayer both testified to and confirmed that extraordinarily vivid and dynamic immediacy of God for the believer. God was "at hand." The whole historic practice of liturgical and private prayer in Israel provided an avenue to glorify the name of God for his greatness and goodness and to bring human needs before him for satisfaction or redirection. It is the little ones in the Kingdom who fulfill man's true vocation to glorify their Father, for "Out of the mouth of babes and sucklings thou hast brought perfect praise" (Matt. 21:16). They are the ones who behold the face of the Father, for the very nature of prayer is a direct meeting in which one must address the other in speech rather than oblique forms of expression. Karl Heim puts it powerfully: "Only one relationship is possible with such a Thou. It is that of personal dialogue between I and Thou, in the waking attitude of prayer."[17]

The Practice of Prayer

Any discussion of Jesus' teaching about prayer ought to begin with a recognition of the reality of prayer in his own life. The Evangelists are able to penetrate only partly into his private experience, but they provide evidence enough of his life of communion with the Father. They make mention of acts of prayer at the time of the baptism (Luke 3:21), outside Capernaum after a busy day of healing (Mark 1:35), after the cleansing of a leper (Luke 5:16), when the twelve were chosen (Luke 6:12), following the feeding in the wilderness (Mark 6:46 par.), at Caesarea Philippi (Luke 9:18), at the Transfiguration (Luke 9:28f.), before the Lord's Prayer (Luke 11:1), at the Last Supper (Mark 14:22f. par.), at Gethsemane (Mark 14:32–42 par.), at the meal at Emmaus (Luke 24:30), and at the raising of Lazarus (John 11:41). Probably the sigh of Mark 7:34 on the occasion of the healing of the deaf and dumb man is to be construed as an inaudible prayer (cf. Rom. 8:26).

Ten prayers of Jesus are recorded, no doubt in fragmentary form: "Our Father" (Matt. 6:9–13; Luke 11:2–4); "I thank thee, O Father" (Q Matt. 11:25f.); "Simon, Simon" (Luke 22:31f.); "Abba, Father" (Mark 14:36 par.); "Father, I thank thee" (John 11:41f.); "Father, save me" (John 12:27f. Gethsemane?); "Father, the hour has come" (John 17:1ff.); and three prayers from the cross: "Father,

[17] Karl Heim, *The Transformation of the Scientific World View,* copyright 1953 by Harper & Row, Publishers, p. 189.

forgive them" (Luke 23:34[18]); "My God, my God" (Mark 15:34 par.); and "Father, into thy hands" (Luke 23:46). A full range of themes finds expression: thanksgiving, forgiveness, deliverance from danger, bestowal of material needs, intercession, guidance in crises, and the coming of God's reign.

Jesus calls his disciples to prayer and promises that this can be a responsive dialogue rather than an empty soliloquy. The alternation of imperative and declaration can be seen clearly in the sayings that are a familiar part of the Sermon on the Mount. "Ask, and it will be given you; seek, and you will find; knock, and it will be opened to you" (Q Matt. 7:7). The emphasis falls on assurance, however, as the following verse makes clear, quite the opposite of a "desperate encounter between human inquiry and the silence of the universe."[19] There is an answering that follows the asking; a finding that follows the seeking; an opening to all who knock.[20] The comment upon this asking, seeking, and knocking is a reminder that God as *Abba* surely provides his children with what they need. "If you then, who are evil, know how to give good gifts to your children, how much more will your Father who is in heaven give good things to those who ask him?" (Q Matt. 7:11). Then employing a common device of rabbinical reasoning, he draws the conclusion *a minore ad maius:*[21] how much more will the Father, who is beyond all fraud and deception, give to those who ask! One asks and seeks and knocks in the simple faith that he is heard and will be given. "Therefore I tell you, whatever you ask in prayer, believe that you receive it, and you will" (Mark 11:24 par.; cf. John 14:13f., 15:7).

The Disciple Prayer

On one occasion, as he was praying, his disciples asked Jesus to teach them to pray, just as John had taught his disciples. In reply

---

18 This prayer exhibits a very uncertain textual history in the manuscript tradition. John Martin Creed doubts its genuineness (*The Gospel According to St. Luke* [London: Macmillan & Co., Ltd., 1957], p. 286); C. S. C. Williams favors it as an original passage in the Gospel (*Alterations to the Text of the Synoptic Gospels and Acts* [Oxford: Basil Blackwell, 1951], pp. 8–9).

19 Albert Camus, trans. Anthony Bower, *The Rebel* (New York: Alfred A. Knopf, Inc., Vintage Books, 1965), p. 6.

20 A gnosticised version of this saying is found in the *Gospel of Thomas,* Saying 2, a form which Clement of Alexandria ascribes to the *Gospel According to the Hebrews* (*Misc.* V.14).

21 *Qal wā-ḥōmer,* lit. "light and heavy."

Jesus proposed a brief prayer that soon became a model for personal devotion and a component of early Christian worship. The *Didache,* a Jewish-Christian document that may be from the closing years of the first century, enjoins Christians to recite this prayer three times daily (*Did.* 8:2f.). Preserved in two separate traditions, the prayer as we have it in Matthew and Luke exhibits a number of differences. It has been conjectured by scholars that the original form may have included five petitions and run somewhat as follows:

> Father, hallowed be thy name.
> Thy Kingdom come.
> Give us this day our bread for the coming day.
> And forgive us our sins, as we also have forgiven those who have wronged us.
> And bring us not into temptation.[22]

Jewish scholars have often pointed out that every clause in it is to be found in Jewish prayers and sayings in the Talmud.[23] Yet there is no single prayer in Judaism that contains just this collocation of petitions; nor, more significantly, correlates in such a manner entreaties for the satisfaction of daily needs with petitions for the establishment of the divine reign.

The Disciples' Prayer or the Prayer of Believers, as it may be called (Matt. 6:9–13; Luke 11:2–4), is intended to supply both a pattern of prayer and also a model to be repeated. It begins with that characteristic faith-name Jesus used in addressing God: *Abba,* which may be translated either "Father" or "my Father" or "our Father." Professor Jeremias captures this note of affectionate intimacy in his translation of *Abba* as "dear Father." In the expanded Matthaean

---

[22] Thomas Walter Manson's reconstruction, *The Sayings of Jesus* (London: SCM Press, Ltd., 1961), p. 266. Joachim Jeremias, *The Lord's Prayer* (Philadelphia: Fortress Press, 1964), pp. 10–15.

[23] Cf. Klausner, *Jesus of Nazareth,* pp. 386f.; C. J. G. Montefiore, *Rabbinic Literature and Gospel Teaching* (London: Macmillan Co., Ltd., 1930), pp. 125ff. Klausner's observations may be summarized thus: Our Father which art in heaven (many Jewish prayers begin thus); May thy name be hallowed and may thy kingdom come (the *Kaddish*); Do thy will in heaven, and on earth give comfort to them that fear thee, and do what is right in thy sight (the "Short Prayer" of R. Eliezer); May it be thy will, Our God, to give to every one his needs and to every being sufficient for his lack (a variant form of the "Short Prayer"); Forgive us, Our Father, for we have sinned; pardon us, O our King, for we have transgressed; for thou dost pardon and forgive. Blessed art thou, O Lord, who art gracious, and dost abundantly forgive (the sixth petition of the *Prayer of Eighteen Benedictions*); Lead us not into sin or iniquity or temptation (a Talmudic prayer still used in the "First Blessings" of the Book of Prayer); (For thine is the kingdom [*Alenu*]).

version, which we follow, there next appear three petitions of an eschatological character beseeching the fulfillment of God's holy will in the coming reign. The hallowing of God's name surely guards against any undue familiarity with the remote God who is so intimate in his dealings with his children. It leaves no room for the presumptuous informality, bordering on disrespect, that approaches the deity in the back-slapping manner of some forms of piety. There remains only the simple entreaty that God be acknowledged as he truly is, apart from every alias: *Abba.*

"Thy Kingdom come" is a clear expression of Jesus' expectation that the fulfillment of the reign of God was still a future hope, to be realized, however, in the imminent future. Luke's version omits the third petition, "Thy will be done on earth". This may be a Christian addition to the prayer from the famous "Short Prayer" of Rabbi Eliezer.[24] It is manifestly intended to interpret the second petition. The coming of the Kingdom signifies a condition in which the divine will is perfectly accomplished through the length and breadth of the universe. The phrase "on earth" must be viewed in the light of our earlier consideration of the coming of the Kingdom. There we saw that the present appearance of the Kingdom on earth referred to Jesus' own presence, words, and works that constituted his mission among men. The future coming of the Kingdom presupposed a radical reconstruction of nature and human nature lying on the other side of the Great Judgment. It would be a new communion between God and man in a transformed environment, symbolized by the prophetic conception of new heavens and a new earth. Thus the coming of the Kingdom and the extension of the will of God throughout the "earth" requires a metamorphosis of the character of human existence and the conditions that can support it.

The difficult but amusing parable of the importunate widow, more accurately named the unjust judge (Luke 18:1–8), may provide a significant commentary on prayers for the Kingdom. A defenseless widow who seeks legal aid is pictured as one who makes such a nuisance of herself in her persistence that a corrupt judge fears she will "beat him black and blue" in a verbal drubbing. He finally grudgingly acts upon her case. But Jesus' comment makes it clear that human disappointments over the delay in the establishment of the Kingdom

---

[24] See note 23. Alternatively, Matthew's form may be colored by the rabbinic view that identified obedience to the Mosaic law as taking upon oneself the yoke of the Kingdom of Heaven.

must be checked by the realization that God is assuredly committed to his own cause. The day of vindication of his people cannot fail to dawn.

With the fourth petition, the prayer turns attention to the common necessities of food, forgiveness, and protection. Only when man has learned to seek first the Kingdom of God, voiced in the first section of the prayer, is he prepared to seek truly God's mind on his present situation within the world. The precise meaning of the fourth petition continues to be uncertain because we do not yet know how to translate the rare Greek word *epiousion*. The King James Version renders it "daily"—a legitimate possibility. "Give us this day our daily bread."[25] Certain ancient Egyptian versions of the Greek New Testament and the *Gospel According to the Hebrews,* however, permit the translation "tomorrow." This Greek word may then be the equivalent of the Latin *diaria,* the rations issued at the end of the working day that provided the slaves and workmen with the bread for the next day's need. It may be that the petition should be translated, "Our bread of tomorrow give us today." The meaning is not really altered by either rendering. After the pattern of Proverbs 30:8, the disciple is to pray to the *Abba*-Father, who upholds all living things, for that food which is needed for sustenance.

This may be a prayer for the necessities for physical livelihood. But it is quite possible that the allusion is to the food of the heavenly banquet, the messianic meal of salvation, anticipated in the table-fellowship of the disciples and Jesus. Like the whole prayer, this would beseech God for the coming of his Kingdom with its bread of life, which alone can satisfy the hungers of the heart.[26]

The emphasis upon forgiveness in the fifth petition is found repeatedly in Jesus' teaching. "Whenever you stand praying, forgive, if you have anything against anyone; so that your Father also who is in heaven may forgive you your trespasses" (Mark 11:25; cf. Matt. 6:14f.). Acceptance of the Father's forgiveness is conditional upon the

25 Cf. Joshua ben Levi (first half of third century) quoting Hillel: "The giving to man of his daily bread is as wonderful a marvel as the dividing of the Red Sea" (*Pesikta Rabbati,* 42a).

26 Jerome translated the Matthean word by the Latin *supersubstantialem,* interpreting this to mean the food of the coming Kingdom, and he is followed by modern scholars like Schweitzer, Jeremias, Lohmeyer, and C. F. Evans ("the heavenly sabbath bread of the Kingdom which had already drawn near" *The Lord's Prayer* [London: SPCK, 1963], pp. 54f.). For an opposite view see Werner G. Kümmel, *Promise and Fulfilment,* trans. Dorothea M. Barton (Naperville, Ill., Alec R. Allenson, Inc., 1957), pp. 51f.

expression of forgiveness in human relationships, for it is only the merciful who understand the nature of *Abba* to be merciful. The importance of demonstrating forgiveness was recognized also in Judaism. "As you withhold mercy, so they [that is, God] withhold mercy from you," reads Midrash *Tannaim* 15.11. A classical statement is found in the Wisdom of Sirach 28:2–5 which begins,

> Forgive your neighbor the wrong he has done,
> And then your sins will be pardoned when you pray.

It is worthy to note that for Jesus this forgiveness is to be extended by the injured party himself; whereas Judaism's principal concern was with the wrongdoer. Both he who has done wrong and he who has suffered it can experience the peace of God only as each seeks a reconciliation beyond cultic sacrifice. Not only is he to pray for forgiveness; he is to enact it by interrupting his service of praise with the congregation in the temple to seek the man whom he has offended (Matt. 5:23f.). It might be said of God as it was of Joseph in Egypt, "You shall not see my face, unless your brother is with you" (Gen. 42:3).

There is no calculation put upon the spirit of forgiveness; seven times or seventy times seven may be the occasions for reaching out toward one another. Matthew follows that reminder with the story of the unmerciful servant who owed a debt to his king impossible to honor (Matt. 18:23–35). Forgiven upon tearful entreaty, he seized his freedom as an occasion to demand the payment of a paltry sum owed to him by a fellow servant. The ratio was $10,000,000 to $20.00! But he found that the king, whose generosity in the act of initial forgiveness went beyond every reasonable or just calculation, could be also more sternly exacting than other men. Thus only those are fitted to appropriate the forgiveness of God who can practice unlimited forgiveness from the heart, for a grudging, vengeful spirit shuts out the mercies of God. "The wrath of God is kindled against the hard and relentless more than the weak and foolish."[27] If one does not extend the forgiveness which is God's gift to him, he forfeits that gift and can expect only the full measure of judgment at the end.

The prayer comes to an abrupt conclusion with the plea for protection against the storms and vicissitudes of everyday experience as well as those untoward persecutions and trials that will mark humanity's

---

27 Manson, *The Sayings of Jesus,* p. 213.

last hours.[28] Temptation is probably to be interpreted, not as the enticements of fleshly appetites, but as the pressure to defect from loyalty to the Kingdom. Deliverance in the sense of removal is impossible, short of death. But the disciple prays for the strength necessary to withstand all the flaming darts of the Evil One who dominates this present age.[29] He prays for the power to overcome evil with goodness. We may compare the Talmudic prayer, "Bring me not unto the power of sin, nor into the power of temptation" (B. *Ber.* 60b).

Publicity and Piety

The foe of all self-display in religious practices and perfunctory prayer, Jesus lampoons certain Pharisees whose daily public prayers are recited with an eye to the admiring bystanders. By contrast, he advises complete privacy in personal prayer, such secrecy in charitable giving that one does not even inwardly gloat over his generosity, let alone seek to impress others. Voluntary fasting too can be practiced in such a way that the pietist advertises his abstinence for the applause of "the lesser breed without the law." Such persons are truly secularists, bogus men of God, as the Aramaic word translated by the Greek *hypokritai* seems to mean (Matt. 6:1–18).

Jesus' criticism of certain popular practices in religious acts did not mean the rejection of the acts themselves as a form of expression and nurture of the religious life.[30] He was not a mere reformer. He developed no rival order of hierarchic leadership, liturgical rites, or esoteric *halakah* as did the secessionists of Qumran. He recognized the legitimate function of the Pharisaic teachers to transmit the authoritative tradition of Moses (Matt. 23:2), and he appears to have accepted the proper duties of the priest (Mark 1:44; Luke 17:14). He and his followers offered their sacrifices of praise and thanksgiving on ordinary and festival occasions in local synagogues and at the national temple. The earliest congregations of Christian disciples after Easter participated regularly in the services of the temple (Acts 2:46; cf. 21:26ff.).

---

28 The doxology which concludes the prayer in Protestant worship, based upon the KJV, is missing from the earliest manuscripts and probably represents an addition to the original text on the pattern of the liturgical form found in *Didache* 8:2.

29 Eph. 6:11–18; cf. Sirach 2:1f.; James 1:2ff.

30 Cf. Thomas, Saying 6, but Sayings 14a and 104a display a strong anti-ritualism.

Nevertheless, his work became radically disruptive to the institutions and forms of Jewish religious activity. "No one puts new wine into old wineskins" (Mark 2:11). He cries down God's judgment upon nefarious practices of the temple clergy, and predicts that it will soon pass before the establishment of the temple of the New Age with its worship in spirit and in truth (John 4:24). For him true religious practices are the spontaneous outworking of a heart touched by the mercy of God, not a labor performed in the hope of winning that mercy. The rabbis taught that there were works of charity beyond the Torah—alms, works of peace, visits to the sick, burial rites, the instruction of children in the Torah—that accumulated special favor to the doer. But Jesus makes no place for any practices that pretend to purchase the divine favor. The whole Pharisaic system of *zâchûth,* or merit, collapses before the severity of the divine demand upon men and the grandeur of a grace which stoops to their weakness. Men may be slaves, but God treats them as sons. So their works of charity are not insurances against an unknown future but celebrations of an identifiable present.

The Father and the Son

From the very outset of the Church's life Jesus was hailed as the Son of David (Messiah), the Son of God, the coming Son of Man. Very soon, many other titles, some clearly associated with the Jewish messianic tradition, others only slightly if at all, were conferred: High Priest, Mediator, Lamb of God, Word of God, Savior, Chief Shepherd, Second Adam, Apostle, Stone of Prophecy, and many others. There can be no doubt that however distinctive each of the names might be, they all point to the common faith-conviction of the early Church that the whole circumstance of Jesus' ministry was the very act of God himself.

Jesus, in a dialogue that may echo the speculations of disciples and commoners about his ministry, sought to know the views of his own contemporaries and invited the disciples to share with him their honest convictions. In answer they reported a confused variety of opinions (Mark 8:27ff. par.; cf. 6:14–16). Those who heard about him or watched his curative activity were divided in their views. To some he was in the prophetic and teaching tradition of Judaism; to others he was the messianic prophet himself, or his herald. Still others rejected him as a Samaritan, that is, a madman in Jewish eyes, a deluded heretic.[31] His own disciples timorously identified him as the Messiah and quickly revealed that their thinking was largely determined by the political messianism of the times.

Unlike his contemporary and former associate, John the Baptist, Jesus does not speak of a Mightier One to come; rather he identifies his own healing activity as that of a Mightier One engaged in binding Satan (Q Luke 11:22). His response to the embassy from John makes the claim that the marks of the expected Kingdom of God are demonstrated in his own activity, thus the eschatological future is already occurring *in and through him.* He replies to those who criticize the neglect of fasting by his disciples by saying that the Bridegroom is here and his presence signifies a time of festive joy that leaves no room for fasting (Mark 2:19f.; cf. John 3:25–30). He comes into a Roman-ruled Jewish province sounding the death knell of the present world-age and announcing the coming of the new world-age, commencing in his own work. He spreads division and disturbance wherever he goes—"I have come to cast fire upon the earth; and would that it were already kindled!" (Luke 12:49).[32] Several sayings of Jesus offer insight into his own self-understanding. We shall look briefly at a few.

1. In several passages Jesus anticipates his forthcoming role as judge and advocate at the right hand of God and asserts that the present decision about him determines the final verdict delivered at the Great Judgment:

> For whoever is ashamed of me and of my words in this adulterous and sinful generation, of him will the Son of man also be ashamed, when he comes in the glory of his Father with the holy angels [Mark 8:38 par.].

This may be compared with the confessing and denying saying preserved in the Q tradition:

> I tell you, everyone who acknowledges me before men, the Son of man also will acknowledge before the angels of God; but he who denies me before men will be denied before the angels of God [Q Luke 12:8f.].

It has often been noted that both Mark and Q draw a distinction here between Jesus and the Son of Man. Some would argue that this

---

[31] In view of the relationship between the Samaritan schismatics and a Trans-Jordan sect of Nasareans, this epithet may explain the puzzling *Natsoraeos* of Matt. 2:23. Was Jesus called a Nazarene as a term of abuse to associate him with a nonconformist, anti-Pharisaic, anti-Jerusalem group?

[32] Cf. Thomas, Sayings 10 and 82.

significance is an original separation of these two figures; hence Jesus was not referring to himself in any way but rather to the majestic figure of the Son of Man who would manifest himself in the future.[33] But the text makes plain, even in its ambiguity, that the relationship is so close that a decision about the one becomes the basis for a verdict by the other. In view of this, we may read the sayings about the rule and judgment of the Son of Man as further evidence of Jesus' belief that the Father had commissioned him to serve both as judge and witness of the Great Judgment (Matt. 19:28; Luke 17:24). This is most dramatically pictured in the eschatological vision of Matthew 25:31–46.[34] A decision now for or against this messenger of the Kingdom will determine a man's portion in that blessed age to come.

2. The saying on mutual knowledge of the Father and the Son in Matthew 11:27, with its parallel in Luke 10:22, has been described as a "meteor from the Johannine heaven." The meaning, of course, is that these words appear so uncharacteristic of the Synoptic writers that they are best explained as an early scribal transfer from a more congenial lodging in the Gospel of John. Its genuineness is still questioned in whole or in part, but in the light of the Qumran hymns it is doubtful that we can dismiss verse 27 as a "typically Hellenistic thought of mutual recognition."[35] As it now appears, the Matthaean passage is in the form of a hymn consisting of three strophes; the first, a prayer of thanksgiving for the revelation which has been entrusted to him to give to others (vss. 25–26); the second, a claim that Jesus is the true revealer of the *Abba*-God (vs. 27); the third, an invitation to a discipleship that leads into the Sabbath rest of the Kingdom (vss. 28–30). These are statements of sovereign authority quite beyond any precedent known among the prophets and rabbis.

3. One of the characteristics of the Gospel of John is the promi-

---

[33] Thus especially Rudolf Bultmann, *Theology of the New Testament,* I, trans. Kendrick Grobel (New York: Charles Scribner's Sons, 1954), 29ff., and the members of the Bultmann school. Support has been adduced from additional passages such as Mark 8:31, 13:26, 14:21, 14:62.

[34] Eduard Schweizer believes Jesus himself spoke only of a witness role he would serve; a Jewish Christian group in the early Church extended this function from witness to judge. See "The Son of Man Again," *New Testament Studies,* IX (1963), 260.

[35] Kümmel, *Promise,* p. 41; Rudolf Bultmann, *History of the Synoptic Tradition,* trans. John Marsh (New York: Harper & Row, Publishers, 1963), p. 159; but cf. W. D. Davies, "Knowledge in the Dead Sea Scrolls and Matt. 11: 25–30," *Harvard Theological Review,* XLVI (1953), 113–39; B. M. F. van Iersel, *'Der Sohn' in den synoptischen Jesusworten* (Leiden: E. J. Brill, 1961), pp. 146–60. See Thomas, Saying 61.

nence of the first personal pronoun in Jesus' sayings. "I am he," he says to the Samaritan woman (4:26) and to the Pharisees standing by the temple treasury (8:24, 28).[36] These are forthright identifications with the Messiah that stand in striking contrast to the Synoptic Gospels where only one such explicit claim is made (Mark 14:62). There are no less than seven other passages in which that simple declarative is joined to a predicate describing the significance of Jesus to the life of humanity. He announces himself to be the Bread of Life, the Light of the World, the Door, the Good Shepherd, the Resurrection, the Way, the Truth and the Life, and the Vine.[37]

These unabashed affirmations are usually taken as expressing the conviction and experience of the early Church, read back in the style of Jesus' formal utterances. Yet it is significant to note that the declaratory "I" is not absent from the Synoptic Gospels either. The impression of direct authority is surely connoted by the simple and forceful, "But I say to you," which introduces each of six antitheses in the Sermon on the Mount,[38] or the commanding word spoken in the exorcism of evil spirits (for example, Mark 9:25; cf. Q Luke 11:20). Prayer regularly concluded with a Hebrew expression, *Amen* (truly, surely), a solemn affirmation akin to an oath endorsing the prayer and pledging a willingness to accept the consequences of its fulfillment. In a fashion without parallel among the teachers of his day, Jesus frequently introduces a teaching with the solemn and authoritative *Amen*. "*Amen* I say to you" is a preamble that assumes an extraordinary authority behind what he had to say. When he says, "Come to me, all who labor and are heavy-laden, and I will give you rest" (Matt. 11:28) or "I came not to call the righteous, but sinners" (Mark 2:17b) or "I came to cast fire upon the earth" (Luke 12:49), we are in the presence of a sovereign ego whose claims are as bold to modern men as they must have been to his first hearers.

Nor is it to be overlooked that the parables and miracle stories of the Gospels conceal a self-assertion whose meaning was sometimes discerned more readily by the enemies of Jesus than by his friends. In what he does and how he defends his mission, in the unity of his preaching and his conduct, Jesus places himself in God's stead and so scandalizes his critics that they demand his blood.[39]

---

36 See also John 8:58; 13:19; 18:5, 6, 8.

37 John 6:35; 8:12; 10:7, 11; 11:25; 14:6; 15:11.

38 Matt. 5:22, 28, 32, 34, 39, 44.

39 Cf. Ernst Fuchs, *Studies of the Historical Jesus,* trans. Andrew Scobie (Naperville, Ill.: Alec R. Allenson, Inc., 1964), p. 21.

Messiah-Son of David

The question of the messianic consciousness of Jesus is probably the thorniest of all issues connected with the study of the Gospels. Did he accept and modify the traditional title for the one anointed by God (*māshīach*) who would be commissioned to lead his people? Did he reject it out of hand, or did he radically reinterpret it so that it had very little relationship to the popular concept? All three views have been strongly championed, though scholars today are disposed to attach less importance to the evidence of titles in the Gospels than to the claim implicit in Jesus' words and deeds.

One ought to remind oneself that designations as such were of little concern to Jesus, partly, perhaps, because he found the nomenclature too rigid for refashioning, partly because he probably was unhappily aware of the slogan-shouting disposition of crowds who often enough made party cries the substitute for active commitment to a cause. "Why do you call me 'Lord, Lord,' and not do what I tell you?" (Q Luke 6:46) has been aptly described as one of the most poignant phrases in the Gospels. On one occasion Jesus replied to a woman's blessing of his mother and her son with the deflecting words, "Blessed rather are those who hear the word of God and keep it" (Luke 11:27f.).[40] He was far more concerned to bring about a meeting of sinful men with the living God that would prepare them to live within and under his fatherly rule.

The concept of messiahship was indivisibly joined to a dream of national restoration and political rule. The *Psalms of Solomon*, the "Marseillaise of the Kingdom of God," heralds the enthronement of the new king, the Messiah ben David, to reign over God's servant Israel.[41] The blood-and-guts character of his rule is a marked characteristic of the "Prince of all the Congregation" in the literature of Qumran.[42] In view of such common opinions, therefore, it is no surprise that Peter's confidence in Jesus as the hoped-for leader was followed by Jesus' strict enjoinders to silence. Without an explicit acceptance or rejection of the title, Jesus proceeds to a new and startling teaching about a suffering Son of Man so foreign to any conventional view as to provoke an impulsive protest from Peter and an even sharper rebuke from Jesus (Mark 8:27–33 par.). If the

40 This saying in the *Gospel of Thomas* (Saying 79) may have been intended to justify the sexual asceticism advocated by Gnostic groups.

41 *Pss. Sol.* 17:26; 18:6, 8.

42 1QSb v.20–29 and 1QM *passim*.

messianic title is not rejected outright here, it is evident that unfamiliar features are introduced into it. Nevertheless the fact of Jesus' crucifixion as a pretender to the throne shows that Jesus was commonly believed to be a messianic aspirant, a reputation no doubt due to the chatter of disciples and friends who held their nationalist hopes to the bitter end.

In Matthew's Gospel Jesus is addressed as Son of David several times, but never by his own disciples. In Mark and Luke the ascription is found only once in the story of blind Bartimaeus (Mark 10:47 par.). It is absent entirely from John's Gospel. Mark records a revealing incident of Jesus' discussion with Pharisees in Jerusalem concerning the popular expectation of a Davidic messiah (Mark 12:35–37a par.). To the scribal view that the messiah is to be a descendant of David, Jesus proposes an interpretation of the 110th Psalm designed to show the superiority of the messianic leader to David. "David himself calls him Lord; so how is he his son?" (vs. 37a). The anecdote certainly does not preserve a tradition of the non-Davidic descent of Jesus, as some have contended, for the early Christian conviction of his royal ancestry is too strong to be denied.[43] But the enigmatic reply of Jesus seems to represent a rejection of a royalist understanding of messiahship and the acceptance of a more transcendental view of "great David's greater Son," signified by the Hebrew word *adon,* or Lord. Genealogy, as such, had little meaning to him, as the saying about his true mother and brothers eloquently testifies (Mark 3:31ff.).

We may then conclude from this summary of the limited evidence that Jesus detached himself from the infectious enthusiasm of a chauvinistic messianic ideal. Certainly his life and work did not fit traditional messianic concepts. This accounts for his reticence to speak about himself and his brusque request that those whom he has healed should not advertise the fact. In part, at least, he preferred an incognito status to avoid illicit appraisals of his work. Professor Turner is quite right: "The Messianic Secret is really a Messianic cross-purpose between Jesus and His contemporaries."[44]

Son of God

Apart from the opening title, there are eight passages in the Gospel of Mark where Jesus is referred to as the Son of God. In two of these

---

43 Cf. Matt. 1:6; Luke 2:4, 3:31; Rom. 1:3; II Tim. 2:8; Rev. 5.5, 22:16; Euseb., *Hist.* III.20.1, 2.

44 H. E. W. Turner, *Jesus, Master and Lord* (London: Mowbray & Co., Ltd., 1954), p. 92.

Jesus himself is said to use the abbreviated form, the Son. One instance is the parable of the wicked tenants in 12:1ff. where the term "a beloved son" is used of the last messenger who goes to collect the fruit for the owner, only to be killed by the tenant farmers. In its present form the story is likely to represent a strongly colored Christological revision of a warning by Jesus of an impending crisis facing the nation. Accordingly, it might be argued that no special importance should be assigned to the identity of the last messenger. Yet the vinedressers' guilt is clearly understood to be decisively heightened by their murder of one who comes as the owner's son rather than as slave. Though the emphasis probably fell on the gravity of the national predicament, as Jesus told the story, the description of the messengers may still hint of Jesus' estimate of his filial relationship.[45]

In addition to this parable there is the familiar repudiation of apocalyptic calculations in Mark 13:32, where Jesus declares that neither the Son nor the angels in heaven but only the Father knows the time and the hour of the New Day. Beyond Mark, a third passage is found in the material common to Matthew and Luke, the famed "Johannine meteor" we have recently been considering (Q Luke 10:22). In addition, all those passages in which God is declared to be the Father of Jesus, whether or not the formal word "son" appears, must be brought into consideration.

The concept of the Son of God has a complex background in both Hellenistic and Jewish piety. To the Hellenistic world the "divine man" (*theios anēr*) or Son of God was one who partook of the very nature of deity, a miracle worker who exercised divine powers in performing signs and effecting cures. It was also one of the royal titles, since the ruler was believed to be the offspring of the gods, and it was claimed by members of the secret societies called Mysteries. In Jewish thought, however, there were no traces of such pagan notions of sonship as physical generation by the deity. The element of majesty and privilege was preserved, but to it the Hebrew understanding added a corresponding sense of subordination and obedience in service. It is just this coalescence of high destiny and lowly service,

---

[45] Cf. Joachim Jeremias, *Parables,* 6th ed., trans. S. H. Hooke (New York: Charles Scribner's Sons, 1965), pp. 70–77. The Thomas form of this parable (Saying 65) is accepted as the most primitive by H. Montefiore and H. E. W. Turner, *Thomas and the Evangelists* (Naperville, Ill.: Alec R. Allenson, Inc., 1962), p. 62; Jeremias, *Parables,* p. 77, and in part by Iersel, *'Der Sohn,'* p. 140.

a mission undertaken under the authority of the Most High yet exercised in humility, that stamps Jesus' whole ministry as remembered by the community of his followers after Easter.[46]

In summary it may be said that to the early Church Jesus was the Son of God in a twofold sense. The content of the title was shaped, in the first instance, by the biblical meaning of sonship. It was a dignity conferred by God's commissioning to a task and a resultant obedience in the execution of that appointment. This conviction of a holy appointment and a devoted submission to that divine purpose determined the form of Jesus' entire ministry. In the struggles with the Tempter throughout his ministry and in the Gethsemane agony, he accepted the concordat sealed centuries earlier by his people: "All that the Lord has spoken we will do, and we will be obedient" (Exod. 24:7).

In the second place, the concept of sonship, however frequently or infrequently Jesus may have employed the actual words, was expressive of his consciousness of being intimately related to and dependent upon the Father. This sense of being bound to the Father's will in a way not shared with other men, this ruling persuasion that he had been given a complete knowledge of the Father-God and the bent of his will toward mankind—this constituted his selfhood and became the foundation of all his work. Presuppositional to and determinative of the task to be performed was the conviction of being the *yaḥid,* the Beloved of God. This did not signify a privilege to be enjoyed, however, but a work to be done. He was to represent *Abba* to the nation as well as to present the true Israel to *Abba.*

Son of Man

Of all the names of Jesus in the Gospels, that of Son of Man appears most frequently. There are about seventy instances of its use in the Synoptics alone, forty without parallels, and the Gospel of John contributes more than ten. But what marks it out for special attention is the unusual fact that of all the titles it alone is used exclusively by Jesus himself. It is never applied by others to him except in John 12:34 where the people puzzle about its significance, "Who is this Son of man?" The single appearance of the term outside the Gospels is to be found in the vision described by the dying Stephen (Acts

[46] See, e.g., such Johannine sayings as 1:51, 3:13; Eph. 4:8ff.; and creedal fragments such as Rom. 1:4; Phil. 2:5–11; I Tim. 3:16; and further Eduard Schweizer, *Lordship and Discipleship* (London: SCM Press, 1960).

7:56). It is sometimes supposed erroneously that this designation expresses the full humanity of Jesus in distinction from the assertion of his deity in the title Son of God. But this certainly cannot be true since a significant group of passages mention this name in speaking of the future glorious manifestation of an eschatological figure. Thus before the high priest Jesus declared, "You will see the Son of man sitting at the right hand of Power [that is, God], and coming with the clouds of heaven" (Mark 14:62).[47] Here and elsewhere the Son of Man is obviously a title of majesty and exaltation, connoting the power and authority of one destined to play a crucial role in the last events of history.

Still other sayings in which the title is found, however, speak solemnly of the way of the cross, a way of rejection, suffering, and death, in stark contrast to the salvation figure appearing at the end of history. Absent from the Q tradition, these Passion sayings of the Son of Man nonetheless occur in the very early Marcan tradition. "He began to teach them that the Son of man must suffer many things, and be rejected by the elders and the chief priests and the scribes, and be killed, and after three days rise again" (Mark 8:31).[48] The bitter word of rebuke to Peter, "Get behind me, Satan!" in Mark 8:34 presupposes an understanding about himself in sharp contradiction to Peter's view of a conquering Messiah.

In a third group, the title Son of Man is used as an oblique reference to the present situation in which Jesus finds himself. "Foxes have holes, and birds of the air have nests; but the Son of man has nowhere to lay his head" (Q Luke 9:58).[49] How are we to understand these passages? What is Jesus saying about himself in terms of an appraisal of his immediate work and an expectation about its outcome when he uses the expression Son of Man in all these varied contexts?

As we might suspect, the concept of the Son of Man was not framed for the first time by Jesus. It has a history that stretches backward

---

[47] Other passages relating the Son of Man to the Parousia are Mark 8:38, 9:9, 13:26, 14:62; Q Luke 11:30; 12:8, 40; 17:22, 24, 26, 30; M Matt. 10:23; 13:41; 16:28; 19:28; 24:30, 39; 25:31; L Luke 18:8. No attempt has been made in this and the following two groupings to distinguish purely editorial work from the basic source materials.

[48] Cf. also Mark 9:12, 31; 10:33, 45; 14:21, 41; (Q? Luke 17:25); M Matt. 26:2; L Luke 22:22, 24:7.

[49] Other passages that refer to the present situation include Mark 2:10, 28; Q Luke 6:22, 7:34, 9:58, 12:10; M Matt. 13:37 (?), 16:13; L Luke 19:10. E. Schweizer thinks the sayings in Luke 11:30, 17:22, and 17:26f. meant originally the earthly career of Jesus.

through Judaism into still earlier areas of thought and life in Canaanite and Iranian myth and ritual, and forward into the world of Hellenistic Gnosticism of the post-New Testament period. There may have been some influence exerted on the New Testament idea by the Hellenistic conception of a Heavenly Man who descends from his celestial home to lead back those mortals who possess a divine light-substance. However, there is a substantial margin of doubt about the pre-Christian circulation of such thought.

Jewish usage provides a more substantial clue, but here too we may quickly get lost in the labyrinth of contrary views. The Hebrew equivalent of the Greek term, *ben adam,* like its Aramaic form *bar nasha* (*bar enash*), may be translated either "man" or "son of man." When the psalmist speaks of the diminutive stature of mortal man before the immensities of the starry heavens, "What is man that thou art mindful of him, and the son of man that thou dost care for him?" he has the frailty and finiteness of man in mind.[50] So it has been suggested that certain of the Son of Man sayings in the Gospels may signify simply generic man. Others would find the clue to the meaning of this designation in the use Ezekiel makes of it,[51] but an open-minded reading of the Gospel passages leads to the conclusion that Jesus is not simply talking about a prophetic role as such, nor even man as he ought to be, when he uses this mysterious term.

It is rather Jewish apocalyptical literature that gives us the best lead. The apocalypse of Daniel, for example (ca. 165 B.C.), depicts in its first vision a heavenly figure who appears to be "like a son of man." He is subsequently identified as a representative figure for the saints of the Most High who "shall receive the kingdom, and possess the kingdom forever, forever and ever" (7:18; cf. vss. 22, 27). In other Jewish writings of the New Testament period, we find this title used to refer to a heavenly being who stands beside the throne of God till his time arrives to judge and rule the world.[52] Perhaps these

50 Ps. 8:4; cf. 1QH iv.30.

51 E.g., G. S. Duncan, *Jesus, Son of Man* (New York: The Macmillan Company, 1949), Chap. xi.

52 Thomas W. Manson, "The Son of Man in Daniel, Enoch and the Gospels," in his *Studies in the Gospels and Epistles* (Manchester: Manchester University Press, 1962), pp. 123–45; James Muilenberg, "The Son of Man in Daniel and the Ethiopic Apocalypse of Enoch," *Journal of Biblical Literature,* LXXIX (1960), 197–209; A. J. B. Higgins, *Jesus and the Son of Man* (London: The Lutterworth Press, 1964); Heinz Edward Tödt, *The Son of Man in the Synoptic Tradition* (Philadelphia: The Westminster Press, 1965); Matthew Black, *The Son of Man Problem in Recent Research and Debate* (Manchester: John Rylands Library Publications, 1963).

apocalyptic images were enriched also by some of the rabbinic speculations in certain circles about the primal man Adam and contributed to such early Christian ideas of Christ as the last Adam and the man of Heaven, Paul's distinctive terminology for the Gospels' Son of Man.[53] E. Schweizer also calls attention to the picture of the suffering righteous man who is finally exalted by God, described in the Wisdom of Solomon and in the 22nd Psalm, and suggests its influence on Jesus' thinking about the Son of Man.[54] He believes this common conception in Judaism of the hard-pressed righteous man who is finally vindicated by God is the real prototype of the Son of Man concept in the Gospels. But all this is far from certain or clear. The plain fact is that Son of Man never was a common title for the messiah in Judaism. A few apocalyptists may have tried to fit it into the traditional messianic pattern, but it seems to be almost wholly absent from rabbinical material.[55]

In my view, Jesus used the title to express his own understanding of his present earthly work and of his future eschatological role. In the latter sense, it spoke of the triumph of God's Day over man's day, the final assessment of all human history—its achievements and its miseries, its cultures and its institutions—before the bar of divine justice. The Son of Man is that divinely ordained deputy of God's righteous judgment who will play the double role of both witness and judge in that last hour. He will intercede for his own before the Father and refuse to defend others (Mark 8:38 par.; Q Luke 12:8f.); but he will also execute judgment in the Father's name. That surely is the claim inherent in the awesome judgment scene depicted in Matthew 25:31–46, and this function is emphatically brought out by John: "He [the Father] has given him authority to execute judgment, because he is the Son of man" (5:27).

There is no individual Son of Man, however, without a community to gather and guide. For Judaism and for Christianity there is no messiah without a people. From the outset of Jesus' proclamation of the reign of God, a community or kingdom is implied. Those who

---

53 Rom. 5:12ff.; I Cor. 15:21f., 45ff.

54 Cf. Wisd. Sol. 2:16–20, 5:1–5; *Jub.* 4:23, 10:17; *II Bar.* 13:3. Eduard Schweizer, "The Son of Man," *Journal of Biblical Literature,* LXXIX (1960), 122–23; and "The Son of Man Again," *New Testament Studies,* IX (1963), 256–61.

55 The Jewish scholar H. J. Schoeps finds only two references in rabbinical literature to Dan. 7:13 interpreted as predictive of the Messiah: *Tanchuma* B. *Toldoth* 20 (70b) and *Sanh.* 97a.

acknowledge him are to share with him in the fellowship, kingly rule, and judgment which mark that society. This is by no means to eliminate the figure of Jesus himself in the use of the name Son of Man. It is rather to recognize that this concept in the Gospels may embrace the total reality of the new community, which will live under the divine rule but which is embodied *par excellence* in Jesus himself who is the acknowledged leader.

The noblest prophetic understanding of the remnant maintained that this faithful minority was placed as God's representative to the nation of Israel and in a more inclusive sense to all mankind. The faithful stood as intercessors for a sinful humanity before the Holy One, who signified his presence in judgment and blessing upon them.[56] Similarly, as Preiss has insisted, the Son of Man concept in Jesus' message and action must also be viewed in terms of his identification with men in need everywhere, not simply with the community of those who acknowledge his rule.[57] This is certainly made explicit in Matthew's judgment scene, in which the Son of Man reproaches some people who count themselves within his loyal company: "Truly, I say to you, as you did it not to one of the least of these my brethren, you did it not to me" (Matt. 25:45). That vision makes it quite clear that the brethren of the Son of Man include the hungry, the thirsty, the foreign, the naked, the sick, and the imprisoned—the least, that is, among the common people scorned by the religious elite.

Here we must leave the matter of Jesus' estimate of himself and his program. The names he accepts and those others assign to him are beyond precise definition. They can never explain him nor authenticate his message and mission. For ancient and modern Christians they serve as ways of interpreting the basic experience of meeting God and his salvation in the person of Jesus of Nazareth. The claim he makes does not rest upon any one of the titles that appear in the Gospels. It is rather in his extraordinary consciousness of serving as the meeting place between the Father and his children that the real clue to his self-understanding is given.

---

56 See, e.g., Exod. 19:4–6; Zech. 8:23; Isa. 42:6f.

57 Théo Preiss' essay on "The Mystery of the Son of Man," in his book *Life in Christ,* trans. Harold Knight (London: SCM Press, 1954).

CHAPTER VI

THE RESPONSIBLE LIFE BEFORE GOD

Whoever keeps his word, in him truly love for God is perfected. By this we may be sure that we are in him: he who says he abides in him ought to walk in the same way in which he walked [I John 2:5–6].

O living Love replacing phantasy,
O Joy of life revealed in Love's creation;
Our mood of longing turns to indication:
Space is the Whom our loves are needed by,
Time is our choice of How to love and Why.*

Responsive Love to God

When Albert Schweitzer was a man of thirty-three, he wrote a brilliant appraisal of the various attempts of German scholarship to write a critical life of Jesus that would reveal him as he really was. Commenting on the way German theology had adjusted the imperious demands of Jesus of Nazareth to fit its own systems of ethical idealism, he said:

Many of the greatest sayings are found lying in a corner like explosive shells from which the charges have been removed. No small portion of elemental religious power needed to be drawn off from His sayings to

* W. H. Auden, "For the Time Being, a Christmas Oratorio," *The Collected Poetry of W. H. Auden* (New York: Random House, Inc., 1945).

> prevent them from conflicting with our system of religious world-acceptance. We have made Jesus hold another language with our time from that which He really held.[1]

It is sadly true that Jesus has often been presented as a somewhat unorthodox Jewish rabbi, formulating a new set of moral rules for an impossibly utopian society. In the interests of practicality and realism, his radical ethic of the coming reign of God has been adulterated into an opportunist, prudential morality. To be sure, he could promise relief to his disciples from the weighty impedimenta of Essene and Pharisaic ritual regulations men were to shoulder.

> Take my yoke upon you, and learn from me; for I am gentle and lowly in heart, and you will find rest for your souls. For my yoke is easy, and my burden is light [Matt. 11:29f.].

But it is soon evident that this promise is no simple annulment of the stringent obligations imposed by the *halakah* of moralists who would not lift a finger to help their students (Matt. 23:4). His own commands are intensified until the total regions of man's personality are affected by them. He interprets them as the firm and legitimate expectation of a Father who requires obedience. "For Jesus," Professor Bultmann concludes, "man is de-secularized by God's direct pronouncement to him, which tears him out of all security of any kind and places him at the brink of the End."[2]

Jesus called for perfect obedience to the will of God here and now in light of the coming of God's righteous rule. "This world is like a vestibule before the world to come," observed Rabbi Jacob (ca. A.D. 200), "prepare thyself in the vestibule that thou mayest enter into the banqueting hall" (*Aboth* 4.16; cf. 3.17). A number of Jesus' sayings call attention to essential conditions for entrance into the Kingdom. "Truly, I say to you, whoever does not receive the kingdom of God like a child shall not enter it" (Mark 10:15). "How hard it will be for those who have riches to enter the kingdom of God!" he observes sadly to his disciples. "It is easier for a camel to go through the eye of a needle than for a rich man to enter the kingdom of God" (Mark 10:23, 25). To be ready to receive or to enter the approaching Kingdom requires something more than eager expectation. These and other sayings delineate a whole new

---

1 Albert Schweitzer, *The Quest of the Historical Jesus,* trans. W. Montgomery (London: A. & C. Black, 1954), p. 400.

2 Rudolf Bultmann, *Theology of the New Testament,* I, trans. Kendrick Grobel (New York: Charles Scribner's Sons, 1954), 29ff.

disposition in man and a corresponding behavior to prepare him for that blessed event. What is often misleadingly termed the ethic of Jesus is more accurately described as the total posture toward and performance of the unconditional demands of God which man must obey.

Love, the Basic Commandment

If entrance into the Kingdom of God is predicated upon a total and absolute obedience to the will of the Father in Heaven (Matt. 7:21), then the seeker is bound to ask, "But what does the Father desire?" The answer is defined and summarized in a single word: love, an utterly full-hearted, unreserved love for God and an uncalculating, energetic set of the will toward the welfare of other men. That the early Church in its preaching and teaching recalled the centrality of love in Jesus' teaching can be seen in the way Paul writes, "Love does no wrong to a neighbor; therefore love is the fulfilling of the law" (Rom. 13:10; cf. I Thess 4:9). When Irenaeus (ca. A.D. 180) comments on Isaiah 10:23, he observes that the "short word" God has spoken summarizing the whole law is love.[3]

The classic instance in Jesus' ministry where this *kelal* or basic commandment summarizing the Torah was identified is found in the story of his encounter with a certain scribe who posed the question: "Which commandment is the first of all?" (Mark 12:28–34 par.). It was a common theological problem of the day, frequently debated in the rabbinical schools. The story is told in the Talmud that a heathen once approached Rabban Shammai (c. 30 B.C.) and asked that he convert him and teach him the law for as long as he could stand on one foot. The quick-tempered teacher pushed him aside with a stick. Then the man went to Rabban Hillel. This wise and gentle teacher said to him, "What is not right for you, do not to your neighbor. This is the whole Torah. All the rest is only a commentary on this; go and learn it" (B. *Shabbat* 31a).

Jesus, replying to the Torah teacher's question, cites first the opening words of the traditional Jewish confession of faith, the *Shema* of Israel (Deut. 6:4–9, 11:13–21; Num. 15:37–41) and correlates with it the Torah command to love one's neighbor (Lev. 19:18).

> The first is, "Hear, O Israel: the Lord is our God, the Lord is one; and you shall love the Lord your God with all your heart, and with

---

[3] Irenaeus, *Presentation of the Apostolic Preaching,* 87.

> all your soul, and with all your mind, and with all your strength." The second is this, "You shall love your neighbor as yourself." There is no other commandment greater than these [Mark 12:29–31 par.].

Of the latter Rabbi Akiba (d. ca. A.D. 135) once observed, "This is a great, inclusive, fundamental truth in the Torah," that is to say, a commandment which epitomizes all the rest.[4] But Jesus' correlation of commands summing up man's duty is without parallel in Jewish teaching.

Early Christians faced no less a problem than we do in trying to express the distinctive character of this relationship of love between man and God as Jesus defined it. They adopted a little-used word in the rich Greek love-vocabulary and spoke of this divine attitude as *agapē*. Greek-speaking Jews and Christians found the term in their Bibles. It had been the choice of the Greek translators of the Hebrew Bible to express *'ahebhah,* the distinctive symbol for the deep affection binding together man and wife, the unselfish devotion of friends, and the mutual loyalty between God and man. In our language the word carries a far wider range of meanings. Still, for ancient as well as modern man it was necessary to differentiate among its varied usages. For that purpose a criterion had to be established, and the Hebrew found it in the covenant-love of God for Israel.

True love, Christians believed, had received its full definition and demonstration in God's action toward men in Jesus' whole ministry, offering them pardon for their sins and releasing them to new possibilities and tasks. Love had as its subject not a proposition nor an attribute, but a person. C. S. Lewis has given pointed expression to Jesus' emphasis on the unexpected, undeserved loving action of the Father toward men:

> You asked for a loving God: you have one. The great spirit you so lightly invoked, the "lord of terrible aspect," is present: not a senile benevolence that drowsily wishes you to be happy in your own way, nor the cold philanthropy of a conscientious magistrate, nor the care of a host who feels responsible for the comfort of his guests, but the consuming fire Himself, the Love that made the worlds, persistent as the artist's love for his work, and despotic as a man's love for a dog,

---

4 *Sifra* on Lev. 19:18. In *Berakoth* 63a, Bar Qappara (ca. A.D. 200) refers to Prov. 3:6 as the basis of the whole law. Rabbi Simlai identified it in Hab. 2:4 (*Makkoth* 23b), and Philo in the principle of the love and fear of God (*De Spec. Leg.* I, 299–314).

> provident and venerable as a father's love for a child, jealous, inexorable, exacting as love between the sexes.[5]

A dual response was called for: an unconditional devotion to God and a loving concern for others that overflows in concrete acts of forgiveness and kindness. Divine love or *agapē* is not some natural instinct to seek God and serve man, else it would be unnecessary to put it under commandment, but rather a free choice of the beloved and a resolute loyalty at any cost. The paradox of commanding love

> . . . is an embarrassment to many students of Jesus' teaching since it seems obvious that love is a matter of human feeling and cannot be ordered about in juridical fashion. But Jesus' mandate, and the Torah precept, recognize that divine love involves a set of the will, a passionate desire, and a resolute seeking after the loved one. It is neither optional nor instinctive. Love is discriminating in its choice of what is love-worthy, and jealously constant in its devotion with a willful strength. The writer of the Gospel of John understands this clearly. That is why he brings love and obedience into the most intimate relationship in his interpretation of Jesus' words. Love arises out of obedience, obedience out of love.[6]

It is this characteristic of divine love that other New Testament writers have in mind when they speak of Jesus' teaching on love as the "law of Christ" (Gal. 4:6), or the "royal law" (Jas. 2:8), and consider it to be both the ground and the goal of all the decretals of discipleship (Rom. 13:10; I Tim. 1:5). "If you love me, you will keep my commandments" (John 14:13; cf. 15:16). No one can really experience God's love without committing himself whole-heartedly to loving all whom God loves and as God loves, though this usually violates impulse and ignores universally accepted community limits.

The order of the commandments in Jesus' summary is of utmost importance. A glowing passion for God is not the end result of a series of charitable actions toward our neighbor. Instead it constitutes the ground of all genuine agapic action toward ourselves and other men. God alone is the only truly love-worthy being. Man's inhumanity to man through the centuries down to the brutalities of the present age is proof enough, if proof is required, of Nicholas Berdyaev's sad

---

[5] Clive Staples Lewis, *The Problem of Pain* (New York: The Macmillan Company, 1943), p. 35.

[6] C. K. Barrett, *The Gospel According to St. John* (London: SPCK 1957), p. 397.

reflection: "Where there is no God, there is no man." An entirely contrary view to both Berdyaev and Jesus is presented by a recent Soviet writer who observes, "When there are no more believers, then things will go very badly for God, not for us!"

The love Jesus enjoins is no dilettante affection conveniently offered and easily withdrawn but so complete in its demand as to enlist the total person. He adds the significant words "with all your mind (*dianoia*)" to the *Shema* as it is found in both its Hebrew and Greek versions. In this respect he is nearer an Essene description of the constituents of selfhood: "All who declare their willingness to serve God's truth must bring all of their mind, all of their strength, and all of their wealth into the community of God" (1QS i.11f.).[7] Nothing less than all that there is of a man is to burn with love's consuming fire.

The Conflict of Loves

The greatest single threat to an unstinted devotion to God is identified by Jesus as the concern for material goods, both in the avarice for possessions and in the anxiety of losing what one has. Property of every sort—the basic meaning of the Aramaic word *mammon*[8]—constitutes a spiritual peril by dividing human loyalties, draining off man's energies, and nullifying the trust that should be vested in God himself. The practical facts of experience, though often more complex, are reduced to a simple either/or, characteristic of Jewish teaching about the two ways of life.

> No servant can serve two masters; for either he will hate the one and love the other, or he will be devoted to the one and despise the other. You cannot serve God and mammon [Q Luke 16:13].[9]

An ungrudging generosity to those in need and voluntary poverty are enjoined. In part this is probably conditioned by the expectation that the last times were at hand, but it is also a radical repudiation of the kind of living thought to be secured by material possessions. The only imperishable wealth is of a spiritual sort, whereas all material wealth is subject to risks of theft, corruption, and decay.

---

[7] Theodor Herzl Gaster, *The Dead Sea Scriptures* (Garden City, N. Y.: Doubleday & Co., Inc., 1956), p. 39.

[8] Cf. Sirach 31:8.

[9] Cf. the expanded version found in the *Gospel of Thomas:* "It is impossible for a man to mount two horses and to stretch two bows, and it is impossible for a servant to serve two masters..." (Saying 47). A Hellenistic parallel is found in the *Corpus Hermeticum* I.iv.6.

> Sell your possessions, and give alms; provide yourselves with purses that do not grow old, with a treasure in the heavens that does not fail, where no thief approaches and no moth destroys [Q Luke 12:33].

We live with what we love. Thus the acid test of the true object of affection is the threat of loss, for one is never parted cheerfully from what he esteems dearest of all.

The incident with the rich man is a dramatic depiction of an alien love that had stolen God's place. (Mark 10:17–21 par.).[10] To a direct question about how one could enter the Kingdom, Jesus replied by pointing to the conditions set out in the Torah, citing the concluding commandments of the Decalogue. His disquiet not easily put to rest, the inquirer answers that he has always obeyed them, even the dictum that one shall not defraud another by withholding his wages.[11] But when Jesus invites him to join his group, with all that implies in the way of severing family and property ties, the wealthy man turns away sorrowfully. He cannot bear to sacrifice his estate. His true love was now unmasked, and it turned out to be not the goods of the New World but the goods of this present world. In contrast, a chief tax collector named Zacchaeus won Jesus' commendation for his decision to make ample return to those he had exploited, dividing half his fortune with the poor and making full legal restitution to those he had cheated (Luke 19:1–10).[12]

Far from providing release from anxious care about the future, the drive for economic security often becomes the source of neurotic anxiety. It is a mark of the secular mind to be busily preoccupied with the basic physical needs of food and clothing (Q Luke 12:30), but the child of the Father, confident of his loving care, has a carefree rather than an anxious mind about such matters. This is neither

---

10 The same point is made in the story of the rich fool, Luke 12:16–20; cf. Thomas, Saying 63; I Tim. 6:18f.

11 It was not unknown; see Jas. 5:2–4.

12 Roman and Jewish law required a fourfold restitution (Exod. 22:1). By the more common standard of Num. 5:7, the publican restored twenty times more than was lawfully demanded. The whole story is probably a secondary composition, a variant form of Mark 2:13–17, but nevertheless, it is faithful to the attitude of Jesus toward the social outcasts and the right use of wealth. Cf. the apocryphal version in the Jewish-Christian *Gospel According to the Hebrews*. See *Gospel Parallels,* 2nd ed. (New York: Thomas Nelson & Sons, 1957), p. 130; M. R. James, *The Apocryphal New Testament* (Oxford: Clarendon Press, 1953), p.6. Jeremias regards it as an independent version of the Marcan story (*Unknown Sayings of Jesus,* trans. Reginald H. Fuller [London: SPCK., 1957], pp. 33ff.).

a call to asceticism nor indigence.[13] It is rather a matter of exchanging a morbid ego-concern and desire to control the future on one's own terms for a courageous willingness to accept one's life from day to day fresh from the hands of God. Jesus' recognition of God's benevolence in the natural order is given unforgettable expression here as he reminds his hearers of the care God lavishes upon such frail creatures as purple anemones, field grasses, and birds. How much more, he reasons, will he be devoted to sustaining human life (Q Luke 12:22–32; cf. vss. 6–7). To love God means to feel safe and secure under his fatherly protection.

Jesus promises that trustful dependence on the Father's unfailing care will ensure the provision of basic material needs (Q Luke 12:31). He recognizes that the goods of this world provide an opportunity to minister to the needs of other people (Q Luke 12:33; Luke 16:9). When the unrighteous mammon of this world is pressed into the service of human need, it wins the appreciation of men and brings the blessing of God's friendship. Responsible administration of the coin of Caesar's realm prepares one to receive the true currency of the Kingdom. "If then you have not been faithful in the unrighteous mammon, who will entrust to you the true riches?" (Luke 16:11) becomes the rapier-like question with which he pricked the pride of the worldly man. David Head draws a profile of the modern affluent society in his prayer:

> We who seek to maintain a shaky civilization do pray most earnestly that the countries which suffer exploitation may not be angry with the exploiters, that the hungry may not harbour resentment against those who have food, that the down-trodden may take it patiently, that nations with empty larders may prefer starvation to communism, that the "have not" countries may rejoice in the prosperity of those that have, and that all people who have been deeply insulted and despised may have short memories.[14]

The place of a Christian ethic of property in the industrially developed and developing societies of today continues to be debated, but there is no mistaking Jesus' warning cry: "What folly to lay up treasures for yourself and be not rich toward God!"

---

[13] Early Gnostic Christians interpreted Jesus' attitude as a world-renouncing asceticism; see Thomas, Sayings 56 and 80.

[14] David Head, *He Sent Leanness* (New York: The Macmillan Company, 1959), p. 23.

Model and Motivation of the Love Ethic

The love ethic of Jesus is to be distinguished from all forms of humanistic ethics essentially autonomous and automatic. Rather, it is theonomous and theomatic, that is, sanctioned and practiced with reference to God. That is the significance of the double commandment of love which affirms the unity of the two loves, the indivisible interrelation and interdependence of faith and ethics. The basis for that intimate association is declared unequivocally in a saying that concludes the discussion about the new law and the old law in the Sermon on the Mount. "You, therefore, must be perfect (*teleioi*), as your heavenly Father is perfect" (Matt. 5:48).[15]

At Qumran, perfectionism meant a total obedience to all that was revealed to the people through Moses and the prophets.[16] Jesus' command is a variant form of the familiar Jewish precept, "You shall be holy; for I the Lord your God am holy" (Lev. 19:2; cf. I Pet. 1:15f.). But it is more than identifying the proper model to be imitated. One is not simply provided with the pattern for upright behavior and then left to do his best with his own resources. Paul's insight that the believer is empowered by the Holy Spirit to be and to do what would otherwise be impossible finds its source in Jesus' own understanding of the "theomatic" nature of the way of righteousness. As Ernst Fuchs has pointed out, perfection does not only mean a scrupulously accurate performance of a good thing.[17] It means also a reckoning with and dependence upon the perfect God, who not only offers the standard but also a share in the powers of the age to come. Thus he is a Father who gives what he demands.[18] "Beloved, if God so loved us, we also ought to love one another" (I John 4:11; cf. 4:19).

The Law of Christ: Responsible Love Toward Men

To Jesus there is no genuine love for God that does not find overt expression in loving service to men. The Father seeks a responsive love

[15] Luke substitutes "merciful" for "perfect" (Luke 6:36), a liturgical designation for God in Judaism of the New Testament period, but the meaning is unchanged. Cf. *Sifra* 8.6b; B. *Sotah* 14a; B. *Shab*. 151b.

[16] Cf. 1QS i.8–9; v.1, 7–11; viii.1,15f.; ix.13,19,24. See Lucetta Mowery, *The Dead Sea Scrolls and the Early Church* (Chicago: University of Chicago Press, 1962).

[17] See his essay in K. Aland, ed., *Studia Evangelica* (Berlin: Akademie-Verlag, 1959).

[18] Compare the similar thought in the Qumran hymn, 1QH iv.30–32.

from men that will transform their relationships with other men from mutual exploitation to responsible love. An aspirant to the Kingdom of the Father must demonstrate his readiness to receive it by such a love toward others as the Father himself shows to all, rich and poor, king and commoner, just and unjust (Matt. 5:45). So the corollary Jesus places upon the *Shema Yisrael,* which the devout Jew recited every morning and evening, was the Levitical injunction, "You shall not take vengeance or bear any grudge against the sons of your own people, but you shall love your neighbor as yourself" (Lev. 19:18).[19]

The range of application of that Torah command was a popular topic of discussion in the rabbinic circles of Jesus' day. It is entirely natural, therefore, that one who was himself a lay teacher of the Torah should have pressed the Galilean teacher beyond the platitudinous principle of general beneficence to ask "Who *is* my neighbor?" (Luke 10:29)—which was the crucial point, of course. It was generally recognized that "neighbor" connoted the fellow-Israelite, including the resident foreigner, and the rabbis widened this to include the full proselyte. Even then, one had to ask what the limits of love were within the community. Can a Pharisee or an Essene, bound by firm oath to cherish and practice the holy law, show love toward the commoner who was often ignorant of or indifferent to the sacred precepts? What if the neighbor is not a friend but a foe or a foreigner? Does one love where love has already been received or may be anticipated? Is it not cheapened beyond worth when it is indiscriminantly bestowed?

The reply of Jesus is so familiar that its subtleties often go unrecognized. His answer is set within a story of compassion upon human suffering, but it is to be noted that in the course of it Jesus reformulates the scribe's question (Luke 10:25–37). The latter had posed the problem of the rabbinical discussions on the Levitical text: "Who is my neighbor?"—that is, Who is the *object* of my neighborly solicitude? Who is legally entitled to be treated as a friend? One can usually protect one's prejudices by raising the wrong questions in discussion. Jesus alters the question to direct concern toward the *subject* of the benevolent action and asks "Which man, the priest, the Levite, or the Samaritan proved to be a neighbor?"

---

19 While I John 4:21 preserves the double form of the Great Commandment, usually it is the love to others that is cited: Rom. 13:8–10; Gal. 5:13–14; Jas. 2:8; I John 2:7–11, 3:11–23; Thomas, Saying 25. But loving the brother is the true evidence of love for God (I John 4:20).

The answer toward which the religious logic of the story moves is an unwelcome and shocking one. The official Judaism of the hierarchy is indicted by the abstention of the priest and the Levite from a ritual defilement incurred by contact with what they probably thought was a dead man. And it turns out also that one whom the scribe would have despised as an apostate Jew and enemy of Israel, a Samaritan, is prompted by love to care for his enemy, an unnamed Jew who had fallen victim to wayside robbers. The force of that offensive conclusion is unrelieved by the substitution of "Israelite" for "Samaritan," as some suggest, for unquestionably Jesus would have had in mind a member of the *'am ha'arets,* whom the scribes often held in contempt. But the contrast is more shocking still if "Samaritan" is retained. The bitter antagonism between these schismatic half-breeds and full-blooded Jews is summed up in the byword of John's Gospel, "Jews have no dealings with Samaritans" (John 4:9). Though the form of this comment may reflect a later situation of strict separation after the Second Revolt, it nevertheless indicates the suspicion and disapproval in which these heretical Jews were held.

Thus the answer is not a legal definition of "neighbor," for that would permit all manner of casuistical evasion of the demand of love. It was a man who was not a neighbor at all by Jewish law who ministered to this unfortunate victim. The Torah defined the neighbor primarily as a fellow-Israelite; love defined the neighbor as any human being who is in need. More important still, however, is the implication that only the love of God moves one to recognize a man as a neighbor and creates that neighborly concern to minister to him. Rules are swept aside. Love is seen to be entirely uncalculating, unrestricted, and unlimited in its manifestation. One must not construe the Torah saying, then, to mean a legal neighbor or a personal friend but simply "others" of any and every sort. Love overrides all reservations and frontiers, if it be in the shape of God's love.

Love of Enemies

The radicalism of Jesus nowhere finds more startling expression than in his call to such reconciling love among men as leads them, like God, to accept and neutralize hostility. "If you love those who love you, what credit is that to you? For even sinners love those who love them" (Q Luke 6:32). This saying provides a revealing comment on the popular maxim, "Practise love to others so that they may practise love to you." In psychological language it could be said that we may be quite devoted to our own ego-image projected into an external love object. We love ourselves by loving our kind. But Jesus talks of something else.

> That one should be amiable toward one's neighbors, serviceable in the community, kind to stray dogs and the grateful poor—that much of Jesus' teaching is accepted by everybody and requires no special depth of moral conviction.[20]

But to belong to God is to behave toward others as God acts toward us. It is clearly God's way to seek out and to restore those who are still impenitent and vengeful, resistant to the divine will and love. But if God extends his merciful love to sinful men and patiently bears with the evil and the unjust, his sons can do no less. "I say to you that hear, love your enemies, do good to those who hate you, bless those who curse you, pray for those who abuse you" (Q Luke 6:27f.).

Few sayings of Jesus have given more offense to men in general and uneasiness to his own followers in particular. The shock of his counsel is intensified when we remember the strife-torn nature of the society in which he lived. We have already noted the bitter hatred toward the occupying power of Rome that saturates much Jewish apocalyptic literature. Although it is certainly right to object to Matthew's quotation by pointing out that the Torah nowhere says, "You shall love your neighbor and hate your enemy" (Matt. 5:43), the Qumran sectarian documents provide much evidence of the total rejection of all those who opposed God's law. The initiate pledged himself "to hate all the children of darkness, each according to the measure of his guilt, which God will ultimately requite."[21] He is called upon "to bear unremitting hatred towards all men of ill repute, and to be minded to keep in seclusion from them."[22]

Voices on the other side were rare, but not absent. The Old Testament occasionally inculcates practical kindness toward personal enemies,[23] and Jewish writers of the intertestamental period urge a similar treatment even to foreigners.[24] Jesus, however, insists that the love of enemies is crucial to the whole concept of holy love. It

---

20 B. Harvie Branscomb and Ernest W. Saunders, *The Message of Jesus*, rev. ed. (New York: Abingdon Press, 1960), p. 106.

21 1QS i.10 (Gaster, *Scriptures*, p. 39); cf. the terrible curse pronounced upon God's enemies (and theirs) in the same *Manual* ii.4–18 and note 1QS i.4; viii.6f.,10; ix.16,21f.; x.20f.; 1QM iii.5f.

22 1QS ix.20 (Gaster, *Scriptures*, p. 60).

23 Exod. 23:4f.; Prov. 25:21.

24 *Mekilta on Exod.* 23:4; *Ep. Aristeas*, 227; Philo, *De Virtut.* 109ff.

distinguishes God's perfect way in this imperfect world, hence he who would be a son of the New Order must also walk this way. So love is to be proffered where there is no expectation of return, beggars satisfied, loans cheerfully made even to the undeserving, hatred expunged, and vengefulness countered with prayers for the persecutors. And the warrant for this strange attitude and extraordinary conduct is simply that this is God's way with men.

The Golden Rule

Against these rivalries and antagonisms that fracture society, the full force of the so-called golden rule must be understood (Q Luke 6:31). The rule internalizes the sanction to action by urging one to have his dealings with others correspond to his desires for himself. Once again, the "others" must be understood to include even the enemy. "Thou" has displaced "I" as the chief object of concern and action in a new centripetal system. Paul has clearly understood the implication: "Let each of us please his neighbor for his good, to edify him" (Rom. 15:2). Read in the light of the great commandment, this rule means to love ourselves and others *as God loves us*. Against a conventional kind of self-respect extended toward other men, Jesus holds up a love of self and others *in God*[25] as the approved way for the man of the Kingdom.

Love, as Jesus understands it, possesses a strange power to bring together national enemies like Samaritans, Romans, and Jews; to dissolve personal hatreds; and to reconcile the sinner and the saint. So he does not restrict his company to the teachers, jurists, priests, and nobility, but welcomes the tax collectors, harlots, and common people. Radical love is known by the company it keeps.

As we have seen, parables like the great supper (Q Luke 14:16–24) and the lost sheep (Matt. 18:12–14) were probably originally spoken to justify Jesus' ministry to the publicans and sinners. Similarly, the rules of hospitality in planning dinner parties were undoubtedly intended in the first instance as an illustration of the inclusive call of the Kingdom and a vindication of Jesus' own ministry.

> When you give a feast, invite the poor, the maimed, the lame, and the blind, and you will be blessed, because they cannot repay you. You will be repaid at the resurrection of the just [Luke 12:14].

---

[25] Note the determinative expression "in the Lord" to characterize Christian family relationships in Col. 3:18–4:1; Eph. 5:21–6:9. Cf. John's reformulation of the Torah precept, John 13:34, 15:12.

A startling contrast to this plea for truly gracious hospitality is furnished in a prohibition of the Damascus Covenant, the rule practiced by the Essenes in the Hauran:

> Fools, madmen, simpletons and imbeciles, the blind, the maimed, the lame, the deaf, and minors, none of these may enter the midst of the community, for the holy angels (are in the midst of it) [CD xv.15–17].[26]

Love and Forgiveness

Involved in any recognition of the guilty, the poor and despised, the weak and the helpless as brothers, is the refusal to pass the judgments of condemnation upon them, in which sanctimonious faith delights. Utilizing proverbs drawn from Jewish wisdom teaching, Jesus advises, "Judge not, and you will not be judged; condemn not, and you will not be condemned; forgive, and you will be forgiven; give and it will be given to you" (Q Luke 6:37–38a).[27] He indulges in a typically Oriental hyperbole by telling a parable that exposes the absurdity of men examining the defects of others when they too suffer from imperfect vision (Q Luke 6:41f.; Thomas, Saying 26). As T. W. Manson observes, "The contemplation of human folly and sin, with the aid of a looking-glass is a less congenial occupation; but very salutary."[28] Obviously this is not a matter of fence-straddling on moral issues, but refraining from self-righteous criticisms of others. That personal appraisals are to be made is presuppositional to the whole concept of a Final Judgment, but it is quite another matter to usurp the prerogative of God and make his decisions for him. So Jesus refuses to play the role of an umpire when it is a reconciliation rather than a judicial verdict that is needed. "Man, who made me a judge or divider over you?" (Luke 12:14).

Instead of being quick to condemn the wrongdoer, the candidate for citizenship in the New Kingdom will want to annul the injury by demonstrating a forgiving spirit. Jesus inverts the old desert formula of vengeance (Gen. 4:24) and urges the injured man to show an unwearying readiness to forgive, if there is any sign of

---

[26] From an unpublished fragment from Cave IV; J. T. Milik, *Ten Years of Discovery in the Wilderness of Judea* (Naperville, Ill.: Alec R. Allenson, Inc., 1959), p. 114.

[27] Cf. Mark 4:24; *Mekilta* 13.19; *Sotah* 1.7; *Sotah T.* 13.1; *Aboth* 2.5.

[28] Thomas Walter Manson, *The Sayings of Jesus,* (London: SCM Press, Ltd., 1961), p. 58.

repentance, on the principle that one can expect to receive the divine mercy in the measure that it is exhibited to others(Q Luke 17:3f.).[29] But this familiar Jewish principle of getting back in the measure that has been given is not intended to suggest a bargaining relationship with God, as though I claimed God's forgiveness by forgiving someone who has injured me. In Jesus' explanation of the dynamics of forgiveness, the man who shuts his heart against an erring brother and nurses his grievances will soon discover that he has likewise barricaded the way against the inflow of God's forgiveness (Mark 11:25; Matt. 5:7, 6:12, 14f.). Such is the corrosive power of hostility rankling in the human heart that it destroys both the power to accept as well as to give pardoning love.

The parable of the unmerciful servant (Matt. 18:23–35) is an example, as we have seen. A situation more akin to a pagan than a Jewish royal court involves a government official who has perhaps misused crown revenues and succeeded in implicating himself in a debt of colossal magnitude, some ten million dollars. Forgiven by his king, the foolish man holds a colleague accountable for a paltry debt of twenty dollars, bringing down the king's wrath upon him. "So also my heavenly Father will do to every one of you, if you do not forgive your brother from your heart" (vs. 35). Perhaps this parable, too, was originally spoken in the urgency of the present hour before the rapidly approaching Last Judgment. Its appeal for a forgiving disposition may be related to the counsel for the immediate reconciliation of friends who had a disagreement, related in the parable of the man on the way to court (Q Luke 12:58f.) and the simile of the temple offering (Matt. 5:23f.).[30] Only those who deal mercifully are prepared to be dealt with mercifully.

A Reversal of Roles

If men are to be guided by divine love in their dealings with God, themselves, and other men, then a radical revision of the concept of leadership is required. This world means one thing by lordship; the New World means quite another. All prideful pretensions, all ambitions

---

29 Cf. Q Luke 6:38; Mark 4:24. The Matthean form (18:15–22) shows clear evidence of development into a community rule. See the interesting form of this saying preserved in the *Gospel of the Nazarenes* (*Gospel Parallels*, p. 99).

30 The priority of restitution and reconciliation over cultic acts is also found in Jewish teaching. Cf. Tos. *Baba Qama* 10.18; Philo, *De Opif.* I, IV.

to greatness and authority must be jettisoned if one would grasp this entirely new attitude. "The kings of the Gentiles exercise lordship over them. . .but not so with you; rather let the greatest among you become as the youngest and the leader as one who serves" (Luke 22:25f. par.).[31] In God's Kingdom the measure of greatness is the measure of service. Jesus' own ministry among them provided the pattern: "I am among you as one who serves" (Luke 22:27b). The Greek verb *diakonein* means literally "to wait at table."[32] So responsible love toward others delivers men from a dictatorial, domineering rule that manipulates other persons into subordinate positions for personal profit. As Dietrich Bonhoeffer observes, "To bear the burden of the other person means involvement with the created reality of the other, to accept and affirm it, and, in bearing with it, to break through to the point where we take joy in it."[33]

The New Righteousness

According to Matthew's form of the Great Sermon, there are two primary conditions for admission into the new and blessed reign of God: a righteousness that exceeds that of the "righteous men" of the day (Matt. 5:20), and a faithful practice of the will of the Father (Matt. 7:21). The biblical words denoting righteousness will help us to understand what is involved. *Zedek* or *Z^edakah,* the most common expression, refers to honesty and uprightness of moral character in a man. It is used also to signify a divinely given deliverance from national foes or the dangers of personal sin. In the few appearances of the word in the Gospels, both meanings are embraced. Jesus enjoins those who would enter God's Kingdom to practice a way of living divided from secular behavior and pious posturing, and thus to be assured that they have received the favorable verdict of the Righteous One. Here again it is not a matter of setting aside the righteousness defined by the Old Testament but a recall to the biblical view of the righteous life by radicalizing contemporary concepts and practices of righteousness.

Blessings and Woes

In the Lucan series of blessings and woes, commonly called the Beatitudes, Jesus contrasts the present situation of God's faithful

[31] Cf. Mark 9:35 par.; Luke 14:7–11; Matt. 18:4, 23:12.

[32] See Luke 17:18; Acts 6:2.

[33] Dietrich Bonhoeffer, *Life Together,* trans. J. Doberstein (New York: Harper & Row, Publishers, 1954), p. 101.

people with the blessedness of the perfected life in the world tomorrow. God's people trust him with child-like confidence, offer to others the gift of divine mercy, build peace where discord prevails, and despite the opposition of unfriendly men, praise God with cheerful heart, refusing to be dismayed.

Each illustrative characteristic of this total disposition is matched by a corresponding condition in the New Age, swinging between the two poles of the empirical and the eschatological. Thus those who now are poor will become the inheritors of all that God's reign signifies.[34] Obviously this is not a beatification of the state of economic poverty as such, but rather a recognition of that kind of deprivation that is the result of one's unconcern for worldly goods in utter obedience to God. There are the Devil's poor and there are God's poor. That Jesus sought and found so many of God's poor among the outcasts of society became socially intolerable and religiously offensive to many of those who entertained a different standard for membership in the Kingdom of God. Yet Scripture testified that it would be just these "terrible meek" who finally would possess the earth (Ps. 37:11).[35]

Those who are now famished for the Word of God and his righteousness will find a welcome contrast in the feast at God's board, Jesus promised. They are really looking for a righteousness that cannot be earned as a reward for acts of piety, but can only be an acknowledgement and acceptance by God's grace. C. H. Dodd translates the Matthaean form, "Blessed are they who ardently desire the vindication of the right, the triumph of the good cause."[36] The cries of God's oppressed people are heard before his throne and will not go unrequited. "Blessed are you that weep now, for you shall laugh" (Luke 6:21b). The hearts that are heavy at the delay in the consolation of Israel, will be lifted up in joy at the reign of God. In God's sight they are really the happy ones, not the seemingly satisfied men who can bear neither hunger nor tears.

There is to be no panic when such a way of living encounters

34 The *Gospel of Thomas* offers a conflate form of Matt. 5:3 and Luke 6:20 in Saying 54. This apocryphal Gospel includes four of the Beatitudes in altered form and adds seven others that are not found in the New Testament. In addition there are two woes which are unknown.

35 Cf. 4QpPs37 i.9, ii.10–11; cf. ii.1–2 which interprets the meek as "the congregation of the poor." The exact phrase "poor in spirit" is found in 1QM xiv.7, *ʿaniyē rûach*.

36 Charles Harold Dodd, *The Epistle of Paul to the Romans* (New York: Harper & Row, Publishers, 1932), p. 12; cf. Luke 18:7.

the hostility and persecution of others, as it surely will. We may catch here an echo of the 37th Psalm, which in many ways seems to provide a model for these blessings. "The wicked watches the righteous, and seeks to slay him. The Lord will not abandon him to his power, or let him be condemned when he is brought to trial" (37:32f.). *Mirabile dictu,* it is even good fortune for those who are counted worthy of suffering, because the patient endurance of slander and ostracism will bring its reward in the Kingdom of Heaven.[37]

To these four blessings Luke appends four corresponding woes, which remind those who have made comfortable adjustments to this world how ephemeral are their pleasures and how dismal their prospects in the New Order (Luke 6:42–46).[38] Perhaps the earliest form consisted of three blessings and their corresponding woes:[39]

> How blest are you who are poor; the kingdom of God is yours.
> How blest are you who now go hungry; your hunger shall be satisfied.
> How blest are you who weep now; you shall laugh.
> But alas for you who are rich; you have had your time of happiness.
> Alas for you who are well-fed now; you shall go hungry.
> Alas for you who laugh now; you shall mourn and weep.
> [Luke 6:20–21, 24–25 NEB]

Here, then, are some features of a whole way of life that brings God's approval and his promise of fulfillment in the Kingdom. The intimate relationship between eschatology and ethics that marks Jesus' preaching about the Kingdom is exhibited clearly here. A religious teaching that penetrates the marrow of existence is strengthened by a firm eschatological sanction. The Beatitudes constitute a summons to the life of the Kingdom before its manifestation. They represent an ethic of obedience that defines a point of view, a posture, and a practice crucially important to participation in God's New Age.

The Old and New Law

This new and more exacting righteousness finds further definition in the Matthaean Sermon in a series of six commands of Jesus

---

37 The eschatological emphasis has disappeared from the gnosticized form of the two Beatitudes on persecution in the *Gospel of Thomas.* See Sayings 68, 69a.

38 Cf. the covenant curses of Deut. 28–29 (called the Commination in the synagogues) and the oath of blessings and cursings taken by the Qumran initiate (1QS i.16–ii.18; Gaster, *Scriptures,* pp. 40–41).

39 Manson, *The Sayings of Jesus,* p. 150.

representing reformulations of Torah rules (Matt. 5:21–48). Dealing with the prescriptions of the law pertaining to such problems as murder, adultery, divorce, perjury, retaliation, and the definition of the neighbor, these new precepts reach beneath the formal letter of the law and identify the basic intention which had been calcified into legal form. In part, also, they deliberately and daringly set aside specific points of the Torah and present substitutes offered with no defense save the authority of the speaker. Some allowance, of course, may be made for a heightening of these contrasts between the old and new law by the Church's situation in Matthew's day, when an unbridgeable gulf yawned between the Christian Church and the Jewish synagogue. Not only Matthew but other writers like Luke, John, and Paul understand that Jesus' teaching on one level fulfills the law of Moses by searching out its basic principles, yet on another level denies and supersedes it with a new Torah of the Messiah.

1. The Sixth Commandment in the Decalogue prohibiting civil murder, Jesus declares, is not observed as long as one permits hostility to fester in his heart against another person, even though he may never resort to an act of physical violence (Matt. 5:21f.). Positively, this can only mean that instead of depriving a person of his life in any way, the child of God will be eager to *give* him his life. So understood, even the rabbinic views providing court penalties against those who grievously insult another person with violent and abusive language are not drastic enough. Even four-letter words like *raka* and *mōre,*[40] considered harmless taunts, destroy the dignity of another by treating him as an object of contempt. A man risks condemnation by making such verbal assaults. Old Testament and rabbinic teaching similarly deplored unseemly displays of anger.[41] But the striking thing about Jesus' prohibition is that he regards the offense as warranting the gravest consequences. One feels this is no artful exaggeration to make a point. Neither God nor men, in his view, ought to tolerate anything less than full love toward other men, whether friend or foe, respecting them as brothers.

---

40 The origin and meaning of these two epithets are still vigorously debated. They may be Greek loan words of uncertain meaning or, as we suppose, they may be Greek transliterations of Aramaic insults (*rêqâ nābāl*). They have been interpreted to mean frivolous or foolish, the little and great synagogue bans, or empty-headed or obstinately wicked. The context suggests that they are words of insult. Both words are found in CD x.18 (G. Vermes, *The Dead Sea Scrolls in English* [Baltimore: Penguin Books, Inc., 1962], p. 112).

41 See Lev. 19:17; Sirach 28:2–5; *Test. Gad* 4:6.

2. The Seventh Commandment, and in part the Tenth, protects the integrity of the family by an interdiction against acts of adultery and the underlying covetousness. Paul apparently regarded the roving eye as the most difficult of all to control. Spinning spider webs to trap victims for personal pleasure without any concern for their rights is nasty occupation for those who petition God for the coming of the Kingdom. Without minimizing for a moment the significance of such behavior, Jesus insists with the prophets and the rabbis that such evil action is rooted in the inner life (Matt. 5:27f.).[42] Clean hands are no certain evidence of a pure heart, but the chaste spirit always declares itself in decent behavior.

What is new here and elsewhere in Jesus' teaching is that he breaks through the juristic form of control on human behavior, both cultic and civil, and interprets the legislation in terms of its implicit moral demand. The radical obedience Jesus seeks to develop exists only "when the whole man stands behind what he does; or better, when the whole man is *in* what he does, when he is not *doing something obediently,* but *is* essentially obedient."[43] The right way of walking before God (*halakah*) must involve not simply the overt action but the whole matter of a man's motivation and disposition. His conduct may be socially acceptable, but he himself may have bowed to a formal authority from which he still reserves his essential self.

3. The third saying in the contrasting expositions of the Torah deals with the Jewish position on divorce (Matt. 5:31f.). Jesus' unconventional approach to the law is illustrated here as he daringly contrasts several variant injunctions regarding marriage and divorce and asserts the chronological and intrinsic priority of the one over the other. Despite the concession that the Torah makes for the dissolution of a marriage under certain conditions (Deut. 24:1), Jesus insists that this cannot nullify the scriptural understanding of the divine purpose in instituting the marital relationship (Gen. 2:24). "What therefore God has joined together, let not man put asunder" (Mark 10:9). The scandalous divorce rate, which the rabbis bitterly

---

42 With oriental exaggeration, vss. 29f. advise drastic self-surgery rather than submission to unbridled passion. In Mark 9:42–48 par. a similar saying is broadened to include anything that leads to sin. Cf. 1QpHab v.7 (Vermes, *The Dead Sea Scrolls,* p. 235); and Solomon Schechter, *Some Aspects of Rabbinic Theology* (New York: The Macmillan Company, 1923), pp. 264ff.

43 Rudolf K. Bultmann, *Jesus and the Word,* trans. Louise Pettibone Smith and Ermine Huntress (New York: Charles Scribner's Sons, 1934), p. 77.

criticized, was the result of rationalizing the intention of the covenant with God until its original meaning was no longer recognizable.

Here and elsewhere in the Gospels the position of Jesus is quite clear. Divorce is simply prohibited as it apparently was in the strict code of the Essenes (CD iv.21). Either the husband or the wife who marries again after divorce is guilty of adultery (Luke 16:18).[44] According to the Mishnah, Rabbi Hillel claimed the law of Deuteronomy 24:1 could be interpreted to mean that a husband may divorce his wife "even if she spoiled a dish for him, for it is written, Because he hath found in her indecency in anything" (*Gitt.* 9.10).[45] Even the failure to fulfill a vow was considered by some rabbis adequate cause for divorce (*Ket.* 7.6),[46] though the conservative view of Shammai's school was that infidelity was the sole ground (*Gitt.* 9.10). In a remarkable recognition of mutual rights and responsibilities, Jesus repudiates any double standard and confirms the permanence of the marital relationship by appealing to God's purpose in instituting marriage (Mark 10:5–9).

4. Jewish law provided stiff penalties against perjury (Num. 30:2; Deut. 23:21ff.), and the Third Commandment sternly prohibits the irresponsible invocation of the divine name in oaths.[47] But the jurists of Jesus' day distinguished between those oaths that were binding because they made reference to the divine name or attributes and those that were not. Jesus denounces the Pharisees for such fallacious and ridiculous discriminations. "Woe to you, blind guides, who say, 'If any one swears by the temple, it is nothing; but if any one swears by the gold of the temple, he is bound by his oath' " (Matt. 23:16)[48]. Against these covert invitations to deal lightly with the truth, Jesus bluntly insists that all oaths implicate God in one way or another. In the simpler form preserved in the letter of James, the saying runs, "But above all, my brethren, do not swear, either by heaven or by earth or with any other oath, but let your yes be yes and your no be no, that you may not fall under condemnation" (5:12; cf. Matt. 5:33–37). It is interesting to note that the Essenes also

---

[44] The Q form in Luke 16:18 would seem to be the earliest in this tradition of Jesus' saying. Mark 10:11–12 probably reflects the Roman law and practice that permitted wives to divorce their husbands.

[45] Herbert Danby, trans., *The Mishnah* (London: Oxford University Press, 1958), p. 321.

[46] *Ibid.*, p. 255.

[47] Exod. 20:7; Deut. 5:11; cf. Lev. 19:12.

[48] Cf. Matt. 23:17–22, and the Mishnaic tractates *Ned.* 3.3; *Sheb.* 4.13.

frowned upon the use of oaths to bolster a pledge.[49] Jesus insists upon such a dependable relation between a man's promise and his performance as to eliminate the necessity for oaths altogether. There is no place for sophistry or double-talk in one who cherishes the word of truth.

5. In its time the *lex talionis* marked a tremendous advance upon the old desert law of blood-revenge (Gen. 4:23 f.). The sages and rabbis had gone far beyond this restrictive retaliation in urging that a man must not rejoice over the misfortune of his enemy, and ought not to recompense evil with evil.[50] The preface to the Levitical law on love toward the neighbor reads, "You shall not take vengeance or bear any grudge against the sons of your own people" (Lev. 19:18a). But with the same impatience we have already noted toward anything less than complete obedience to God's will, Jesus declares, "You have heard that it was said, 'An eye for an eye and a tooth for a tooth.' But I say to you, Do not resist one who is evil" (Matt. 5:38f.).

What is involved in nonretaliation is concretely specified in the amplifications of the fifth antithesis. It means the refusal to requite in kind the personal injury suffered in an insulting slap[51] or court action (Luke: robbery) or the requisition of one's property by the military.[52] There is to be no retaliation, no revenge, no petulant self-defense. However, this is not to be a passive acceptance of exploitation, but rather the requital of active love for aggressive hatred. Even the nagging beggar and chronic borrower are not to be turned aside but greeted with open-handed generosity (vs. 42). It need not be concluded that Jesus is unaware of the occasional need "to close the open hand out of love," since he is not covering every conceivable situation but illustrating a total attitude. If God is so good to the poor and needy, can the righteous man be any less? Nor is the law of proportionate recompense enough. Love is to be given where none

---

49 Cf. CD xv.2–5; Jos., *War* II.8.6; *Antiq.* XV.10.4; but the initiate to the Order swore a solemn oath to obey the Torah.

50 Prov. 20:22; 24:17f., 29; Sirach 28:1–12; B. *Shab.* 88b; *Mek. on Exod.* 20:23; 1QS x.18.

51 *Baba Kamma* 8.6 (Danby, *The Mishnah,* p. 343) prescribes a fine of 400 *zuz* for a slap with the back of the hand. In the Essene community gesticulation with the left hand (considered unclean) was punishable by doing penance for ten days (1QS vii.15).

52 The verb translated "to force," *angarenein,* is a Persian loan word used to refer to the requisition of a peasant's pack animal or the impressment of civilians into service by the Roman militia. Cf. Mark 15:21.

may be returned; personal property shared beyond either the legal or illegal demand.

6. This refusal to repay evil with evil but rather to overcome evil with good is finally confirmed by the sixth contrast, which exposes the radical dimension of the neighbor-love counsel. We have seen how discussion of that Mosaic admonition led Jesus to argue that love redefined the meaning of neighbor until it included not simply the fellow-Israelite but embraced even schismatic Jews like the Samaritans. That Samaritan merchants, Greek businessmen, and Roman civil officials were to be met not with suspicion or animosity but with friendship is a complete reversal of reaction for a hard-pressed subject people.

> Not by way of retaliation, and not by the way of friendliness to the one belonging to one's own group and hatred toward the one not belonging, but only by the way of love which overcomes hostility because one is for the other is the torn community repaired.[53]

It is a striking fact that the only two instances in which Jesus speaks of men becoming sons of God occur in contexts where the problem of hostility in human relationships is being discussed. Those who represent in their active peace-making God's own generous offer of amnesty toward rebellious mankind are his real sons (Matt. 5:9). And those who requite aggressive love for aggressive hatred similarly publicize the parentage of their Father who is in Heaven (Q Matt. 5:45). So seriously were these words taken by the early Church that for the first two centuries most Christians seem to have abstained from military service, and the Church fathers repudiated Christians' participation in war. "We who formerly murdered one another," writes Justin, 'now not only do not make war upon our enemies, but that we may not lie or deceive our judges, we gladly die confessing Christ."[54] "We do not fight under the emperor although he requires it," says Origen,[55] to which his pagan critic makes scornful reply, "If all men were to do the same as you, there would be nothing to prevent the king from being left in utter solitude and desertion and the forces

---

53 Walter Grundmann, *Die Geschichte Jesu Christi* (Berlin: Evangelische Verlaganstalt, 1961), p. 123.

54 Justin, *Apol.* I.39. "From the end of the New Testament period to the decade A.D. 170–180 there is no evidence whatever of Christians in the army." (Roland H. Bainton, *Christian Atttitudes Toward War and Peace* [New York: Abingdon Press, 1960], pp. 68f.). Cf. Cecil John Cadoux, *The Early Christian Attitude Toward War* (London: Headley Bros., Ltd., 1919).

55 Origen, *Contra Celsum* viii.73.

of the empire would fall into the hands of the wildest and most lawless barbarians."[56] Although their conviction of the imminent end of the world and their attitude toward the Roman state may have influenced the Christians' position toward military service, their basic objection centered in the conviction that such intentional and organized bloodshed was incompatible with the demand for love.

Hearing and Doing

This ethic of obedience is further confirmed in several stories Jesus tells. To make these commandments the source of obedient action is to make the wise choice of a foundation site that will provide secure anchorage against all the violence of the elements. This is the point of the parable of the two houses (Q Matt. 7:24–27). There is obviously no insurance that guarantees perpetual fair weather, but a man's way of action will enable him to stand up against the great flood of the final tribulation that brings ruin to another.[57]

Amid a collection of parables exhorting watchfulness in the face of the approaching eschatological crisis, Matthew places a story of three servants employed by a wealthy man who sets out on a long journey. They are entrusted with portions of his property commensurate with their ability (Matt. 25:14–30).[58] Two of the men proceed to put their loans to work, doubling the original amount they received. But the third is reproached by the returning householder for his cautious "safety first" procedure in simply burying his thousand dollars. The money is taken from him and given to the one who has the most, for "to everyone who has will more be given, and he will have abundance; but from him who has not, even what he has will be taken away" (Matt. 25:29). The point of the whole story is that men are not privately self-employed but are the managers of divine resources and are strictly accountable before God for what they do with them. The meaning of their existence is to be realized in loyal and devoted service in God's employ.

Bertolt Brecht gives us a bitter Marxist critique of this parable of the talents-pounds in his *Threepenny Novel.*

---

[56] *Ibid.,* viii.68–69.

[57] A similar parable of two houses is told by Rabbi Elisha b. Abuya (ca. A.D. 120); cf. B. T. D. Smith, *The Parables of the Synoptic Gospels* (Cambridge: Cambridge University Press, 1937), pp. 70–71.

[58] Cf. the variant versions in Luke 19:12–27 and the *Gospel of the Hebrews* (*Gospel Parallels,* p. 161). Both Synoptic forms cast the story in an eschatological setting that may not have marked the original.

> "My friends," began the judge in a respectful tone; "can you tell me anything about the reason why some of us, the minority, increase their goods and make five or even ten pounds out of one pound, as the Bible commands; while others, the great majority, after a long and hard working life, increase, if anything, only their misery? What my friends, is this pound of the fortunate, which produces such enormous profits and around which, so I have heard, such a desperate battle rages?"

With the discovery that it is the oppressed proletariat who constitutes the pound of the privileged minority, the judge turns to the accused "religious teacher," who had naively taught that *everybody* receives a pound as a gift from God, and screeches his verdict:

> "You are convicted! Nothing but misrepresentation! You have spread this! Therefore I condemn you! As an accessory! Because you gave people this parable, which is also a pound! Out of which profit can be made! And all who pass it on, all who dare to relate such things, I condemn! To death!"[59]

Such an economic interpretation of the parable along the lines of the class struggle represents a tendentious perversion of Jesus' story, however. Jesus' message is the plan of a way to be traveled, a narrow path that threads its way across the landscape of this world until it issues in the royal realm of God. That way recognizes no dichotomy between hearing and doing, believing and behaving. In his account of the life of responsible love toward other men, Jesus probes both the dynamics of conduct and the specific behavioral forms, insisting that the outward way must be a spontaneous expression of the inward way.

In summary, we have seen that the responsible life before God is the human response to Jesus' mandate for a total commitment of the self in love to the *Abba*-God. It finds concrete manifestation both in acts of prayer and praise and in loving service to men. But that mandate is put to its severest test when conventional definitions of the neighbor are revised to include even the enemy. Thus to look, feel, and act is to reflect the outlook, attitude, and action of God who gives himself and his Kingdom with undeserved generosity as his "reward" to the faithful disciple. The disciple-life is an ethic of "love's unforced obedience" to a commanding God and an ethic of grace from a forgiving and enabling God.

---

59 "The Pound of the Poor" in Bertolt Brecht, trans. Desmond I. Vesey and Christopher Isherwood, *Threepenny Novel* (New York: Grove Press, Inc., 1956), pp. 392, 396.

CHAPTER VII

THE CURATIVE POWER OF THE NEW AGE

> Our Savior's works were permanent, for they were true—those who had been healed and had risen from the dead did not merely appear healed and risen, but they endured not only during the Savior's stay on earth, and after his departure they continued for a considerable time, so that some of them reached our own times.*

> But miracles are miracles, are God:
> And when we are dismayed, when most we stray,
> They suddenly surprise us in the way.†

The Meaning and Function of the Miracle Stories in the Early Church

The Gospels present the new life of God's order, not simply as the subject of conversation and debate between Jesus and others, but also as a gift of health that he transmits in his encounters. We have been considering the description in Jesus' message of the disruptive and restorative power of God's sovereign rule brought to bear upon the present world. But the gospel of the kingly rule of God was not confined to oral communication. Isaiah's ancient promise, "Peace,

---

* Quadratus, early second century, quoted by Eusebius, *Church History,* IV.3.2.

† Boris Pasternak, "The Miracle," in *In the Interlude: Poems, 1945–60* (London: Oxford University Press, Amen House, 1962), p. 79.

peace to the far and the near, says the Lord; and I will heal him" (Isa. 57:19), found accomplishment in Jesus' attack upon the sickness, disease, and psychological disturbances of men. Regarding illness to be contradictory to God's reign, he was not content simply to announce the imminent end of the present age and to issue an invitation to the Father's house. He demonstrated the curative power of God in concrete acts of service to human need in which sickness was overcome and health restored. The healing miracles represent a deliverance Jesus effected from the paralysis of pain, the crippling power of guilt, self-alienation, and that estrangement from nature which robs men of true life and contributes to the tragic element in human experience.

The Gospels speak of these deeds of Jesus as acts of power (*dynameis*), signs (*sēmeia*), and works (*erga*), terms expressive of the common biblical conception of God as power. Our word "miracle," which popularly conveys the sense of a *deus ex machina* in a closed system of natural law, is obviously unsuitable to an age that held no such conception of nature.[1] To the people of the first-century Roman world, unusual and marvelous demonstrations of supernatural power could be performed by properly qualified persons, revealing the divine order which occasionally penetrated the world of men and matter. For biblical man God could only be known insofar as he chose to reveal himself by his activities.

To Jesus, it would appear, these mighty works were seen as evidence that the decisive moment had arrived in redemptive history. "Wisdom [God] is justified by her deeds" (Matt. 11:19). These acts performed by him and his disciples were manifestations of the presence and action of God, and signaled the eventual defeat of demonic power in the world and the vindication of the divine purpose. Satan, the strong man, was being robbed of his power (Mark 3:27; Q Luke 11:21f.). Their purpose was to display glory, evoke repentance, arouse faith, and make possible true existence in a world of phantasy and disorder. But this, of course, was nothing else than what the preaching of the Kingdom intended (Mark 1:15).

---

1 The Latin word *miraculum,* which appears often in patristic and later theology, is never used in the Vulgate to translate any of the Greek words rendered "miracle" in English. Its presupposition of universal and inexorable laws of nature finds no place in the biblical concept of the world, which is seen as God's creation and subject to his control.

Views of Illness in the Ancient World

In the Jewish and Greek worlds of the first century, disease and other calamities were attributed to demonic activity preying upon helpless mortals. The intention of physicians and exorcists was to drive out the evil spirit that had taken possession of a person and had either enslaved his own spirit to his control or expelled it completely. But the early Church was confident that the King of life had appeared to do battle with the King of death. "The reason the Son of God appeared was to destroy the works of the devil" (I John 3:8).

This "lost Archangel," as John Milton called Satan, was much more than a "mythological representation of a sinister squint in human nature or an evil trend in history."[2] He was the ruler of this world (John 12:31, 14:30, 16:11) who could bind human lives and rack their bodies with pain (Luke 13:16). His minions could invade the citadel of the self and evict the owner. It was the voice of the demon with whom the victim had completely identified himself who cried out in the wretched man's delusional state: "What have you to do with us, O Son of God? Have you come here to torment us before the time?" (Matt. 8:29).

This was one of the commonest explanations of physical and mental illness in Jesus' day. The whole world lay under the power of the Evil One, either because of the very nature of things or because of human and angelic rebellion against God. Nevertheless the dominion of Satan was doomed, it was firmly believed. With the coming of God's messiah, his rule would be vanquished, his captives released, and the foundations laid for a New Order where sin, suffering, and death would have no part. God's righteous rule would prevail throughout the earth, indeed, through all creation.[3] Such is the mythological background against which we must study and interpret the curative work of Jesus. Like the parables, these "mighty works," as they are usually called, are one of the ways of understanding the mystery of the Kingdom of God and observing its power in action.

---

[2] J. A. Mackay, *God's Order* (New York: The Macmillan Company, 1953), p. 28.

[3] On the dethronement of Satan, see Isa. 24:22f.; *I Enoch* 10:11f., 54:4f.; *Test. Levi* 18:12; *Test. Sim.* 6:6; *Test. Jud.* 25:3; *Jub.* 23:29; *Asmp. Moses* 10:1. Isa. 25:8 and 35:10 are the background for the promise of Rev. 21:4 that suffering and death shall be no more.

Use of the Miracle Stories in Teaching

Martin Dibelius has suggested that the miracle stories were told by Christian storytellers after the fashion of other short stories and wonder-working tales of the time. Their form precludes a use in missionary preaching as such, but they served a propaganda purpose, nonetheless, by convincing hearers of the superior power of the Lord Jesus over all the other miracle workers, saviors, and cult gods of healing in the Hellenistic world.[4] Within the community of faith, the stories as enacted parables may have served a teaching purpose by conveying the significance of Christ's work and the character of discipleship. So for Luke the story of the miraculous catch of fish (Luke 5:1–11) is a symbolical prefiguration of the universal outreach of the gospel. Indeed he may have converted Mark's episode of the unfruitful fig tree outside Jerusalem (Mark 11:12–14) into a parable of God's judgment upon the spiritually bankrupt nation (Luke 13:6–9). In Mark's combination of a miracle story involving a paralyzed man (Mark 2:1–5a, 10b–12) and an apothegm on the forgiveness of sin (Mark 2:5b–10a), we can hear the kerygmatic witness of the primitive Church that promised forgiveness of sins in Christ's name (Acts 2:38, 3:19).

John's Gospel offers striking instances of the symbolic teaching value of these stories from the life of Jesus. The "first of his signs," Jesus' miracle at the wedding festival in Cana, for example, signifies to the Evangelist the superiority of the new wine of the gospel over the old wine of Judaism (John 2:1–12). Both propagandist and instructional purposes were served through these accounts of the healing power operative in Jesus' relationships with the sick and ailing. Though many form critics believe that a number of the miracle stories have been embellished with features of Jewish and Hellenistic wonder stories or are borrowed complete, a study of these non-Christian narratives points up the remarkable sobriety and restraint of the Gospel stories.

Some Facts and Fancies

It may be noted that the healing strength which brought relief to pain-racked bodies and disturbed minds was never understood to be

---

[4] Martin Dibelius, *From Tradition to Gospel,* trans. Bertram L. Woolf (New York: Charles Scribner's Sons, 1935), p. 96. Cf. Rudolf Bultmann, *History of the Synoptic Tradition,* trans. John Marsh (New York: Harper & Row, Publishers, 1963), pp. 218–44.

an exclusive gift of Jesus; others besides him were able to expel demons. Jesus himself recognized the successful work of Jewish healers who had no relationship with him.[5] His own disciples were trained and given authority over the unclean spirits,[6] a therapeutic power that extended into the life and work of the post-resurrection community.[7] The early Church believed the power to work miracles was demonstrative of the reality of the New Age now experienced in the eschatological gift of the Holy Spirit. They were "tasting the goodness of the word of God and the powers of the age to come" (Heb. 6:5).

It is true that the early Church soon appealed to these stories to support its confession of Jesus as Lord, believing that these were the mighty works of the Messiah, the Son of God. Nonetheless it was recognized that the wonderful acts of power were corroborative and confirmatory rather than constitutive of his divine nature. As early as the second century Marcion of Pontus was arguing that Jesus proved himself to be the Son, Messenger, and Christ of God by the evidences of the miracles. But it was a hard-headed Christian lawyer named Tertullian who tersely objected that even false messiahs, according to the teaching of the New Testament, can perform signs and wonders.[8]

Obviously there was nothing *coercive* about the miracles of Jesus to drive spectators to a single conclusion about him. The sharply divided response among the people is proof enough of that. There were those who marveled at his success in healing the sick and who concluded that he must possess the authority of a prophet, perhaps even of the Mosaic prophet (John 9:16f.).[9] Others who were eyewitnesses to the self-same events came to opposite conclusions. The Synoptic Gospels record a semiofficial investigation of Jesus' Galilean work by the theological experts of the Pharisaic brotherhoods in which the opinion was given that Jesus was an ally of the Evil One. The cures, the reality of which was never questioned, were concluded to

---

5 Mark 9:38–41 par.; Q Luke 11:19.

6 Mark 6:7 par.; Luke 10:19.

7 Acts 2:43, 3:1–10, 9:32–43; Gal. 3:5; I Cor. 12:10, 28; Heb. 2:3f.; etc.

8 Tert., *Against Marcion* III.3; Mark 13:22 par.; II Thess. 2:9; Rev. 13:13f. Cf. Deut. 13:2–6; Origen, *Contra Celsum* I.68.

9 References to signs validating a prophetic testimony are found in *Sifre* (on Deut. 18:19), #177 (108a); B. *Sanh.* 93b, 98a. Apparently miracles were never considered as signs validating the Messiah, however. See George F. Moore, *Judaism,* II (Cambridge, Mass.: Harvard University Press, 1944), 349.

be the artifice of Satan to deceive and entrap God's faithful. "He is possessed by Beelzebub, and by the prince of demons he casts out the demons" (Mark 3:22;[10] Q Luke 11:15). John reports a similarly sharp division among the observers. "Many of them said, 'He has a demon, and he is mad; why listen to him?' Others said, 'These are not the sayings of one who has a demon. Can a demon open the eyes of the blind?' " (John 10:19–21; cf. 7:20, 8:48). The most surprising evidence of a negative appraisal of Jesus' work is furnished by the earliest Gospel, when it is intimated that Jesus' own family feared that he was demented and they sought to take him into protective custody (Mark 3:19b–21, 31–35).[11]

No less than the utterances of Jesus, the mighty works that he performed invited contradictory opinions. In and of themselves the miracles of the Gospels at best can only demonstrate that Jesus of Nazareth was a good and compassionate person who was helpful to persons in need.[12] His therapy was astonishingly, but not exclusively, effective. Both words and works, however, pose a situation that challenges faith to recognize in them something contrary to veiled demonic activity, on the one hand, and beyond sheer humanitarianism, on the other. "To the 'outsider' the miracles were mere portents, the acts of one wonder-worker amongst many; to the believer they were unique—not so much in outward form or action, as in their inner spiritual significance as *Gesta Christi*."[13]

That marvelous acts of control over sickness and disease were constituent to Jesus' work is testified by a variety of non-Christian witnesses, although the appraisals of their meaning and significance are varied. Both Mandaean and Islamic literature refer to Jesus as a miracle worker, and the earliest strata of the Jewish Talmudic literature do not question the fact of healings performed by Jesus

---

10 Mark represents the judgment to have been passed by scribal authorities who had come from Jerusalem for the express purpose of investigating Jesus. This suggests more nationwide notoriety than is likely at this stage of Jesus' ministry. The Q context of an act of exorcism is to be preferred.

11 Cf. John 7:5. The translation "friends" in the KJV and RSV does not suggest, as the Greek expression *hoi par'autou* does, that these may be immediate members of his family. Read with the NEB: "When his family heard of this, they set out to take charge of him; for people were saying that he was out of his mind."

12 Cf. *Gospel of Peter* VIII.28: "If such mighty signs are wrought at His death, consider how righteous a man He is."

13 Alan Richardson, *The Miracle-Stories of the Gospels* (London: SCM Press, 1941), p. 49.

and his associates. "On the eve of Passover," reports an early *Baraita,* "they hanged Yeshu [of Nazareth] and the heralds went before him for forty days saying, '[Yeshu of Nazareth] is going forth to be stoned in that he hath practiced sorcery and beguiled and led astray Israel' " (B. *Sanh.* 43a; cf. 107b). His disciples are said to have performed cures in his name.[14] The charge that Jesus executed signs and wonders as acts of black magic is found in both Jewish and Greek critics of Christianity and is echoed in medieval Jewish literature.[15] No such acts were claimed for John the Baptist, however.[16]

Interpreting the Miracle Stories

Our study of the miracle stories will be aided by a consideration of a few presuppositions.

1. We ought to be clear about the words the New Testament uses to refer to these acts of Jesus and his disciples, as well as to miracles in general, and what they signified. Four different Greek words are employed, none of which is strictly compatible with the most popular definition of "miracle."[17] *Dynamis,* a word meaning physical force or power, is used in the sense of a work of power or a mighty deed. *Terata,* used only in the plural and in combination with the word for signs, is usually translated "wonders." This word calls attention to an extraordinary occurrence that is interpreted to be an omen or a portent. In the Gospels it is used only once in reference to Jesus' own activity (John 4:48), otherwise, of the eschatological events. *Sēmeion,* or "sign," a favorite word of John's Gospel, is used by the New Testament writers about an act certifying the authority of a speaker or an event revelatory of the power and glory of God. The latter is the sense that the word *erga* or "works" also has in the Gospel of John.

These "miracles" of the New Testament, as of the Old Testament, are regarded to be particularly striking demonstrations of the continual activity of God, who can be described as the one who works wonders (Ps. 77:14). In the New Testament, too, it is God who is understood

---

[14] T. *Hul.* II.22–23. See also P. *Shab.* 14d. Morris Goldstein, *Jesus in the Jewish Tradition* (New York: The Macmillan Company, 1950), pp. 27, 96.

[15] Cf. Justin, *Apol.* I.30; *Dial.* 69 and the tenth-century Jewish polemic *Tol'doth Yeshu,* where it is alleged that Yeshu worked miracles with the use of the Ineffable Name by means of the magical arts for evil purposes.

[16] Jos., *Antiq.* XVIII.5.2. Cf. Luke 7:28; John 10:41.

[17] E.g., Mark 6:2; John 5:36; 10:32, 37, etc.; Acts 2:22, 3:12, 10:38; Heb. 2:3f.

to be the source of the wonder-working power manifest in the acts of Jesus and the Church. "Whatever the Lord pleases he does, in heaven and on earth, in the seas and all deeps" (Ps. 135:6; cf. II Macc. 15:21). Nevertheless, there is an orderliness and a regularity, ordained by the Creator, displayed in the natural world; God honors his own handiwork (Ps. 148:6). Thus we may continue to use the word "miracle" biblically to refer to an act or event in nature and history which strikingly expresses the divine presence and action, evoking the responses of awe, gratitude, and praise.

2. Any appraisal of the miracle stories of the Gospels must reckon seriously with the biblical understanding of nature, man, and God, as well as with the New Testament interpretation of Christ and the goal of history. The God of the Bible is never viewed as a *deus ex machina* who is frantically introduced to resolve the complexities of a mechanistic natural order. There is no thought of an independent, self-sustaining order of nature made out of eternally existent matter, as the Stoics held. Nor is there any notion of an inviolable causal nexus in nature, as Aristotle taught, and which became the basis of the medieval conception of miracle as an interruption or a suspension of the world-order by divine supervention.

God is the Lord of nature and history, and both are imprinted with his purposes and plastic to his touch, so that in more or less veiled form they disclose his glory and greatness (Ps. 135:6; Q Luke 12:27f.). Potentially any event can represent a revelatory sign to men from the Father-Creator. Since he is the master and not the slave of his creation, the ranges of his possible actions can neither be anticipated nor prescribed by man.

> I know that thou canst do all things,
> and that no purpose of thine can be thwarted,

is the conclusion to Job's interrogation of the Almighty (Job 42:2).[18]

3. In the biblical view, God's Day stood in judgment and condemnation upon the disease and distortions that left life broken and incomplete in this present age. It is of critical significance to understand that the salvation the Bible associates with the new era is never conceived as some exclusively spiritual experience, but a restoration of man's total life to unity and wholeness. In the Old Testament the verb "to save" (*yasha*) means to make spacious, to bring victory in

---

18 Cf. Gen. 18:14; II Macc. 15:21; Luke 18:27.

battle, or to grant safety from enemies and the vicissitudes of life. Like the word *shalom,* salvation therefore signifies the total condition of welfare of a person or a people in a right relationship to God. There is no health-salvation apart from this. "Heal me, O Lord, and I shall be healed; save me, and I shall be saved" (Jer. 17:14).[19] We shall see that in the New Testament the verb *sōzein* is often used in the sense of healing, where the correlative religious meaning is never far away.[20] To declare that the Day of Salvation is at hand is to announce the end of sickness and suffering and God's offer of fullness of health for all who will receive it.

Not only would the coming of the New Age be heralded by the healing of the sick (Isa. 35:5f., 61:1f.), it also would be attended by physical signs and wonders throughout the universe. The later literature of the Old Testament and Jewish writings in the period between the Testaments frequently allude to the awesome events that will accompany the New Age.[21] Thus both miraculous healings and extraordinary occurrences in nature were anticipated in apocalyptic Judaism as eschatological events fulfilling God's promise to redeem his creation. There would be new men, thoroughly sound in mind and body, set in a suitable environment of new heavens and a new earth. The Bible recognizes astutely that men are not "saved" *in vacuo* but in relationship with a social and a natural environment. The cosmic signs and wonders at the End would herald a renovated and redeemed environment coming into being, a suitable setting for a new and perfected form of human existence.[22]

4. Every critical study of miracle, biblical or otherwise, must not only begin by defining its terms but also by recognizing the determinative influence of its presuppositional views of nature, man, and God. If natural law is misconstrued as a kind of enacted legislation, and the physical universe conceived along the lines of the closed system of mechanistic Victorian science, then miracle is ruled out *ex hypothesi,* except for the poets and the painters who delight in figurative language. But it is open to consideration that twentieth-century physics and psychology offer understandings of nature and human nature congenial

---

19 Cf. Pss. 3:8, 30:2, 41:3, 116:4, 6, 8; Zeph. 3:19. An excellent description of the physician as the agent of God's healing is found in Sirach 38:1–15.

20 Some fourteen times in the Gospels, e.g., Mark 5:34; Luke 7:50, 8:36.

21 Micah 7:15; Wisd. of Sol. 5:17–23; IV Ezra 7:27, 13:50; *II Bar.* 29:6, 51:7.

22 Isa. 65:17, 66:22; cf. Rom. 8:19ff.; II Pet. 3:13; Rev. 21:1.

to, though scarcely corroborative of, the signs, wonders, and mighty works described in the New Testament.[23]

Thus it is nonsense to state that the issue for modern man is whether or not he can subscribe to the naive credulity of the first-century mentality. Simple, prescientific credulity there was, which men have not wholly outgrown. But there were also deep intuitive insights into the interaction of spirit and matter and a realization of the unitary nature of personality which modern man is in process of recovering and elaborating. Were cures actually performed and natural forces tamed as visible phenomona? Physics and psychology must engage one's theology in answering that question. To many it will appear that the supreme miracle in the Gospels is the evidence of the total fact of Jesus himself and the presence of the Spirit of God in him creating new life in men. Once again, the miracles, as the message, drive us to the mystery of Jesus' person.[24]

Miracle Stories in Roman Hellenism and Judaism

Hellenistic Stories

Wonder-working and miraculous cures were widespread claims in the Roman world in which the Christian faith was cradled. Grandiose titles like "Son of God" and "Divine Man" were frequently assigned to men who were believed to possess marvelous curative powers. The healing of the blind, lame, and sick was credited to famous Pythagorean philosopher and contemporary of Jesus named Apollonius who came from Tyana in Asia Minor and whose amazing adventures are recorded by a certain Philostratus a century and a half later (ca. A.D. 215). The legendary embellishment of his exploits may be illust-

---

23 For non-Kantian conceptions of space and the new concept of nature, see such books as Werner Heisenberg, *Physics and Philosophy* (New York: Harper & Row, Publishers, 1958); A. Koyré, *From the Closed World to the Infinite Universe* (New York: Harper & Row, Publishers, 1958); Karl Heim, *The Transformation of the Scientific World View* (New York: Harper & Row, Publishers, 1953).

24 Among recent helpful books on the subject, attention may be called to Reginald H. Fuller, *Interpreting the Miracles* (Philadelphia: The Westminster Press, 1963); J. S. Lawton, *Miracles and Revelation* (London: Lutterworth Press, 1959); Ronald S. Wallace, *The Gospel Miracles* (Edinburgh: Oliver and Boyd, 1960); I. T. Ramsey *et al.*, *The Miracles and the Resurrection* (London: SPCK, 1964); H. Van Der Loos, *The Miracles of Jesus* (Leiden: E. J. Brill, 1965).

rated by this account of the philosopher raising a dead girl to life, a story the biographer gives some reason to doubt:

> A young woman had apparently died at the time her marriage and the bridegroom was following the bier, greatly lamenting his unfulfilled marriage, while Rome sorrowed with him, for the girl was of a family of consular rank. Apollonius, seeing their grief, said: Put down the bier, for I will stay your tears over this maiden. Then he asked what her name was. The multitude thought that he was going to deliver a speech, one of those funeral sermons which stir up lamentation, but he only took hold of the maiden and whispering something secretly, awoke her from her seeming death. At this the maiden spoke aloud and returned to her father's house, as Alcestis did when brought back to life by Herakles. When relatives of the girl wanted to present Apollonius with 150,000 drachmas, he said to give the money to the maiden as a dowry [Philostratus, *Apollon.* IV.45].

Excavations at the famous healing shrine of Asklepios at Epidaurus in southern Greece have disclosed votive tablets inscribed by grateful invalids who had experienced cures of paralysis, blindness, and aphasia through the healing touch of the god.

> A dumb boy came to the sanctuary seeking to recover his voice. As he was presenting his first offering and performing the usual ceremony, the acolyte who bears the fire for the sacrifice to the god turned and said to the father of the boy, "Will you promise, if you get your wish, between now and the end of the year to bring the offering you owe as a fee for the healing?" At once the boy cried out, "I promise!" The father was greatly astonished, and told him to say it again. The boy said it again and was made whole from that moment.[25]

An inscription on another stele recovered at this ancient Lourdes records a cure of blindness:

> A blind man. He lost his ointment bottle in the bath. As he lay down to sleep, he dreamed that the god said he should seek it in the larger shelter, to the left as he entered. When it was day, the attendant led him to seek it. Entering the shelter he saw it immediately and thereupon was healed.[26]

It was said that the emperor Vespasian himself had performed a miracle of healing a blind man.[27]

---

[25] From *Hellenistic Religions*, edited by Frederick C. Grant, copyright © 1953, by The Liberal Arts Press, Inc., reprinted by permission of the Liberal Arts Press Division of The Bobbs-Merrill Company, Inc., p. 57. n. 5.

[26] Quoted in Lawrence J. McGinley, *Form-Criticism of the Synoptic Healing Narratives* (Maryland: Woodstock College Press, 1944), p. 138.

[27] Dio Cassius, *Roman History* LXVI.8; Tacitus, *Hist.* IV.81; Suetonius, *Vespasian* 7.

Magical incantations employing esoteric and unintelligible words were sometimes used:

> Then enter straightway and gazing intently draw the breath into thyself from the divinity. When thy soul has been restored, say: Draw nigh, O lord, archandara photaza puriphotoza buthix etimenmerophoratherieprothriphorathi.[28]

It may be something of this sort that Jesus described as the babblings of the heathen (Matt. 6:7).

But there were sharp critics of these Hellenistic miracle stories, just as there were of the Christian cures. One of the best known is the satirist Lucian of Samosata in northern Syria (ca. A.D. 125–190) whose writings include both vigorous polemics and clever parodies on the credulity of his contemporaries in accepting seriously these extravagant tales.[29]

Jewish Stories

The prominence of stories in the Gospels manifestly concerned with mental and emotional illness has no counterpart in the Hellenistic literature of the period.[30] For similar accounts of such healings attributed to the expulsion of a demonic spirit that had temporarily usurped the normal self, we must go to the literature of Judaism and the Orient. In both the Mesopotamian region and in Egypt the conviction was centuries old that illness was caused by demonic possession. There can be little doubt that in the postexilic period the Jewish communities in Babylon, Palestine, and Egypt were strongly influenced by Oriental demonology in their diagnosis and treatment of illness. References to Jewish exorcists appear in the New Testament and in Talmudic literature. A recently discovered scroll from Qumran describes an exorcism supposedly performed by Abraham at Pharaoh's

---

28 Paris Magic Papyrus, Bibl. Nat. Suppl. Graec., 574; 628–33, quoted in McGinley, *Form-Criticism,* p. 139. Cf. Lucian, *The Lover of Lies* XII.30f.; Martin P. Nilsson, *Greek Piety* (Oxford: The Clarendon Press, 1948), Chaps. vii-x: C. K. Barrett, *The New Testament Background: Selected Documents* (New York: The Macmillan Company, 1957), pp. 31–36.

29 His account of a charlatan prophet named Alexander makes entertaining reading and provides accurate information on the wiles of an ancient demagogue. See Grant, *Hellenistic Religions,* pp. 95–98.

30 Hellenistic literature records several instances of demon-possession and exorcisms, however. See Lucian, *Lover of Lies,* XVI and XXX; Philostratus, *Apollonius,* III.38, IV.20, the latter an account of an exorcism by Apollonius himself.

court.[31] Josephus tells of a certain Eleazer who proved that demons actually left their victims when the spirits were ordered to overturn basins of water in the presence of spectators.[32] In the Acts of the Apostles Luke mentions by name a Jewish high priest of Ephesus whose sons attempted unsuccessfully to employ the name of Jesus in their adjurations.[33]

Rabbinic contemporaries of Jesus such as Jochanan ben Zakkai, Eliezer ben Hyrcanus, and Chanina ben Dosa are reported to have performed successful cures by exorcising demonic spirits from their helpless human victims.[34] Even resuscitations from the dead are claimed.

> Antoninus came to Rabbi. He found him sitting with his disciples before him. Antoninus said to him: Are these the disciples of whom thou speakest with such praise? He answered: Indeed! The least among them can raise the dead. Some days later a servant of Antoninus became sick unto death. Antoninus sent word to Rabbi: Send me one of thy disciples to make this dead man live again! He sent him one of his disciples; some say it was R. Simon ben Ḥalaphta. The disciple went and found the servant lying prostrate. He spoke to him: Why liest thou prostrate, while thy master stands upon his feet? Immediately he stirred and stood up [*Levit. Rabba* 10.111d].[35]

Paddy Chayefsky's play, *The Tenth Man,* movingly depicts an exorcism ceremony in a modern orthodox synagogue based upon the old Jewish legend of dybbuks, the anguished spirits of the wicked dead who invade the bodies of living persons.

Such stories bear witness to the popularity of marvelous cures and miracle workers in the Roman world of the first century. The miracle stories of Jesus in the Gospels must be seen in such an environment of naive wonder and expectation to appreciate what may be genuinely distinctive to them.

---

31 The *Genesis Apocryphon* xx.21f. (G. Vermes, *The Dead Sea Scrolls in English* [Baltimore: Penguin Books, Inc., 1962], pp. 219f.).

32 Jos., *Antiq.* VIII.2.5.

33 Acts 19:13–20. Cf. 13:6–12; Mark 9:38–40.

34 *Yoma* 39b; *Hagiga* 17b; *Taanith* 25b; *Baba Metzia* 59b. Cf. Moore, *Judaism,* I, 376–79; II, 349; C. J. G. Montefiore and H. Loewe, *A Rabbinic Anthology* (London: Macmillan and Co., Ltd., 1938), pp. 690–93, n. 97.

35 On resuscitations of the dead see Philostratus, *Life of Apollonius of Tyana,* IV.45; Lucian, *Lover of Lies,* XI; Pliny, *Nat. Hist.* VII.124, XXXI.7; Apuleius, *Florida,* 19f.

Jesus as Therapist

The Gospels record many stories of Jesus' work as an exorcist and healer. A variety of physical as well as mental illness finds mention: cases of high fever, leprosy,[36] hemorrhage, paralysis, blindness, epilepsy,[37] aphasia, deafness, dropsy, and body deformities. "He healed many who were sick with various diseases, and cast out many demons" (Mark 1:34a). The stories exhibit certain features paralleled in the techniques employed by so-called "divine men" who were practitioners of the healing arts in the Roman world, yet there are significant differences, too. Basically, though, it is Jesus' own explanation of these cures in relation to the total proclamation of the reign of God which is of principal interest to us.

Certain texts appear to distinguish demon-possession from sickness, for example, Mark 1:32, 34; Matthew 4:24. But it is doubtful that the Evangelists intended to assign separate causes to mental and physical illness. In Luke's version of the healing of Peter's mother-in-law, Jesus is said to "rebuke" the fever (Luke 4:39). The blind and dumb are said to be demon-possessed (Matt. 12:22), and lameness and epilepsy are attributed to malevolent spirits (Luke 13:11; Mark 9:17–18). Illness in all its forms represented demonic power at work disfiguring God's creation and defying his right to rule. The coming of the Kingdom meant the defeat of all these alien authorities and the release of their human victims.

At this point we want to investigate in some detail several healing stories that may be considered representative of Jesus' therapy with the sick.

Healing a Demoniac

The story of the deranged man of Gergesa[38] who was healed by Jesus on a visit to the eastern shore of the Galilean lake may be examined as representative of Jesus' activity in exorcising evil spirits (Mark 5:1–20 par.). It is possible that this man, ostracised from his

---

36 The rabbis held that this disease and the raising of the dead were subject only to God's control, B. *Sanh.* 47a.

37 Known as the sacred disease in the Hellenistic world.

38 Probably, as Dalman suggested, we may think of the ancient city of Gergesa, now called Kersa, on the southeast coast of the lake. A ruined tower nearby, known as Gurza, testifies further to this place name. Gustaf Herman Dalman, *Sacred Sites and Ways,* trans. Paul P. Levertoff (London: SPCK, 1935), pp. 177–78.

friends and neighbors because of his disturbed condition, was a Gentile. Mark may have intended the story to establish a basis in Jesus' ministry for the rapidly developing Gentile mission of the Church in his own day, though this can only be conjectured.

Modern psychiatry might speculate that the Gergasene was a manic-depressive psychotic whose acute mania was abruptly quieted by this contact with Jesus. Here and elsewhere, however, the scanty details of the report make any diagnosis conjectural. Bound under the power of Satan, as he believed, this poor fellow exhibited such frenzied strength in these states that a primitive strait jacket of chains and fetters was useless to restrain him. "No one could bind him any more, even with a chain." A modern patient described these attacks in similar terms,

> It just comes, and I can't do anything to prevent it. I tear up and break everything within my reach. Afterwards I am very sorry, but that is the way it is. Either an attack of mania comes or I must remain silent or wander about.[39]

As Jesus landed on the shore with his disciples he was met by the demented man, who made a reverential act of obeisance and greeted him with a wild cry, "What have you to do with me, Jesus, Son of the Most High God? I adjure you by God, do not torment me." Evidently Jesus' reputation as a skilled antagonist of evil powers had preceded him. Jesus' request for the stranger's name reflects ancient views that the identity of the evil spirit must first be established if the healer is to gain control over it. In attacking the name, the symbol of the alien self, by the use of the more powerful name of the deity, it was believed that the demon would be brought under the control of the healer. The victim's intuitive insight into the complexities of his personal condition can be discerned in his reply, "My name is Legion; for we are many."[40] His plea to be left alone may have been a reaction of fear to these men who might make him the object of their sadistic sport as others had done. But Mark wants us to understand that the request was provoked by a sudden, intuitive recognition of the Galilean as God's appointed deliverer who would perform the messianic task of restoring men to health.

Jesus' word of firm authority "Come out of the man, you unclean

---

[39] A twenty-two year old female patient of the famed psychiatric nurse Gertrud Schwing, quoted in Schwing, *A Way to the Soul of the Mentally Ill* (New York: International Universities Press, Inc., 1954), p. 37.

[40] The Roman legion numbered 3,000 to 6,000 men.

spirit!" lacks the solemn oath or threatening curse which characterized most of the formulas of exorcism. Suddenly the tumult subsided and peace replaced the paroxysm, just as in the previous story described by Mark in which Jesus' rebuke effected a great calm over the storm-churned waters of the lake (Mark 4:35–41). Perhaps the Evangelist's mind recalled in the consecutive position of these two miraculous narratives the familiar words of the Psalmist as he described the effect of God's activity in the world of nature and men.

> [Thou] who dost still the roaring of the seas,
> the roaring of their waves,
> the tumult of the peoples.
>
> [Ps. 65:7[41]]

In any event the Gergesene responded to the presence and declaratory word of Jesus by becoming calm and rational. When the neighbors came, they found the two in quiet conversation. The vivid detail of the herd of swine stampeding to destruction over the cliff provided the first-century storyteller with dramatic evidence that the demons had been driven out of the sufferer (Mark 5:10–14a). Unless we think of the story as a secondary elaboration of the original, we may explain the animals' panic as the result of the screaming and raging of the tormented man.[42]

Characteristically, the recovery of health is interpreted by Jesus as the therapeutic energies of God at work through the instrumentality of the healer. "Go home to your friends, and tell them how much the Lord has done for you, and how he has had mercy on you" (Mark 5:19). The relation of dependence is broken. Jesus refused the plea of the healed man to remain with him, urging him instead to make a personal witness among his own people to the goodness and power of God toward those who are in need. The expulsion of Satan, the deliverance from disordering psychoses, had to be followed by a new and purposive activity if the results of the cure were to be conserved.

---

41 Suggested by Edwyn Hoskyns and Noel Davey, *The Riddle of the New Testament* (New York: Harcourt, Brace & World, Inc., 1931), pp. 69–71.

42 Mark 5:10–14a. Joachim Jeremias, *Jesus' Promise to the Nations* (Naperville, Ill.: Alec R. Allenson, Inc., 1958), p. 31, suggests that the Latin loanword *legio* is a misunderstanding of the Aramaic original which should be translated "soldier." Thus, the man really said, "My name is Soldier, since we are a great host." The confusion of meaning is responsible for the insertion of the secondary details of the swine in vss. 12–13 to account for the disappearance of the evil spirits.

Healing Methods

Several healing stories mention certain techniques employed by Jesus which are suggestive of the procedures of Hellenistic thaumaturgy. Describing the treatment of a deaf man further handicapped by a speech disorder, Mark relates that Jesus touched the man's ears and tongue with saliva, commonly believed to be an effective agent in breaking a charm or warding off evil (Mark 7:32–37).[43] A cure in stages is reported in Mark 8:22–26 where in a private meeting Jesus touches the sightless eyes of a blind man with saliva and then asks, "Do you see anything?" Only a partial restoration of sight, however, accompanies the first treatment. When once again Jesus touched the eyes, the man's vision was fully restored.[44] The disciples, engaged on a preaching mission through Galilee, are said to have anointed the sick with oil and healed them, a practice continued by the elders of the early Church upon the sick in the congregation (Mark 6:13).[45]

Though these primitive medicines were utilized, the Gospel accounts do not suggest that any magical potency was ascribed to them. It is the word of command and the prayer of faith that make the cure possible. To the sick person, the very presence of the healer is so charged with therapeutic energy that he believes he can be cured by the touch of the healer's hands. A story is told of a woman who had suffered recurrent hemorrhages over a period of many years and believed that if only she could touch the Galilean's robe she would be healed (Mark 5:25–34 par.). And so it happened. It is interesting to compare the impassioned cry of a modern schizophrenic patient. The girl is reported to have pleaded with her therapist, "Say to me: 'Elly, you are going to get well, your heart will again be peaceful and strong; then I can believe it. But touch me with your hands, please, please. . . ."[46]

Whereas wonder-working and magic made extensive use of incantations and magical formulas, the therapy of Jesus is conditional upon faith, prayer, and a word of command. We hear of a sharp word of

---

[43] Cf. Mark 8:22–26; John 9:1–7.

[44] Compare the account of a miraculous cure, probably credited to the god Asclepius: "To Valerius Oper, a blind soldier, the god revealed that he should go and take the blood of a white cock, together with honey, and rub them into an eye-salve and anoint his eyes three days. And he received his sight, and came and gave thanks publicly to the god." Quoted in C. K. Barrett, *The Gospel According to St. John* (London: SPCK, 1957), p. 293.

[45] Cf. James 5:14.

[46] Schwing, *A Way to the Soul,* pp. 42–43.

rebuke devoid of any magical words or names: "Come out of the man, you unclean spirit!" In contrast, note the following formula employed by a Jewish exorcist:

> To a demon one should say in order to drive him out: Be what is stopped up; be what is stopped up; be cursed, broken and banned, son of mud, son of the unclean, son of clay, in the name of Norigo, Moriphath and his Seal.[47]

Faith and Love as Preconditions

Faith is the indispensable condition of the cures Jesus performs. Mention of it always appears in close association with the unusual *tours de force* of Jesus. The revolutionary effect of dynamic faith at work upon the ills and wrongs of human life staggers the imagination. That which appears to be an immovable mountain obstructing man's way yields to the presence of such a faith and can be displaced.[48] "Nothing will be impossible to you" (Matt. 17:20b; cf. Mark 9:23). Of God alone is it said in the Old Testament that he can move mountains (Zech. 14:4). Jesus' word is an invitation to work the works of God by a full and complete trust in his promises. What appears ridiculous or impossible to faithless men becomes sensible and possible to faithful men.[49]

Paul is persuaded that the precondition for the effective use of miracle-working faith, however, is *agapē,* love. "If I have all faith, so as to remove mountains, but have not love, I am nothing," he concludes (I Cor. 13:2). Often enough, the Evangelists make special mention of the compassion of Jesus in the face of human sickness and suffering[50] and his emotional involvement in these crises.[51] His reaction to the power of sickness to cripple and pervert human life was said to be one of anger or strong agitation.[52] There are no independent

---

47 Quoted in S. V. McCasland, *By the Finger of God* (New York: The Macmillan Company, 1951), p. 102, from H. Strack and P. Billerbeck, *Kommentar zum Neuen Testament aus Talmud und Midrash,* IV (Münich: Beck, 1922–1956), 532ff.

48 Mark 11:22f. par.; Matt. 17:20. In Thomas, Sayings 48 and 106, this power is the outcome not of faith but the result of recovering the primordial, androgynous state of man. A Jewish-Christian tradition identifies the mountain as the heavy load of human sufferings which is susceptible to a removal by faith, Ps. Clem., *Recog.* V. 34.

49 Mark 11:24 par.; Q Luke 17:6; I Cor. 13:2. The figure is changed to the deep-rooted *shikmaha* or sycamore tree in Luke's account, 17:6.

50 Matt. 9:36, 14:14; Mark 1:41; Luke 7:13; etc.

51 Matt. 9:30; Mark 1:43, 3:12, 9:25; John 11:33, 38.

52 Mark 1:25, 41 (Codex Bezae and certain Old Latin mss.).

displays of power for personal advantage. Instead his ministry to the sick gives expression to the love of God for this divided and disordered world in rescuing the distressed, quieting the disturbed, and actualizing their manhood.

Love as Jesus practices it is the means whereby another person is understood in his uniqueness, accepted in his own essential being and potentiality, and helped to affirm this of himself. It is to confront another person with an inherent preparedness for devotion, to grasp intuitively his needs, and to make his well-being as important as one's own. Jesus established just such relationships, believing that he was doing something more than voicing his own heartbreak for those others had forgotten. He was expressing instead the fundamental attitude of God himself toward stricken and maimed humanity. Wherever faith came to effective expression in love, it signaled a new relationship with God and the release of divine energies into human life, reversing the processes of disintegration and destruction. "Take heart!" is his word to the depressed and the chronically ill, "Your faith has made you well."

Where no movement of faith is evoked by the preaching of the gospel, as at the synagogue in Nazareth, no work of healing is accomplished. To a paralyzed man he met by the Bethesda pool in Jerusalem, Jesus pointedly asked, "Do you *want* to be healed?" (John 5:6). He knew that a mark of deep sickness was the unconscious desire to be sick, a negative faith not to get well.

Prayer as an Instrument

So constant is the reference to the expectations of the patient and the association of prayer with the actual therapy that they may be presumed presuppositional even in those accounts where no specific mention of them is made. To Jesus transformative faith in God's concern and curative intervention for the sick involves ranges of prayer beyond ordinary imagining. In the previously cited case of the deaf mute, it is probable that the reference to Jesus looking up to heaven and sighing before he utters the command describes an impulsive and urgent appeal to the Father in prayer.[53] To his disciples who complained about their failure in helping an epileptic boy, he observes quietly, "This kind cannot be driven out by anything but prayer" (Mark 9:29). Matthew omits this word and substitutes the rejoinder

---

[53] Cf. Rom. 8:26; II Cor. 5:2, 4.

that the measure of their faith was inadequate to the special demands of this situation. But the meaning is unchanged. Prayer is a seeking, an asking, a knocking, in the acute realization of the reality, nearness, and power of God and of his loving concern to help the supplicant.

Jesus' concern clearly went beyond bringing relief to the immediate problem of painful symptoms through a supportive relationship. He wanted to establish the permanence of the new condition of health by a basic change in personality structure requiring new personal attitudes, relationships, and commitments.[54] There are indications that he did not always succeed in his efforts to cure in this more inclusive sense. Every physician and psychiatrist is unhappily aware that the return of a patient to an unchanged environment may subject him to destructive pressures that can quickly undo the accomplished reconstructive work. Momentary successes are a familiar accompaniment of some forms of healing. So in the language of first-century psychotherapy, Jesus describes the predicament of a man restored to health only to be subject to new and more acute attacks by evil spirits. The result is that his final condition is worse than the original one (Q Luke 11:24–26).

Levels of Health-Salvation

When is a patient cured? This is a question very difficult to answer, for cure is a relative term; it proceeds on a number of different levels and may be arrested in its early stages. The insistent contention of the Gospels is that fullness of health, that is to say salvation, is achieved only when men seek first the Kingdom and devote themselves in preparation for God's promised salvation. In this sense the moral and spiritual realignment signified in the injunction to become again as a little child and begin life all over again is also an essential part of the therapy of Jesus. This principle of regression, as Jesus urges it, obviously does not mean the resumption of infantile behavior, but rather the experience of a personality change analogous to the experiences of birth and childhood. Mere exorcism was not enough. Unless commitment were made to the word of Jesus and the rule of the Kingdom, relapse into a more serious illness was a real risk.

Then as now men looked for healing without salvation. They sought medical cures to facilitate a happier existence in the present world, whereas Jesus was concerned to give them the life of the new creation.

---

54 Cf. Carl W. Christensen, "Faith, Its Genesis and Its Function in Psychotherapy," *Journal of Pastoral Care,* XIII (1959), 140–41.

Perhaps this explains those intimations in the Gospels of Jesus' reluctance on occasion to expand his ministry of healing. He was frustrated by those who refused to recognize the deeper meaning of his acts but clamored for immediate relief for themselves or their friends. "Truly, truly, I say to you, you seek me, not because you saw signs, but because you ate your fill of the loaves" (John 6:26). He leaves Capernaum while people there are still anxiously seeking him, perhaps to solicit his help for their sick.[55] Thus the healing activity of Jesus cannot be limited to its physical and psychophysical effects. It must be viewed broadly enough to include the radical personality renewal of "normal" persons like Levi and Zacchaeus, the tax collectors, or the sinful woman who anointed his feet, all of whom are truly raised from death to life and share in the salvation of new creation. The health-salvation he bestowed went beyond ancient and many modern views and centered on a proper relationship with men and God.[56]

A New Heaven and a New Earth

For modern man, the miracle stories in the Gospels that present the major problems to credibility are those that tell of Jesus' power over the forces of nature. They have not enjoyed that return to favor in the post-Freudian public mind achieved by the healing stories. Such stories as Jesus' stilling the storm, walking on the sea, feeding the multitude despite insufficient rations, blasting the fig tree, and converting water into wine have only occasional parallels in ancient literature and no counterparts in the life of a modern scientific age.[57]

Unlike the Greeks, who believed in the uncreated, endless existence

---

[55] Mark 1:35–38 par.; cf. Luke 5:15f.; Matt. 8:18.

[56] Compare the aims of the modern school of logotherapy and existential analysis. See Viktor E. Frankl, *The Doctor and the Soul: An Introduction to Logotherapy* (New York: Alfred A. Knopf, Inc., 1955); R. May, E. Angel, and H. F. Ellenberger, eds., *Existence: A New Dimension in Psychiatry and Psychology* (New York: Basic Books, Inc., Publishers, 1958); and Rollo May, ed., *Existential Psychology* (New York: Random House, Inc., 1961). Dorothee Koch's *Healing and Salvation* (London: SCM, 1958) is a reverent and insightful examination of the biblical evidence and the implications for miraculous cures today. See also Aarne Siirala, *The Voice of Illness* (Philadelphia: Fortress Press, 1964).

[57] The stilling of the storm, Mark 4:37–41 par.; walking on the water, Mark 6:45–52 par.; feeding the multitude, Mark 6:34–44 par. (8:1–9 par.); the catch of fish, Luke 5:1–11; the cursing of the fig tree, Mark 11:12–14, 20; the coin in the fish's mouth, Matt. 17:24–27.

of matter, the Jews were convinced that the world of nature was no rival of God but a work of his own hands. He was the Lord who

> . . . created the heavens and stretched them out, who spread forth the earth and what comes from it, who gives breath to the people upon it and spirit to those who walk in it [Isa. 42:5].

To be sure, other powerful wills in rebellion to the Lord of creation were at work in the natural order, usurping his sovereign position and enticing men to swear fealty to them. But to those who faithfully adhered to God's covenant there was the promise that this world of nature would not finally be harsh and hostile. God would wrest out a new way in the wilderness for his people as once he had stretched a path through the sea. Jewish teaching voiced Israel's faith that man, deprived by sin from dominion over the world of nature, would someday reclaim that prerogative ordained by the Creator (Gen. 1:29).

Rescue from a Storm

Once the disciples were in mortal terror for their own safety when a sudden storm churned the placid waters of the Sea of Galilee into raging waves that threatened to engulf their little fishing boat (Mark 4:35–41 par.). Such sudden squalls and violent thunderstorms are still a common occurrence on that inland water. On this occasion the disciples were reduced to wonderment about the Teacher when, in response to his cry of rebuke "Be muzzled; be still," the storm suddenly passed and the waters quieted. The same stern command had once quieted the ravings of a demon-possessed man in Capernaum (Mark 1:25). It is questionable whether they misunderstood Jesus' rebuke of their own nervous complaining for a word spoken to the demon of the storm, as some propose. Perhaps it was a pure coincidence that the wind ceased abruptly as he spoke. Perhaps the whole story is an adaptation by the early Christians of one of the many accounts in the Roman world of the miraculous abatement of a storm's fury. But the gospel storyteller who first told the anecdote to a congregation of worshippers was sure that the ship came to a safe harbor and that the frightened Galileans attributed their rescue to the one who asserted authority over the storm god.

It is not difficult to imagine the meaning the early congregations would find in the story. Christ, the present and living Lord, offered succor to all who came into peril and guided them into the haven of peace. No doubt the Marcan story had special meaning to his Roman community threatened with the shipwreck of their faith by the savage attacks of Nero and others. To these frightened people the promise of final deliverance through faith must have brought sorely needed assurance and a reborn hope in the God who does not forsake his people even in the midst of their deepest distress. Behind the story there probably stands some actual incident in the Galilean mission, but the historical details are irrecoverable.

What is the relationship of the natural order, the organic and inorganic worlds, and this strange realm of mind which alone knows that it has a beginning and an ending in this world? The advance of science since the Middle Ages is, in one significant sense, a chart of nature's progressive submission to the authority of the human mind. The uneasiness that grips our time is that man shall have subjected the powers of nature to do his will without himself becoming master of his own will. The outcome may be the ruination of the natural order and self-destruction. With good reason men fear lest a presumptuous, self-assertive mastery spells a mortal wounding of this planet and its inhabitants and a contamination of others.

If the New Testament is to be believed, the powers of redeemed man can be enormously extended, but always in the measure of a responsive relationship between man and God. The so-called nature miracles indicate that even the apparently hostile forces of nature can be tamed by the mind and brought into the service of men. Such acts fulfill the primordial decree of God at creation: "Fill the earth and subdue it; and have dominion over the fish of the sea and over the birds of the air and over every living thing that moves upon the earth" (Gen. 1:28).[58]

Signs of the Kingdom and Acts of the Messiah

In our study of the meaning of the Kingdom in Jesus' teaching, we had occasion to point out that Jesus interpreted his acts of power as an integral part of his total ministry of proclaiming the imminent beginning of God's New Age. Preaching and healing belonged together as twin testimonies to the single reality of the Kingdom's approach. The Heavenly Raider was already binding Satan and releasing the wretched victims of his tyranny. Jesus' work is driven by the purpose of bringing men to repentance and making their salvation possible. If

---

[58] Ancient man regarded even inanimate objects as living things.

one can perceive the miracles as decisive acts of God, then only one legitimate conclusion can be drawn: "the kingdom of God has come upon you!" (Q Luke 11:20; cf. Luke 20:9). True heavenly joy arises not so much over the vanquishing of Satan and his evil host as from the exciting anticipation of God's New Order. Jesus reproves his disciples who are enthusiastic over their success in healing by reminding them that the collapse of Satan's treasonable assault on Heaven is not so significant as their own participation in the coming Kingdom (Luke 10:18).[59]

Further confirmation of this meaning of Jesus' acts is to be seen in his claim that the prophetic promises are now materializing. Both healing and nature miracles are said to move Isaiah's predictions from the status of hope to that of reality. "Go and tell John what you have seen and heard," he advises the deputation of John's disciples; "the blind receive their sight, the lame walk, lepers are cleansed, and the deaf hear, the dead are raised up, the poor have good news preached to them" (Q Luke 7:22). So Isaiah had heralded the blessings of the future:

> Then the eyes of the blind shall be opened,
> and the ears of the deaf unstopped;
> then shall the lame man leap like a hart,
> and the tongue of the dumb sing for joy.
> [Isa. 35:5f.]
>
> . . . .
>
> the Lord has anointed me
> to bring good tidings to the poor;
> he has sent me to bind up the brokenhearted
> [Isa. 61:1]
>
> . . . .
>
> The dead shall live, their bodies shall rise.
> O dwellers in the dust, awake and sing for joy!
> [Isa. 26:19]

Early Christians recognized the true import of Jesus' acts, claiming them to be manifestations of the powers of the age to come and finding preliminary influence in the immediate present (Heb. 6:5). Here indeed were glimpses of the New Reality that exposed the mischief

---

59 Cf. John 12:31; Isa. 14:12.

of popular views of reality and offered men in the present hour a life determined by a new future.

To the writers of the Gospels there is no room for doubt that these powerful and benevolent works of Jesus are a testimony to his royal authority and divine mission.[60] Yet in the Synoptic Gospels Jesus never uses the word "sign" to refer to his work as a healer or to any of his acts. To the strident demand for a sign from Heaven he brusquely replied, "No sign shall be given to this generation" (Mark 8:12).

The Sign from Heaven

In the Q collection of sayings, which probably preserves the oldest form of the saying about the sign from Heaven, a qualification is made: "No sign shall be given to it [this generation] except the sign of Jonah" (Q Luke 11:29). This, to be sure, is a difficult and obscure statement. Since both Luke and Matthew speak further of the repentance of the Ninevites at the preaching of Jonah, we are probably to find here the clue to the original meaning of the Jonah sign. As Jonah called for repentance before God's act in judgment upon that wicked city, so Jesus proclaims repentance and faith before the advent of God's judgment. But this preaching of repentance, with its call to turn to God, is not restricted to the spoken words of Jesus. When he bitterly criticized the Galilean cities for their indifference to the good news of God that he brought, Jesus declared, "If the mighty works done in you had been done in Tyre and Sidon, they would have repented long ago, sitting in sackcloth and ashes" (Q Luke 10:13). The acts of healing, the subduing of the destructive forces in nature—these were intended to lead to repentance and to evoke faith. Both the spoken and acted word—the total reality of Jesus, who he is and what he does—is the true and only sign to those who can discern that the presence and power of God is at work in their midst.

To conclude that this man is a brilliant teacher who speaks old truth with new authority, or to recognize and accept his skill simply as a healer, or worse, to dismiss him as a demagogue, this is to misconstrue the sign from Heaven for which they clamor and to evade the gospel. He doesn't *perform* signs; he *is* the sign. As Jonah became a sign to the men of Nineveh and as King Solomon became a sign to Sheba's queen, so Jesus himself is a sign to the men of his generation (Luke 11:30). The wisdom of Solomon and the preaching of Jonah

60 Matt. 11:2; they are "deeds of the Messiah"; John 5:36, 10:25, 32, 38, 14:11.

were declarations of God's word to their generations; now the more crucial message of salvation is being proclaimed. Yet it goes unheard. The true light is now shining, yet men prefer the darkness (Q Luke 11:33).[61] The New Temple is soon to be established, yet men cling stubbornly to the old ritual practices while supplicating God for the New Age. They neither submit to the witness of the Scriptures (Luke 16:31; John 5:39, 45–46) nor receive Jesus' words as God's word nor recognize that his works are the works of God.

It took a special kind of vision and an acute hearing to see, hear, and understand.

> Earth's crammed with heaven,
> And every common bush afire with God;
> And only he who sees takes off his shoes—
> The rest sit round and pluck raspberries.[62]

The Gospel parallel to this poem is readily available: "Truly, truly I say to you, you seek me, not because you saw signs, but because you ate your fill of the loaves" (John 6:26). But men must be free to make their own decisions, not stampeded by displays of the divine power and glory. That would be beyond mortal endurance anyway. So the Kingdom must in this life be a hidden Kingdom and the Messiah one who might easily be lost among the crowd.

---

61 Cf. Mark 4:21 par.; Thomas, Saying 33b.

62 Elizabeth Barrett Browning, "Aurora Leigh," Book VII.

CHAPTER VIII

DISCIPLESHIP AND THE KINGDOM

> Draw near to me, you who are untaught,
>   and lodge in my school.
>
> . . . .
>
> Put your neck under the yoke,
>   and let your souls receive instruction;
>   it is to be bound close by.
> See with your eyes that I have labored little
>   and found for myself much rest.
>
> [Wisdom of Sirach 51:23, 26f.]

> I am learning to see. I don't know why it is, but everything penetrates more deeply into me and does not stop at the place where until now it always used to finish. I have an inner self of which I was ignorant. Everything goes thither now. What happens there I do not know.*

"Follow Me"

Of those who listened with interest to Jesus' message of the approaching rule and realm of God, there were some who attached themselves to him as sympathizers and followers. The gathering of a group of loyal adherents about a teacher of acknowledged learning

* Rainer Maria Rilke, *The Notebooks of Malte Laurids Brigge* (New York: Capricorn Books, 1958), pp. 14f.

in the rules of Jewish life and faith was common enough. The men of the Great Synagogue were reported to have said, "Be deliberate in judgment, raise up many disciples, and make a fence around the Law" (*Aboth* 1.1). In Jesus' day, the rabbinical school under the leadership of Shammai was dominant in Galilee, in sharp contention at many points of interpreting the oral and the written law with the more liberal school of Hillel. The community at Qumran was pledged to a common way of life and the strict rule of the new covenant under the leadership of their beloved teacher and his priestly associates and successors. John the Baptist, while attracting large audiences, had a smaller band of companions who shared with him an ascetic life of prayer and fasting (Luke 5:33). Jesus too, while devoting himself to preaching the message of the Kingdom to the common people and helping the sick and needy, gathered about him a circle of men and women, committed to a discipline of preparation for the event of the Kingdom's arrival. It was from this larger group of disciples that the twelve were to be chosen.

The Call for Associates

In all probability the account of the call of the first disciples (Mark 1:16–20 par.) is an idealized scene, though it may be based on actual reminiscences. Through constant retelling in Christian preaching and teaching, the story has been compacted into a form that omits mention of any previous relationship between the Galilean teacher and the Gennesaret fishermen. John's Gospel adds certain details that may well be historical. Here we are told that two of these men, Andrew and presumably John, had previously been disciples of John the Baptist. Together with Simon, Andrew's brother, they had allied themselves as *talmidim* or disciples of Jesus during John's ministry at Bethany beyond the Jordan (John 1:35ff.).

All these stories bring into clear focus the two essentials of discipleship: the call and the obedient response. Jeremiah had spoken of fishermen from beyond Israel who would be sent in divine judgment to "catch" these rebellious people who had forsaken the covenant (Jer. 16:16).[1] But Jesus' men were to be sent in the interests of the divine salvation. He even appealed to some people whose occupations were of questionable status according to a strict interpretation of the Torah, inviting them to join with him in recruiting men for the

[1] Cf. Amos 2:2; Hab. 1:14–17; 1QpHab vi.1f.

Kingdom of God. Whole-hearted commitment was required, but no attempt was made to build a holy community as at Qumran.

He summoned them much as any rabbi might receive an application and invite a candidate to join his band of *talmidim*.[2] But there are significant differences. His mission is already announced to prepare people of the entire nation for the reign of God which is at hand. Attachment to him, therefore, could not mean matriculation in a rabbinical school, assembled daily in an appointed study center to engage in discussions on the teaching of the Torah according to the traditions of the elders. Some of the people were asked to travel with him as he acted as God's courier of the good tidings of salvation to everyone, from the learned doctor of the law to the hopeless sinner, including even the Greek and Roman aliens in the land. Those who shared that task with him engaged in more advanced discussions and practice of his way in order to be trained for the same service of preaching and healing. This teaching presented Jesus' own requirements of the New Age as he saw its relationship to the present situation of men. Those who worked with him must want to do the King's will with eager and passionate devotion. Jesus was convinced that their "redemption is no longer a question of pursuit but of surrender to Him who is always and everywhere present."[3]

The Membership

Equally unparalleled was the character of the group Jesus gathered together. They were selected from the ranks of those whom Pharisees, Sadducees, and Essenes would have regarded as under divine condemnation because they neither knew nor dutifully practiced the law (John 7:49). Fishermen, tax collectors, lepers, prostitutes, shepherds, and peddlers, even Roman centurions and Canaanite women—all were confronted by the call to repentance and the demand to live in the light of the coming Kingdom. They were the sick who knew their need to be healed (Mark 2:17). They were the hungry sheep who must be fed (Mark 6:34; Matt. 10:6; Luke 12:32). They represented the harvest to be reaped for God's use (Q Matt. 9:37; John 4:35; Thomas, Saying 73). They were the "little ones," a term of tender affection, who were the object of the Father's loving concern. "Whoever causes one of these little ones who believe in me to sin, it would

2 In rabbinical usage, the expression "follow me" meant literally the act of the pupil in walking at a respectful distance behind his teacher. Cf. Mark 10:32.

3 W. H. Auden, "For the Time Being," *The Collected Poetry of W. H. Auden* (New York: Random House, Inc., 1945), p. 454.

be better for him if a great millstone were hung around his neck and he were thrown into the sea" (Mark 9:42).[4]

The Gospels refute the popular assumption that Jesus' disciples numbered only twelve.[5] The call went out to all Israel, impelled by their desperate need, to run toward the God of forgiving love and to begin now to prepare themselves for family fellowship in the Father's house. Many responded. Both the righteous according to the law and sinners were addressed with the word of invitation. But the former were seldom willing to be torn loose from their familiar ways and follow this unfamiliar way. Even more surprising from the standpoint of Jewish amenities was Jesus' conversations with and acceptance of women into the fellowship of those preparing for the onset of God's New Age.[6] This was no conventional rabbi, this Galilean who urged all sorts of people to follow him and who claimed to possess the authentic truth about God and the approaching judgment.[7]

Only a few of those who heeded his call were remembered by name in the Church's tradition, and there is confusion about their identities. The rest remain anonymous. Those who responded to his invitation as the Father's messenger were to constitute a different kind of Israel than the sanctimonious brotherhoods who rebuked Jesus for offering the good news to the unwashed multitudes. But these decisions took no single form. Some people were called to accompany him on his tours throughout the province, leaving behind their families and giving up their possessions and trades (Mark 10:28–30 par.). Another, perhaps a Gentile, was told to go home to his friends and tell them about the greatness of God's kindness toward him (Mark 5:19). One was advised to put his loyalty to a supreme test by giving away all his property and joining the little band (Mark 10:21). But Zacchaeus was commended for promising to make legal restitution for his frauds (Luke 19:8f.) without disposing of his entire estate. Certain women of private means helped to finance the little company in its work, presumably without becoming bankrupt (Luke 8:1–3; cf. 16:9–12). For all, however, discipleship was a sign of the approaching reign of God.

The movement cannot be regarded as a group with a fixed member-

4 Originally, perhaps, this saying and its Q parallel in Luke referred actually to children, though Jesus certainly did speak of penitent sinners as children; cf. Matt. 18:10–14; and probably Mark 9:37; Matt. 10:42 and 25:40, 45.

5 Mark 3:13f., 35; 4:10; Matt. 8:21, 10:42; Luke 6:13; John 6:60, 66.

6 Mark 3:35, 15:40f.; Luke 8:1–3, 10:38–42; John 11:1ff.; *Aboth* 1.5.

7 Matt. 23:8–12; Q Luke 6:39f.; Matt. 10:24–25a, 15:14.

ship. During the main period of Jesus' mission in Galilee there were crowds who followed him to hear him speak and to solicit his help. Obviously they did not really belong to him.[8] We hear of other acknowledged disciples who were offended at certain words of the Teacher about the bread of life and who severed their relationship with him from that point on (John 6:60, 66). The parables of the wheat and the weeds and the seine-net emphasize that there can be no superfine separation of the true sons of the Kingdom from the sons of darkness until the End.[9] Then it became God's exclusive prerogative.

The Twelve

From the larger group of his apprentices, Jesus made a selection of twelve who were to accompany him on his evangelistic travels. After training they were to be sent out as *sh^eluchim,* or envoys, bearing the good news of the Kingdom and manifesting its healing power (Mark 3:14f.). Luke reports that this was a solemn, deliberative moment in Jesus' mission, faced after an all-night vigil of prayer (Luke 6:21). The earliest reference in Christian literature to this special group is to be found in Paul's writings. He understands that Jesus appeared in risen form to the twelve, following the initial manifestation to Peter (I Cor. 15:5).

There is no substantial reason to doubt this selection of an inner group, for they play a larger part in the tradition of the earthly ministry of Jesus than they do in the actual life of the primitive community.[10] The frank recognition of a traitor within the group is hardly credible if the list is simply a predating of the role they played in the post-Easter community. But we may ask what the special purpose was in the choice of this smaller group. Professor Taylor has proposed to find the answer in a Galilean mission in which they were sent out two by two to proclaim the coming of the Kingdom of God and to heal the sick (Mark 6:6–13).

---

8 Mark 3:7f., 11:8f.; John 6:2, 25f.

9 Matt. 13:24–30; Thomas, Saying 57; Matt. 13:47f.; *contra* the holy community at Qumran, CD xv.15–17, xx(ii).13ff. For a later sarcastic criticism of the social make-up of the early Church in the empire as rabble, see Origen, *Contra Celsum* III.44, 59; Lucian, *The Death of Proteus Peregrinus* 13.

10 *Contra* J. Weiss, *The History of Primitive Christianity,* I, trans. Frederick C. Grant, ed. (New York: Wilson-Erikson, Inc., 1937), 47f.; Maurice Goguel, *Life of Jesus,* trans. Olive Wyon (New York: The Macmillan Company, 1949), p. 341.

> Before and after this mission they are merged in the larger group of "the disciples"...The conclusion to be drawn is that the appointment of "the Twelve" was of the things that pass, because its original purpose was fulfilled.[11]

Yet Paul refers to the twelve as witnesses to the resurrection, as we have just noted, and Luke's history of the primitive Jerusalem congregation describes the otherwise puzzling insistence on choosing a successor to the traitorous Judas to complete the original number (Acts 1:15–26).[12] Clearly something more than an *ad hoc* appointment is understood.

It seems that the choice of twelve men was just as deliberate an act on Jesus' part as the appointment of the same number of laymen at Qumran, who with three priests composed the Community Council.[13] In both instances there was a symbolic intention of specifying the true Israel that would become the nucleus of the new humanity of the Kingdom of God. These men were the representatives of the twelve-tribed nation who were sent out to gather in the lost sheep of the house of Israel, and who would exercise prominent roles of leadership in the New Age (Matt. 19:28; cf. Luke 22:29f.).

Immediately we are confronted by the nettlesome problem of Simon Peter's position within the inner circle of Jesus' disciples. Centuries-old disputes about the primacy of Peter arise to haunt the Christian, inflame prejudice, and make difficult an honest interpretation of the biblical sources. There can be no question, however, quite apart from the controversial passage in Matthew 16:18, of Peter's prominence among the twelve. Paul makes special mention of him.[14] He may be offering his own comment on the tradition of Peter's special appointment by the Lord when he observes to the Corinthians, "No other foundation can any one lay than that which is laid, which is Jesus Christ" (I Cor. 3:11).[15] The appendix to John's Gospel similarly

---

[11] Vincent Taylor, *The Life and Ministry of Jesus* (New York: Abingdon Press, 1955), p. 99.

[12] Luke's restriction of the number of apostolic leaders to that of the former twelve disciples and his presentation of them as the official rulers of the community may be questioned in view of Paul's wider usage of the term apostle.

[13] 1QS viii.1f. The text is ambiguous and may mean a total college of fifteen or even of twelve. In any event the twelve undoubtedly represent the twelve tribes of Israel.

[14] Gal. 1:18, 2:7ff.; I Cor. 1:12, 9:5.

[15] The story of Jesus' reproof of the ambitious designs of the Zebedee brothers (Mark 10:35–45 par.) may reflect the position of the partisans of Peter in tensions over leadership in the early Church. Note the prominence of James and Thomas over Peter in the *Gospel of Thomas* (Sayings 12, 13) and generally in the Jewish-Christian tradition.

reflects a tradition of Peter's rehabilitation after the crucifixion and resurrection, based upon the prediction that Peter would become the great evangelist-pastor to Israel before his death as a martyr.[16] Luke, too, knows of such a responsibility vested in the "Rock-man," for he reports a prayer of Jesus anticipating Peter's leadership. "Simon, Simon, behold, Satan demanded to have you, that he might sift you like wheat, but I have prayed for you that your faith may not fail; and when you have turned again, strengthen your brethren" (Luke 22: 31–32).[17]

It is evident, however, that Peter is not "appointed" to a position of superiority over his brethren. Any notion of such unrivaled primary and exclusive authority, let alone its transfer in some sort of apostolic succession, is foreign to the teaching of Jesus and the realities of early Church life. It is significant that the Evangelist does not quote Jesus as saying, "You are Peter, and upon you, Peter, I will build my Church," an exact transliteration of the *kêphā-kêphā* that would be susceptible to strongly monarchic meaning.[18] Instead he gives the real sense of the play on the Aramaic word by the translation "Peter-rock" (*Petros-petra*). Thus Peter is not *primus super allos* but rather *primus inter pares,* the spokesman and representative of the entire fellowship of the disciples. This is seen in the way the authority given to Peter according to Matthew 16:19—"I will give you [singular] the keys of the kingdom, and whatever you bind on earth shall be bound in heaven"—is subsequently assigned to the whole body of disciples, not simply to the twelve (Matt. 18:18; cf. John 20:23). "Binding and loosing," that is to say, declaring the word of judgment and forgiveness, are tasks shared with the whole group, though Peter will be a special guide and stay. Elsewhere, too, the foundation rock of the Church is identified not simply with Peter, but with the apostles and other leaders[19] and pre-eminently with Christ himself.[20] As Origen would put it later, "Every Christian can and ought to be Peter."[21]

16 See Gal. 2:7f. where Paul compares his commission to the Gentiles to Peter's appointment to work among the Jews.

17 Cf. also Luke 5:1–11, 8:45, 9:32, 12:41, 22:8, 61; 24:34.

18 Henri Clavier, *"Petros kai Petra"* in *Neutestamentliche Studien für Rudolf Bultmann* (Berlin: Alfred Topelmann, 1957), p. 108.

19 Gal. 2:9; Eph. 2:20; I Pet. 2:5; Rev. 21:14.

20 Mark 12:10; Acts 4:11; I Cor. 10:4; Eph. 2:20; I Pet. 2:4. Cf. *Shepherd of Hermas, Simil.* ix, 12:1. See Oscar Cullmann, *Peter: Disciple, Apostle, Martyr,* 2nd ed., trans. Floyd V. Filson (Philadelphia: Westminster Press, 1962).

21 Origen, *Comm. on Matt.* XII.10 – 11.

Though little enough is known of the other disciples, it is certain that they too were chosen by Jesus from the common people whom he describes as the lost sheep of Israel. Galileans all,[22] with the possible exception of Iscariot, five of them receive some attention in the record with respect to their call, which might explain the curious Talmudic note that Jesus had only five disciples.[23] By the time the earliest Gospel was written there was already some haziness of memory concerning the precise identification and special function of the twelve. Differences may be observed in the four listings of the disciples.[24]

The brothers of a fisherman named Zebedee, like Simon Peter, are given a byname, the meaning and spelling of which is quite uncertain. But in view of Old Testament and Ugaritic references to thunder as the utterance of the divine voice, it is likely that the obscure word *Boanerges,* which Mark translates "sons of thunder" (Mark 3:17 par.), means, "men who hear and declare the heavenly voice, the *Bath Qol.*"[25] They are, so to say, spokesmen of the Almighty God.

The Johannine tradition says that the brothers Simon and Andrew as well as Philip came from Bethsaida, "Fisher-home," a city lying on the eastern shore of the mouth of the Jordan as it empties into the lake of Gennesaret.[26] Established as his capital by the tetrarch Philip shortly after his accession to rule, the city, along with the neighboring towns of Capernaum and Chorazin, was one whose obstinate refusal to hear the call to repentance wrung from Jesus a prophetic commination (Q Luke 10:13).

Bartholomew is actually a patronymic, like Bar-Jonah; hence it is often conjectured that this is the Nathanael named by John, his full name being Nathanael bar-Ptolemy. It may have been on a visit to Nathanael's village of Cana in Galilee that Jesus first met this "Israelite in whom is no guile" (John 2:47, 21:2).

The confused manuscript tradition testifies to the uncertainty of the Gospel tradition about the disciple named Thaddeus by Matthew and Mark, for the name sometimes is given as Lebbaeus. It is a common speculation to identify him with Judas, son of James, mentioned in Luke 6:16, but there is no real evidence to support it.

---

22 The famed Stoic teacher Epictetus is quoted by Arrian as saying that the followers of Jesus were Galileans (Epic., *Disc.* IV.7.6; cf. II.9.19ff.).

23 B. *Sanh.* 43a, bottom.

24 Matt. 10:2–4; Mark 3:16–19; Luke 6:14–16; Acts 1:13.

25 Cf. Pss. 18:13, 29:3ff., 68:33; Job 37:1–5; IV Ezra 13:4, 11, 27, 37; *Aqhat* I.1.46; *Baal* II.v.8.

26 Mark, however, relates Simon and Andrew to Capernaum (1:29).

According to the Gospel of Matthew, a tax collector named Matthew once heard Jesus' challenge "Follow me" as he was engaged in his daily routine (Matt. 9:9). Pushing the ledger aside he rose and went after him. This identification may represent an early copyist's gloss, since Mark and Luke speak of a *publicanus* named Levi but fail to include him within Jesus' inner circle.[27]

John's Gospel reminds us that the name Thomas is not a proper name at all, but rather the Aramaic word for twin (*thoma*), for he translates it into the Greek equivalent *didymos* (John 11:16, 20:24, 21:1). Who is this twin who plays a much more prominent role in this Gospel than in the Synoptics? Syriac-speaking Christianity early identified him with Judas, the brother of Jesus (Mark 6:3).[28] The second-century apocryphal *Gospel of Thomas* begins with the words, "These are the secret words which the Living Jesus spoke and Didymos Judas Thomas wrote." Luke's list makes mention of a Judas who might be understood to be the brother of James, hence one of the Nazareth family,[29] but he clearly distinguishes this Judas from Thomas (Luke 6:16).

Sometimes a man is remembered by the very special company he keeps. This appears to be the case with a second Simon numbered in the private circle of Jesus. Matthew and Mark refer to him as Simon the *Kananaios,* a Greek transliteration of an Aramaic word that Luke preferred to translate into Greek as "zealot" or enthusiast. We have already learned of an extremist political party that played an incendiary role in the uprising of the Jews against Roman suzerainty in A.D. 66. That Jesus' disciples probably included even political hot-heads is further evidence of what a nondescript cross-section they were of the conflicting sympathies and points of view represented in Jewish society of the day.

Each Evangelist reserves the last and the least position in his survey to that disciple who became a symbol of apostasy in the Church. His full name is given by John as Judas the son of Simon Iscariot (6:7, 13:2, 26), and he refers to him contemptuously as *diabolos,* Satan's

---

27 Several ancient manuscripts read "James the son of Alphaeus" in Mark 2:14, a conjecture that may have given rise first to the (mistaken) insertion of the occupation in Matt. 10:3 before the name of James, and a subsequent alteration of that name to Matthew in 9:9 to correspond with 10:3.

28 See, e.g., *Acts of Thomas* 1, 10, 11, 31, 39, 47, 78; and cf. Euseb., *Hist.* I.13.11.

29 The Greek "Judas of James" permits a relationship of either son or brother.

ally (6:70, 13:2). The meaning of the surname is uncertain, and various guesses have been made about it. Since the Greek word may signify a compound of two Hebrew words, it is sometimes held that the reference is to a Judean village of Kerioth (Josh. 15:25) or to a town in Moab (Jer. 48:24, 41; Amos 2:2). The meaning then would be "a man of Kerioth (*'ish qᵉriyyoth*)." Others hold that Iscariot is a corruption of *sicarius* and refers to the band of assassins or extremist Zealots who are mentioned by Josephus in connection with a later messianic uprising.[30] Again, it is argued that it is a corrupted form of an Aramaic word meaning "false one" or "liar." Of these possibilities, the first seems most plausible.

Such then was the motley crew of *talmidim* that Rabbi Jesus called to himself to announce the acceptable year of the Lord. Rough fishermen, who knew more about hauling nets than about rhetoric, an internal revenue agent who had turned his tax farming into personal profit, a model Israelite who was an earnest student of the Torah,[31] an enthusiast who may have had subversive sympathies, and a keeper of the purse who may have displayed that common haughty superiority that marked the Judean's attitude toward his countrymen from the north. From the standpoint of the political authorities, it is not surprising that this band of wandering Evangelists appeared to be a peasants' revolt. To the priest, the theologian, and the holy man, as to Saul the Tarsian Pharisee, they made claims both ridiculous and blasphemous when they charged God's rejection of the national leadership and announced the promise of messianic salvation upon them and their ilk. But to their teacher, this little coterie of followers had the makings of true Israel; they were destined to exercise governing roles in the fulfilled Kingdom of God. They and the wider company of his disciples, God's beggars,[32] were the long-suffering dispossessed who were to inherit the vineyard of God now despoiled by the leaders of the people (Mark 12:1–9). They were the terrible meek who were to inherit the whole earth under the fatherly judgment of the God who abased the proud and exalted those of low degree (Matt. 5:5; Luke 1:52).[33]

---

30 Jos., *Antiq.* XX.8.10; *War* II.13.3. Cf. Acts 21:38.

31 Jesus observes Nathanael sitting under a fig tree (John 1:48), the place and posture the rabbis recommend for studying the Torah.

32 The phrase is Jeremias' (*The Parables of Jesus,* 6th ed., trans. S. H. Hooke [New York: Charles Scribner's Sons, 1963], p. 209).

33 Cf. Matt. 18:4, 23:12; Luke 18:14.

The Galilean Mission of Jesus' Disciples

The training and activity of the disciples is presented in some detail in the story of an evangelistic mission that they carry on in the cities and towns of Galilee. Varied versions of this missionary enterprise are to be found in all four of our basic sources, Mark, Q, M, and L.[34] It is, therefore, one of the best attested narratives in early Christian tradition. No doubt it has been enlarged and adapted to fit the needs of the burgeoning missionary program of the early Church.[35] The very fact that early Christians believed that there was authority in Jesus' own teaching and in actual journeys of the disciples to proclaim the coming Kingdom of God for their own missionary work in the empire is significant, however. We shall want to consider whether this later extension of a preaching mission into the Gentile world is likely to have been part of Jesus' own instructions to his disciples.

At what point in his Galilean ministry the mission of the twelve occurred is beyond identification. Mark certainly understands that it has something to do with attracting the unwelcome notice of the political authorities to the work of Jesus. He connects the story with a report that Herod Antipas, evidently alarmed at the growing popularity of the movement, was convinced that his old foe John the Baptist had returned from the dead to make his life miserable (Mark 6:14–16). Other than that, Mark regards the mission simply as an extension of the teaching ministry of Jesus.

The mission story probably details a representative situation, one of several occasions in which the disciples were sent out as accredited envoys of Jesus. The narrative of one such expedition, perhaps the first, provided an appropriate setting for the Evangelist to gather together a number of mission charge sayings that were preserved in the community tradition. In this sense Luke may possibly reflect a

---

34 Mark 6:6b–13 par.; Matt. 9:35–11:1 (M and Q); Luke 10:1–16 (L and Q). S. E. Johnson believes that the Lucan form (10:1–16) is the earliest form of the mission charge, preserving a more Semitic flavor than Mark's (Sherman Eldridge Johnson, *The Gospel of Mark* [Harper & Row, Publishers, 1960], pp. 114f.). F. Hahn regards Luke 10:8–11 as closest to the intention of Jesus (*Mission in the New Testament,* trans. Frank Clarke [Naperville, Ill.: Alec R. Allenson, Inc., 1965], p. 46).

35 Against the skeptical judgments of those who consider this simply an assignment to Jesus' program of the first Christian missionary work in Palestine is the multiple evidence in the Gospels. Furthermore, passages such as Matt. 10:23 were certainly not constructions of the early community. Compare the directions for traveling apostles and prophets in *Didache* 11:3–13:5.

memory of several evangelistic forays. On a later occasion he repeats essentially the same mission charge delivered to the twelve, involving a larger group of seventy-two missioners.[36]

The Charge

These apprentices of the Kingdom were sent out in pairs after their preliminary training, perhaps on the Torah principle that a testimony is sustained only on the evidence of two or three witnesses (Deut. 19:15). The workers were all too few. "The harvest is plentiful, but the laborers are few; pray therefore the Lord of the harvest to send out laborers into his harvest" (Q Luke 10:2). Their task was identical with his task: to preach the Kingdom of God and to heal the sick. As they themselves were awakened and forgiven men, so they were freely to share with others what they had received (Matt. 10:8). The specific instructions recorded in the several accounts eloquently reflect the crisis that Jesus believed confronted men. They go, as T. W. Manson says, like an invading army, prepared to live a hand-to-mouth existence from house to house, town to town.[37] Under the conviction that this gospel must first be offered to the people of Israel, who would become finally the rallying center of all the nations of the earth, the disciples are enjoined to go only to the lost sheep of the house of Israel.[38] "Heal the sick...and say to them, 'The Kingdom of God has come near to you' " (Q Luke 10:9; cf. Mark 6:7 par.).

The disciples were asked to see this task as a holy mission of great urgency. The devout Jew refrained from carrying a staff or sandals or a wallet into the temple precinct or walking with dirty feet on those sacred pavements out of respect for that meeting place of God and man.[39] So also the eager herald of God's salvation would take with him nothing that would signify disrespect for his mission or convey anything less than that the divine judgment was imminent. They must

---

36 Luke 10:1–9. The manuscripts variously cite the number of missioners as 70 and 72. The evidence, with the support now of P^{75}, seems to indicate that 72 is the earlier reading. Seventy nations of the earth were traditionally counted from the Hebrew catalog of Gen. 10. The Septuagint lists 72.

37 Thomas Walter Manson, *The Sayings of Jesus* (London: SCM Press, Ltd., 1961), p. 181.

38 Matt. 10:5; cf. 15:24. The firm conviction, too, of the early Church; see Acts 3:26, 13:46, 15:16f.; Rom. 1:16, 2:9, 10.

39 *Berakoth* 9.5; Herbert Danby, trans., *The Mishnah* (London: Oxford University Press, 1958), p. 10. Mark 6:8f., probably a later form (see vs. 13), does permit both sandals and staff.

depend for their food and lodging[40] upon the hospitality of friendly homes upon which they will invoke a *shalom* benediction, "for the laborer deserves his wages."[41]

These messengers of the Kingdom take their lives in their hands. So their enthusiasm must be tempered with a cold, sober realism about the deceptions and the difficulties they will encounter among a people who may stubbornly refuse to believe they are on the King's business. "Lo, I send you out as sheep in the midst of wolves," to which Matthew appends a bit of proverbial advice, "So be wise as serpents and innocent as doves" (10:16).[42] Even as Jesus has reminded them that he meets them in the poor and needy,[43] so now he speaks of his identification with the disciples in their missionary task. Together they are bound in an indissoluble triangular unity. "He who hears you hears me, and he who rejects you rejects me, and he who rejects me rejects him who sent me" (Q Luke 10:16). As Jesus has been sent from the Father, so these disciples, trained and commissioned, have been deputized for service (John 17:18). And the divine intention behind this chain of relationships is to one end: that men may be called back, turned from their flight into a far country, and encouraged to start the long trip home to the waiting Father. Of a rabbi's official delegate on a mission it was said: "A man's *shaliach* is as the man himself."[44] As the *sheluchim* of Christ, the disciples were empowered to act on his behalf, not only to bear witness to the approaching reign of God, but in some real sense to exemplify that blessed rule. They were plenipotentiaries whose credentials bore the seals of the seeking and waiting Father.

The Return of the Missioners

We cannot be certain about the original setting of the saying of Jesus that Luke represents as spoken upon the return of the seventy-two missioners (Luke 10:17–20). He draws upon his own special source to preserve a saying of Jesus certainly spoken in some situation involving the work of his disciples as exorcists. The preliminary con-

40 Cf. Thomas, Saying 14, which twists this saying to an antiritualistic purpose.

41 Luke 10:6–7; Matt. 10:10b, a saying known to Paul (I Cor. 9:14; cf. Gal. 6:6); referred to as Scripture in I Tim. 5:18 and quoted in *Didache* 13:1.

42 The *Gospel of Thomas* combines this saying with Jesus' condemnation of the Pharisees, Saying 39.

43 Cf. Mark 9:37 par.; John 13:20.

44 *Berakoth* 5.5; Danby, *The Mishnah*, p. 6.

quest of Satan is signified by the words, "I saw Satan fall like lightning from heaven" (10:18). In some visionary experience Jesus saw the one who is man's fateful accusor before God already condemned and banished from the heavenly court, as indeed he would be forever at the End (Rev. 12:10). As unclean spirits were yielding now to the work of Jesus and his colleagues, the powers of the New Age were already affecting the tyranny of Satan in the present order (Q Luke 8:20).

The point of special interest here is that it is this and only this realization, Jesus contends, that ought to be the source of the disciples' joy. Pridefully, they reveled in the power at their command to sway others with their words and to exert authority over the evil spirits. But if it is the humble and not the aggrandizers who are to inherit the earth, they must continually resist the temptation to revert in attitude from "thine be the glory" to "mine be the glory." The disciples are not to rejoice in their curative power over disease and suffering. Rather they are to rejoice that *Abba*-God cares for them and for the sick and the outcast. They are not nameless nobodies; they are known to him by name (Luke 10:20). Discipleship means mission. And mission is one of the Father's sons saying to another, "Come behold the wonderful works of God; let us rejoice and be glad in them."

The Scope of the Mission

What was the scope of the mission planned and carried on by Jesus and his disciples? The answer is by no means simple. The tradition that has been filtered through the life and experience of the primitive Christian communities was surely not impervious to the reality of the Gentile mission developed early in the Church. By the time the first of the Gospel writers was collecting and combining his material, the Church was predominantly a Gentile movement, with both Jewish Christianity and the mission to the Diaspora rapidly fading into the background.[45] Jewish Christianity survived as a minority group within the churches, becoming increasingly reactionary and isolated. Believing that the Messiah had come to affirm the Torah and to expound it more fully, not to abrogate it, its members continued to abide by all the ritual requirements. They considered Paul an apostate because he

45 A large-scale mission to the Gentiles in the fifties resulted in the development of a Gentile Christianity that eclipsed the Jewish-Christian mission to the Dispersion.

refused to make these rules prerequisite for the acceptance of Gentiles into the synagogue of the Messiah Jesus. They bitterly denounced the scribes and Pharisees who refused to believe that the messianic promises had been fulfilled in Jesus of Nazareth, and hence that the days of the Messiah preparatory to the New Age were shortly to dawn.

In view of this turn of events it would be understandable if the writers of the Gospels identified Jesus' movement, not with his own people who spurned him and his message, but with the non-Jewish world that entered the fellowship of the Church. They may have rationalized the historical fact of Gentile Christianity as the intention of Jesus to have his followers preach the gospel to all the nations.

But this matter may not have been within the original plan of Jesus. It is the measured judgment of a number of modern interpreters of the Gospels that Jesus never intended that he or his disciples would ever extend their mission on a worldwide basis.[46] To be sure they believe that Jesus anticipated the eventual inclusion of the Gentiles in the Kingdom, but this would result, not from missionary preaching, but by an eschatological act of God who would gather them by his holy angels. Such sayings as Mark 13:10 and 14:9, which allude to a missionary program of universal dimension, may have developed from the missionary activity of the early Church. But this does not mean that Jesus excluded from consideration the peoples outside the national boundaries of Judaism. Far from it, for he renounced unequivocally any chauvinistic understanding of the Kingdom and confirmed the Old Testament promise to the nations that they too would participate in the New Age God was preparing to begin.[47] But with such a view, the development of a *mission* to both Jews and Gentiles by the post-Easter community is left completely unexplained. A review of Jesus' activities and preaching will suggest another understanding about the scope of his mission.

The Church and the Nations

Although we cannot be certain what was in the mind of Jesus in restricting his ministry to the Jewish people,[48] it is important to recog-

46 See, e.g., J. Jeremias, *Jesus' Promise to the Nations* (Naperville, Ill.: Alec R. Allenson, Inc., 1958), pp. 19–39; W. G. Kümmel, *Promise and Fulfilment,* trans. Dorothea M. Barton (Naperville, Ill.: Alec R. Allenson, 1957), pp. 84f.; R. K. Bultmann, *Jesus and the Word,* trans. Louise Pettibone Smith and Ermine Huntress (New York: Charles Scribner's Sons, 1934), pp. 46f.; David Bosch, *Die Heidenmission in der Zukunftsschau Jesu* (Zürich: Zwingli Verlag, 1959), pp. 97–200.

47 Matt. 8:11, 25:31ff.; John 11:51f.

48 See Matt. 10:5, 15:24; Luke 13:28, 19:9; John 4:22. Only a few specific

nize that this order of mission, "to the Jew first and also to the Greek," was the firm conviction of the preachers and teachers of the early Church. First Israel must hear the message and then become the bearer of good tidings to all the peoples of the earth, a position that even the great Apostle to the Gentiles held at first. Such a proclamation to the Gentiles was understood as a stage in the eschatological program which began with Jesus' suffering, death, and resurrection.

In Jesus' earlier work in Judea, Samaria, and Galilee, John emphasizes in his Gospel, he was aware that his words and signs were preparatory to the crucial event of his suffering and death. "My hour has not yet come," he reminds his mother at Cana (2:4) and the Evangelist repeats this observation on several other occasions.[49] It is only when Andrew and Philip inform Jesus at the Passover feast about a group of Greeks who are anxious to meet him that Jesus announces solemnly, "The hour has come for the Son of man to be glorified" (12:23). Then referring to his forthcoming death and exaltation he declares, "I, when I am lifted up from the earth, will draw all men to myself" (vs. 32). The hour of his death will be the hour of his glorification as the Son of God and the removal of all hindrances to the full manifestation of his glory to men everywhere (13:1, 17:1). Both John and Luke recognized in the traditional story about a miraculous catch of fish by Jesus' disciples an allegory of the coming of the Gentiles into the Kingdom of God in the last times.[50] Until then, Israel must be brought to repentance and the accomplishment of her divine vocation in the world.

It is even possible that the references by Mark to Galilee in relationship to the resurrection appearances presume that Galilee of the Nations, as it was called, would be the chosen place of eschatological fulfillment, the symbol of the salvation which was to extend into all the world.[51] The Evangelists and the early churches that stand behind them interpreted the significance of the Easter event as the risen Christ's commission of his followers to preach the gospel of salvation throughout the world. Matthew states it most directly and convincingly

---

instances of Jesus' engagements with proselytes and foreigners are known to the Evangelists: a Roman centurion (Q Luke 7:1–10; cf. John 4:46–53), a Phoenician woman (Mark 7:24–30 par.), and perhaps the Gergesene demoniac (Mark 5:1–20 par.).

49 Cf. John 7:6, 30, 39; 8:20.

50 Luke 5:1–11; John 21:1–14.

51 Mark 14:28, 16:7. The mention of the peoples from Tyre and Sidon in Mark 3:8; 7:24, 31, may signify the prefiguration of the Gentile mission to the Evangelist.

in his account of the great commission (Matt. 28:16–20), but the charge to make disciples of all the nations is repeated in several forms in each of the other Gospels.[52] There is no doubt that the Church recognized its task to extend the mission of Jesus beyond his Jewish homeland into the nations of the world.

Jesus and the Nations

Since the middle of the third century B.C. Judaism had carried on a missionary activity that reached a peak in the time of Jesus and the apostles, a period that has been described as "*par excellence* the missionary age of Jewish history."[53] Jesus' bitter reproach of the intensive proselyting activities of the Pharisaic *Ḥabērīm* (Matt. 23:15) finds corroboration in Paul's own words about a missionary zeal more intent on converting others than in correcting the self (Rom. 2:17–23). A sizeable missionary and apologetic literature of Hellenistic Judaism bears testimony to Josephus' word, "There is not one city, Greek or barbarian, nor a single nation, to which our custom of abstaining from work on the seventh day has not spread. . . ."[54] Jesus' proclamation of the comprehensive salvation of the Kingdom could not ignore this zealous missionary universalism.

Although the explicit command to evangelize the Gentiles, as it is formulated in Mark 13:10 and 14:9, may well have been sharpened after the early Church decided about the Gentile mission, we may doubt the categorical rejection of such a mission in Jesus' mind. It would be strange indeed for Jesus to have read in Isaiah about Israel as a light to the nations and then to call his disciples to be light and salt to a world that was restricted to the national boundaries! There is some evidence for the view that the reception of the Gentiles into the Kingdom would come about wholly as an eschatological act of God without any human proclamation. But the extensive Jewish missionary literature of the time and the remarkable success of the proselyte movement in the Roman world surely mean that the mission was not left entirely in God's hands. Judaism, in any event, insisted that propaganda and preaching among the Gentiles prepared the way for the establishment of the Kingdom of God. If the impending

---

52 Mark 13:10, 14:9; Luke 24:47–48; Acts 1:8; John 20:21–23; cf. 10:16.

53 Jeremias, *Jesus' Promise to the Nations,* p. 12.

54 *Against Apion* II. 282. Cf. W. G. Braude, *Jewish Proselyting in the First Five Centuries of the Common Era* (Providence, R.I.: Brown University Press, 1940).

catastrophe of the Judgment Day did not vitiate preaching to Israel by Jesus' disciples, it is improbable that it excluded the word spoken to the Diaspora and even beyond Israel.[55]

To be sure Jesus does not undertake any deliberate missionary work among the Gentile peoples, but he does not turn aside from appeals for help raised by a Roman centurion or a Phoenician woman (Matt. 8:5–13 par.; Mark 7:24–30 par.). We have already seen the unconventional attitude he assumed toward the heretic Jews who lived in Samaria, attacking deeply ingrained Jewish prejudices by introducing a Samaritan as the hero of a tale about true neighborliness (Luke 10:30–37), and describing another as the only one in a crowd of Jews who gave thanks to God for an act of mercy (Luke 17:12–19; cf. John 4:1ff.). His parables of the wheat and the weeds (Matt. 13:24–30) and the seine-net (Matt. 13:47) emphasized that the new community was not meant to be an association of the ritually pure and the cultic undefiled but one that admitted into its life all sorts of people. To a serious practitioner of the law, such Jews in name only were not far removed from the condition of despised foreigners.

Although Jesus predicted the vindication of God's elect over their oppressors, the prospect of the eschatological destruction of the Gentiles finds no place in his teaching. A study of late Jewish literature dealing with the Last Judgment reveals a recurrent emphasis on God's vengeance upon the heathen in the final assessment of the nations. The dominant popular expectation was that either they were to be made the slaves of the elect or they were to be utterly destroyed.[56] It is surely significant that the teaching of Jesus is unmarked by any expression of hatred toward the foreign lords who controlled the land or by any threat of divine retaliation visited upon them in the great Assize. Perhaps the surprise and annoyance of the Nazareth townsmen at Jesus' exposition of the passage from the prophet Isaiah in his synagogue sermon was precipitated by the omission of the dark words about the day of vengeance that follow in the

---

55 It may be argued that Jesus believed that at his death the Kingdom of God would be established in power; hence there would be no time to extend the mission beyond Israel. But there are hints in Jesus' sayings that he did not regard his death and the Parousia to be simultaneous events. He anticipated persecutions and trials for his disciples and evidently believed that they would continue their fellowship together after his death (Mark 14:25). In the interval, the mission he had begun would be carried on by his followers.

56 Isa. 61:5f.; *I Enoch* 91:12; 1QS ii.5–9, viii.6f., 10f., ix.23; 1QpHab v.3–5; 1QM *passim;* etc. "No Gentile will have a part in the world to come," avowed R. Eliezer ben Hyrcanus (ca. A.D. 90). T. *Sanh.* 13.2.

prophetic lection.[57] These townsmen were further provoked when Jesus appealed to the historic stories of two foreigners, the widow of Zarephath and Naaman the Syrian, to demonstrate the deliberate visitation of God's mercy upon Gentiles in the past. If they had their way they would have hurled him to his death then and there (Luke 4:28–30).

Jesus replies to the inquiry of the disciples of John the Baptist about the significance of his work by drawing upon several scriptural texts, but in each instance the texts are quoted freely and partially. The original mentions of divine vengeance have disappeared.[58] Professor Jeremias has proposed that the concluding admonition, "Blessed is he who takes no offense at me" (Q Luke 7:23) may mean, "Happy is the man who is not offended because the messianic age wears a different aspect from that which he had expected, and that, instead of God's vengeance, it promises God's tender mercy for the poor."[59]

In flat contradiction to the Jewish expectation that the Gentiles, especially the Romans, would experience the full fury of God's wrath in the Last Judgment, Jesus exceeded John the Baptist in his bitter reproaches of Jewish pride in blood and soil. Such heathen peoples as those of Sodom, Gomorrah, Tyre, Sidon, Nineveh, and Sheba will fare better in the final Judgment than unrepentant, cocksure Israel (Q Matt. 10:15, 11:21–22, 12:41–42). In the apocalyptic vision of Matt. 25:31–46, "all the nations" appear for judgment before the throne of the Son of Man and listen to some shocking decisions. No discrimination is made here between Jew and Gentile or heathen and Christian. Those anywhere and everywhere who have shown merciful love toward the Son of Man, who has met them in every sufferer and needy person, hear the welcome invitation. But a denial of compassion and acts of mercy toward the "least of the brethren" by anyone, including his own followers, is a denial that results in banishment from the heavenly fellowship.[60] Like

---

57 Isa. 61:2b; Luke 4:16–30.

58 Cf. Isa. 29:20, 35:4, 61:2.

59 Jeremias, *Jesus' Promise to the Nations,* p. 46. K. Schubert proposes to interpret the saying on the love of enemies (Matt. 5:43f.) as a reference to eschatological powers of evil and the Gentiles ("The Sermon on the Mount and the Qumran Texts," in Krister Stendahl, ed., *The Scrolls and the New Testament* [New York: Harper & Row, Publishers, 1957], p. 121).

60 This Judgment scene has been considerably colored by the Christological views of the early Church, but the nature of the judgments rendered corresponds to the position Jesus takes in his teaching. Cf. Luke 10:30ff. where he emphasizes the duty of helping everyone who is in need. Kümmel, *Promise and Fulfilment,* pp. 92–95.

the leading prophets, Jesus rejoiced in the prospect of the gathering in of all the nations, and he reminded unrepentant Israel that the privilege of being Abraham's children was without benefit apart from wholehearted contrition, submission to God, and indiscriminate acts of love without respect to frontiers.

Nowhere does Jesus attack national snobbery more daringly than in his claim that the Gentiles would precede the children of Abraham into the Father's house and take their places at the messianic banquet. An anonymous apocalypse of the third century B.C. had given voice to this promise of the full fellowship between God and man that would mark the life of the Kingdom.

> On this mountain the Lord of lords will make for all peoples a feast of fat things, a feast of wine on the lees, of fat things full of marrow, of wine on the lees well refined [Isa. 25:6].

Confronted by the stubborn obstinancy of those who were the spiritual leaders of the people, Jesus boldly declared, "Many will come from east and west, and sit at table with Abraham, Isaac, and Jacob in the kingdom of heaven, while the sons of the kingdom will be thrown out into the outer darkness; there men will weep and gnash their teeth" (Q Matt. 8:11f.).[61]

Although no specific mention is made of the Gentiles in the parable of the great supper (Luke 14:16–24), they are probably to be identified with the poor, the suffering, and the outsiders who take the places reserved for the original guests at the festive board. From the standpoint of a religious particularism, these latecomers would be considered no more fit than *goyim* to share in that blessed eschatological feast.

Without denying Israel's great heritage, Jesus viewed its historic election as defining the possibilities for serving God, but never as a guarantee of salvation nor a substitution for a direct and decisive meeting with the living God. It is especially significant that Jesus describes the Court of the Gentiles in the holy temple as having been converted into a den of robbers by the merchants who served the worshipping pilgrims. In a fury of indignation he reminds them of the prophet's words, "My house shall be called a house of prayer *for all peoples*" (Isa. 56:7c). The New Temple of God's coming Age will receive those within Israel as well as those in the nations

---

61 Cf. Isa. 49:12. By contrast, as Jeremias points out, the rabbinic interpretation of Isa. 25:6 emphasized the wrath and sufferings destined for the Gentiles (*Jesus' Promise to the Nations,* p. 62).

of the world who were now excluded by cultic law from appearing before God in his sanctuary.

Jesus devoted his energies and those of his disciples to the announcement of the imminent onset of the reign of God among his own people, believing that the people of Sinai must first be prepared to meet this crisis. Through them, the peoples of the world would hear the gospel, for the righteous among the Gentiles as among the Jews would be gathered in at the Last Judgment to share the joys and responsibilities of obedience to the divine rule. The oldest tradition in the Gospels contains no mandate of Jesus for a mission to the Gentiles by his disciples. But that mission was the consequence of his rejection of Israel's claim to priority in the Kingdom and of his understanding that a new day was dawning for all men, including the Gentiles.[62]

It was not the *right* to preach salvation to the Gentiles that constituted the nettlesome problem dividing the early Church. It was rather a question of the *terms* on which Gentile converts might be received into the Christian community. Ultra-conservative members insisted that full proselytism to Judaism or at least circumcision was a *sine qua non*. Others like Paul insisted that the law no longer could be made conditional for salvation, only complementary at most (I Cor. 7:18–20).

But it was true missionary obedience to what the disciples remembered as Jesus' own words and behavior that led them to inaugurate a mission to Samaria and to the Dispersion, refusing to turn away from the Gentiles who were attracted to their word. Struggle though it surely was, the inclusion of the Gentiles into the early Church represented the inescapable conclusion to Jesus' concern that *all* Israel, not just the spiritually elite, must be confronted with the claim of God's kingship.

---

62 Cf. F. Hahn, *Mission in the New Testament*, Chap. ii.

CHAPTER IX

CONTROVERSIES AND A CRISIS

[The men of the Great Synagogue] said three things: Be deliberate in judgment, raise up many disciples, and make a fence around the Law [*Aboth* 1.1].

For Christ ends the law and brings righteousness for everyone who has faith [Rom. 10:4 NEB].

The Basis of the Conflict with Sectarian Judaism

The traditions of Jesus' mission embedded in all four Gospels are unanimously agreed on the hostility that Jesus encountered from leaders of the major Jewish parties of the day. Pharisees, Sadducees, and Herodians sharply attacked his work as a prophet of the coming reign of God, finally overcoming their own intramural differences by joining together to remove him from the scene. Indeed much of Jesus' teaching consists of vigorous controversies with these party leaders in which he vindicated his message and work and counter-attacked with pointed and polemical words. "If all the controversial discourses and sayings and answers to questions, which were so to speak wrung from Him, were subtracted from the sum of His utterances, how much of the didactic preaching of Jesus would be left over?" asks Albert Schweitzer.[1] The answer obviously is, remarkably little, remarkably, that is, if one entertains the erroneous notion that Jesus was principally a teacher of the scribal sort, dispensing instruction on religious and moral issues, based upon Scripture and tradition.

---

1 Albert Schweitzer, *The Quest of the Historical Jesus*, trans. W. Montgomery (London: A. & C. Black, 1954), p. 353.

Yet it would be a mistake to imagine that the mission began in an atmosphere of unfriendliness and hostility, or that Jesus had no sympathy for nor elicited any favorable reaction from the Pharisees. The Gospels reflect their mutual efforts to establish communication with each other. Jesus was once invited to the home of a Pharisee named Simon, where he received an unknown woman's act of homage (Luke 7:38ff.). In the home of a synagogue official who was a member of a Pharisaic community he healed a man afflicted with dropsy (Luke 14:1ff.). One of the discussions about ritual purity took place in the home of a Pharisee where he was a dinner guest (Luke 11:37). Certain manuscripts of Mark's Gospel preserve a curious divergent reading in 2:15f. where it is said, "Many people followed him, even some scribes of the Pharisee."[2] Although it is not certain that he numbered Pharisees among his disciples, we read of Pharisaic Jews, members of the early Jerusalem church, whose conservative views were sharply challenged by another Christian Pharisee, a Jew from Tarsus named Saul.[3] Though Jesus had been sharply critical of them, it is a fact that the early Palestinian churches, under such leadership as James the Righteous, lived in peace for years with their non-Christian neighbors. That is, until the events of the Jewish Revolt of A.D. 66 divided them. Once again it is Luke, with a special interest in these relationships of Jesus, who tells of an occasion when Jesus' life was threatened by the tetrarch of Galilee. He was warned to flee for safety by some of the Ḥabĕrîm, the Associates, as they preferred to call themselves (Luke 13:31).

The Conflicts with the Pharisees

What, then, precipitated the differences between Jesus and the Pharisees, leading to the rupture of their relationships? As we study the Gospels' accounts of his work, it seems certain that the collision occurred primarily over the problem of righteousness and its meaning in terms of the reign of God. Righteousness, or *zedek,* to these earnest students of the Torah was preconditional to a share in the messianic age and the world to come; and righteousness, they firmly believed, was the result of a life faithfully regulated by the full demands of the law. Standing in a natural succession to Father Abraham and

---

2 Mss. S, L, Δ, 33.

3 Acts 15:5; cf. Mark 12:34.

confirming their special privilege as the elect of God[4] by their study and practice of the law, they believed themselves certain of a place in the Kingdom. But Jesus insisted from the outset of his mission that the gospel was not discriminate of audience. It was God's good news to the poor as well as the privileged. In fact it was specially intended as a blessed word to the outcasts and the wretched, the sick and suffering, and all those who were the victims of society, for these were the consciously sick who were in need of the services of a doctor (Mark 2:17). From the standpoint of the "Separatists," this was to make a mockery of the law as God's covenant requirement on the daily lives of his people. If the God of Israel decreed that his people should be holy as he is holy, how could one wink at the flagrant impurity of these *'am ha'arets* without questioning God's word and insulting those devoted men who patiently and joyfully accepted the yoke of the law?[5]

The grievances of the Pharisees with Jesus' strong convictions are clearly expressed in several stories. For example, a banquet is arranged by a revenue agent named Levi who quit his job at the customs desk at Jesus' invitation to follow him (Luke 5:29–32 par.). Some scribes and Pharisees who may even have been adherents of Jesus' growing group of associates were offended that he should defile himself by associating with such untouchables. "Why do you eat and drink with tax collectors and sinners?" They might have quoted such a saying as is found in the tractate B. *Berakoth* 43b: "A disciple of the wise must not sit at table with the *'am ha'arets*."[6] In reply Jesus justified his ministry among them with the simple observation: they need me. "Those who are well have no need of a physician, but those who are sick." He adds with irony, "I have come not to call the [self-styled] righteous, but sinners to repentance" (Luke 5:31f.

---

[4] Cf. the use of this term also among the brothers of Qumran, who call themselves "Elect of Favor" (1QS viii.6) and "Elect of Righteousness" (1QH ii.13).

[5] *Supra*, pp. 37ff. The name Pharisee (*Pĕrīsha*), or Separatist, was used in contrast to the *'am ha'arets*. "When I was an *'am ha-arez*, I used to say that if I had a scholar I would bite him like an ass," said Rabbi Akiba (*Pesaḥim* 49b). On the antagonisms between the scholars and the peasants, see Louis Finkelstein, *The Pharisees*, I, 3rd ed. (Philadelphia: The Jewish Publication Society of America, 1962), 24–37.

[6] Cf. the problem of Christian table-fellowship between Jews and Gentiles which arose later in Antioch and elsewhere (Gal. 2:12). Such continuing tensions explain the preservation of the story in the tradition.

par.). Perhaps he was making sharp rejoinder to intolerant hatred of the outsider by the Qumran exclusivists when he concluded the parable of the dishonest steward with the words, "The sons of this world are wiser in their own generation than the sons of light" (Luke 16:8b).

A cutting refutation of any pretensions to priority in the divine favor appears in the story of the laborers in the vineyard, or rather, to put the emphasis where it belongs, the good employer (Matt. 20:1–15). From the standpoint of a sound labor policy in any economic order, the account of this grape farmer certainly raises its problems. Even though all the workers received a fair day's wage in terms of the wage scale of the day, it would be a strange kind of employer who gave a full day's pay to hands who had only worked one hour of the normal twelve. Surely they deserved to receive only a *pondion*, a twelfth of a denarius. But in plain fact the same pay was given to all the laborers without respect to the number of hours they put in.

God, says Jesus, has such compassion upon the poor and the unemployed that though they only lately have begun to give him what is due they are not deprived of a share in the life of the Kingdom. The repentant sinner, in fact, may actually *precede* the veteran workman in the Lord's vineyard (Matt. 21:31f.). A strict bargaining relationship established on a fair return on one's investment, the popular view of *zâkûth* or merit gained through obedience to the Torah, is obviously set aside for the superior relationship of love in which one is always treated better than one deserves. That is what the New Testament means by grace.

In sharp counterattack against the exclusivism of the Pharisees and Essenes, therefore, in their hostility to his mission to the people of the land and their criticism of his gospel, Jesus retaliated through argumentative stories and sayings. His critics understood little of the fatherly goodness of God, he believed. Though they themselves, with all their faults and frailty, would never deny food to their own hungry children, they imagined that the *Abba*-Father would (Q Matt. 7:9–11). Behind their distorted conception of the Father's true relationship to his children lay a confused understanding of the whole scriptural revelation. They were the very men who were the specialists in the amenities of the Torah and how they were to be made relevant to the present life of man under the covenant. But they knew neither God nor his word. With that, the attack mounted an offensive against what the Torah and the tradition meant to them and the concomitant feelings of self-assurance and self-righteousness that were evoked.[7]

Jesus and the Law of Moses

> It is surely a striking and significant fact that the New Testament presents Christianity, among other things, as a movement which not only denies the old Torah on one level and affirms and fulfills it on another, but also introduces a new Torah.[8]

As the foe of rabbinical Judaism with its preoccupation with casuistic niceties and legalistic elaborations of the law, Jesus exercised a force that was disruptive to the Pharisees. Though the original context of the twin metaphors of the patch and wineskins is conceded to be lost, it is certain that they point to the disturbance of the inbreaking Kingdom upon the traditional ways and beliefs of Israel (Mark 2:21f. par.).[9] A patch of undressed cloth sewn to an old garment is bound to shrink and cause a worse tear. And wine not yet fully aged is never put into old skin bags which cannot yield to the continuing fermentation without bursting. John probably interpreted Jesus' figure of wine as a reference to the way in which the wine of the gospel replaces the water of Judaism, for that seems to be the allegorical meaning he intended to convey through the story of Jesus' miracle at the wedding feast in Cana (John 2:1–12). The new has come, revealing the provisional character of the old and bringing it to completion. This was to be the proper function of the priestly messiah when he came, the covenanters of Qumran believed. As the interpreter of the law (*dôrēš hattôrah*), he would proclaim a

---

7 On Jesus and the Pharisees see further, Samuel Umen, *Pharisaism and Jesus* (New York: The Philosophical Library, 1963); Marcel Simon, *Les sectes juives au temps de Jésus* (Paris: Presses universitaires de France, 1960); Asher Finkel, *The Pharisees and the Teacher of Nazareth* (Leiden: E. J. Brill, 1964). On Jesus and the Essenes, see Ethelbert Stauffer, *Jesus and the Community at Qumran,* trans. Hans Spalteholz (Philadelphia: Fortress Press, 1964).

8 William David Davies, *Torah in the Messianic Age and/or the Age to Come* (Philadelphia: Society of Biblical Literature, 1952), p. 91. References to the new Torah may be found in Matthew's conception of the teaching of Jesus; John 13:34, 14:15; Gal. 6:2; I Cor. 9:21; Rom. 8:2. Cf. B. *Niddah* 61b; Philo, *Life of Adam* I.13; *Life of Moses* III.22; *Targum* on Isa. 12:3; *Midr. Levit. R.* on 11:1; Justin, *Dial.* 11.

9 Cf. Thomas, Saying 47.

new and final Law that would complete and replace the new covenant now observed.[10]

Jesus' Approach to Scripture

We may note three characteristics of Jesus' attitude toward and use of the law of Moses that set him apart from the official exposition and jurists of his day.[11]

1. He draws a critical distinction between specifically ethical and cultic rules, emphasizing the superior importance of the prophetic-ethical and religious injunctions over the cultic prescriptions.

> Woe to you, scribes and Pharisees, hypocrites! [that is, profane persons], for you tithe mint and dill and cummin, and have neglected the weightier matters of the law, justice and mercy and faith; these you ought to have done, without neglecting the others. You blind guides, straining out a gnat and swallowing a camel! [Matt. 23:23f.; cf. Luke 11:42].

It is true that the teachers drew distinctions between light and heavy precepts, but Rabbi Judah warned that even the light precept must be calculated in terms of the reward that might be gained or lost as it was obeyed or transgressed.[12] It was just this neatly calculated arithmetic of merit and reward that Jesus firmly repudiated. The net result of treating the Mosaic law as statutory legislation, considered to be infallible and immutable, was to regard cultic rules on the same level with ethical mandates. The earnest scribe who joined the discussion on the summary of the law in a basic *kelal* shrewdly distinguished between the cultus and the love of God and man, as the prophets had done (Mark 12:32f., par.). But the tone of Jesus' reply, "You are not far from the kingdom of God," suggests that there was something out of the ordinary about such an answer. The typical Pharisee would certainly have been offended at the value

---

10 CD vii. 15–17; 4Q *Florilegium* i.10; *Comm. on Micah* i.16; cf. J. T. Milik, *Ten Years of Discovery in the Wilderness of Judea* (Naperville, Ill.: Alec R. Allenson, Inc., 1959), p. 114; Davies, *Torah in the Messianic Age*.

11 "Great is Torah, for it gives life to them that practice it both in this world and the world to come" (*Aboth* 6.7). See Bennett Harvie Branscomb, *Jesus and the Law of Moses* (New York: R. R. Smith, Inc., 1930), Chap. ii; George F. Moore, *Judaism,* I (Cambridge, Mass.: Harvard University Press, 1944), Pt. I, Chaps. iii–vi. William David Davies, *Christian Origins and Judaism* (Philadelphia: The Westminster Press, 1962); H. Kleinknecht and W. Gutbrod, *Law* (*Bible Key Words,* London: Adam and Charles Black, Ltd., 1962), pp. 67–92.

12 *Aboth* 2.1.

distinctions Jesus draws between the rules that he discusses in the Sermon on the Mount, radicalizing some maxims of righteous conduct and dismissing others as faulty or inferior.

Beyond the matter of the written Torah, Jesus divided sharply with the Pharisees in their estimate of the traditions of the Elders, which they held fully consonant in origin and authority with the written law. For them the *mitzvoth,* the rules of the Torah, and the *halakoth,* the rules of tradition, together constituted the Torah in the broadest sense. Consequently they were shocked by Jesus' liberal practices concerning fasting, ceremonial hand-washing, and sabbath observance. Although he did not declare the scribal cultic purity rules null and void, Jesus challenged their mandatory observance, maintaining that they assumed a tyrannical form over conduct when they were woodenly practiced. Rejecting the claim of divine authority for the *halakoth,* he accused the Pharisees of employing them to nullify the full demands of the Word of God (Mark 7:6f., 9–13 par.).

By contrast, Jesus centered his ethic of obedience upon the twofold law of love in such a way that though the cultic rules are not rejected, they recede into the background. Since this violated the concept of the Torah and tradition as an indivisible whole, he incurred the wrath of the official Torah teachers. He was accused of bringing an unauthorized relief to his disciples in their life under the law by releasing them from many of the externalities of the Pharisaic *halakoth.* "My yoke [that is, my teaching] is easy, and my burden is light" (Matt. 11:30).[13]

2. Jesus differentiated ritualistic legalism from obedience, refusing to make the simple identification of the will of God with the Torah rules. The distinction must not be blurred between the word of Scripture and the Word of God that preceded and authenticated it. For the rabbis the entirety of God's decisions about the true form of human outlook and action was expressed in a code of living, authoritatively defined and applied in their tradition and teaching. Though Judaism knew that the law was only a juridical expression of a covenant between man and God, in actual practice it concentrated on the Torah itself. To Jesus, obedience was being directed to the Torah of God, rather than to the God of the Torah.

But the mere adjustment of one's pattern of conduct to a code of orthopraxis was not deemed sufficient by Jesus. He broke open the

---

[13] *Contra* Matt. 23:4; *Aboth* 3.5.

requirements as such and declared that men must come face to face with the absolute, unconditional will of God, which is only partially expressed in the prescriptions of the Torah and tradition. Above all they must meet not the law, the symbol and instrument of the covenant, but the living God who is the maker of the covenant. It is the knowledge of this absolute, holy, and unconditional will of God that leads him, not only to radicalize the laws about murder, adultery, and perjury, but even to set some aside in the conviction that they represent unwarranted compromises with the divine demand. The regulations regarding divorce and oaths or the limits imposed on neighbor love are examples. "Unless your righteousness *exceeds* that of the scribes and Pharisees, you will never enter the kingdom of heaven" (Matt. 5:20). There is a more exacting kind of righteousness, shaping not simply the behavior but the very center of selfhood, than what results from a juristic exegesis and formal practice of the Torah.

One can subscribe to coercive rules and still maintain an inner freedom of self-rule. A man may dutifully perform the requirements of ritual and cult, be quite correct in his dealings with others, and still cherish his own rights, hiding his privacy from divine search. Or he may imagine that he has discharged all the specific rules and thus more than met the divine demand. The law was not adequately understood for what it was: a disclosure of God's will for men. It had become an intermediary, separating God from men; they could hide from him by imagining that they had only to deal with his representative, not with him. Where men have lost a vivid consciousness of being confronted by the living God himself in their decision-making, it is possible to make his demands manageable in morality and cultic codes, which conceal his stringent imperative under fussy activity.

3. As we noted earlier Jesus enunciates new commandments with the self-conscious authority of one declaring a new and final law. Some interpreters urge that the "I say unto you" introductions to the six antitheses of the Sermon on the Mount are only customary forms for introducing a contradictory opinion in rabbinical debate. But the total effect of these corrective interpretations, together with the solemn Amen-sayings in Mark and the absence of references to scribal decisions to defend his sayings, is to mark Jesus as an authoritative teacher who stands above Moses.[14] Formerly the relationship to the

[14] Walter Grundmann, *Die Geschichte Jesu Christi* (Berlin: Evangelische Verlaganstalt, 1961), p. 124.

law determined a man's relationship to God; now it is declared that the relationship to Jesus and his commandments determines the relationship to God.[15]

The New Torah

We have asked, What is Jesus' relationship to the law of Moses? Are we to conclude that he played the role of the reformer, decrying contemporary interpretations and practices of Scripture and calling his people back to the primacy of the written word, stripped of its ceremonial features? Does he simply reinstate a revised Torah, construing it in terms of the faith and spirit of the prophets? This was not the conviction of his first followers in the early Church. They believed that he was the heralded Messiah who removed the obscurities of the Mosaic revelation and inaugurated the new law of the Kingdom, the Torah of the Messiah. And there is evidence that Jesus himself was moved by a similar conviction. In the metaphors of the patch and the wineskins he speaks of the new and disruptive power that is extending its challenge to the traditional cultus and community life. There is an even more striking word wherein Jesus claims that the divine declaration through Moses and the prophets came to a climax in the work of John the Baptist, opening the way for the new and final fact of the Kingdom. "The law and the prophets were until John; since then the kingdom of heaven has suffered violence, and men of violence take it by force."[16]

What follows in Luke, however, seems to contradict any such understanding. When it is said, "It is easier for heaven and earth to pass away, than for one dot[17] of the law to become void" (Luke 16:17; Matt. 5:18), the law in its minuscule detail appears to be regarded as possessing validity until the very end of time. Did Jesus mean that the period of the law's sovereignty would be brought to an end with the fulfillment of salvation history? It would seem that he did. The coming of the Kingdom which was at hand would usher in a new and perfect understanding of God's holy will.

A striking parallel to the conservatism of Matthew 5:18 may be

---

15 Mark 8:38; Q Luke 12:8; John 6:28f.

16 Combining Luke 16:16a with Matt. 11:12, as many scholars propose. The same juxtaposition of Moses and Christ is emphasized even more strongly in the Fourth Gospel, viz. 1:17, 3:14, 5:39–47.

17 The "dot" probably refers to the ornamentation with which copyists of the Torah manuscripts adorned certain letters of the alphabet. Others consider it to be the tiny mark that distinguishes certain Hebrew letters from one another.

be seen in a passage from the *Manual of Discipline* in the Dead Sea Scrolls: "Until the coming of the Prophet and of both the priestly and the lay Messiah, these men are not to depart from the clear intent of the Law to walk in any way in the stubbornness of their own hearts" (1QS ix.10). Here too there is a temporal restriction upon the period of the Torah's authority. But for the Gospels, that hour of divine action was actually at hand, indeed already present in Jesus' own program. The present was a time of eschatological fulfillment, as he said, "Truly I say to you, many prophets and righteous men longed to see what you see, and did not see it, and to hear what you hear, and did not hear it" (Matt. 13:17). Jesus makes the extraordinary claim that his knowledge of God and God's demand of men is of imperishable validity, holding for this present age and for the coming New Age. "Heaven and earth will pass away, but my words will not pass away" (Mark 13:31). He himself was the Way *(halakah)*.[18]

Against these daring claims the Torah teachers in the Pharisee and, we may presume, Essene brotherhoods rose up in arms. To them the Galilean teacher was guilty of undermining the Torah and setting aside much of the protective and interpretive tradition which they believed was as inviolate as the Torah itself. This unwillingness to respect and defend the whole national heritage from Abraham and Moses through the prophets and sages down to these scribes "who sit on Moses' seat" constituted a sinister threat that must be repulsed. Nowhere does the conflict become sharper than in the controversy about Sabbath observance.

A Test Case: Sabbath Observance

No less than six stories are preserved in the Gospels describing Jesus' quarrel with the Pharisees over the proper observance of the Sabbath.[19] There were many controversial rulings about the Sabbath that were not firmly established as authoritative and were debated among the rabbis. Jews in Galilee, with its predominant rabbinical school of Shammai, followed some religious customs which differed from those in the south. The Galilean rabbis complained about the indifference and outright opposition of the peasantry to approved practices, though even scribal rulings differed between the two districts.

---

[18] John 14:6.

[19] Cf. Mark 2:23–28, 3:1–6; Luke 13:10–17, 14:1–6; John 5:1–19, 9:1–41.

Milk was served with meat, contrary to the Pharisaic interpretation of Exodus 23:19. Tithing of vegetables and herbs was not rigorously adhered to, and it is said that the citizens of Capernaum held it permissable to ride on the Sabbath day, a deliberate flouting of the Pharisaic position. "The rules about the Sabbath," observes the Mishnah tractate *Hagigah,* "are as mountains hanging by a hair, for [teaching of] Scripture [thereon] is scanty and the rules many" (*Hag.* 1.8), a clear admission of custom beyond scriptural specification.

Mark's initial collection of conflict stories concludes with an incident about a healing that took place in a synagogue one Sabbath day (3:1–6 par.). In form, however, it may be classified as a pronouncement story, for the emphasis falls not upon the cure but a word of Jesus about the relation of human need to Sabbath observance. "Is it lawful on the sabbath to do good or to do harm, to save life or to kill?" In the Matthaean version, a reference is made here to a rabbinical provision for rescuing a sheep that had accidentally fallen into a pit on the Sabbath, without violating the work interdictions. The Essenes not only prohibited this rescue in their ultraorthodox Sabbath rule (CD xi.13f.) but forbade coming to the assistance of human beings in distress, for the Damascus Document reads at xi.16f.: "A living man who falls into a water pit or pond on the Sabbath may not be drawn out with a ladder, nor with a rope, nor with any other device."[20] The more lenient view of the scribes and Pharisees finds expression in the Mishnaic dictum, "Whenever there is doubt whether life is in danger, this overrides the Sabbath" (*Shab.* 18.3).[21]

A saying which Matthew inserts into the story of the controversy in the grainfield is pertinent here (12:5–7). Jesus reminds his critics that even sacerdotal service in the temple takes priority over the injunction against work on the Sabbath. If so, then surely those who perform acts of mercy on this holy day must be guiltless too, for God regards mercy above sacrifice (Hosea 6:6). But the objection of the Pharisees to this and other acts of healing was that there was no immediate threat to life; hence the medical care could easily have been postponed to one of the work days of the week. Jesus maintains that restoration to wholeness of life was an imperative and urgent necessity that brooked no postponement for fast or feast day. The Father offered bread to those who were hungry now, medicine to

---

20 The text may be corrupt here, but the strict Sabbatarianism of the Essenes is convincingly affirmed.

21 Cf. *Yoma* 8.6; *Erub.* 10.13–14.

those who now were in pain. Something greater than the Sabbath, the new life of the Kingdom of God, was powerfully present.

A Test Case: Purity Laws

The disagreements between Jesus and the Torah specialists soon widened to include the theory and practice of ceremonial purity. Mark 7:11–23 represents a topical collection of Jesus' sayings bearing upon his attitude toward the unwritten law or tradition of the Elders. For the benefit of Roman readers, the Evangelist recalls some of the practices that marked the Jews as a strange people in Roman society, such as ceremonial handwashings and purification rites after contact with unclean persons or objects (vss. 3f.).

The sectarian rules of conduct practiced at Qumran show that their legalistic puritanism outdid the more moderate position of the scribes and Pharisees. All those who entered the new covenant of the Essenes were obligated to "distinguish between clean and unclean and . . . proclaim the difference between holy and profane" (CD vi.17f.). Only after the novice had completed a full year of his novitiate was he permitted to join the members of the sect in the daily ritual ablutions. So highly did they value these cultic disciplines that they spoke of entering through them into fellowship with the sons of heaven. They robed themselves in white garments, priestly vestments that signified the highest degree of purity.[22]

To the blunt query "Why do your disciples not live according to the tradition of the elders, but eat with hands defiled?" Jesus made sharp reply. He cited a prophetic denunciation upon a people who were as adept in their cultic confessions as they were delinquent in whole-hearted devotion. And he made an accusation so devastating as to threaten the pattern of life of these tradition enthusiasts. In the bluntest terms he denounced their sacred *halakah* as the clever fabrication of human ingenuity rather than a true exposition of the Torah statutes. "You leave the commandment of God, and hold fast the traditions of men!" (Mark 7:8). Clearly these scribal and Essene practices, binding upon the priests and no doubt emulated by pious laymen,[23] were judged to be ritual embroideries that too often became substitutes for the plain sense of the divine imperative.

---

22 Jos., *War* II.8.3, 5.

23 See the Mishnah tractate *Yadaim* and compare the very important role of ritual washings at Qumran. CD x.10–13; 1QS iii.4f., 9; iv.21; v.13; Jos., *War* II.8.5–13.

To Jesus such cultic acts were too often shocking burlesques in which men profaned[24] God's holy name by solemnly invoking it in a piety divorced from daily life. Acts of supplication must be acknowledgments before God of an obedience that has already been expressed in meeting and serving one's neighbor. Instead they had become substitutes for it. The unconditional demands of God were being domesticated into manageable requirements men could fulfill and even supplement, resulting in an overbearing pride. In truth, man's careless and spasmodic obedience to the expectations of the Holy Father made the plea for mercy more appropriate than the word of self-congratulation. Converting ethical demands into the statutes of a code only meant that the individual was less sensitive to his immediate responsibility to the God who stands behind the façade of requirements. He was not *deus absconditus,* the God who is hidden, but rather *deus dicit,* the God who speaks. With conduct quite proper to the sanctuary, one may yet hide from such a God, meanwhile offering himself to other men as a guide, presumptuously leading the blind, though blind oneself.

Abuse of abstention vows was another case in point. By such a vow one renounced the use of a thing or an act which was ordinarily permissable. It might be that one thus dedicated it as an offering to the temple. In second-century Judaism it was common to employ a dedicatory word, *Korban* or offering, as an oath or vow confirming a resolution. So a man might say "*Korban!* if I eat of thine" or "*Korban!* if I ever again plough my field with your cow."[25] Mark reports a practice in Jesus' time whereby a man might actually deprive his parents of support, in violation of the Fifth Commandment, by declaring that support *Korban,* that is, consecrated as a gift to the temple (7:9–13). One conjectural reading of a passage in the *Damascus Document* (xvi.14, 15) prohibits the use of the related *Ḥerem* vow to deprive a workman of his food.[26] In the

---

[24] The Greek word *hypokritai* (actor, interpreter) was chosen in the Gospels to convey the meaning of the Aramaic *chanêfā,* a profane person.

[25] See the tractate *Nedarim,* Herbert Danby, trans., *The Mishnah* (London: Oxford University Press, 1958), pp. 264–80.

[26] A Jewish tomb from the first century, recently discovered in the area southeast of Jerusalem, contains the *Korban* formula in an inscription that reads: "All that a man may find to his profit in this ossuary [is] an offering [*Korban*] to God from him who is within it" (J. A. Fitzmyer, "The Aramaic Qorbān Inscription from Jebel Ḥallet eṭ-Ṭûri," *Journal of Biblical Literature,* LXXVIII [1959], 60–65). The Mishnaic *Nedarim* 2.4 implies that Galileans did not use the ban formula for things dedicated to the temple.

Mishnah such deception in the name of piety was criticised by the sages, who urged the prior responsibility a man owed to his father and mother.[27] But the Gospels are evidence that in the days before the triumph of Pharisaic Judaism contentious Galileans often thus deprived their fellow citizens and even their own relatives of a share in their possessions. Such injustice in the guise of piety was reproached by Jesus; it was further proof that the sacred tradition often became an excuse for nullifying the Torah.

This sharp antithesis between the tradition of men and the commandment of God, expressive of Jesus' radical criticism of ritual regulations comes to its most piercing form in an independent saying on defilement preserved in Mark 7:15. "There is nothing outside a man which by going into him can defile him, but the things which come out of a man are what defile him." Matthew's form of this saying (15:11) restricts it to dietary matters and immoral actions (vss.17,19), but the Marcan version, which is more sweeping, is probably earlier.[28] In their concern that men approach God with clean hands, the ritualists had depreciated the importance of an inward purity of heart. For Jesus it is the pure in heart who see God; this alone is the condition for fellowship with him.

In such judgments about the meaning of purity, Jesus brings his criticism beyond a polemic against the venerated tradition of the Elders. As H. Braun points out, the sayings about handwashing and Sabbath observance are criticisms of the *halakah,* the traditional interpretation of the Torah. But the principle that nothing external defiles a man strikes at the ceremonial law within the Torah itself.[29] Though one may find occasional parallels in the Essene writings to the strictures in the Gospels about the traditional rules of purity, there is nothing corresponding to such radical criticisms of cultic practices and the Torah as we find here. The teachers at Qumran, like Jesus, maintained that the Pharisaic *halakah* served to soften the stringency of God's commandment. But they called for a more thoroughgoing Torah piety developed along the lines of a stricter

---

27 *Ned.* 9.1.

28 Cf. Luke 11:39–41; Rom. 14:14–23; I Tim. 4:3–5; Titus 1:15; Thomas, Saying 14; Mark 7:17–23 represent early Christian applications of this basic saying to the problem of table-fellowship between Gentiles and Jews in the Christian societies (see Gal. 2:11–14; Acts 15:20f.). See *Numbers Rabbah* 19.2 for a Jewish reply to this position.

29 Herbert Braun, *Spätjüdisch-häretischer und frühchristliche Radikalismus* (Tübingen: J. C. B. Mohr [Paul Siebeck], 1957), II, 72f.

understanding of the written law than the rabbis themselves, whereas Jesus issued no call to stricter obedience to the Torah but instead summoned men to be confronted now by the living God. He does not tell them to return again to Moses and the fathers and to devote themselves to a patient, intensive study of the law as foundation for the proper kind of action.[30] "The letter and the intent of the Torah were no longer regarded as inviolable. Something else was now superior to the Torah, something the rabbis found incomprehensible."[31]

Mutual Accusations

It would be as egregious an error to let the Gospels determine our picture of first-century rabbinism as it would be to accept the Talmudic portrayal of Jesus. Both represent caricatures in some measure, shaped by the bitterness of attack and counterattack. Both reflect the strains and stresses that continued to divide the synagogue from the Church in the early years of the Christian movement. In certain passages the Synoptists, Matthew especially, give the impression that the entire system of Pharisaism was polemized as corrupt by Jesus. But these are surely instances of generalization. We have already noted some unobtrusive evidences of more friendly relationships between Jesus and certain Pharisees. That there were pious frauds among the *Ḥaberim* was recognized by themselves. Said a second-century rabbi: "There are ten portions of hypocrisy in the world, and nine of them are in Jerusalem!"[32]

Holiness, Hustle, and Hypocrisy

Some of the specific accusations Jesus leveled against the teachers of the Pharisaic societies and, we believe, the Torah community of Qumran are collected in three of the principal strands of tradition in the Gospels: a warning against the scribes, Mark 12:38–40; six woes in the Sayings Source, Luke 11:37–12:1 (Q or L); and seven

---

30 1QS i.7–9, v. 8ff.

31 Hans Windisch, *The Meaning of the Sermon on the Mount,* trans. S. M. Gilmour (Philadelphia: The Westminster Press, 1951), p. 147.

32 Cf. *Pss. of Sol.* 4; *Asmp. Moses*; Jos., *Antiq.* XVII.2; J. *Ber.* 9, 14b; J. *Sotah* 5, 20c. middle; B. *Sotah* 22b, 41b–42a; B. *Yoma* 86b; I. Abrahams, *Studies in Pharisaism and the Gospels,* Second Series (Cambridge: Cambridge University Press, 1924), pp. 30–32.

woes in Matthew 23:1–36 (the latter a synthesis of material from both Mark and Q with Matthew's own private source). These indictments deal with matters of practical living, ceremonial purity, tithes, and status-seeking.

Alas for you scribes, Jesus sighs, you embroider the law of Moses with your *halakoth* so that men are dismayed by their failures and transgressions before God without help or much hope of ever pleasing him (Luke 11:46). As for the scribes themselves, they are too often more adept at a study of the law than in regulating their conduct by the commandments which they enjoyed discussing (Matt. 23:3). They remind one of a fast-talking son who is usually reluctant to match his deeds with his mouth (the parable of the two sons, Matt. 21:28–31). As any farmer knows, the kind of fruit harvested says something important about the condition of the orchard (Q Matt. 7:16–20); just so, pious words must be backed up by a holy life. There are those who ostentatiously wear throughout the day the phylacteries and prayer shawls which are the proper vestments of the devout Jew at the hours of morning and evening prayer (Matt. 23:5).

Rabbi Judah the Prince, compiler of the Mishnah, once observed, "Which is the straight way that a man should choose? That which is an honor to him and gets honor from men" (*Aboth* 2.1). Rabbi Jesus disclaimed seeking honor from men (John 5:41) and accused some of the Pharisees of being more concerned about making a good showing and receiving admiring glances than in rendering homage to God. Thus they enjoyed deferential salutes accompanied with a courteous bow: "Peace, my great One [Rabbi]; Peace, Father [Abba]," as they walked in the town market place (Mark 12.38 par.; Q Luke 11:43). They relished the positions of honor both in the synagogue and at the banquet table (Mark 12:39)[33] where their learning and social standing received public recognition. Sensing the attractiveness of such recognition, Jesus warned his disciples against similar ambitions, reminding them that they should acknowledge only one *Abba,* the Father God, and one Teacher, Jesus himself (Matt. 23:8–10).

Jesus is especially caustic about the spiritual pride betrayed by such preening before the public and by a censorious attitude toward the common man. The self-admiring prayer of the virtuous Pharisee in his familiar story (Luke 18:9–14) may not be too gross an

---

33 Cf. Q Luke 20:46; Luke 14:7–11.

exaggeration of some of his contemporaries.[34] Status-seeking not only feeds on social approval; it shows that confidence is based on oneself rather than on God. The rabbis were not unaware of the problem. A renowned rabbi warned against putting trust in oneself and once observed, "My abasement is my exaltation and my exaltation is my abasement."[35]

With fussy preciseness, these holy men wash their cooking utensils and tableware but are unmindful of the inner purification so badly needed, Jesus claims. Indeed, he adds bitterly, they who so desperately avoid any uncleanness are a contaminating influence upon other men, like unmarked graves which can defile the unsuspecting who pass by them or yeast which pervades the dough.[36] They refuse to hear God's own messenger when he comes and thus prove themselves to be sons of their fathers, who in their time spurned the judgmental word of God that was spoken through the prophets, and they struck them down in hot violence. It may be that by "prophets" and "messengers" (apostles) (Q Luke 11:49) Jesus refers not simply to earlier men of God but to his own followers who as heralds of the Kingdom already experienced the rebuffs and the thirty-nine lashes of synagogue scourging instigated by these devout students of the Torah.[37] With their fathers they became blood-guilty of the murder of righteous men, from the innocent Abel to the priest Zechariah, who was slain, like Canterbury's Thomas à Becket, as he served before the altar of God.[38] They belong to the prophet killers of every age who

---

[34] Jeremias quotes a Talmudic prayer (B. *Ber.* 28b): "I thank thee, O Lord, my God, that thou hast given me my lot with those who sit in the seat of learning, and not with those who sit at the street corners; for I am early to work, and they are early to work; I am early to work on the words of the Torah, and they are early to work on things of no account. I weary myself, and they weary themselves; I weary myself and profit thereby, while they weary themselves to no profit. I run and they run; I run towards the life of the Age to Come; and they run towards the well and the pit of destruction" (*The Parables of Jesus,* 6th ed., trans. S. H. Hooke [New York: Charles Scribner's Sons, 1963], p. 142; cf. Phil. 3:4ff.).

[35] Rabbi Hillel (ca. 20 B.C.), *Lev. Rab.* v.1.5.

[36] Cf. Num. 19:16. The qualifying adjective "white-washed" in the Matthean form (23:27) alters the meaning of the saying and is probably an editorial addition.

[37] The members of the sect at Qumran seem to have thought of themselves as prophets inheriting the persecutions that befell these earlier spokesmen of God's will.

[38] Cf. II Chron. 24:20–22. This is probably the correct identification of this man whom Matthew mistakenly confused either with Zechariah the prophet or Zechariah ben Baris (d. A.D. 67).

think to silence the voice of God through his envoys by hatred and violence.[39]

The Scribes' Rebuttal

In the judgment of Jesus, the lay theologians and brothers were in fact blind guides, insensitive to the wideness of God's mercy to the poor, the wretched, and the needy, and guilty of a damnable disposition to reform others without beginning with themselves. They, in turn, were convinced that in him Satan had disguised himself as a reformer and worker of miracles.[40] Their solemn judgment was that he was mad and that entering into a pact with the Evil One, he had gained the power to accomplish these feats of healing.

> Either Jesus was greater than they, a divine emissary, an individual with authority: In this case their elaborate system of Torah teaching and of tradition had collapsed. Or, Torah and tradition remained inviolate: In this case Jesus was no emissary but a false teacher, a false prophet, a pseudo-Messiah. The rabbis decided upon the second alternative, and thus the external fate of Jesus was sealed.[41]

Jesus, the Sadducees, and the Liberation Front

On other national fronts also Jesus criticized and was criticized. It is certain that the wealthy and influential bourgeousie opposed him and eventually took the leadership in bringing him to his death. And it is possible to read between the lines of some of his sayings to discover something of his attitude toward the revolutionists and political radicals of his day. Here again our new knowledge of apocalyptic Essenism in the last period of the Qumran community's history throws some light on the tangle of relationships with the state and provides new dimensions of meaning into Jesus' own mission.

---

39 Directed against Pharisaic and scribal critics were such parables as the talents (Matt. 25:14–30; Luke 19:12–27), the great supper (Matt. 22:1–14; Luke 14:16–24; Thomas, Saying 64), the servant with authority (Q Luke 12:42–46); and such sayings as blocking the way to the Kingdom (Matt. 23:13; Luke 11:52; cf. Thomas, Saying 39) and the uprooted plant (Matt. 15:12; cf. Thomas, Saying 40).

40 Mark 3:20–22; Q Luke 11:14–16; John 10:20. *Beelzebul* (*Baalshamaim*), perhaps the name of an early Canaanite deity meaning "Lord of the Heavenly House," may have been coined by Jesus' critics in derision of his assumed role of leadership in God's house, i.e., the Kingdom. Cf. Matt. 10:25; Mark 3:27.

41 Windisch, *Sermon on the Mount*, p. 149.

Critique of the Aristocracy

The Evangelists tell us, with considerable plausibility, that both the parables of the two sons and of the wicked husbandmen were spoken to members of the Sanhedrin, hence to members of the priestly and lay aristocracy as well as to the Pharisees and Elders (Matt. 21:23; Mark 12:12 par.). They were the leaders who had betrayed their appointed responsibilities and were threatened in the impending Judgment with the loss of their privileges and prerogatives. The Sadducees had defiled the Court of the Gentiles in the house of God by converting it into a den of thieves and refusing to prepare it as the place where ultimately the righteous Gentiles from all the nations would assemble to worship the true and living God (Isa. 56:7; Mark 11:17). Because of their secularizing of the sacred cultus in Jerusalem, the presence of the Holy One of Israel no longer overshadowed the temple. "O Jerusalem, Jerusalem. . . Behold your house is forsaken!" (Q Luke 13:34f.).

It is possible that many of Jesus' sayings about those who trafficked in the mammon of unrighteousness and who made the acquisition of material goods the major ambition of their lives were pointed to the Sadducees as the monied and propertied class in Jewish society.[42] At opposite extremes from such puritanical ascetics as the priests of Zadok at Qumran, they were men who had to maintain their social standing and exercise of power at all costs. "He went away sorrowful, for he had great possessions," could have been said of a Sadducee.

In the parable of the rich man and Lazarus (Luke 16:19–31) Jesus etches with acid words a portrait of a typical Sadducee of his time: smart clothes, luxurious living, gourmet appetite—*la dolce vita,* and a flint-hearted disregard for the lame beggar who lay on the street outside his gate hoping for some of the sops of bread he and his carousing friends tossed away for the dogs to pick up. The identification is made virtually certain when we see the reversal of fortunes that begins after the death of these two men. Lazarus enjoys the blessedness of fellowship with Father Abraham in the heavenly banquet. The unfortunate aristocrat discovers to his sorrow that there is in fact an afterlife, though his Sadducean theology had admitted no place for such a belief in the resurrection (vss. 28, 30).

Jesus makes pointed comment on the rigidity of their exclusively

---

42 Luke 16:14, for example, is more likely spoken of Sadducees than Pharisees; cf. Jos., *Antiq.* XIII.10.6.

this-world theology and their callous indifference to the plight of the needy. "If they do not hear Moses and the prophets, neither will they be convinced if some one should rise from the dead" (Luke 16:31). Of what use would it be to send someone to warn the five brothers, who share the same Sadducean creed, of the fate that is in store for them unless they recognize that there is an afterlife and a retribution to be reckoned with? The very Scriptures on which the Sadducees base their eschatology refute them, though they do not recognize it.[43] They neither comprehend the full meaning of God's sovereign rule and realm as the real goal of history nor do they respond to the holy imperative of love to share cheerfully and compassionately with those who are destitute. On their account, the liturgies are celebrated in a deserted temple, for God has forsaken a dwelling place in which his name is desecrated and his law distorted (Q Matt. 23:38).

The National Resistance Movement

Such were the political tensions in first-century Palestine that it is quite unthinkable that Jesus' mission was conducted without contact or reference to the revolutionaries who had particular strength in the upcountry districts of Galilee. The "signs of the times" must surely have included sensitivity to the rapidly worsening relations between the Roman overlords and their Jewish subjects, which provoked varied recommendations for solution. Many of Jesus' sayings that appear to be counsels to the disciples on how to withstand persecution may originally have been addressed to the peril confronting the nation from those who advocated a trust in God's salvation supported by armed violence.

Since the days of the rebellion led by Judas the Galilean against the imperial order for a census of property, there had been no lack of insurrectionists and their sympathizers who represented the hope of the Jew's deliverance secured by bloodshed and violence, with divine aid. Luke reports one local skirmish where Tiberius' representative massacred a group of Galileans (13:1). Out of this movement, as we have seen, came the party of Zealots and the cut-throat Sicarii who played so prominent a role in the First Jewish Revolt (A.D. 66–73). Judging from the bloodthirsty *War Scroll*, the second and final phase of the Essene occupation of Qumran was strongly influenced by these revolutionist programs. No longer were the men of the new covenant to

43 Cf. the discussion with the Sadducees on the resurrection, Mark 12:18–27 par.

hasten the coming of the Era of Favor simply by their holy life in the desert retreat, studying and practicing the Torah according to the secret understanding revealed to them. Now they planned their strategy and practiced their maneuvers as the battle troops of God who would actively fight in the forty-year Holy War that was soon to break out.

Against the agony of these times one must listen again to a saying previously heard: "From the days of John the Baptist until now the kingdom of heaven has suffered violence and men of violence take it by force" (Q Matt. 11:12). If indeed it is precarious to identify the "men of violence" with any special group, it remains true that allusion is surely made to the confusion and unrest of the day.[44] In their misguided efforts some whom Jesus identifies as antagonists are actually robbing men of the Kingdom of God. The way of physical violence and revolution is unequivocally renounced. Modern man's reluctance to believe that such peaceful alternatives to the resolution of personal and social conflict are practical and possible has often led to a strained exegesis of Jesus' words and acts to claim his support. But the testimony is clear enough. Those who are devoted to the making of peace where enmity now exists are the blessed ones who are promised a place in the Father's Kingdom (Matt. 5:9). The Leviticus love-commandment is interpreted contrary to popular contemporary views to mean that even the enemy is to be loved and prayed for (Matt. 5:43f.). "There was nothing in Leviticus 19:18," observes Professor Manson, "to indicate to a Jew in the days of Jesus that he ought to love Pontius Pilate!"[45]

Jesus and the State

But if Jesus held no sympathy for the answer of militant nationalism to the problem of his day, what is to be said about his attitude toward the state? He certainly did not share the Romans' conviction that the divine Augustus, "Father of the Fatherland and Savior of the People," had inaugurated a universal empire of peace. Instead he speaks of leadership in the Kingdom as the very antithesis of the kind of lordship

---

44 In the Qumran *Commentary on Habakkuk* the phrase "men of violence" seems to refer to the Jewish collaborators with the Seleucid kings who were severely dealt with by the Hasmonean rulers Jonathan and John Hyrcanus (1QpHab viii.11). Cf. Prov. 3:31, 16:29; 1QH vi.5; 4Q *Testimonia* 25. In each instance the phrase refers to evil men who oppress the righteous.

45 Thomas Walter Manson, *The Sayings of Jesus* (London: SCM Press, Ltd., 1961), p. 161.

that marks the Gentile kings and benefactors (Luke 22:25 par.). A sharp contrast is drawn between the opulence of a royal court and the austerity of the desert preacher, John the Baptist. Obviously those who responded to John were not in search of political patronage (Q Matt. 11:8).

It is, however, the question of the tribute money which gives us a surer insight into Jesus' attitude toward the state (Mark 12:13–17 par.).[46] In the tense atmosphere of Passover time, with the city swollen with pilgrims and Pilate's police force, strengthened by troops who had marched from Caesarea to ensure order, Jesus' foes contrived a strategem that would expose him to the authorities. They chose the age-old problem of taxation as the pretext, for no single stand on that controversial matter won majority approval. Since Pompey's campaigns in the East, Syria and Palestine had been forced to contribute their revenues to the coffers of the Roman state. To freedom-loving Jews the tax was a galling reminder of their servitude to foreign control. It dramatized the desperate privation of a well-nigh bankrupt people.[47] But its worst offense was the public submission it demanded to one who was revered across the world as a savior and lord. How did the imperial silver coin read? On the obverse appeared the words: "Tiberius Caesar Augustus son of the divine Augustus"; on the reverse: "High Priest."[48] Even the titles of his step-father were to be found on some of Tiberius' coins: "The Worshipful One, the Image and Manifestation of the King of Heaven on earth." To the people of God this was idolatry, whether or not other peoples shrugged off the titles as merely honorific.

With a deferential address calculated to disarm this suspected revolutionist, the Pharisees and Herodians raised the question: "Is it lawful to pay taxes to Caesar, or not? Should we pay them or should we not?" They refer to a particular tax as a test case: the head tax or land tax exacted of every subject of the crown in the provinces and client states. Should we agree or should we refuse to pay the

46 Cf. Thomas, Saying 100, and see the fragment of a variant version of this story in an early second-century papyrus owned by the British Museum. *Gospel Parallels,* 2nd ed. (New York: Thomas Nelson & Sons, 1957), p. 145.

47 Double taxation is estimated to have consumed 30 to 40 per cent of the family income. The *tributum,* paid to Roman revenue agents, included land and head taxes; the *publicum,* collected by Jewish employees of the Romans, represented taxes levied on sales, customs, salt, manumission, business concessions, etc.

48 *Tiberius Caesar Divi Augusti Filius Augustus. Pontifex Maximus.* See Figure 9; cf. Figure 3.

Fig. 8. Stone discovered in the summer of 1961 in Caesarea containing the name of Pontius Pilate, procurator of Judea (A.D. 26–36). Probably from a temple built by Pilate in honor of the Emperor Tiberius, the Latin inscription reads in translation "Tiberium [? of the Caesareans ?] / Pon] tius Pilate / Pref] ect of Jude [a." *By courtesy of the Israel Department of Antiquities and Museums.*

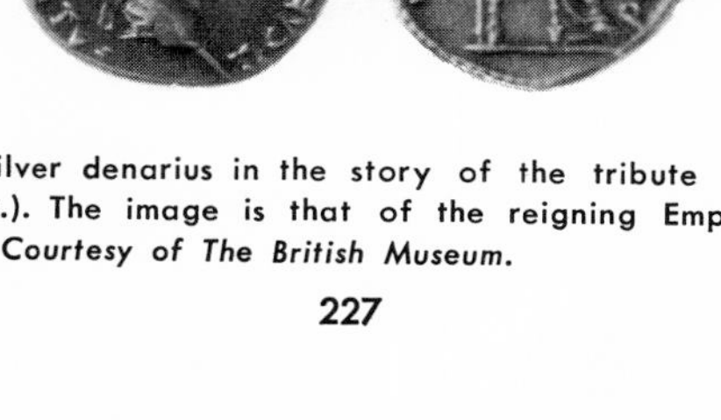

Fig. 9. The silver denarius in the story of the tribute money (Mark 12 : 12–17 par.). The image is that of the reigning Emperor Tiberius (A.D. 14–37). *Courtesy of The British Museum.*

tributum? Their theological protest was well known. Indeed at the outset of his term of office Pilate had been humiliated by delegations of Jews who came to Caesarea to implore him to recall from Jerusalem the imperial troops who had carried ensigns bearing the effigy of the reigning emperor. Yet the same people now continued daily to use the Roman silver *denarius* with the image and blasphemous titles of the Caesar in their business dealings. The sole stipulation was that it must be converted into Tyrian coinage for use in the temple area. Its very use signified that they too benefited from the vast economic, legal, police, and governmental system that marked the *imperium.*

After forcing from them the grudging admission that the coin was actually Caesar's to begin with, Jesus concluded with the enigmatic words: "Render to Caesar the things that are Caesar's, and to God the things that are God's" (Mark 12:17). It is certain enough that Jesus recognized the legal and moral responsibility of the citizen and provincial to support the government by the payment of taxes.[49] Caesar is to receive back a token of what he has already given. However disgruntled the subjugated Jew might be, he could not deny the benefits of a dependable and peaceful social order. The people of God were not to be in monastic seclusion from the world, but to live responsibly in it. At the same time they were to acknowledge the rightful claims of God upon them. Similarly a second-century rabbi advised, "Give unto him what is his for thou and what thou hast are his" (*Aboth* 3.7). "Holy Week is the existential exegesis of His words: submission to the dominion of Caesar, submission to the dominion of God. . . ."[50]

No parallel is to be found in Jesus' teachings to the fierce hatred of the Seleucids and Romans which colors the *Rule of the War* and the biblical commentaries of the Qumran community. Still there can be no doubt that Jesus anticipated collision between the demands of the *imperium Dei* and the *imperium Caesaris.* "You will stand before governors and kings for my sake to bear testimony before them," he warned his disciples. Such predictions of conflict with the authorities may indeed be colored by the experience of the early Church, but there is no reason to suppose that Jesus was unaware of the threat posed

---

49 Cf. *Aboth* 3.2. Strangely enough, Jesus' critics were to make deposition before Pilate later that he had incited the populace to refuse to pay taxes to the empire, associating him with the revolutionist party (Luke 23:2).

50 Ethelbert Stauffer, *Christ and the Caesars,* trans. K. and R. Gregor Smith (London: SCM Press, 1955), p. 135.

by the political order to the gospel of the Kingdom. The saying that has so often been used as a liniment for minor aches and pains—"If any man would come after me, let him deny himself and take up his cross and follow me" (Mark 8:34 par.)—was a sober calculation of the cost of discipleship.[51] The disciples would never have understood it as economic privation or a migraine headache to be endured patiently for Christ's sake. Crucifixion meant only one thing in their day: the terrible death that the Roman courts meted out to convicted bandits, rebels, slaves, or provincials. To take up the cross was tantamount to a declaration of war between the Kingdom of God and the kingdoms of this world in which the disciple knew himself to be expendable in the interests of the final victory of God's rule over the kings and nations of the world.

The Climax of the Galilean Mission

Herod's Suspicions

Exactly when the tetrarch began to interest himself in the movement led by Jesus is uncertain. It is clear that Mark's account of Herod's speculations and the report of the death of John the Baptist is an interlude without organic connection with the context of the commissioning and the return of the mission teams of disciples (Mark 6:14–16, 17–29). In any event the work of Jesus and his disciples had been discussed throughout the district so that notice had come to the tetrarch's palace in Tiberias on the lake. Herod's attitude toward Jesus is difficult to determine from the Gospels. At this juncture his curiosity at least was piqued. He was appraised of the views of the rabble who considered Jesus to be a prematurely risen John the Baptist or even Elijah *redivivus,* the Prophet of the Last Days. Concerned no doubt about the political implications of such a populist movement, the puppet ruler anxiously queried, "John I beheaded; but who is this about whom I hear such things?" Luke, who seems to have had access to special information about the royal court, brings the incident to conclusion with the observation, "He sought to see him" (Luke 9:9).

---

[51] The authenticity of this saying is questioned by some interpreters who feel that it is a prediction *post eventum,* framed by the Christian community. However, the common reality of crucifixion in Roman Palestine as a form of capital punishment and the increasing hostility Jesus experienced from the authorities make it extremely likely that his warning of suffering was given just such a setting.

It is most unlikely that Antipas, "the fox," had any friendly intentions behind his decision for a personal investigation. Luke reports one of those rare friendly encounters of Jesus with the Pharisees when, on some unspecified occasion, they warned Jesus to flee for safety because Herod had put a bounty on his head (13:31–33; cf. Acts 4:27). Jesus discounted the threat, declaring his deliberate intention to continue his healing ministry "today and tomorrow," that is, for some time yet. He is already persuaded that there is a divine obligation upon him to declare the gospel in Jerusalem itself, even though the price may be death. An interesting suggestion has been made by Jeremias that the parable of the lamp (Mark 4:21f.; Q Luke 11:33) was Jesus' figurative rejection of the proposal that he seek refuge from this immediate danger. "The lamp has been lit, the light is shining, but not in order to be put out again! No, but in order to give light!"[52]

The Lakeside Meal

Shortly after the return of the disciples from their preaching tour, there occurred an event that held far-reaching implications for the whole program of Jesus. It was about Passover time when the disciples rejoined him, probably in Capernaum,[53] and reported with excitement the remarkable success that had attended their work in the towns and villages throughout the district. Tempering their enthusiasm with the reminder that their success was no occasion for a Pharisaic self-esteem (Luke 10:17–20), Jesus suggested that they get away from the confusion of the busy fishing port and seek rest and refreshment in a desert retreat. The geographical references are very puzzling and obscure. Mark speaks vaguely of a lonely place to which they repaired. After the meal Jesus dismissed the crowd and sent his disciples off by caique to Bethsaida while he himself went into the hills to pray (6:46). Luke, however, understands that the meal took place near Bethsaida Julias, the home of Peter, Andrew, and Philip and capital city of Philip the tetrarch. A famous Aramaic scholar, Gustaf Dalman, has conjectured that the wilderness area where Jesus sought solitude with his disciples was near the midpoint of the eastern shore just south of Wadi es-Samak, called today Moḳa' 'Edlo.[54] He believes that this was also the place where the Gergesene demoniac was cured by Jesus (Mark

---

52 Jeremias, *Parables,* p. 121.

53 John 6:4, and note the "grass" (i.e., wild herbs) of Matt. 14:19; Mark 6:39; John 6:10; which give a clue to the season.

54 Gustaf Herman Dalman, *Sacred Sites and Ways,* trans. Paul P. Levertoff (New York: The Macmillan Company, 1935), p. 173.

5:1–20 par.). Perhaps Jesus sent out the disciples from here, intending to rejoin them at Bethsaida Julias in order that he might continue the journey with them. The storm that arose during the night may have driven the little boat towards the village of Gennesaret just below Capernaum.[55]

To some such spot on the eastern shore a crowd numbering several thousands had followed Jesus and his disciples. Moved by their interest in his message, he talked to them about the blessed New Age soon to dawn. According to the story, when evening came Jesus insisted on acting as host for the evening meal over the protests of his disciples. It was immediately obvious that they were quite unprepared to entertain so large a group of people. All they had were their own meagre provisions, a hamper containing five loaves of bread and two smoked fish. John points out that even these belonged to a little boy who was standing by. Forty dollars would not be enough to purchase sufficient bread for the people who had gathered here (Mark 6:37). Where were they to get the daily bread for which he had taught them to pray?

But after the crowd had been seated on the ground in small groups of hundreds and fifties, looking for all the world like the separate plots in a Palestinian garden, Jesus began to recite the traditional Jewish table blessing: "Blessed art thou, O Lord, King of the world, who bringest forth bread from the earth." As the sun set, he broke the flat loaves and gave the pieces to the disciples to begin to distribute to the hungry and tired families who sat around him. When the distribution was complete everyone had received something to eat and there were enough food scraps left over to fill several reed baskets!

The prominence the Evangelists give the episode—it is told no less than six times—suggests that they regard this as a parabolic action of Jesus, dramatizing the message of the Kingdom of God. John certainly recognizes its symbolic significance (John 6:26; cf. Luke 14:15). The *form* has probably been shaped by the Old Testament narrative of the miracle of Elisha (II Kings 4:42–44) and perhaps by features of the Lord's Supper observed by the early Church. But the *substance*

---

55 Dalman reports an interesting personal experience: "On April 6, 1908, a journey over the lake by the staff of the Institute resulted in a similar experience. Coming from the eastern edge below Hippos, we wished to sail northward along the shore in order to land again in Bethsaida. But a strong wind rising at noon from the east made it impossible to land and drove us to Capernaum" (*Sacred Sites and Ways,* pp. 175–76). The Dalmanutha of Mark 8:10 may be Magdala, an important fishing center not far from Gennesaret.

reflects the popular and recurrent symbol of the Kingdom: the banquet with the Messiah in the Father's house.[56] With good reason Albert Schweitzer referred to this meal as a "veiled eschatological sacrament." Here the parable of the great supper already had become reality (Q Luke 14:16–24).

> With the morsel of bread which He gives His disciples to distribute to the people He consecrates them as partakers in the coming Messianic feast, and gives them the guarantee that they, who shared His table in the time of His obscurity, would also share it in the time of His glory.[57]

The meaning of the meal as a dramatic statement of conviction about the Kingdom is corroborated by a crucially important detail of the day's events which John alone preserves. He writes, "Perceiving then that they were about to come and take him by force to make him king, Jesus withdrew again to the hills by himself" (6:15). Stirred by Jesus' description of how this present age was destined to yield to the glorious Kingdom of God, the excitement of the crowd may have led to a mob action of which Jesus was the target. Surely this was the Prophet who was to come into the world in the last time; perhaps he was the royal Prince himself (6:14).[58] Was not this the act by which he threw off his incognito disguise and revealed his true identity?

But their high hopes were dashed by his protest. So deep was the disappointment over Jesus' refusal to declare himself in favor of such messianic leadership that many turned against him. Nazareth neighbors had been scandalized by his refusal to predict God's judgment upon the Gentiles in the final hour of the nations of mankind. Now some of his own disciples were perplexed by his words about the real meaning of the reign of God. They became disillusioned and impatient at his continuing aloofness from their hopes for the ransoming of Israel. In disappointment and disgust they turned away; they had pinned their hopes on him in vain (John 6:66).

---

56 On the Messianic banquet: Isa. 25:6–8; *I Enoch* 62:14–15; *II Baruch* 29:3–8; Ezek. 44:3; Qumran, *Serek ha'edah* (1QSa).

57 Schweitzer, *The Quest of the Historical Jesus,* p. 376. Compare the cult meal at Qumran: Jos., *War* II.8.5; 1QS vi.2–8. K. G. Kuhn, "The Lord's Supper and the Communal Meal at Qumran," in Krister Stendahl, ed., *The Scrolls and the New Testament* (New York: Harper & Row, Publishers, 1957), pp. 65–93; Matthew Black, *The Scrolls and Christian Origins* (New York: Charles Scribner's Sons, 1961), pp. 102–15.

58 The detail in John 6:15 is dismissed by some scholars as a Johannine alteration of the Kingdom saying in Q Matt. 11:12.

CHAPTER X

JOURNEY TO JERUSALEM

This decision to go to Jerusalem is undoubtedly the turning-point in Jesus' life.*

I have come to set fire to the earth, and how I wish it were already kindled! I have a baptism to undergo, and how hampered I am until the ordeal is over! [Luke 12:49f. NEB]

Peter's Confession and the Secret Teaching About the Suffering Son of Man

To the Synoptic Evangelists, certain experiences of Jesus and his disciples which occurred in the vicinity of Philip's Caesarea focus on the major turning point of the whole mission.[1] In the first phase of Jesus' work the preaching of the Kingdom elicited broadly based popular support and a large following of disciples. In the latter period of his Galilean work, however, criticism by the religious authorities hardened, political suspicions were aroused, the response to his mission was far more restricted, and some of his own disciples deserted him. In consequence, he concentrated much more of his time upon the instruction of the twelve. In the Gospels these disturbing events, pyramiding

* Günther Bornkamm, *Jesus of Nazareth,* trans. Irene and Fraser McLuskey with James M. Robinson (London: Hodder and Stoughton, 1960), p. 154.

1 Mark reports activity of Jesus alone and also in the company of his disciples in the Tyrian district north of Upper Galilee, ranging from the coastal region eastward to the vicinity of the tetrarch Philip's residence at Caesarea Philippi, territory considered by the rabbis as part of the traditional homeland of the Jews (Mark 6:45–8:26). The section is omitted entirely by Luke and may be considered of questionable value although the individual experiences may come from an early tradition.

to the point of Jesus' decision to carry the crusade to Jerusalem are colored by the approaching martyrdom in Jerusalem and the work of the Son of Man accomplished through suffering, death, and vindication.

The Scene

According to Mark's second narrative of the events associated with the lakeside meal (8:1ff.; cf. 6:30–7:37), Jesus and his disciples, after returning from Magdala to Bethsaida, travelled north toward Caesarea Philippi where the events of the confession and the transfiguration took place.[2] Some scholars accept this as the older account, believing that this journey immediately followed the meal with the multitude. In that case it could be argued that Jesus, still dogged by the eager crowds who clamored for a miracle worker and the promised New Day for Israel, once again sought privacy for rest and planning. Others identify an older form of the double tradition and suggest that after a few months of solitude in the Tyrian country following the wilderness meal, Jesus rejoined his disciples and shortly afterwards came into the vicinity of Philip's residence at Caesarea. In this instance, the mission team would have been separated for some months from the stormy experiences of the Galilean activity.[3] This much is sure: the Evangelists believed that escape from public pressures figured less significantly in Jesus' plans than his desire for conversation and prayer with his disciples.

The old village shrine sacred to Pan that Philip had rebuilt into a modern Roman city lay about twenty-five miles north of Bethsaida on the lower slopes of Mt. Hermon. Dalman proposed that any one of several volcanic eminences extruded above the plateau of Golan might have marked the site of the Transfiguration.[4] Perhaps the conversation centering in Jesus' question to his disciples occurred in the neighborhood of Bethsaida, as Luke suggests, while the men were en route toward Caesarea Philippi. Several days later, at the outskirts of the tetrarch's residence, Peter experienced the heavenly confirmation of his messianic confession, termed the Transfiguration.

---

2 A, Mark 6:30–7:37; B, 8:1–26.

3 F. C. Burkitt estimated a period of eight months for these journeys. John's Gospel suggests an interval of five or six months between the lakeside meal and the arrival at Jerusalem (Passover to Sukkoth) (John 6:4, 7:2).

4 Gustaf Hermann Dalman, *Sacred Sites and Ways,* trans. Paul P. Levertoff (London: SPCK, 1935), p. 205. Tradition assigns it to Mt. Tabor.

Critical Views of the Narratives

Some interpreters of the story of Jesus are convinced that the confession of Peter and the Transfiguration represent the Easter experiences and Christological faith of the early Church, antedated to the close of the Galilean mission. To Professor Bultmann, for example, Peter's testimony is cast in the form of the earliest Christian creed: "I believe that Jesus is the Messiah [Lord]." Since it was probably Peter who was first convinced that Jesus had been raised from death to become the triumphant Lord, this story traces the beginnings of the Christian community to the resurrection faith based on Peter's experience.[5]

A much larger number of scholars share Bultmann's view that at least the Transfiguration was originally a manifestation of the risen Christ to some of his disciples, which has been read back to this juncture as a sign of things to come.[6] They point out that the declaration of Jesus' identity as Messiah appears in the Gospels in the context of solemn predictions of the suffering, rejection, death, and resurrection which will be the lot of the Son of Man. But the disciples' faith in the messiahship of Jesus did not develop in his lifetime; it came as a corollary to the historical events of Golgotha and Easter. It was only after the climactic events of the national condemnation of Jesus as a crypto-king and the dialectical response of resurrection faith that Peter and his companions became fully convinced that Jesus had been appointed by God as the Messiah. In his lifetime they knew him simply as prophet, healer, and teacher. So the confession and the Transfiguration are symbolic narratives proleptic to the faith that dawned with Easter. Others who point out the incongruity of the details with other resurrection Christophanies consider the story a mystical preview of the Parousia or the enthronement of the Messiah,[7]

---

5 Rudolf Bultmann, *History of the Synoptic Tradition*, trans. John Marsh (New York: Harper & Row, Publishers, 1963), pp. 257–61.

6 Cf. Bultmann, *ibid.*, pp. 259–61. Cf. e.g., Maurice Goguel, *Life of Jesus*, trans. Olive Wyon (New York: The Macmillan Company, 1949), p. 343; and C. E. Carlston, "Transfiguration and Resurrection," *Journal of Biblical Literature*, LXXX (1961), 233–40. Carlston emphasizes that the function of the story to declare the heavenly authority of the Messiah and to invoke obedience to him was precisely the function of the early Christian preaching.

7 An interesting instance of the Transfiguration viewed as a foreshadowing of the Parousia is provided already within the New Testament, viz. II Pet. 1:16–18. See further, G. H. Boobyer, *St. Mark and the Transfiguration Story* (Edinburgh: T. & T. Clark, 1942).

either an actual experience of Peter's or a highly symbolic allegory created by the early Church.

It seems to us, however, that the Easter event was not so much the origin of the disciples' faith as it was the confirmation and elaboration of a faith presupposed by it. Without doubt Jesus' disciples regarded him at first as an unconventional Galilean rabbi and even as the Prophet who was to come in the End-time. Still it is very likely that the ground for the early Church's faith in him as the Son of God is to be staked out within the response his disciples made to his leadership in the later period of his ministry.

Peter's Bold Faith

On the road Jesus inquired about the various opinions the people held about him. "Who do men say that I am?" (Mark 8:27 par.). The disciples replied with the same estimates of his mission previously reported to the tetrarch. Then, quite unexpectedly perhaps, the question was turned in upon the reporters. But what do you yourselves think? The community survey of religious beliefs was no longer adequate. They were not neutral observers. Where some said one thing, "He is the eschatological Prophet who comes in the last days," and some said another, "He is demon-ridden," they could not be without an opinion. Fanatic, madman, reformer, teacher of a new *halakah,* messianic prophet—who was he? Peter speaks for the whole group, "We believe that you are the Messiah." To Mark, this was an opening of the blind eyes of the disciples not unlike the hard-won cure of the blind man near Bethsaida only a few days earlier (Mark 8:22–26). Now they saw things clearly, though not yet in a depth of focus that brought vicarious suffering and atoning death into view. Another version of this statement of faith by Peter and the eleven is found in the Gospel of John, where it is placed in the context of an experience in a Capernaum synagogue following the meal on the eastern shore (John 6:66–69).

The form of the story in Mark and Luke is puzzlingly incomplete. Neither joy nor surprise greets Peter's declaration. In fact there is no proper reply at all to Peter's words, only a command to silence so that Jesus' true identity remain concealed from the people. Matthew adds a paragraph from his special source which seems to help solve but actually only complicates the reader's problem. Replying to Peter, Jesus makes it clear that this identification must be understood, not as a gradually dawning insight on Peter's part, but the gift of a supernatural wisdom. "Blessed are you, Simon Bar-Jona! For flesh and blood have not revealed this to you, but my Father who is in heaven" (Matt. 16:17).

Storms of controversy have raged over the meaning of the words that follow in Matthew's special tradition. "You are Peter, the Rock; and on this rock I will build my church, and the forces of death shall never overpower it"[8] (Matt. 16:18 NEB). Present-day scholarship remains sharply divided on the authenticity of the saying. To E. Schweizer, for example, Jesus "did everything to attain no success, no growth, and no fortifying of the Church, but to allow himself and his followers to be broken in pieces—for the world." Accordingly, the saying is to be seen as a product of the experience of his followers after Easter. Neither during nor beyond his lifetime did Jesus envisage an obedient remnant or an exclusive congregation distinguished from Israel and representing the true people of God of the last days.[9] Cullmann, on the other hand, is convinced that we have here a genuine word of Jesus, originally set in the context of the Last Supper when Jesus spoke of his prayerful hope that Peter would become the strength and stay of his brethren in the dark days that lay ahead (Luke 22:31–32).[10] The problem is exceedingly complex and answers must be framed with caution.

That Peter could be surnamed the Rock can only mean in a biblical context that he is a *witness* to the true Rock, God himself. In the Old Testament secure faith in God constitutes the tested stone that is the foundation of Zion.[11] The faith of Israel is the hitherto rejected stone that is to become the keystone in the temple of the New Age (Ps. 118:22). The altar of burnt sacrifice in the great temple of Jerusalem once was believed to stand upon a holy rock marking the gate of heaven and the entrance to the world of the dead. Later that holy stone was identified with the foundation of the Holy of Holies.[12] The early Christians saw in Christ the precious stone on which the new

---

8 *Supra*, Chapter VIII, pp. 189–90.

9 Eduard Schweizer, *Church Order in the New Testament*, trans. Frank Clarke (Naperville, Ill.: Alec R. Allenson, Inc., 1961), p. 33, an opinion shared by such widely differing scholars as W. G. Kümmel, R. Bultmann, M. Goguel, E. Lohmeyer, A. Schweitzer, M. Enslin.

10 Oscar Cullmann, *Peter: Disciple, Apostle, Martyr,* 2nd ed., trans. Floyd V. Filson (Philadelphia: Westminster Press, 1949), pp. 182–84. The authenticity is defended by such men as K. L. Schmidt, A. Oepke, M. Kaiser, J. Jeremias, J. W. Bowman, T. W. Manson, R. N. Flew, etc. Bultmann sees Matt. 16:17–19 as the original conclusion to the (Easter) messianic confession of Peter (*History of the Synoptic Tradition,* p. 258).

11 Isa. 28:15–16; cf. Pss. 18:1f., 46; 28:1; 40:2.

12 *'eben shattiyyāth;* cf. Joachim Jeremias, *Golgotha* (Leipzig: Verlag von Eduard Pfeiffer, 1926), pp. 65–66.

community, conceived as God's temple, was being built. Christ was the Rock on which the new temple was built.[13] In his confession, "You are the Messiah," Peter believed that he had found the only secure foundation for God's dwelling place on earth, just as for Isaiah the tested stone consisted of the assurance, "He who believes will not be in haste" (Isa. 28:16). This is the only security against the ravages of the final disasters (Isa. 28:15; Matt. 7:25).

Like the penitents of Qumran who saw themselves as men of the Rock, the Israel of the last days established on God's rock,[14] the *ekklesia* of Jesus was also a community of the last days founded upon God's faithful word of judgment and salvation. For Jesus, too, the concept of the Church was closely related to the Kingdom of God viewed either as the House or the City of God. When he said he would build his *ekklesia* and when he promised to destroy the Jewish temple and build another (Mark 14:58), he spoke of the same thing: the establishment of the eschatological community.[15] Peter had voiced the faith which would form the bed-rock of the new community: recognition of Christ as the true revealer of God and adherence to him and his cause in the world.

The members bore no special name. They were called apart not to become a separatist movement, intent on preparing their own ways, but to return and give themselves like their Teacher for the sake of the needy sons of the world who were called to become sons of God's world. They constituted the renewed people of God, who existed not for their own sake but for the sake of those not yet aware of God's claim and gifts.[16]

Forebodings of Tragedy

Turning to the Marcan account of the incident, we note that Jesus gives neither approval nor disapproval to the conviction Peter has voiced, but he proceeds immediately to pledge the disciples to strict

---

13 Mark 12:10; Acts 4:11; I Cor. 10:4; I Pet. 2:4. Cf. *Odes of Solomon* 22:12.

14 Cf. 1QH vi. 24–27 (G. Vermes, *The Dead Sea Scrolls in English* [Baltimore: Penguin Books, Inc., 1962], p. 171); 1QS viii.7–8, ix.5f.; xi.4f.; 1QH iv.1, vii.8f.; *Comm. on Ps. 37* Frag. 1, ii.16. In 1QH vii.8f. the Teacher declares that he has found safety on the rocky wall of God's truth.

15 See the excellent discussion by Ernst Lohmeyer in his *Lord of the Temple,* trans. Stewart Todd (Richmond, Va.: John Knox Press, 1962), Chap. iii, now illuminated further by the Qumran sectarian documents.

16 The real question is not so much whether Jesus intentionally founded the Church in history, but whether the Church that came into existence following Easter is and continues to be an authentic expression of his mission.

secrecy about the whole matter. We are left to speculate about the reasons. But the outcome of the whole story makes it very probable that Jesus seals them to silence because they entertain false expectations. They were still infected with the imperialistic hopes that bewitched the crowds a few months earlier as they heard him describe the New Age. These dreams of the Davidic warrior-messiah explain Peter's shocked reaction to Jesus' grim anticipation of the dangers that lie ahead for him and the severe rebuke it elicits, "Get behind me, Satan!" (Mark 8:33).

The prediction of these tragic events, the first of the so-called Passion predictions, warns that the Son of Man is to be the victim of suffering, rejected by officialdom, done to death, and then, after a short interval of time, brought back to life again. (Mark 8:31; cf. 9:31, 10:32–34, 10:45). It is certain that this national repudiation is viewed as something other than a personal defeat. The emphatic "must suffer" found in Mark 8:31 and Luke 17:25 is to be understood as a conviction about a divinely ordained program. A common view about the final events anticipated a general suffering of the wicked and sore tribulations that would even try the faith of the righteous.[17] Jesus is convinced that he will take upon himself, as a representative of the people, these divine afflictions. He will drink the cup of God's wrath served up to a wicked and adulterous generation. And the suffering concentrated upon him will become the deed of expiation effecting atonement for the guilty.

Quite apart from the Evangelists' insistence that Jesus conceived his role from the time of his baptismal experience in terms of the Servant mission in Isaiah, Jesus must have brooded over the arrest and martyr's death of John. He was not insensitive to the suspicion of some and the outright enmity of other Pharisees. The fickle popularity he enjoyed with the crowds who came to watch and listen did not deceive him. There is good reason to believe that Jesus advised men and women who responded to his preaching to calculate realistically what discipleship involved and to make generous allowance for rebuff and opposition. In his reply to Herod's decision to deal with him as he did with the Baptist, Jesus reflects his own ponderings on the fate of Israel's prophets: "I must go on my way today and tomorrow and the day following; for it cannot be that a prophet should perish away from Jerusalem." In the same breath, Jesus appears

[17] *Jub.* 23:11–25; IV Ezra 5–6; 1QH iii.7–12, which may refer to the birth pangs of the messiah.

to anticipate his own death by stoning, which is a Jewish method of execution (L Luke 13:34). Again, answering the question why his disciples do not fast like those of John, Jesus speaks of the appropriateness of their conduct to the present time of fulfillment when the salvation of the Kingdom was already a blessed reality. But the words "Can the wedding guests fast while the bridegroom is with them?" anticipate a time to come when this situation will not be true and when fasting as a sign of mourning will be fitting enough.[18]

Thus the calculation of risk and the prospect of consequences that would probably result from Jesus' chosen mission were likely soberly considered long before this point in his ministry. Nevertheless it is patent that from this turning point Jesus' thought and disciple-teaching center upon a suffering both representative and redemptive. Under varied figures of a baptism to be undergone, a cup to be drained, a road to be walked, a ransom to be paid, and a covenant to be sealed, he teaches his disciples what is the divinely determined lot of the Son of Man.

In their present form the Passion predictions in Mark are secondary. That is to say, they represent the thinking of Jesus drawn out of a prophetic and apocalyptic background but shaded by the writers with the actual experiences that marked the last days of Jesus' life. Behind the precision of the predictions, however, there is evidence that Jesus brought his expected death into relationship with his total mission of preaching and healing and with the full coming of the reign of God. He anticipated a humiliation at the hands of Jewish leaders, a martyr's death, and a triumphant vindication of his message when he would be exalted by the Father and, in due season, the Kingdom would be fully established.

The Martyred Servant of God

Renewed investigations of Jewish religious thought in the period contemporary with the work of Jesus show that "the idea that God chooses a righteous man in expiation of sins, who is regarded as a pawn for the sins of the people, seems to have been very widespread."[19]

---

[18] As W. G. Kümmel has shown in *Promise and Fulfilment,* trans. Dorothea M. Barton (Naperville, Ill.: Alec R. Allenson, Inc., 1957), pp. 76 - 77.

[19] Hans Joachim Schoeps, *Paul,* trans. Harold Knight (Philadelphia: The Westminster Press, 1961), p. 129. The discussion that follows is indebted to Schoeps' summary of expiatory sacrifice and the suffering messiah in Judaism. Cf. Eduard Schweizer, "The Son of Man Again," *New Testament Studies,* IX (1963), 256–61.

Built into an ordered theory of suffering in the period after A.D. 70, the understanding of the redemptive significance of suffering was generally accepted in Jesus' day. Undoubtedly it is rooted in the biblical idea of sacrifice as the offering of a life which could procure atonement (*kephar,* covering) for the sins of the worshipper. "The innocent effects atonement for the guilty," is the teaching of the Talmudic treatise on the Day of Atonement (*Yoma* 43b).[20] The idea is to be found in apocryphal and sectarian literature of the Jewish community even earlier than the time of Jesus. The refugee priests and laymen in the monastic community on the bluffs overlooking the *Lacus Asphaltitus* believed they represented an atoning sacrifice for the nation.[21]

It is of course another matter whether the messiah of Israel was ever conceived at this time as the embodiment of the Servant figure of Isaiah and hence subject to shame, reproach, and even death. It has usually been held that a messianic interpretation of Isaiah 53 is not to be found in Judaism before the advent of Christianity. More recently, however, some Jewish and Christian scholars have come to recognize that the Suffering Servant of the Lord may have been occasionally understood as a prototype of the Messiah.[22]

Thus the sufferings of individual righteous men availing for needy men, even the use of the language of Isaiah 53 to describe their afflictions must be reckoned as factors in the Jewish doctrine of vicarious sacrifice in Jesus' day. It would be strange indeed if it were wholly unknown to him. While it is self-evident of the *ebed Yahweh* figure, it may be added that the Son of Man figure in Ezekiel, Daniel, and Enoch is not unrelated to the problem of persecution and pain.[23]

---

20 The *Mekilta on Ex.* 20:23 and *Sifre on Deut.* 6:5 contain a number of statements on the value of suffering credited to the Tannaim. See C. J. G. Montefiore and H. Loewe, *A Rabbinic Anthology* (London: Macmillan and Co., Ltd., 1938), pp. 225–32.

21 1QS v.6, viii.6–10, ix.4; *et passim.* Language reminiscent of the suffering Servant is used in 1QH ix.26–27 and iv.27 (cf. Isa. 53:12). Cf. also *IV Macc.* 6:27–29, 17:20–22; II Macc. 7:37–39.

22 Schoeps, *Paul,* p. 139, citing the Qumran Psalms. Jeremias argues for a pre-Christian messianic interpretation of Isa. 53 in Walther Zimmerli and Joachim Jeremias, *The Servant of God*, trans. Harold Knight, *et al.* (Naperville, Ill.: Alec R. Allenson, Inc., 1957), p. 77; cf. William David Davies, *Paul and Rabbinic Judaism* (London: SPCK, 1958), p. 283. See Justin, *Dial.* 39, 49, 68, 69; B. *Sanh.* 88a, 93b, 98a; *Targum of Jonathan* on Isa. 53:12.

23 See, e.g., Ezek. 4:9ff.; 5:1ff.; 12:6, 11, 17ff.; 21:11, 17; 24:16ff., 27; Dan. 7.

The transcendent figure of the Son of Man in the apocalypses of Enoch, Baruch, and Ezra is described in terms drawn partly from Isaiah's Servant figure. So the concept of a suffering Son of Man is not totally unknown in canonical and apocryphal Jewish literature of the time, even though this understanding of his function appears to be restricted to a limited circulation.

Two sayings have a special bearing on our discussion of Jesus and the Servant: the ransom saying of Mark 10:45 and the covenant saying of Mark 14:24. An impressive number of scholars believe that the words, "The Son of man also came not to be served but to serve, and to give his life as a ransom for many," are a doctrinal reformulation along the lines of a Pauline theology of the cross. They contend that the earliest form of this saying on service is found in the Lucan Passion narrative (Luke 22:27), where no mention is made of vicarious sacrifice.[24] Its contribution to our study is therefore debatable. Still, assuming that it might be genuine, what is the significance of the words "a ransom for many"? The reference is unmistakable. This is the central theme of the greatest of the Servant Songs, eulogizing the sacrificial ministry of the *ebed Yahweh*.

> Yet it was the will of the Lord to bruise him;
>   he has put him to grief;
> when he makes himself an offering for sin (*asham*),
>   he shall see his offspring, he shall prolong his days;
>
> . . . .
>
> He poured out his soul to death,
>   and was numbered with the transgressors;
> yet he bore the sin of many,
>   and made intercession for the transgressors.

In this case, Jesus believes himself to be the *asham,* the vicarious sin offering, which would bring estranged men back to God. In words that were to become "a sort of kerygmatic formula" based on the characterization of Isaiah's *ebed,* he interprets the program of his mission. Though the precise form of this saying may be influenced by the Servant theology of the community after Easter, we believe it still preserves the dominant consciousness of Jesus. He was the bearer of

---

[24] Bultmann, for instance, maintains that it has been formed by "the redemption theories of Hellenistic Christianity" (*History of the Synoptic Tradition,* pp. 144, 407). A summary of representative views may be read in Vincent Taylor, *The Gospel According to St. Mark* (London: Macmillan & Co., Ltd., 1953), pp. 445f.

the sins of the people whose death, like that of the Servant, was to be an offering of the one for the many through whom healing and restoration would occur.

The Transfiguration

It was about a week after these conversations of Jesus with his disciples that Peter, James, and John had an experience which they interpreted as a divine confirmation of Jesus' messiahship (Mark 9:2–8 par.). It is said that they beheld a vision of an unearthly, radiant figure whom they recognized as none other than their own beloved rabbi. Whatever also was meant by this strange happening, it certainly signified to them God's approval of their teacher as the messianic deliverer.

The story of the Transfiguration in the Gospels is replete with symbolic details of the wilderness tradition of Israel expressive of a faith that the greater exodus is beginning. In allusions to the first redemption of Israel under Moses' leadership, we are reminded of that earlier vision of the glory of God symbolized by the cloud that hovered over Mount Sinai and the voice that spoke out from the cloud (Exod. 24:12–18).[25] This time the voice or *Bath Qol* utters the same solemn words that were used to report Jesus' baptism in the desert. Again it is the language of the Servant Song (Isa. 42:1): "This is my beloved Son." The dumbfounded hearers are commanded, "Listen to him." In garments of dazzling white, a heavenly attire,[26] Jesus is seen in conversation with two figures from Israel's past. The presence of the wilderness prophets Moses and Elijah in conversation with Jesus would signify to the enraptured Peter the final hour of history to be heralded by the reappearance of these two great representatives of Israel's prophets. A rabbinic tradition had it: "God said to Moses: 'When I send the prophet Elijah, both of you shall go together.' "[27]

Old Testament prophecy and rabbinic teaching had commonly made use of the theme of Exodus as a popular model for the expecta-

---

25 The correspondence of the chief features of the Transfiguration story and this wilderness tradition is convincingly set out by Ulrich Mauser in his study, *Christ in the Wilderness* (Naperville, Ill.: Alec R. Allenson, Inc., 1963), pp. 110–19.

26 Cf. *Test. Levi* 4:5; Mark 16:5; Rev. 7:14; and see the description of the heavenly Son of Man in Rev. 1:13–16 (Dan. 7:9).

27 Mid. *Deut. rabba* 3.10.1; J. *Targum* on Exod. 12:42; cf. Rev. 11:3ff. Note, too, the prophet, the priestly and the lay messiahs of Qumran's expectation, 1QS ix.9–11.

tion of the final redemption of Israel.[28] The rich symbolism of the Transfiguration story is intended to portray Jesus as none other than the second Moses who will lead the people of God in the new exodus and establish the full and final meeting between Heaven and earth. Through him the Promised Land is reached; the Kingdom of God becomes reality. As the story stands, this is the significance of the epiphany of Christ's glory which is disclosed to the astonished disciples in this hour.

Luke interprets his basic source quite correctly here by making an explicit reference within his account of the mountain vision to the approaching passion of Jesus. He tells us that the subject of the conversation among Jesus, Moses, and Elijah was the *exodos* shortly to be accomplished in Jerusalem (9:31), that is, Jesus' death in the holy city and subsequent exaltation to the presence of God.[29] But the disciples, heavy with sleep, are not aware of this heavenly revelation to Jesus of the necessity of suffering and death in relation to the messianic redemption. They waken, says Luke, to see the glorious sight of Jesus with the two men and to hear the heavenly voice identifying Jesus as the Beloved Son. At this juncture of affairs, the Evangelists all believe that the disciples were unable to comprehend the extraordinary fact to be confirmed on Good Friday and Easter. The unity of the eschatological Son of Man, leader of the new exodus, with the martyred Servant of the Lord quite escaped them.[30] The destination of the new way through the wilderness was to be accomplished only through the mystery of Jesus' suffering, death, and resurrection. The way of the Kingdom must first run through the urban wilderness of Jerusalem, as the disciples would soon see.

The Journey to Jerusalem

The Fateful Decision

"When the days drew near for him to be received up, he set his face to go to Jerusalem" (Luke 9:51). What was the meaning of this sense of necessity to visit the holy city? All the Gospel writers were convinced that the journey to Jerusalem was a death march deliber-

---

[28] See Isa. 10:24–26; 11:15f., 40–55 *passim;* Ezek. 20:33ff.; Hos. 2:14f.; Mic. 7:15; and Mauser, *Christ in the Wilderness,* pp. 55f.

[29] So John A. T. Robinson, *Jesus and His Coming* (New York: Abingdon Press, 1958), p. 133.

[30] For the association of Moses with the Suffering Servant of Isaiah, see Thomas Francis Glasson, *Moses in the Fourth Gospel* (Naperville, Ill.: Alec R. Allenson, Inc., 1963), pp. 18f.

ately undertaken out of the conviction that it was according to God's plan. Yet they hint that those who were with him had other expectations.

The Johannine narrative preserves a separate tradition of the departure for Judea that is curiously cryptic. The brothers of Jesus urge him to go to Jerusalem for the celebration of the autumn feast of *Sukkoth*. They propose that he perform some dazzling demonstrations of his prowess to persuade some among the crowds that he is the Messiah. They obviously speak in irony. "No man works in secret," they tell him, "if he seeks to be known openly. If you do these things, show yourself to the world" (John 7:4). Jesus rejects the suggestion, however, electing to remain in Galilee while they go ahead. Thereupon, without explanation, he decides to follow them, only secretly. But that pose is not retained long, for as soon as he arrives in the city he begins to teach openly in the temple precinct. Evidently Jesus planned to go to the capital city, but not for the reasons they suggest or John implies. Perhaps his own intention was to carry the crusade to the focal center of national life. With the doors of Galilee closing behind him, he felt he must continue the mission on which he had been sent. The good news had to be preached in Jerusalem, come what may!

The disciples may have greeted with excitement the decision to move south into Judea. They were mindful that the site of God's sanctuary was commonly believed to be the center from which his judgment and salvation would someday flow out to the far places of the earth. Here, according to prophetic dream and apocalyptic promise, the messiah would manifest himself triumphantly on the Mount of Olives and rally the people for the final assault upon the Romans. "The Lord whom you seek," an anonymous prophet had intoned, "will suddenly come to his temple" (Mal. 3:1). Here in David's city perhaps their hope in the prophet-teacher would be vindicated, their prayers answered as he dropped his cloak of anonymity. Jesus would perform a brilliant *tour de force* and bring every loyal Jew to his side. Luke specifically defines these expectations: "He was near to Jerusalem, and. . . they supposed that the kingdom of God was to appear immediately" (Luke 19:11; cf. 24:21).

It is more certain that out of his confidence that his life was in the Father's hands Jesus was convinced that the hour had arrived for a fresh stage in his mission. Could the gospel of the Kingdom be preached wholly outside the walls of Jerusalem, "the city of the Great King?" The course must rather come to climax and completion there.

There where other prophets had preached and perished the expiatory suffering and death would take place that would be a prelude of pathos to the victorious reign of God. "It cannot be that a prophet should perish away from Jerusalem" (Luke 13:33). That sardonic word flung in Herod's face came from a heart heavy over the rebellion of his people yet assured of the invincibility of God's government in the world. Long since now, their holy house was bereft of the *shekinah,* God's glorious presence. Despite the pageantry of their celebrations, the temple was a throne without a king, a house without a host, a shrine without a God. But the Master of the house was returning. Would he be recognized and welcomed? "You will not see me until you say, 'Blessed be he who cometh in the name of the Lord!' " Until that joyful recognition of his true identity, the temple would be deprived of the divine presence. He himself would be stricken from the land of the living (Q Luke 13:34f.).

Duration of the Visit

The Synoptic writers are agreed in assigning the entry into Jerusalem a few days before the Passover celebration. But we have already noted the chronology in John's Gospel which extends Jesus' ministry in Jerusalem to a much longer period of time, from the festival of *Sukkoth* in the early autumn (John 7:2) to the festival of *Ḥannukah* in December (John 10:22). With that, he left the city and crossed the Jordan to Perean Bethany (John 10:40). After some time there and in an obscure village of Ephraim near the Samaritan border, Jesus returned to Jerusalem five days before the beginning of the *Pesach* festival (John 12:1, 12).

There are hints in Luke, however, that Jesus' relationships with the chief city were not restricted to the last few crowded days of his life. A pre-Galilean ministry in Judea is affirmed by a superior manuscript tradition for Luke 4:44.[31] Moreover, the Q tradition of Jesus' lament over Jerusalem, "How often would I have gathered your children together as a hen gathers her brood under her wings" (Luke 13:34b; cf. 19:42), may suggest repeated attempts to win the hearts of the people of Jerusalem. The heated debates with the scribal leaders, Sanhedrin representatives, and temple authorities, which Mark crowds into the few days before Jesus' arrest, undoubtedly represent a topical grouping of conflicts drawn from a much longer activity in the capital city than his brief temporal notices suggest (cf. Mark 10:1).

---

31 Supported now by the early third-century Bodmer Papyrus 75.

The Ministry in Jerusalem and Judea

That there was no simple recollection in the early Church of the course of events that followed Jesus' arrival in Judea is clear enough when we compare the variant accounts in Mark, Luke, and John. Instead of an immediate arrest and trial following the first provocative events, Mark compresses within a space of three days a rapid series of head-on collisions with the authorities. It is evidently his purpose to show his readers how the expectation of any last-hour reprieve for the unrepentant nation was dissipated as the capital dwellers reacted in no different fashion than the Galileans. The specialists in the Torah as well as the official priesthood tried to balk him at every point.

It is generally recognized that Mark had no detailed knowledge of the ministry in Jerusalem comparable to the Passion Story that begins in chapter 14 of his Gospel. From a collection of episodes that may have been used first for instructing converts in the clash between the gospel and the law, Mark, or an earlier compiler, has chosen five stories to relate.[32] The group is prefaced by a symbolic incident about a fruitless fig tree and some scattered sayings about the meaning of faith and prayer (Mark 11:12–14, 20–25). We hear in rapid succession of (1) a challenge to the sanction for his unconventional teaching and healing (Mark 11:27–33); (2) a debate about the payment of the imperial tax (Mark 12:13–17); (3) a response to the Sadducean arguments against the resurrection from the dead (Mark 12:18–27); (4) a friendly discussion with a Torah teacher about the greatest of the commandments (Mark 12:28–34); and (5) an academic discussion about the doctrine of the Messiah (Mark 12:35–37a), followed by renewed strictures against the malpractices of the scribes (Mark 12:37b–40). Throughout, the Evangelist underlines the unscrupulous efforts of the leaders to incriminate the Galilean teacher through rabbinical rhetoric, and to discredit him in the eyes of the people. Mark aims to demonstrate to his readers the dialectical skill of Jesus in discerning their ulterior motives and springing their traps.

These thrusts and parries are climaxed by a lengthy conversation of Jesus with his disciples in which the issues of the future are discussed and Jesus solemnly predicts the destruction of the whole system of Judaism and God's final judgment upon the world (Mark 13:5–37). Whether in fact these encounters occurred at such a time or in such an order is, of course, quite immaterial. As we have seen they are

---

32 Compare the similar grouping of five controversy stories in Mark 2:1–3:6.

insights into the thinking of Jesus as well as the kind of reaction his message provoked among the stalwart defenders of the Torah, tradition, and temple. Nowhere do we see more clearly the agility of a nimble mind that could turn the sharp edge of a question back upon these schoolmen. He cross-examines the examiners and withal shows that his driving concern is not with theological gymnastics but a direct meeting with the living God.

John's Account of the Ministry

John maintains his characteristic individuality. According to him Jesus traveled from his home province to Jerusalem at the time of the autumn festival of *Sukkoth.* In the midst of the week-long festivities that centered in the temple, Jesus suddenly appeared and began to teach with a brilliance and authority that won the admiration of all who heard him (John 7:14ff.). Against the background of the ancient rain-making ceremony, Jesus offers the living water and the light that wards off darkness, provoking the denunciation of the Pharisees. "Are we not right in saying that you are a Samaritan and have a demon?" (John 8:48).

In the same setting, John's narrative locates a prophetic accusation of Jesus spoken against the leaders of his people as undependable shepherd-rulers of their flock (10:1–5). The imagery is familiar enough. Ezekiel's indictment of the mischievous political guides of his day (Ezek. 34) and Deutero-Zechariah's cry, "Woe to my worthless shepherd who deserts the flock!" (Zech. 11:17), come to mind.[33] In contrast to their negligence, the ministry of Jesus to the poor of the land is dramatically depicted in pastoral language already familiar from the Synoptic Gospels. "I am the good shepherd who lays down his life for the sheep" (John 10:11).

It was at the mid-December festival of *Ḥannukah* that Jesus was accused of the religious crime of blasphemy and his life again placed in jeopardy by those who heard him teaching in the temple (John 10:22ff.). In reply Jesus invites them to let his work speak for itself; they might perceive that this is indeed God's work being accomplished in their midst. But they angrily seek his life and he is forced to leave the city, crossing the Jordan to Perean Bethany in the region where John had first begun to preach judgment and baptism to the nation.

---

33 Cf. also the polemic against the Maccabean priest-kings in *I Enoch* 89:59–90:38.

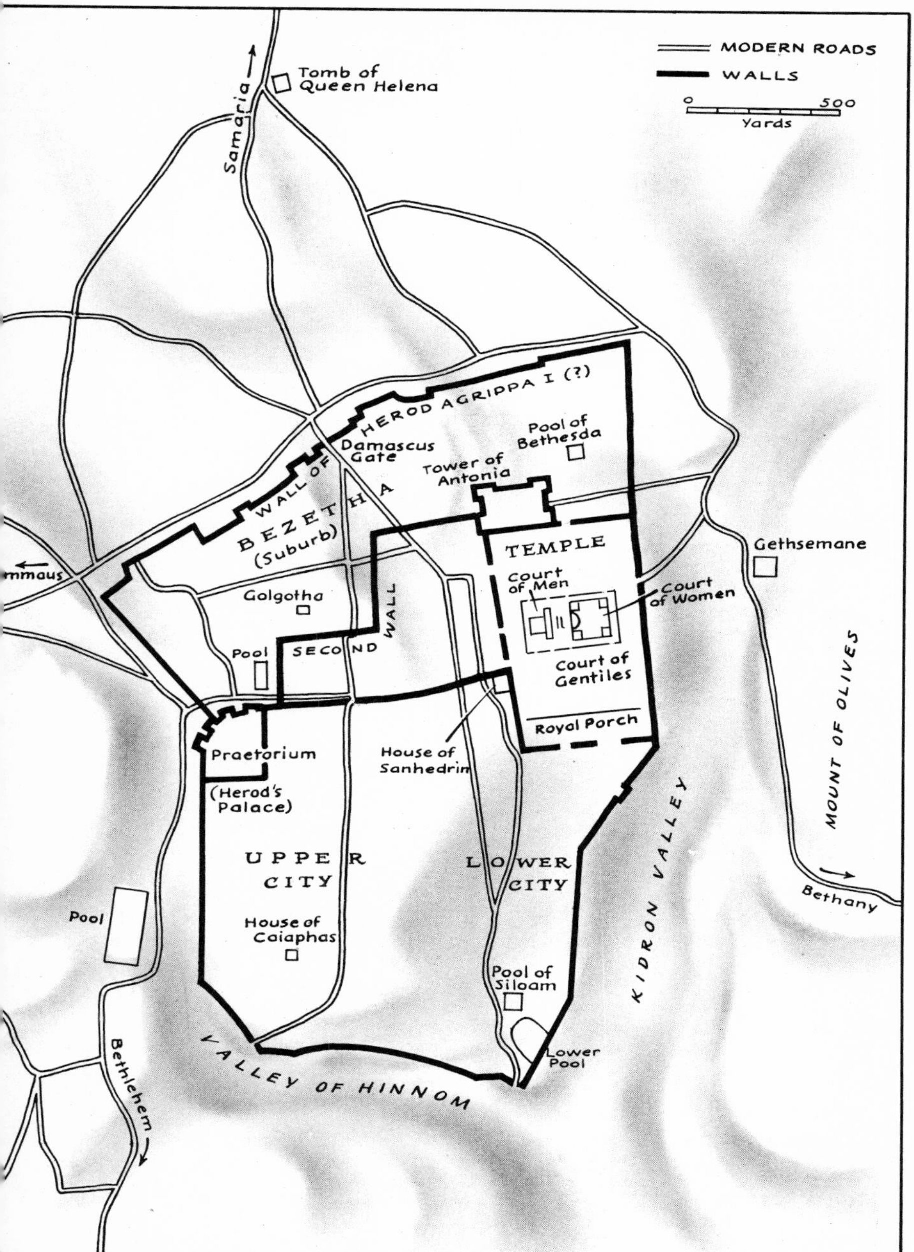

Fig. 10. Jerusalem in New Testament times.

Here he won the sympathetic response Jerusalem denied him (John 10:40–42).

Sometime during these months, according to John, a special session of the Sanhedrin was convened which sealed Jesus' fate (John 11:45–53). The council members fear that the people will be completely led astray and that the Roman military administration will not tolerate even a minor disturbance among the people without reprisals. With their verdict that Jesus must be destroyed and the movement promptly checked, Jesus goes into hiding in an obscure village on the northern border of Judea (John 11:54). He does not emerge again in public until the Passover season in March-April. John dates the official decision to cope with Jesus and his followers months earlier than the Synoptic writers. We have reason to doubt the precipitating cause which he recognizes. But there is a ring of reality behind the explanation that the authorities are distressed at the continuing popularity in which Jesus is held by many people and nervous over the prospect of a Roman intervention that may recoil upon the leaders themselves. We must return to this later for a full assessment.

Two Messianic Signs

The Approach to the City

All the Gospels agree that it was at the approach of the Passover season when Jesus and his friends joined a group of Jewish pilgrims walking to the holy city to celebrate the great freedom festival. To the hard-pressed peasantry, Passover and the exodus from Egypt had become a divine guarantee of the final and complete deliverance the God of Israel would effect for his people. It was the time within the whole year when nationalist feelings and hopes rose to feverish height. Some held that it would be during these days of grateful celebration of God's historic act of redemption that the Anointed One would suddenly appear. Mindful of the swollen population of Jerusalem and the ominous sounds of excitement and unrest, the authorities saw to it that the Roman garrison was always strengthened on these occasions. The Roman governor himself took up residence in the northwest quarter of the city in the splendid palace built by Herod the Great. During these preparatory days Jesus made ready to join the worshipping throngs that packed the city streets and taxed its limited hostel accomodations.

The Evangelists' reports of that approach and the turbulent series of incidents which ensued are heavily imprinted with their own realization that the fateful hour had arrived. In everything that occurs they recognize parallels to the words of prophet and psalmist that they believe to be predictive of the way of the Messiah. He is Isaiah's Prince of Peace, the blessed Son of David who comes in the name of the Lord, Zechariah's King who will establish the New Era of peace among the nations.[34] But he will not be received. He will be scorned by those he seeks to save, persecuted and reviled like the suffering son of God described in Israel's hymn book. Of him Isaiah had truly said, "He poured out his soul to death, and was numbered with the transgressors; yet he bore the sin of many and made intercession for the transgressors" (Isa. 53:12). Some of the passages of Scripture were already given messianic interpretations by the specialists who searched the holy books for signs of the Messiah's coming. Others were identified by the partisans of Jesus as they reviewed the whole succession of these final events from the vantage point of their Easter faith in him as the living Lord.

The principal access led through Jericho, a luxuriant oasis in the Judean desert some fifteen miles north-northeast of the mountain city and the site of a magnificent, recently excavated winter palace of Herod the Great.[35] On the outskirts of the city the pilgrim procession passed a blind man begging by the roadside, a common enough sight in the Near East. The interest of the Evangelists is not in his cure as such but rather in the maimed beggar's cry to Jesus for help. "Jesus, Son of David, have mercy upon me!" he wails (Mark 10:47 par.). It is no simple salutation and appeal. It is a messianic address, expressive of the fervent hopes for the Davidic Prince, but a title that Jesus elsewhere contends to be an inadequate designation for one destined to be the exalted Lord (Mark 12:35–37a par.). Mark undoubtedly tells the story of blind Bartimaeus at this point as a preparation for the acclamation of Jesus as the messianic Son of David by his companions as they enter the city of Jerusalem.

It may be about this time that another incident occurred, which, to the Gospel writers, was fraught with deep symbolic meaning in view of the ministry now rapidly approaching its climax. The relationship among the several recitals of how Jesus was once the recipient of a

---

[34] Isa. 9:6f.; Zech. 9:9f.

[35] See James L. Kelso, "New Testament Jericho," *The Biblical Archaeologist*, XIV (1951), 34–43; *ibid.*, XVI (1953), 14.

woman's grateful devotion as she anointed him with an expensive oil of nard is exceedingly difficult to determine.[36] To Mark, followed by Matthew, the scene took place in the Bethany home of a leper named Simon (Mark 14:3). John, however, sets the story in the house of Jesus' friends, Mary, Martha, and their brother Lazarus, and identifies the unnamed woman of Mark's episode as Mary herself (John 12:1ff.). In the Gospel tradition the simple act of grateful devotion was seen as prophetic of the death Jesus was to die. "She has done what she could," is Jesus' reply to the protest and charge of shameful extravagance, "She has anointed my body beforehand for burying" (Mark 14:8b).[37]

The Entry

Two decisive events mark the arrival of Jesus and his disciples in Jerusalem for the last time: the ovation that marked his entry and the collision with the temple authorities that followed. From the standpoint of those responsible for peace and order within the city both were inflammatory acts calculated to set off public demonstrations of a seditious sort. The timing was clearly Jesus' own. He had deliberately chosen this great Jewish festival to make his last appeal to the nation. The baleful word of holy wrath upon a covenant-flaunting people and the blessed word of forgiveness freely offered the penitent had to be spoken.

From Jericho the road ran through the village of Bethany, two and a half miles from Jerusalem, and the cross-roads hamlet called the House of Figs, or Bethphage. Mounting the eastern slope of the Hill of the Olive Orchards, it came down the western side and across the Kidron watercourse to begin the ascent to the eastern gate of the city. A few days before the Day of Unleavened Bread, the first day of the week-long celebration, Jesus and his friends joined the crowds of pilgrims on their way from Jericho to Jerusalem.

A later Passover legend, depicted in medieval Jewish art, identifies the ass as a messianic symbol and represents the messiah on the beast of burden, led by the prophet Elijah. Recent excavations in Israel have unearthed such pictures on catacombs in Beth Shearim (Sheikh

---

36 Three forms of the story of the anointing survive: Mark 14:3–9 par.; Luke 7:36–50; and John 12:1–8; but the last appears to be a combination of the other two, and Luke may refer to a separate incident entirely. Later Church tradition identified the woman as Mary of Magdala who subsequently became Mary of Bethany, the disciple of Jesus.

37 The authenticity of 8b is debated; vs. 9 is generally recognized as secondary.

Fig. 11. The Palm Sunday Donkey by Richard Scheibe. Courtesy Foto Marburg.

Abreiq).[38] There is good reason to suppose that the prophetic picture, no doubt elaborated in the Gospel narrative, was deliberately staged by Jesus himself on this occasion to make renewed declaration of the messianic vocation of peace and humble service. Arrangements had

---

[38] Cf. Cecil Roth, "Messianic Symbols in Palestinian Archaeology," *Palestine Exploration Quarterly,* LXXXVII (1955), 151–64. The Midrash *Tanḥuma* on Gen. 22:6 explains the ass as a reference to the King-Messiah.

probably been previously made with the owner of a colt in Bethphage; and the two disciples were instructed to remind anyone who challenged them that they had proper permission.[39] Returning with the colt, they prepare for the last few miles of the trip still unaware of what Jesus has in mind.

When the holy city comes into sight as they pass the crest of the Mount of Olives, the tired but happy pilgrims give vent to their feelings in the familiar words of a Hallel hymn.

> I thank thee that thou hast answered me
>   and hast become my salvation.
> The stone which the builders rejected
>   has become the chief cornerstone.
> This is the Lord's doing;
>   it is marvelous in our eyes.
> This is the day which the Lord has made;
>   let us rejoice and be glad in it.
> Save us [*Hoshianna*], we beseech thee, O Lord!
>   O Lord, we beseech thee, give us success!
> [Psalm 118:21–25]

It was a *Sukkoth* psalm principally, but known to have been used in the liturgies of the feasts of Dedication in the winter and Passover in springtime.[40] Originally it was a cry of glad thanksgiving for God's blessings upon this covenant people who were to become the keystone of the temple he was to build in the world. It was an invocation, too, for the heavenly help which alone could bring complete and final deliverance from their foes. *Hoshianna,* Save us! With that cry, the *lulabs* or bundles of palm, myrtle, and willow branches, symbols of salvation,[41] were waved, and the whole procession moved toward the temple mount. From within the temple precincts the priests hailed the approaching worshippers, "Blessed is he who enters in the name of the Lord! We bless you from the house of the Lord."

Christian tradition through the centuries, taking its clue from the Evangelists, has portrayed the historic event of the entry as an enthusiastic, messianic ovation. There is little doubt that the writers of the gospel history believed that Jesus rode the crest of popular

---

39 Matthew, with an impossibly literalistic reading of prophecies of Gen. 49:8–11 and Zech. 9:9, mentions *two* animals, an ass and her foal, on which Jesus rides into the city!

40 II Macc. 10:6f.; *Jub.* 16:20–31; Jos., *Antiq.* III.10.4, XIII.13.5; *Sukkah* 3.9; and cf. the seizure of the Acra by Simon Maccabeus in 142 B.C. (I Macc. 13:51).

41 Cf. the heavenly acclamation in Rev. 7:9f.

acclaim as the messianic king for one brief moment until the wave broke and subsided, leaving him spent and alone.[42] But this interpretation probably owes more to the universal hunger for a messianic sign than it does to the facts. An earlier stratum of the tradition, gleaming here and there within the canonical rewriting, suggests that it is far from certain that this was a messianic entry except for the small circle of those accompanying the Galilean leader. To onlookers who inquired with curiosity what the shouting was all about, the crowd responds (according to an editorial note of Matthew's), "This is *the prophet Jesus* from Nazareth of Galilee" (Matt. 21:11). Nor does the alleged acclamation lead to anything once the procession disbands. There is no need for the intervention of city or imperial police. Luke understands the Jerusalem Pharisees to reproach the enthusiasm of Jesus' own disciples rather than the throng (Luke 19:39). In all likelihood those who joyfully recited the familiar Hallel strophes were shouting the praises of Israel for God's historic and anticipated deliverance of his people. Soon, perhaps even in this very Passover festival, God would fulfil his promise to send his sore bestead people their Davidic Prince and restore their rightful heritage to them.

It may be, however, that his own close friends discerned a deeper meaning in the familiar chant of the people and the quiet solemnity of their leader. Was the day of salvation dawning at long last? Did they wave their *lulabs* and cry their Hosannas in jubilant praise of him who rode beside them with never a sign of approval or disapproval? We do not know. Still, it must remain uncertain whether his own disciples related these acclamations to Jesus. It is more likely that the entry into the city had messianic meaning only for the Galilean who sat astride the little donkey. As for the rest, disciples and pilgrim host, the chants were for the opening of the paschal festival, couched in the time-honored language of the Hallel.

When all necessary allowance has been made for the adaptation of the circumstances to the details of the prophecy of Zechariah 9:9, it is best to see the solemn entry as a historical occurrence deliberately contrived by Jesus with the messianic prediction of the prophet in mind. The king who comes is not the imperious war lord but the humble peacemaker. W. Grundmann and E. Lohmeyer have called attention to an early Talmudic tradition, ascribed to Rabbi Joshua ben Levi (ca. A.D. 250), which reads: "Behold the Son of Man comes

---

42 Note the way Matthew and Luke make Mark's understanding more explicit by converting his benediction on the messianic kingdom into a blessing upon Jesus as the messianic king (Matt. 21:9; Luke 19:38; Mark 11:9).

on the clouds of Heaven, and poor and riding upon an ass. If they [Israel] are worthy of him, he will come on the clouds of Heaven; if they are not worthy, he will come as a poor man riding upon an ass" (B. *Sanh.* 98a).[43] "Israel is unworthy; he comes humbly as the king of poverty; he comes as the king of peace and not of strife; of salvation and not of judgment."[44]

The Judgment on the Temple

It was on the next day, as Mark reports, that the second messianic sign occurred.[45] Three weeks before the beginning of Passover the annual temple tax paid by every male Jew was due. For the convenience of the pilgrim, money-changers were authorized by the temple authorities to set up benches in the Court of the Gentiles. There the hateful Roman tetradrachmae and denarii could be exchanged for Tyrian shekels that bore no evidence of Caesar's claims. Other merchants offered for sale the traditional poor man's sacrifice, the pigeon (Lev. 12:8), and the ceremonial wine, oil, and salt. In itself this was a convenience appreciated by the traveler who had journeyed many miles to join his fellow worshippers in the house of prayer. But the bitter jibes against the hierarchy in the popular literature of the time reveal that abuses of several sorts had crept in, resulting in a spoils system of private benefit to the chief priests and the high priest. We may recall the secession of the Zadokite priests to form a priestly commuinty in exile at Qumran and their boycott of the regular temple services for fear of contaminating their own offerings.[46]

---

43 Also J. *Taanit* 63 d; *Berak.* 56b; Walter Grundmann, *Die Geschichte Jesu Christi* (Berlin: Evangelische Verlaganstalt, 1961), pp. 300–301. G. F. Moore holds that both Dan. 7 and Zech. 9 were interpreted messianically in first-century Judaism (*Judaism,* II [Cambridge, Mass.: Harvard University Press, 1944], 337).

44 Grundmann, *Die Geschichte Jesu Christi,* p. 301.

45 John's Gospel, for theological reasons, locates the episode of the judgment upon the temple at the outset of Jesus' ministry (John 2:13–22). Goguel, following the Johannine chronology, has conjectured that a strong prophetic indictment after the fashion of John 2:19 was made by Jesus at the time of the winter festival of Dedication and was the reason why he was forced to leave the city for Perea (*Life of Jesus,* pp. 418–25). He regards the incident itself as a legendary embellishment of this protest against the profanation of the temple. Some assign the story to the Sukkoth festival, e.g., T. W. Manson, "The Cleansing of the Temple," *Bulletin of the John Rylands Library,* XXXIII (1951), 271–82.

46 It remains a debatable point whether the men of Qumran abstained completely from the temple worship, offering their own sacrifices at Qumran, or, as some think, conducting private ceremonies at the Jerusalem temple (so Matthew Black, *The Scrolls and Christian Origins* [New York: Charles Scribner's Sons, 1961], p. 40).

Jewish literature of the period frequently excoriates the corruption and malfeasance of the Sadducean priesthood and hails the day of the messiah who will purge the cultus. A Talmudic saying bitterly upbraids the avarice and cruelty of the rival houses of high priests: "They are high priests, and their sons are treasurers, and their sons-in-law are superintendents, and their servants beat the people with sticks" (*Pesaḥim*, 57a).[47]

Amidst the stifling confusion, the sweat and smells of a court that had become a bazaar and traffic corridor, Jesus begins to cry down the judgment of God.[48] His words recall the impassioned invective of the prophet Jeremiah centuries earlier as he was stirred to shrill at the worshippers: "Has this house, which is called by my name, become a den of robbers in your eyes? Behold I myself have seen it, says the Lord" (Jer. 7:11). With the prophets Jesus shared the conviction that the glory of God had long since departed from this house and left it forsaken and desolate, a vacant dwelling place.

But even more significant is Jesus' reference to the words of Trito-Isaiah as that prophet heralded the establishment of the temple of the New Age that would be the gathering place of peoples from all over the earth:

> These I will bring to my holy mountain,
> and make them joyful in my house of prayer;
> Their burnt offerings and their sacrifices
> will be accepted on my altar;
> for my house shall be called a house of prayer
> for all peoples.
>
> [Isa. 56:7]

A persistent strain of Jewish apocalyptic thought looked to the day when the worship of the Jewish temple would be perfected. The temple would become a center of prayer and praise for Jews and Gentiles everywhere, and the God of Israel would be acclaimed the true and sole Lord of the nations of mankind.[49] Jesus seems to have

---

47 On criticism of the temple officials, see Chap. II note 28. On the profanation of the temple, see *Asmp. Moses* 5, 7:3–10; *Test. Levi* 14–16; *Pss. Sol.* 4, 8:12f.; 1QpHab viii.8–13, ix.4–7, xi.4–8, xii.7–9; CD iv.18, v.6f., xii.1f., xx.22–24. See I. Abrahams, *Studies in Pharisaism and the Gospels,* Second Series (Cambridge: Cambridge University Press, 1924), I, 82–89.

48 Jer. 12:7; Ezek. 10:18f., 11:22f.; cf. Jos., *War* VI.5.3; Q Luke 13:35.

49 Cf. also Pss. 22:28, 96:7f.; Ezek. 40–48; Mal. 3:1–3; *Test. Benj.* 9:2; Tobit 13:10, 13, 16; IV Ezra 9:38–10:27; *I Enoch* 10:21, 48:5, 89:73f., 90:28f.; *Pss. Sol.* 17:30f.; *Targum* on Isa. 53:5; 1QS ix.6. It is interesting to note that the early Church imagery of the faithful community as a spiritual house is also found as a self-designation in the brotherhood of Qumran (1QS v.6, viii.8, ix.6).

identified himself with this universalist position, declaring that the old order would terminate with the destruction of the present temple.[50] This would give way to the New Order, symbolized as a world sanctuary constituted by true worshippers who would offer spiritual sacrifices to the Most High.

Thus the episode in the temple is far more than an act of reforming zeal or spirited protest against the flagrant injustice and abuse of a center of sacrificial worship. John's Gospel makes this most pointed by correlating the action of Jesus on this occasion with a prediction of the destruction of the temple and the building of the spiritual temple of true believers (John 2:19). The hope of any national repentance has been surrendered. Jerusalem refuses to acknowledge her opposition to the ways of God. Proud and secure in the confidence that she enjoys special favor of God as his elect people, she will not confess her guilt nor submit to that radical turning which could bring salvation. In consequence, therefore, the people must bear the dreaded word of excommunication. "I will have nothing to do with you" (Q Matt. 25:12).

But the consternation and wrath of the city's leaders are aroused by something more than this symbolic act of judgment on the temple. Prophets before and after Jesus upbraided the people for the national wickedness and cultic arrogance that mocked God's will. The final scandal was occasioned by the insinuation that Jesus himself in some authoritative way would be involved in the destruction of this present order and the coming of God's Kingdom. To the officials it seemed that he claimed to be the messianic priest and king who would be the builder of the New Temple. That Jesus was not arrested on the spot by the temple police for this provocative act is probably to be explained by the presence of Galileans among the worshippers and the popular sympathy for this fearless denunciation of a corrupt and illegitimate priesthood.

If this is the true meaning of the cleansing of the temple, it is with ample reason that Mark and Luke represent it as the turning-point in the story of the Jerusalem ministry, precipitating the collusion of the Torah and temple leaders against Jesus. The climax of the whole mission has arrived, and it will be marked by violence and submission, by war and peace, by death and resurrection. "Something greater than the temple is here" (Matt. 12:6).

---

50 On the destruction of the temple see also Mark 13:1f., 14:58, 15:29f.; John 2:19; Acts 7:48–50.

CHAPTER XI

THE FACE OF DEATH

And so for this in early spring
My friends and I together meet,
And our evenings are departings,
And all our parties testaments,
That a hidden stream of suffering
May warm the coldness of existence.*

In order to mount to the Cross, the summit of sacrifice, and to God, the summit of immateriality, Christ passed through all the stages which the man who struggles passes through. That is why his suffering is so familiar to us; that is why we share it, and why his final victory seems to us so much our own future victory.†

The Passion Narratives

Our study of the earliest forms of the tradition of Jesus' sayings and career led us to conclude that from a very early time the story of the last hours of his life was told as a coherent whole in a consecutive order of events. At the very heart of the early Christian preaching was the declaration and brief description of his death, interpreted as an expia-

* Boris Pasternak, "The Earth," *In the Interlude: Poems, 1945–60* (London: Oxford University Press, Amen House, 1962), p. 83.

† Nikos Katzantzakis, *The Last Temptation of Christ,* trans. P. A. Bien (New York: Simon & Schuster, Inc., 1960), p. 2.

tory sacrifice for the redemption of Israel. A more detailed account of the circumstances and the meaning of his death undoubtedly was recited to the new members of the community in answer to their questions about how and why he had met his end. The simple kerygmatic formula, "He died for our sins according to the Scriptures," was thus expanded into a brief descriptive account of his arrest, trial, and death. How did the authorities arrest him without raising a public tumult? How did he face his accusers? Who was really responsible for his death? How could God's Messiah be subject to the scheming of wicked men? To whom did the risen Lord first make himself known? Why do the Jewish people refuse to recognize that Jesus is the messianic deliverer? Such questions reflected existential rather than biographical interests. They were the substance of pagan objections to the Galilean faith as well as of Christian perplexity about the demands of discipleship.

In Matthew's retelling of the Marcan report we may see how the interests of the growing Church have led to the inclusion of additional material, some of it in the form of legendary embellishments such as the story of Pilate's wife or the resurrection of some pious persons in the hour of Jesus' demise or the posting of the Roman guard at the sepulchre. Out of such pious imaginings the Passion Gospels of the apocryphal Christian literature were to spring and flourish.

Each of the Gospels discloses the influence of Old Testament passages in the description and interpretation of details in the story. A comparison of the betrayal of Judas with the allegory of the false shepherds in Zechariah 11 will make this clear. Similarly Psalms 22, 41, and 68 have undoubtedly shaped the form of the story of the crucifixion. In part these Old Testament passages were recalled because of their correspondence with particular details of the actual event. In part, especially in the developed tradition, they were drawn upon to enrich the memories of that final hour out of the conviction that they were divinely inspired previews of what finally came to pass in the death of Jesus.

Behind even Mark's narrative of the Passion (14–15) it is likely that a pre-Marcan report may be found that has undergone revision and expansion, though estimates vary about the original form.[1] When

[1] According to F. C. Grant, it may have consisted of the episodes of the conspiracy, betrayal, Last Supper, arrest, verdicts of the Great Sanhedrin and Pilate, procession to Golgotha, crucifixion, and death of Jesus. This nucleus was expanded by Mark with other groups of stories. See Frederick C. Grant,

we compare the canonical forms of the story, it appears that we may distinguish three: Mark-Matthew, Luke, and John. Obviously all are rooted in a common tradition, but Luke and John differ in so many respects from the Marcan account, to which Matthew loyally adheres, that we may conclude additional, independent sources of varying worth are available to them.[2]

The Conspiracy of Judas and the Hierarchy

It is probable that Jesus was arrested within a day or two after his last arrival in Jerusalem.[3] The provocative act in the temple court could not be ignored. Such an insult against the custodians of God's dwelling place could not go unanswered. The Synoptic writers believe that this event precipitated a plot to bring the offender to book.[4] The reason for the secrecy involved in arresting Jesus would be evident to anyone who knew of the risks of a public uprising at festival time among the holiday-making, Roman-hating crowds that jostled in the city's streets and squeezed into every public house and courtyard. Mark represents the situation accurately when he writes, "The chief priests and the scribes were seeking how to arrest him by stealth, and kill him; for they said, "Not during the feast, lest there be a tumult of the people" (14:2).

John believes that the leaders were prompted to act in concern for their prestige and in fear of Roman reprisals if they failed to take

---

The Gospels: Their Origin and Their Growth (New York: Harper & Row, Publishers, 1957), p. 79. Bultmann's more drastic analysis recognizes the oldest account in a short narrative of the arrest, the condemnation by the Sanhedrin and Pilate, the journey to the cross, the crucifixion and death (*History of the Synoptic Tradition,* trans. John Marsh [New York: Harper & Row, Publishers, 1963], p. 279). Taylor identifies an old Roman form of the Passion Story in Mark 14:1f., 10f., 17–21, 26–31, 43–46, 53a; 15:1, 3–5, 15, 21–24, 26, 29f., 34–37, 39, 42–46 (*The Gospel According to St. Mark* [London: Macmillan & Co., Ltd., 1953], pp. 660–62.).

2 Cf. Alfred Morris Perry, *The Sources of Luke's Passion-Narrative* (Chicago: University of Chicago Press, 1920); N. A. Dahl, "Die Passionsgeschichte bei Matthäus," *New Testament Studies,* II (1955) 17–32; P. Borgen, "John and the Synoptics in the Passion Narrative," *New Testament Studies,* V (1959), 246–59.

3 Maurice Goguel, *Life of Jesus,* trans. Olive Wyon (New York: The Macmillan Company, 1949), p. 424; Günther Bornkamm, *Jesus of Nazareth,* trans. Irene and Fraser McLuskey with James M. Robinson (London: Hodder and Stoughton, 1960), p. 159.

4 Matthew changes this unofficial arrangement of a group of senators in the Sanhedrin into a formal decree of the whole court (26:3–5).

action against the Galilean trouble-maker (John 11:47ff.). More plausibly than Mark, he sets the decision to arrest and execute Jesus some time before the beginning of the Passover and before his arrival in the city. In the discussion that ensued, it was the crafty president of the Court, Joseph Caiaphas (A.D. 18–36) who convinced the neutrals that immediate action was imperative. Their problem was how to bring Jesus into custody without risking a demonstration by the Galilean supporters and Jerusalem sympathizers. They needed to seize him when he was alone and hurry him to his execution before any public notice could be taken and before the sunset hour which marked the beginning of the Octave of the feast of Passover. Otherwise they must wait until the feast was concluded.

The Role of Judas

Speculations have been offered freely and frequently to explain what impelled Judas Iscariot to supply the authorities with the information they needed. Apart from the legendary insinuation of John that Judas was a money grubber and embezzler (12:6), the tradition itself furnishes no clue. But in view of the expectation on the part of his followers that Jesus would accept the role of the Davidic national deliverer, it is possible that Judas found his hopes undergoing attrition by the puzzling refusal of Jesus to fulfill that part. Judas' last hope vanished as the program in Jerusalem, which might have opened the holy messianic war, repeated the familiar pattern of collision with the interpreters of the Torah, a fickle popular enthusiasm, and the stubborn rejection of the messianic task. Jesus was clearly not the one who was to come. Judas had hoped in vain. This interpretation would be given further support if, as some believe, Judas' surname is actually a party label, associating him with a radical group of freedom fighters. In bitter disappointment he made ready to renounce his allegiance to this false prophet. In order to safeguard the gullible peasantry from any further deception, he decided to deliver the imposter into the hands of the city's officers. Alternatively, it has been conjectured that the conspiracy was entered into in the last desperate hope that the hand of this reluctant Messiah might be forced so that he would have to assume the responsibilities assigned to him by providence.

In any case the early Church knew that it was Simon's son, Judas, who agreed to betray Jesus to the authorities. With his characteristic concern for Scripture fulfillment, Matthew draws the action into correspondence with the story of the disillusioned shepherd-ruler of Zechariah 11:4ff. who sold out his people Israel to their enemies for thirty silver shekels. The secret information Judas confided to the chief priests is not defined in the Gospels. In all likelihood it was an agreement that Judas would lead a posse to the place where Jesus repaired regularly after nightfall just outside the city. If Jesus could be brought into custody under the cover of darkness and separated from the Galilean pilgrims who were often with him in the city, he could be quickly brought to justice without exciting general notice. This Judas consented to do.[5]

The Last Supper

Convinced that the end was very near, Jesus prepared to share an evening meal with a group of his disciples. This supper in Jerusalem carried the same eschatological reference as the supper by the Sea of Gennesareth. Now, however, the Kingdom of God was drawn unmistakably into relationship with the death of the host who reclined in their midst and assumed the role of the house-father, as he had done on the many occasions in which they had broken bread together. On later reflection, after the horror of these next eventful hours was a thing of the past, those who shared the meal with him became convinced that he meant to interpret to them the meaning of his whole ministry among them. They believed that through this tragic end he had re-established the covenantal relationship with the *Abba*-God broken by man's infidelity and disobedience. The supper was a prophecy of denial, of death, of glorious vindication and triumph, placed by the Synoptic writers in the setting of the paschal feast. But it was not until the Easter experience that the full significance of what transpired dawned upon the disciples.

The Earliest Account

Certain troublesome but subordinate questions about the narrative must first be faced. To begin with, we ought to recognize that we are dealing with at least three separate accounts of the Supper, that of Mark (14:17–25), followed in the main by Matthew (26:20–29); of Luke, who has introduced several special items (22:14–38); and

---

5 Two different legends are preserved about the result of Judas' treachery: Matt. 27:3–10 (influenced by Zech. 11:17; Jer. 18:1ff., 32:6–9), and Acts 1:16–20.

of Paul (I Cor. 11:23–26). The Fourth Gospel assumes, but does not describe, the sharing of the bread and the wine, substituting for these details a special report of an act of humility and service on the part of Jesus as he washed the feet of his disciples during the meal (13:1–11).

Strong and learned defenses for the priority of each of the three accounts have been made.[6] In the discussion which follows it will be seen that we have depended upon Mark for the form of the bread parable and have turned to Paul for the text of the wine parable. In all, there are three sayings of critical importance, spoken, as the several traditions agree, at the time of this last meal: (1) an explanatory statement following the blessing and breaking of the bread, (2) an interpretive saying following the traditional benediction over the cup, and (3) a prophetic word about the coming Kingdom of God.

The Problem of the Date

Another nettlesome, and probably insoluble, problem centers on the date of the meal (and hence of the execution of Jesus). There can be no gainsaying the divergence within the tradition at this point. No dogmatic principle, wishful thought, nor adroit manipulation of the records can obscure the disagreement between the Synoptists and the writer of the Fourth Gospel about whether the Jerusalem meal was an official Passover or a pre-Passover celebration. According to one source drawn upon by the primary Synoptist, Jesus made deliberate preparations for a celebration of the Seder supper that he ate with his disciples in the privacy of an unidentified house within the city (Mark 14:12–16). This would be on Nisan 15, by Jewish reckoning, marked by the appearance of the first evening star on the day the Roman time scale would denote as the fourteenth. If this is correct—and it is to be noted that this is the only section which specifies that the meal was a Passover—then Jesus was arrested, tried, condemned, and executed on the first and principal day of the week-long festival. Although this is not impossible according to some later rabbinical notices, it would certainly be an extraordinary procedure. The opening day of the Passover feast, the Day of Unleavened Bread, was always

[6] For summaries of the leading arguments as well as the defense of individual positions, see Joachim Jeremias, *The Eucharistic Words of Jesus,* trans. Arnold Ehrhardt (New York: The Macmillan Company, 1955); Angus J. B. Higgins, *The Lord's Supper in the New Testament* (London: SCM Press, 1952); Reginald H. Fuller, *The Mission and Achievement of Jesus* (Naperville, Ill.: Alec R. Allenson, Inc., 1954), pp. 64–77.

regarded in Pharisaic Judaism as a strict Sabbath whether or not it actually fell on the Sabbath day. It would be profaned by any official business or work done on it. Accordingly, it is of no casual interest to notice the variant tradition preserved by John and verified indirectly by Paul and Talmudic tradition which predates these events by a full twenty-four hours.

All the Gospels are agreed that Jesus met his death on the afternoon of a Friday, the day of preparation for the holy Sabbath. However, John testifies that this was at the time that the Passover lambs were being slain in preparation for the Seder supper of the evening. In such a case, the meal Jesus shared with his disciples was a pre-Passover meal, on the evening of Nisan 14 by Jewish reckoning, or the night of the thirteenth by Roman calculation. Jesus was thus taken into custody and put out of the way just before the actual festival began. The problem is not simply chronological. It has bearing upon the meaning that is to be attached to this symbolic meal and its larger theological implications.

In a brilliant essay, Mlle. A. Jaubert has recently proposed that Jesus and his disciples ate the Passover meal on Tuesday evening, following an old solar calendar observed by the Essenes of Qumran and perhaps still widely used outside the official Pharisaic circles in Jerusalem. Such a theory would reconcile the paschal features of the Supper in the Synoptics with the chronology of John, but it opens up new problems about the dating of the succeeding events of the trial and execution.[7]

A more promising parallel may be found in the daily cult meal shared by the members of the Council of the community in Qumran. The regimen included the traditional cultic offerings of bread and sweet wine which were blessed in the name of the God of Israel and distributed among the participants.[8] A careful study of the two principal Qumran texts along with the references in Josephus' writings and in some fragmentary texts suggests that the sacred meal had a two-fold significance to these desert ascetics. On the one hand, as the Qumran priests shared the loaf representing the sacred bread of the

---

7 Annie Jaubert, *La Date de la Cène* (Paris: J. Gabalda, 1957), supported by Matthew Black, *The Scrolls and Christian Origins* (New York: Charles Scribner's Sons, 1961), pp. 199–201, and critically evaluated by J. Obermann, "Calendric Elements in the Dead Sea Scrolls," *Journal of Biblical Literature,* LXXV (1956), 285ff.; and J. T. Milik, *Ten Years of Discovery in the Wilderness of Judea* (Naperville, Ill.: Alec R. Allenson, Inc., 1959), pp. 107–12.

8 Jos., *Antiq.* XVIII.1.22; *War* II.8.5; 1QS vi.2–8; 1QSa ii.11–22.

Presence in the temple, the historic deliverance of Israel in the exodus was recalled. Furthermore, the cultic meal had a festal, messianic meaning, anticipating the glorious banquet that the Davidic Prince would hold in the restored temple of the New Jerusalem.

In view of all these complex considerations, it is best not to be limited strictly to the chronology of either the Synoptic Gospels or the Fourth Gospel. We may conclude that this last meeting of Jesus with his disciples took place at Passover time, without specifying the day.[9] Any Jewish meal eaten in the shadow of the approaching festival would naturally be influenced by the celebration of the historic act of Israel's deliverance from Egypt. This explains in part the paschal allusions in the Gospels. Beyond this, allowance must be made for the early understanding of Christ's death as a paschal sacrifice, expressed already by Paul and John, which led to the interpretation of the final meal itself as a Passover celebration. Behind it all, we may see the early Palestinian church striving to articulate in its daily common meals the momentous significance of the death Jesus died as the sacrificial offering whereby salvation was procured for sinful men.[10]

The Saying About the Two Swords

A strange and unparalleled saying of Jesus is found in Luke's Passion source. It is an enigmatic word of Jesus that might be presumed upon first inspection to mean that Jesus had made the march to Jerusalem in the expectation of rallying an army for the final holy war. "But now, let him who has a purse take it, and likewise a bag. And let him who has no sword sell his mantle and buy one" (22:36). At this point the disciples are said to brandish two swords they were carrying, perhaps as a protection against highwaymen, and Jesus replies cryptically, "It is enough." But a counsel of aggression would fly in the face of Jesus' consistent practice of nonviolent resistance. He rebuked the last, desperate show of resistance at the time of his arrest in the Oil-Press Garden on the Mount of Olives.

The most plausible interpretation is that which sees in his reply a word of grim irony at the fatuous proposal by these Galilean companions that they are a match for the hostility of the authorities.

---

9 Cf., e.g., Bornkamm, *Jesus of Nazareth,* p. 160; Théo Priess, "Was the Last Supper a Paschal Meal?" in his *Life in Christ,* trans. Harold Knight (London: SCM Press, 1954), pp. 81–99.

10 Note how Matthew transfers the kerygmatic phrase "for the forgiveness of sins" from an association with John's baptism, as Mark understands it, to the word spoken over the eucharistic cup (26:28).

When they had gone in pairs throughout the Galilean countryside preaching the good news of the Kingdom, had they lacked anything despite the fact that as God's *ḥasidim* they were like lambs among wolves? They had to admit that though they traveled as mendicants without extra food or change of clothing or protective staff against attack they still were unharmed. But times had changed! Did they suppose now that they could bribe or murder their oppressors? Their pitiful arsenal offered no guarantee, but its inadequacy was enough, for their trust must not be in Mammon or Mars, but rather in the Father into whose keeping they had entrusted themselves. Two swords indeed! Enough of such talk! What fortified them ought not to be any secret weapons but the assurance of the protecting love of God, even when they stared into the grinning countenance of death itself.

The Farewell Meal

Taking deliberate steps to ensure privacy and safety, Jesus had evidently made plans with a householder in Jerusalem for the use of a large guest room where he might meet together with his friends for an evening meal. So runs the legendary story of the preparation which exhibits some striking parallels to the account of the entry into the city.[11] Two of the disciples are to be escorted to the house by a water-carrier they meet outside the city gate. Whose house it was to which they were guided is unknown. A tradition that can be traced back at least to the sixth century identified it with the home of Mary, the mother of John Mark, which seems to have been a favorite meeting place of the Jerusalem society (Acts 12:12; cf. 1:13). But the tradition has no support from the New Testament. The Gospel writers apparently understand that only the twelve were present with Jesus on this occasion. However, the mention of an unidentified young man who fled from Gethsemane before the arresting officers (Mark 14:51f.) and the incident of a certain Cleopas and a companion who recognized the risen Lord in Emmaus (Luke 24:13–35) permit the possibility that other disciples of Jesus were also present.

Whatever influence early eucharistic liturgies may have had upon the accounts of the Supper, we have sufficient reason to believe that in the course of the simple meal Jesus made use of common bread and wine as parabolic symbols. Through them he reaffirmed his faith in the certainty of the Father's rule and promised his companions a share in the redemptive significance of his approaching death. Under-

---

[11] Cf. Mark 14:12–16 with 11:1–6.

lying the present liturgical formulation of Jesus' words are two parables and a Kingdom saying, which interpret his death as the suffering Servant who is destined to be the Son of Man in the coming Kingdom.

The Parable of the Bread

As they sat together at the common table, Jesus, as the priest-father of the little family, took the loaf and pronounced the prayer. "Blessed art thou, O Lord our God, King of the Universe, who bringeth forth bread from the earth." Then he broke and distributed it. It was the traditional *berakah* or prayer of blessing through which the devout Jew gave thanks to God daily for the food which nourished his life. But as he distributed the fracted pieces Jesus made a brief explanation that was no part of Jewish practice, "Take; this is my body."[12] It is by no means easy to determine what the original Aramaic form, and hence the meaning, actually was. But it seems most likely that his words meant, "This is [signifies] I, my very self."[13] But in what sense are they thus invited to share in the reality incarnate in him? Usually the words are construed in relationship to the approaching death whose sombre prospect weighs heavily upon him. Just as the worshipper and priest shared in the significance of the sacrifices offered in the temple by eating a portion of the food, so these who had kept Jesus faithful company are invited to participate in advance in the atoning power of his sacrifice. They, too, will eat with him the bread of affliction. They, too, will take up their cross in bold discipleship. But the way of dying to this world is the way of living into God's Kingdom. Receiving the bread, they are promised the benefits of the vicarious atonement that his death will effect.

Walter Grundmann has proposed another interpretation of this saying which throws the emphasis not upon the fact of the broken bread, hence the death, but rather upon the bread itself as a parabolic interpretation of Jesus' whole mission. With rich insight he proposes that the words of the Fourth Gospel, "I am the bread of life" (John 6:35, *et passim*), offer a commentary upon this saying in the upper room. This has been the meaning of Jesus' mission: to bring to men the nourishment of God's own life which can cleanse and rejuvenate their lives. The two Sabbath loaves symbolized for the Jew the manna

---

12 Accepting the form in Mark 14:22 as the oldest.

13 In Aramaic, *dēn ha gūphī,* a circumlocution for the first personal pronoun.

which miraculously saved the lives of the fathers in the wilderness.[14] Just so, Jesus is God's manna, bread from Heaven, which feeds the hungry souls of men unto everlasting life.[15] To accept from his hands this earthly bread is symbolically to receive that living bread which is the staple of the messianic meal and thus to be identified with his whole ministry among men.

The Parable of the Wine

The parabolic act and interpretive word spoken about the bread in the farewell supper is followed by a similar act with the wine after the meal had been eaten. The disciples heard first the solemn and familiar words of the wine *berakah*. "Blessed art thou, O Lord our God, King of the Universe, who createst the fruit of the vine." But now as the cup circulated about the table, Jesus spoke again in a laconic language that puzzled them. Paul has perhaps preserved the oldest form of the cup-saying: "This cup is the new covenant in my blood" (I Cor. 11:25a),[16] although this has already been expanded to include the command to repeat this rite regularly. Since for Paul a representative significance is already attached to the bread-saying ("for you"), we may conjecture that an earlier form ran, "Take, this cup is the new covenant in my blood which is shed for many." The "cup of blessing" which the disciples are invited to share is a representation of the eschatological covenant that marks God's New Order now made possible through Jesus' death.[17]

In the Old Testament the cup is a symbol of both the divine judgment and salvation.[18] The purgative act of judgment is only the negative aspect of God's final act of redemption. There is a positive side, too. The cup is at once a cup of wrath and a cup of consolation

---

14 B. *Shab.* 117b; B. *Berak.* 39b.

15 The first-century Hellenistic Jewish story, *Joseph and Asenath,* speaks of the bread of the cult meal as the "bread of life" (8:5, 9; 15:5; 16:6; 19:5).

16 Cf. W. G. Kümmel, *Promise and Fulfilment,* trans. Dorothea M. Barton (Naperville, Ill.: Alec R. Allenson, Inc., 1957), p. 120, and the authorities he cites. Jeremias leads a large group of scholars who defend the Marcan form as the most primitive. Goguel argues for the "shorter" text of Luke (omitting 22:19b–20) which has only an eschatological reference. Others regard this latter saying as the only word, omitting both the bread and cup sayings.

17 The "many" of Mark 14:24, an allusion to Isa. 53:12, is to be understood in the inclusive sense of "all." Cf. I Tim. 2:6; Titus 2:14. At Qumran, *rabbim* had a more exclusive reference to the community.

18 Ps. 75:8; cf. 11:6; Jer. 25:15f.

and salvation; to the enemies of God a lethal poison, to his true sons a life-giving tonic. "I will lift up the cup of salvation and call upon the name of the Lord" (Ps. 116:13; cf. Jer. 16:7). On Jewish coins struck in the short-lived period of national independence under the Maccabees, the cup appeared as a symbol of the messianic salvation that would stabilize a hard-won peace.[19] Together with the palm branch and the menorah, the cup became a popular messianic symbol. Now this is precisely the referent of the word Jesus utters. To partake of this cup, then, is to participate in advance in that glad event when God's rule would be fully established among the nations and the earth would be fecund with blessedness and peace.

A second symbol in the cup-saying supports this interpretation. The emphasis of the Pauline formula clearly falls upon the word "covenant" rather than the word "blood." It is the cup of a covenant now to be sealed in Jesus' death. That promised covenant described by the prophets was believed to bring to fulfillment the several covenants God had concluded with the fathers, beginning with Noah and renewed with Abraham, Moses, and Phineas.[20] In the Qumran documents the specific term new covenant (*berîth ḥadasha*) is used several times;[21] in other instances it is called the covenant of mercy or the covenant of repentance.[22] Though the covenant was to be completed at the end of the present age, this apocalyptic community by the Dead Sea seems to have regarded itself as living under the prophetic ideal in advance, a community of the future actualized in the present.

No direct line is drawn between the new covenant and the Kingdom of God in the saying of Jesus, but there is at least one saying that points to such an association. Preserved in the special Lucan tradition it reads: "As my Father appointed [that is, established or founded, a term used to specify a covenantal agreement] a kingdom for me, so do I appoint for you that you may eat and drink at my table in my kingdom . . ." (22:29). Rudolph Otto believed that this was the original form of the cup-saying. R. Fuller sees in it the earliest form

---

19 C. Roth, "Messianic Symbols in Palestinian Archaeology," *Palestine Exploration Quarterly,* LXXXVII (1955), 151–64. See Figure 4.

20 Exod. 24:4–11; Jer. 31:31–34; Isa. 42:6, 49:8; Zech. 9:11.

21 CD vi.19, viii. 21, xix (i).33, xx(ii).12; 1QpHab ii.3. The institution of the new covenant is described in CD iii.12–iv.12; the oath of entry in xv.5–23; and the ceremony of entry in 1QS i.16–ii.18.

22 E.g., 1QS i.8; CD xix (i).1,16. They commonly refer to themselves as the congregation of the Covenant or the New Covenant.

of the covenant word which may have been part of an address Jesus made to his disciples before the meal began.[23] In such a case Jesus defines the content of the covenant that is to be ratified by his death. The new covenant into which they will enter is nothing other than the forthcoming Kingdom of God. It marks the consummation of the old covenant concluded with the fathers and the beginning of a new community securely bound to God.

The Saying of the Kingdom

The double sayings of the bread and the wine find further explanation in Jesus' word about the messianic banquet (Mark 14:25 par.). Introduced by the solemn formula, "Amen, I say to you," this eschatological saying predicts that he will no longer enjoy such a table-fellowship with his disciples after this meal. At the same time he expresses his confidence that there will be a reunion when the Kingdom of God has been established. This meal they share together is a prototype of that festive banquet where they will be the guests of the Father in his house, just as once Moses and the elders "beheld God, and ate and drank" (Exod. 24:11) or as Ezekiel pictured the messianic prince entering the New Temple "to eat bread before the Lord" (Ezek. 44:3). In this present moment, marked by Jesus' vivid sense that they were soon to be separated and scattered, his unshakable conviction found voice that in due season this too would give way to the deathless perfected society. The storm about to break over them could not destroy that.

Bread and wine—ancient cultic offerings once presented to Abraham by a priest of God Most High (Gen. 14:18)—are symbols too of the regular priestly meals in the temple and certainly the staples of the typical Jewish family meal. These simple commodities are used by Jesus to portray in retrospect his ministry among his people, to declare the atoning significance of his coming death, and finally, to give prospect to that future when all the scattered and harassed children of God would be brought together into the new community of the faithful. Remaining loyal to him in his life and being united in his death, the disciples are permitted to experience in prospect that redeemed existence which will characterize the new day.

---

23 Rudolf Otto, *The Kingdom of God and the Son of Man,* trans. Floyd V. Filson and Bertram Lee Woolf (Grand Rapids, Mich.: Zondervan Publishing House, 1938), p. 268; Fuller, *The Mission and Achievement of Jesus,* pp. 72–4.

The Arrest and Trial

Rising from the table after the singing of a psalm, Jesus and his companions threaded their way through the darkened streets of the city. Leaving by the eastern gate of the lower city, they crossed the Kidron valley and climbed the western slope of the Hill of the Olives. Here centuries earlier Ezekiel had seen his vision of the glory of the Lord retreating from the sanctuary demolished by the Babylonians. Here, the rabbis testified, would be the site of the resurrection of the dead and the glorious appearance of the Messiah to Israel. On the lower western slope was an orchard with an oil press called in Hebrew *Gat Shemanim,* Gethsemane in Grecianized spelling, that may have been a favorite place of retreat for Jesus and his disciples. The Gospel storytellers inform us that it was here that Jesus had a sorrowful premonition of the tragedy that would befall him on this particular night. Shortly afterwards, he was arrested.

On route, according to Mark, Jesus shared with his friends the disheartening realization that despite their protests of undying loyalty they would desert him in his extremity. In the tradition followed by Luke and John, the prophecy that they would forsake him, even deny him, occurs during the course of the supper and is focused on Peter.[24] It may be, of course, that we have here a backward projection of what actually happened at the time of the arrest, out of the conviction that Jesus must have forseen clearly the whole course of events that would carry him to his death. But it is reasonable to accept the predictions of a defection emerging from weeks of discussion with his disciples about the way God's salvation would come to Israel and the nations.

Peter would have none of this talk. "God forbid, Master! This shall never happen to you." But he stoutly swore his allegiance, come what would (John 6:66–69). His confidence that he would remain faithful when everyone else had panicked and deserted the Teacher may have prompted Jesus to warn him that he too would prove no match for this dark hour into which they were entering. Indeed, by the time that the Roman bugle call sounded the fourth watch in the city, shortly before daybreak, the burly Galilean fisherman would try to save his own skin by denying that he ever had anything to do with Jesus.[25] It must remain uncertain, however, whether the prediction

---

[24] Luke 22:31–34; John 13:33–38.

[25] A reference to the *gallicinium* signal announcing the beginning of the fourth watch, or three A.M.

that Peter will finally prove to be a strengthening influence among the brethren (Luke 22:31) is a genuine word of Jesus or an ascription by the early Church.[26]

The Battle Ground of Gethsemane

That there are difficulties in vouching for the accuracy of all the details in the prayer agony of Gethsemane is obvious enough. The records themselves indicate that Jesus withdrew some distance, presumably out of earshot, from the three who had gone with him and had fallen asleep promptly. But the candid portrayal of his struggle to accept the cup of affliction is evidence enough that we are in touch with a primitive tradition preserved in apostolic recollection. Mark's description is astonishingly frank: Jesus began to be terribly agitated and distressed (Mark 14:33).[27] Such an admission of Jesus' acute conflict and failure of heart before the prospect of death was not easy to come by in the circles of those who believed that he was the Son of God, the risen and reigning Lord. It may be on that account that John speaks only of the arrest in an unspecified garden beyond the Kidron valley (18:1ff.). A clue to John's knowledge of the tradition of Jesus' anguish in the face of death is found in a passage John assigns earlier in that last week. Jesus cries, "Now is my soul troubled. And what shall I say? 'Father, save me from this hour?' No, for this purpose I have come to this hour. Father, glorify thy name" (John 12:27f.). Still, here the anguished protest has given way to an assurance that his death marks the consummation of his mission from the Father.

These blunt acknowledgements give ample testimony to the integrity of the early Church in preserving the genuineness of Jesus' humanity in its portrayals of his earthly life. "One who does not understand that the whole power of the spirit is required for dying," observed Kierkegaard, "and that the hero always dies before he dies, that man will not get so very far with his conception of life."[28]

Mark 14:34 presents a problem to the translator and exegete. The

26 Cf. the rehabilitation of Peter and his pastoral leadership in the Church prefigured in the resurrection appearance found in the appendix to the Fourth Gospel (21:15–25).

27 Though Luke omits this phrase he adds a symbolic detail that describes the distress of Jesus in the garden with a realism which later copyists found offensive and suppressed (22:43f.). An early tradition is represented in Heb. 5:7f.

28 Søren Kierkegaard, *Fear and Trembling* (New York: Doubleday and Company, Inc., 1954), Prob. III, p. 126.

usual interpretation is repeated by the New English Bible, "My heart is ready to break with grief," a rendering slightly more restrained than the RSV, "My soul is very sorrowful, even to death." This would seem to be more consonant with the way that the Evangelist and the author of Hebrews portray Jesus' horror of death as a separation from God and a sentence of judgment upon human sins than an alternative view that understands Jesus to mean that he actually wished for death instantly to put an end to his soul's unutterable grief.[29]

"Abba, Father, all things are possible to thee; remove this cup from me." Prophets and psalmists had spoken with awe of the bowl of wrath the Lord God would pour out for all the wicked of the earth to drain. It was this cup of the divine judgment Jesus was to drink, the lot of all the wicked, God-defiant, self-possessed, and sinful men into whose pretensions and estrangement he had entered and taken upon himself. Could it be that in the loneliness of this latest hour the black night of the soul enveloped him again as he searched to know how *this* rejection and *this* death could be any worth? Satan was back on the scene!

"Not what I will, but what thou wilt." It was through such an outpouring of his life that the righteous Servant would "make many to be accounted righteous" (Isa. 53:11). In the mystery of God's providential activity the bowl of wrath might prove to be the cup of salvation (Ps. 116:13). It was an insight already hinted at in the theory of martyrdom entertained in Jewish theology of the time. In the death he is to die Jesus steps into the place of a sinful people to make intercession for them before the Father. His wrestling afresh with Satan led to the conclusion that he was not to die like some trapped animal but as a sacrifice to make reparation and reconciliation for his people.

The Arrest

As Jesus senses the commotion of the approaching band of police, he returns to his exhausted companions who have lapsed again into heavy sleep. There is some difficulty in understanding what is meant

---

29 Adopted by Lohmeyer and Klostermann and recently restated by J. Héring in *Neotestamentica et Patristica,* ed. W. C. van Unnik (Leiden: E. J. Brill, 1962), pp. 64–69. Héring also revives Loisy's conjecture that in the tradition beneath the Marcan form of verse 38 Jesus asked his disciples to watch and pray that he might not succumb to the temptation to avoid death on the cross.

by the words preserved in the Greek Gospels at this point. The reconstruction proposed by V. Taylor is suggestive.

> Still asleep? Still resting? The End is far away? The hour has struck! Behold, the Son of Man is being delivered into the hands of sinners. Arise, let us be going. Behold he who delivers me up is near.[30]

He turns to face the arresting officers.

The Synoptists suggest that Jesus was accosted by a hired mob hastily conscripted into service (Mark 14:43 par.), including, perhaps, some temple police (Luke 22:52). John's version identifies them as a cohort of Roman soldiers, perhaps the *Cohors Secunda Italica* that formed part of the Roman garrison in Judea. They are evidently acting on orders from the procurator, Pontius Pilate (John 18:3; cf. 18:12).[31] For reasons that will become apparent as we continue, it is likely that the High Court of Justice had ordered the Jewish police to assist a detachment of imperial forces in rounding up the Galilean and his associates to bring them in for investigation preparatory to a Roman judicial verdict.[32]

What we are meant to conclude from the brief details of the seizure is that the associates of Jesus made some show of resistance, probably more in self-defense than in any loyal protection of their leader. But with the odds overwhelmingly against them, everyone of them fled in terror from the scene. To this straightforward note, Mark has added some stray traditions. Jesus, left alone, faced the posse with a taunt that they had come out after him as if he were a political insurgent who carried on his seditious work in an underground movement.

> Have you come out as against a robber [or rebel leader], with swords and clubs to capture me? Day after day [or in broad daylight] I was with you in the temple teaching, and you did not seize me. But let the scriptures be fulfilled [Mark 14:48f.].

---

30 Taylor, *The Gospel According to St. Mark,* p. 557, who takes the opening words as a question and follows the longer text of Codex Bezae. Perhaps the saying originally ended with the words, "The hour has come."

31 A cohort normally included about six hundred soldiers, far more than this circumstance required. John may be guilty of exaggeration or free imagination. On the other hand *speira* was sometimes used of a maniple consisting of two hundred men.

32 If we are to imagine that the crowd was a hired mob, it is still likely that they were led by the temple police. I acknowledge my obligation in this section to some of the views expressed in a brilliant study by the Jewish scholar Paul Winter, *On the Trial of Jesus* (Berlin: Walter de Gruyter & Co., 1961).

Without further protest he submitted to the curt command of the arresting officer and commenced the march from the olive orchard to the home of the high priest in the southwest section of the city.

The Tradition of the Trial

The accounts of the hearings and trials that follow bristle with difficulties for the historian as he attempts a collation of the Gospel records in the light of what is known about Jewish judicial procedures under Roman rule. Anywhere from fourteen to twenty-seven instances of violations of the rules of procedure governing the juridical work of the Great Sanhedrin as set out in the Mishnaic treatise *Sanhedrin* have been counted. To be sure it is by no means certain that these regulations from a later period necessarily obtained in the first seventy years of the Christian era, but they cannot be wholly set aside. A study of the Gospel narratives, furthermore, points unmistakenly to the conclusion that these accounts betray apologetic motives. We must bear in mind that they were written at a time of increasing hostility between the churches and the synagogues and a heightening of tension between Christians and the political authorities. They reveal a progressive tendency to exonerate the Roman officials from responsibility in the death of Jesus and to affix the blame firmly on the Jews. There is little room for doubt that ultimately the initiative for the seizure of Jesus and the decision that he should be put to death are to be assigned to the High Court. At the same time it is certain that the Romans played a far more responsible role in the disposition of the case against the Galilean leader than the records would lead us to suppose.

It would be tempting simply to harmonize these several records on the thesis that a complete account can be gained by weaving together all the special features of the individual records, even if this requires the conclusion that an interval of several days separated the arrest from the crucifixion.[33] The Gospels present us with descriptions of no less than seven different judicial proceedings. But such compilation fails to recognize that each of the Evangelists intends to give a complete account of the proceedings. Moreover it would fail to take account of something we have discovered throughout the gospel tradition, namely,

---

33 Matthew Black argues for an interval of several days between the arrest and the crucifixion. "The Arrest and Trial of Jesus and the Date of the Last Supper," in *New Testament Essays,* A. J. B. Higgins, ed. (Manchester: Manchester University Press, 1959), pp. 19–33.

that there are primary and secondary strata, together with editorial modifications, to be distinguished if we are to arrive at the oldest reliable form of the Church's recollections. In full recognition that any reconstruction is highly tentative we propose to discuss the following outline of these hours.

1. An examination by Caiaphas and a consultation among numbers of the Supreme Council.
2. The trial of Jesus before the Roman tribunal, issuing in the death verdict.
3. The official scourging preparatory to carrying out the sentence and the impromptu torment by the Roman guard.
4. The execution on Golgotha.

The Jewish Hearing

It is necessary, first of all, to determine as best we can what were the limitations imposed upon the juridical system of Judaism by the military government that prevailed. According to a note found in the Fourth Gospel, the Jews reminded their diffident Roman governor, "It is not lawful for us to put any man to death" (John 18:31). This is commonly interpreted to mean that under Roman suzerainty, the Jewish supreme judiciary was deprived of the right to pronounce and to execute any capital sentences. Some support for this conclusion is found in a Talmudic *Baraita,* which alleges that forty years before the destruction of the temple, the right of pronouncing capital sentences was taken away from Israel.[34]

But there is impressive evidence to the contrary which raises the question of whether the Jewish situation before the catastrophe of the First Jewish Revolt (A.D. 66–70) can be fixed from the far more detailed knowledge we have of conditions afterwards.[35] The New Testament itself provides at least two instances. The Acts of the Apostles describes the trial of an early Jewish-Christian leader named Stephen before the Sanhedrin, resulting in the death sentence for blasphemy and his execution by stoning (6:12–7:60). This was one of the four approved forms of capital punishment according to Jewish law.[36] The arrest of Paul in Jerusalem and his two-year imprisonment

34 B. *Sanh.* 1.1, 7.2; *Shab*. 15a.

35 See the astute analysis summarizing our present state of knowledge in Winter, *On the Trial of Jesus,* pp. 67–90. Cf. T. A. Burkill, "The Competence of the Sanhedrin," *Vigiliae Christianae,* X (1956), 80–96; "The Trial of Jesus," *Vigiliae Christianae*, XII (1958), 1–18.

36 The others were burning, beheading, or strangling (M. *Sanh.* 7.1). According to B. *Sanh.* 43a, Jesus was said to have been stoned and hung because he practiced magic, led Israel astray, and stirred the people to rebellion.

in Caesarea indicate that the Council had power of life and death over the defendant, even a Roman citizen, if they could charge him with criminal infraction of the Torah.[37] In view of these and other instances[38] of direct action by the Jewish Court, we must conclude with a number of modern scholars that before the First Revolt the Sanhedrin had full authority to try any case that involved a violation of Jewish law, and to pronounce and execute the death penalty where such was the prescribed punishment. Where the charge involved political activity, the Roman authority may have reserved the right of final decision.

It is likely that Jesus was escorted from the Mount of Olives to the home of the high priest and kept there for private examination until the morning. Even if the order for his arrest had actually been issued by the procurator and the arresting officers were members of the Roman city garrison, it would have been in order for the president of the Great Court to examine a Jewish citizen to be arraigned before the Roman tribunal on a charge of seditious activity. Some specific indictment might well have been required by Pilate before he was ready to examine the prisoner.

The decision to apprehend Jesus and put an end to the popular movement he was leading may have been reached by the Sanhedrin some time earlier. According to a note found in John's Gospel, this had been done by the Council in an administrative session before Jesus had returned with his disciples to Jerusalem for the last time. "If we let him go on thus, everyone will believe in him, and the Romans will come and destroy both our holy place and our nation" (11:48). We may be in touch here with a very early tradition according to which the Council determined to move against the Galilean prophet, partly in concern for their own safety, partly in an honest concern for the nation as a whole. The growing authority of Jesus could easily precipitate a dangerous excitement among the people that would provide a pretext for a new outbreak of oppressive measures by the Roman authorities in reprisal. With Jesus safely in his hands without immediate risk of a public uprising, the high priest, Joseph called Caiaphas,

---

37 Cf. also Jos., *Antiq.* XX.9.1; *Sanh.* 7.2.

38 The famous inscription stone found in 1871 in Jerusalem warns that death would be the penalty for any foreigner who went beyond the boundaries of the Court of the Gentiles in the temple. Cf. Acts 21:28f.; Jos., *Antiq.* XV.11.5; *War* V.5.2, VI.2.4.

grilled his prisoner to substantiate the accusation of sedition the Council had agreed to swear against him.[39]

The Synoptists agree that Jesus also appeared before an official session of the Sanhedrin. If so, it is most likely that the Court convened in the chambers sometime during the morning hours. But there is no hint that a formal verdict was delivered at the end of the prescribed waiting period. It is difficult to understand, furthermore, why any sentence handed down was not executed by the authorities. Probably we are to understand that the Sanhedrin conducted a private hearing during which they condemned the Galilean as guilty of blasphemy, and then endorsed the indictment of Jesus as a seditionist and agitator already drawn up by the president of the Court. That he was extradited to the Roman tribunal may be explained as an arrangement that the legislative officers had made with Pilate to seize the leaders of the resistance movement and make a public example of them.

According to the basic narrative in Mark, the Jewish examination centered in the accusation that Jesus had predicted the destruction of the temple and insinuated that he would bring about its collapse and institute the New Temple in its place. "We heard him say, 'I will destroy this temple that is made with hands, and in three days I will build another, not made with hands' " (Mark 14:58). Though Mark and the early Church evidently stumbled over this saying, believing it to be too radical to be attributed to Jesus, it is without doubt an authentic saying. The newly discovered *Gospel of Thomas* preserves a form of the primary tradition: "Jesus said: I shall destroy this house and no one will be able to build it again" (Saying 71). Combined with the claim of Jesus in the Fourth Gospel, "In three days I will raise it up," this may approximate the offensive promise.

Jesus was here announcing an eschatological event. It is a declaration that the revelation which has come in him spells the collapse of the temple in the old age and the imminent construction of the New Temple in the dawning Kingdom of God.[40] The offense of Jesus' claim to his critics and foes lay in the messianic implication that *in him* the eschatological moment had arrived; the end had come upon the

---

39 Winter conjectures that the earliest form of Luke and John and the earliest chapters of Acts named (mistakenly) the officiating high priest at Jesus' death as Annas (probably Ananus II). See Winter, *On the Trial of Jesus,* pp. 31–43.

40 A note missing from Josephus' story of the prediction of the destruction of the temple by a certain Jesus bar Ananias about A.D. 62 (*War* VI.5.3).

old. Through him the New Temple of the messianic era was to be established very soon, the shrine that would be the gathering point of God's faithful people now scattered through the world.

The threat against the temple in the testimony of the plaintiffs, therefore, is of a piece with the question the presiding officer puts to him: "Are you the Messiah, the Son of the Blessed?" (Mark 14:61). The second Gospel understands Jesus to have made a full acknowledgement: "I am." In the same breath he predicts the speedy enthronement of the glorified Son of Man who would perform the final act of judgment at the close of the age. "You will see the Son of man sitting at the right hand of Power [that is, God], and coming with the clouds of heaven" (Mark 14:62).[41] Perhaps the reply, though affirmative, was more enigmatic, as Matthew and Luke suggest, "You say that I am" (Matt. 26:64; Luke 22:70). It is often noted by interpreters that Jesus' response speaks of the coming Son of Man in a curiously oblique way, as though of another figure entirely. But the innuendo was caught by the court. Their reaction, if it is to be accepted, shows they understood that the accused man spoke of himself.[42]

That the scandalized chief justice tore his robe according to the prescribed procedure for pronouncing that an act of blasphemy had been committed may seem surprising, since the holy name of God had not been uttered. "The blasphemer is not culpable," declares the Mishnah, "unless he pronounces the Name itself" (*Sanh.* 7.5).[43] It is possible, however, that the hidden name of God that the devout Jew of Jesus' time refused to take upon his lips, preferring instead to use the recognized surrogates, was not simply the sacred tetragrammaton Yahweh. When Moses first confronted the God of Sinai, he is said to have asked his name that he might tell his people. The only answer he received was the enigmatic word, "I am I AM [= Yahweh]" (Exod.

---

41 The language here is not, as commonly supposed, the language of the Second Advent, but rather of vindication and sovereignty, as the biblical allusions testify. Cf. Dan. 7:13; Ps. 110:1.

42 The conclusion that it was the early Church that first identified all the Son of Man sayings with Jesus, though a popular view among present-day scholars, is too facile. The view of Jesus as a prophet who warned of the end of the age and the coming of God's glorious vicegerent scarcely explains the plotting of officials against him and the crucifixion.

43 Cf. B. *Sanh.* 60a. Such an offense was punishable by extirpation from the community (Num. 15:30; *Kerithoth* 1.1) or in extreme cases by death (Lev. 24:10–16; *Sanh.* 7.5).

3:14).[44] Was Jesus' reply, "I am he" understood by the High Court as a naming of the holy hidden name of God? If so, it was a claim that the speaker stood in some special relationship to God, and the reaction of the Court is quite understandable. "In this age," observed Rabbi Pinchas ben Jair (A.D. 130–160), "the prayer of the Israelites is not heard because they do not know the *shem hammephorash;* but in the Age to Come God will reveal it to them." He considered the *Ani hu* (I am He) of Isaiah 52:6 as the secret name. To sensitive Jewish ears, what appeared to be a straightforward answer to the messianic question at the Jewish hearing may have carried a shocking innuendo of a self-description in the same terms as the eternal and self-existing God.[45]

The Roman Trial

By prearrangement with the imperial representative, the prisoner was brought under guard to Pilate's headquarters in Herod's former palace located in the northwest corner of the Upper City.[46] It is not at all unlikely that the Galilean's name was by this time known to the Roman governor as a typical trouble-maker who was stirring up the people by arousing their hopes of a free Jewish kingdom. Perhaps it was on the basis of a complaint sworn out against Jesus that the governor had ordered soldiers from the city garrison to arrest Jesus and bring him into custody. "Are you the King of the Jews?" Pilate asks. To the Roman, unaware of the diverse nuances of the title, any claim to messiahship would be seen in terms of the popular hopes for the re-establishment of the old Davidic monarchy. His own counselors and secret police probably kept him informed of the peasantry's desperate longing for a leader variously known as Son of David, Anointed One of Israel, King of Glory, Prince of the Congregation, and Prince of Light. These were royal titles; as such, they challenged the supremacy of the *imperator et rex* who governed the whole world from his headquarters in the Eternal City. The Jewish writ of indictment is detailed by Luke: "We found this man subverting our nation, opposing the payment of taxes to Caesar, and claiming to be Messiah,

---

[44] See the note on Exod. 3:14 by Norman Walker in the *Journal of Biblical Literature,* LXXIX (1960), 277.

[45] John 4:26; 8:24, 28, 58; 9:9; 13:19; 18:5, 6, 8. Greek, *ego eimi;* Hebrew, *ani hu.* Cf. Isa. 41:4, 42:8, 43:10, 11, 13; 52:6; etc.

[46] Here, at least, was the residence of later procurators. See Jos., *War* II.14.8, 15.5.

a king" (Luke 23:2 NEB). "Are you the King of the Jews?" The reply of Jesus was equivocal: "You have said so." That is to say, these are *your* words, not mine.

There is no mistaking the views of the Evangelists that Pilate is not convinced at all of Jesus' guilt, and that the responsibility for his death must be placed squarely upon the Jewish officials who persist in their accusations. John implies that they threaten to lodge a complaint with the emperor if Pilate refuses to order the prisoner's execution (John 19:12). Pilate's reluctance to pass sentence is strikingly exhibited in the proposal that he acquit the Galilean and execute instead a convicted murderer and resistance leader named Barabbas, or to use his full name, Jesus bar (R) Abba (n). To the Gospel writers, especially Luke, this episode is further evidence that Pilate was convinced of the innocence of Jesus and only pronounced sentence against him under persistent pressure by the hierarchy.

A problem is posed by the combined testimony of Mark and John that it was a regular custom at Passover time for the crowds to choose among several prisoners one whom the governor would pardon and release. No such paschal custom is known, however. There is only slender evidence that governmental officials such as legates, proconsuls, and civil servants of lesser stature like procurators exercised the power of suspending a suit in process or granting an *indulgentia* to a condemned criminal.[47] Yet there is no ground for dismissing the story as a fictitious detail, if for no other reason than that the revolutionist's very name proved so offensive to the tastes of the Christian community that efforts were made to disguise it.[48] P. Winter has offered an ingenious conjecture that Pilate was not appealing to any distinctive paschal custom but inquiring of the guards and plaintiffs whether the man who stood before him for examination and sentence was Yeshua, the son of Joseph, or Yeshua the son of (R) Abba (n), both of whom

---

47 Dubious instances are sometimes recognized in the practices of a first-century Roman governor of Egypt (Pap. Flor. 61.59ff.), cited by Adolf Deissmann, *Light from the Ancient East* (London: Hodder and Stoughton, 1910), p. 267; and for Pliny the Younger, governor of Bithynia ca. A.D. 110 (*Epistles* X. 40, 41). J. Blinzler thinks that support may be found for the paschal custom in an allusion in the Mishnah tractate *Pes.* 8.6 (Herbert Danby, trans., *The Mishnah* [London: Oxford University Press, 1958], p. 147); *The Trial of Jesus,* 2nd ed., trans. Isabel and Florence McHugh (Westminster, Md.: The Newman Press, 1959), pp. 218–21. But see Winter, *On the Trial of Jesus,* pp. 91–99.

48 There is little doubt that the oldest form of the name in Matt. 27:16f. was Jesus Barabbas, and that this represents a primary tradition. It is not certain whether this should be Aramaized as Jesus bar (son of) Abbas (a known rabbinic name) or Jesus bar Rabban (son of Rabbi).

had lately been taken into custody for revolutionary activities.[49] Seated upon the raised platform from which official decisions were announced (John 19:13), the governor delivered the verdict of guilty.

Whether the interrogation of Jesus before Pilate is considered to be a formal trial or not, the final decision about the disposition of the case certainly rested with the imperial representative. Jesus of Nazareth was tried and condemned to death by crucifixion for the *crimen laesae maiestatis,* high treason against the Roman state, and punished according to the method prescribed by Roman law. In accordance with that law affecting condemned slaves and rebel provincials, he was subject to flogging before the actual execution.[50] Tied to a flagellation post, the victim was severely beaten with leather whips stiffened with metal rods or bones. In John's Gospel the scourging takes place as part of the brutal third-degree methods; in the more accurate Synoptic accounts it is said to follow the death verdict.

Further indignities were heaped upon the exhausted prisoner by the Roman legionaries who prepared to conduct him to the execution spot. Here indeed was a ridiculous candidate for royal honors. They make sport of him after the fashion of the carnival kings or the burlesques on unpopular civic officials mimed by street actors in the great cities of the Roman Empire. Over his shoulders they throw a soldier's worn cloak, the *chlamys,* as token of the imperial purple. They weave a crown out of thorny branches or date palm leaves and press it on his head, then pay homage to him with a parody on the royal salute (*Ave, Caesar, Victor, Imperator*): "Hail, King of the Jews" (Mark 15:18).[51] Then, tiring of their buffoonery, a detachment leaves the Praetorium for the execution site.

The Execution

The Via Dolorosa

It was a common Roman practice in executing sentence on a condemned criminal to announce his crime on a placard carried before

---

49 Winter, *On the Trial of Jesus,* p. 99. Goguel speculates that a later episode involving such a rebel leader became confused in the tradition and related to the the trial of Jesus (*Life of Jesus,* p. 520).

50 Jos., *War* II.14.9, V.11.1, VI.5.3.

51 Note the correspondence with the third Passion prophecy, Mark 10:34. Winter argues that this is the original occasion of the mockery, the ridicule in the high priest's home being an instance of the anti-Jewish attitude of the Gospels (*On the Trial of Jesus,* p. 106). Cf. a parallel story of a mockery of an Alexandrian ragamuffin named Karabas reported by Philo, *Against Flaccus,* VI.

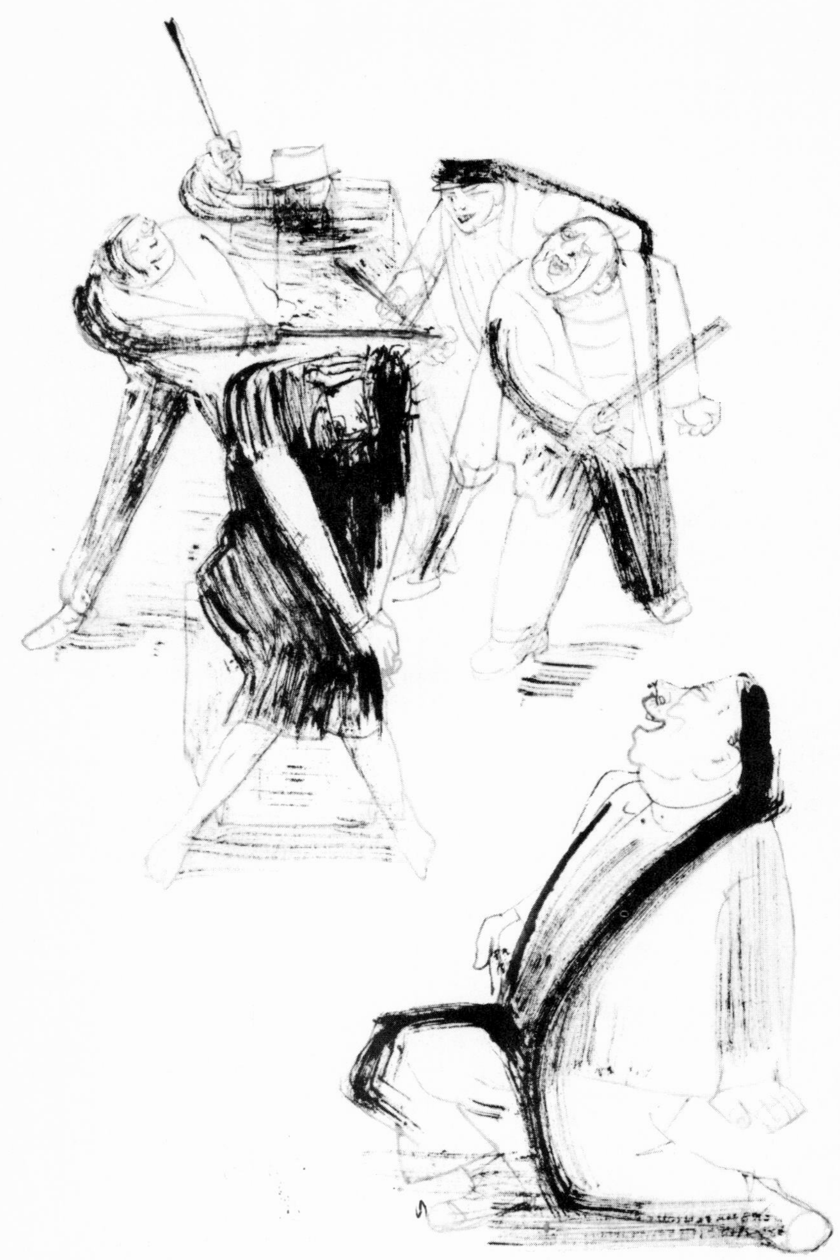

Fig. 12. The Scourging by Josef Hegenbarth (1884-1962). Courtesy of *Hanna Hegenbarth.*

the procession or affixed to the death rack.[52] That the Gospels make passing reference to the use of the *titulus* is further evidence of their familiarity with Roman procedure. Probably the earliest form of the inscription preserved in the tradition were the words found in Mark 15:26: "The King of the Jews." Variants of this formula are given in each of the Gospels. The most elaborate appears in John, where it is said that the announcement was trilingual, published in Hebrew, Greek, and Latin, and read "Jesus of Nazareth, the King of the Jews" (John 19:19). To the subtle mind of this Evangelist, the words were not an accusation but an unconscious recognition of the true sovereignty of the crucified man, just as he interpreted the high priest's comment earlier to be an unconscious prediction of Jesus' sacrificial death (John 11:51f.). The Jewish leaders protest the identification, but to no avail. The obdurate procurator is unmoved: "What I have written, I have written" (John 19:22).

The death march moved out from the Praetorium perhaps through the Gennath Gate, the "Gate of the Garden," to a spot north of the Upper City and west of the suburban wall called in Aramaic *Galgaltha,* so designated either because it was a rocky eminence resembling a skull or head or because it had become associated with many executions. Since the time of Constantine, tradition has identified the site marked by the Church of the Holy Sepulchre as the scene of the crucifixion. Other locations have been proposed, but this remains the most likely, though there is no conclusive identification.[53]

According to the practice of the time, the *patibulum* or heavy wooden cross bar, perhaps with the *titulus* attached, was placed across Jesus' shoulders and his outstretched arms lashed securely to it.[54] It was mandatory for the condemned man thus to carry the cross to the place of execution. It would appear that Jesus, exhausted by a sleepless night of questioning by the high priest and the morning session of the Council and weakened from the beatings he had endured, collapsed before they had gone the whole way. The Roman squad of execu-

52 Cf. Suetonius, *Lives of the Caesars: Domitian* 10, *Caligula* 32. Dio Cassius, *Roman History* LIV.8. Euseb., *Hist.* V.1.44 (Gal. 3:1?).

53 See Gustaf H. Dalman, (*Sacred Sites and Ways,* trans. Paul P. Levertoff [London: SPCK, 1935], Chap. xxi) who supports the traditional identification. Cf. Joachim Jeremias, *Golgotha* (Leipzig: Verlag von Eduard Pfeiffer, 1926); André Parrot, *Golgotha and the Church of the Holy Sepulchre,* trans. Edwin Hudson (New York: Philosophical Library, 1957).

54 Plautus, *Miles Gloriosus,* 359; Plutarch, *De sera numinis vindicta,* 9. The Synoptic Gospels do not say that his hands and feet were nailed, a detail in the Passion Story which arose later (John 20:25).

tioners was forced to commandeer the services of a Jewish civilian form North Africa, a certain Simon of Cyrene who had lodged near the city for the Passover celebration, to carry the timber the remaining distance.[55]

Golgotha

The account of the crucifixion is told in starkly realistic language with no attempt to play upon the emotions of the readers. "They crucified him." The tradition differs about the hour. Mark reports that it was nine o'clock (15:25); John, that it was sometime after twelve o'clock (19:14). The gibbet was a diabolical form of capital punishment, practiced by the Romans since the Punic Wars and reserved for runaway slaves, insubordinate provincials, and common criminals. Josephus says that after the capture of Jerusalem in A.D. 70 Titus crucified so many Jews that "there was not enough room for the crosses, nor enough crosses for the condemned" (*War* V.11.2). The Roman senator Cicero spoke of it as "the most cruel and hideous of tortures."[56]

The executions usually took place along a roadside or at a cross roads where passers-by could watch and yell their curses and jibes. The victim, stripped of his clothing, was lifted into position so that the *patibulum* rested upon the top of the upright pole, or *simplex,* which had been driven into the ground. Sometimes it was fastened a little below the top so that the doomed man's legs dangled a short distance from the ground or were fastened to the post by ropes. Part of his body weight was borne by a peg under his crotch or his feet. There he hung, scarcely able to move a muscle, stricken by the heat of the day, tormented by insects and the pangs of hunger as the hours wore on, pilloried by passers-by, his life's blood draining away through the wounds inflicted by the flogging. Even so it was not unknown for a man to clutch at life for many hours, even extending for two or three days, before death brought an end to his agony. The swiftness of death's release to Jesus' suffering on the cross, which surprised the governor when he heard the news (Mark 14:54; John 19:33), is further evidence of the complete exhaustion brought on by the events

---

55 The Greek verb here is the same Persian loan word referring to the requisitioning of services for the royal post which Jesus uses in speaking of the disposition with which the aspirant for the Kingdom faces cruelty and duress (Matt. 5:41). Is Simon the Negro Christian of Acts 13:1?

56 *"Crudelissimum taeterrimumque supplicium," In Verrem* V.64. Cf. Tacitus, *Hist.* IV.3.11; Jos., *Life* 75.

of the last hours. The immediate cause of his death is unknown. Thirst, exposure, an embolism, or the infection of the victim's wounds were frequent causes.

Before he was hoisted upon the upright pole, Jesus was offered a narcotic of drugged wine customarily given to deaden the pain, perhaps made available by a group of charitable women from Jerusalem.[57] He refused it. Here and elsewhere in the Passion Story the details have unquestionably been colored by certain scriptural passages that came to be construed as prophetic witnesses to the course of the Messiah. Matthew altered the myrrhed wine of Mark 15:23 to "wine mingled with gall" (27:34), to bring it into stricter conformity to the words of the 69th Psalm:

> They gave me poison for food,
> and for my thirst they gave me vinegar to drink.
> [Ps. 69:21]

Thus too the recollection of Roman executioners gambling for the few rags of clothing they stripped from Jesus' body before he was crucified led John to quote a sentence from the 22nd Psalm:

> They divide my garments among them,
> and for my raiment they cast lots.
> [Ps. 22:18[58]]

The Words from the Cross

The traditions of the last words of Jesus from the cross vary among the Gospels. According to the earliest, some six hours after Jesus had been hanged, bystanders heard an almost inarticulate hoarse cry from his lips that sounded like the name of the prophet Elijah (Mark 15:34, 37). In Jewish folklore Mar Elijah is often recognized as the source of miraculous help and rescue from situations of danger. Would Mar Elijah now appear to deliver the doomed man? Actually, say the Evangelists, Jesus was not calling upon the good Jewish saint, but instead reciting the familiar cry of despair with which the liturgical hymn known as the 22nd Psalm commences. In Mark the Hebrew

---

[57] Cf. Prov. 31:6. The drink that was hastily offered to Jesus in his last moments of consciousness was not the original opiate of myrrhed wine but probably *posca,* a favorite drink of Roman soldiers (Mark 15:36 par.; John 19:29). It may be that vss. 34–36 are a secondary elaboration of vs. 37, however.

[58] The incident of the two robbers who were crucified with Jesus may have been inspired by Isa. 53:12, although Mark gives no hint of its symbolic significance. Luke alone elaborates the account (Luke 23:39–42).

Fig. 13. Calvary (1912) by Marc Chagall. Collection, The Museum of Modern Art, New York. Acquired through the Lillie P. Bliss Bequest.

hymn is quoted in the folk-speech of the day: "My God, my God, why hast thou forsaken me?"

The cry cannot be dismissed as an imaginary detail framed by early Christians who piously believed that the proper way to die was to take words of holy Scripture upon one's lips. For this was a hard word, intimating a despair in the last moment that he was bereft of the One whom he had claimed to make known to men. Was it a resurgence of that awful doubt, faced in other moments of inner anguish, that death after all was the final victor? Could it be that he who had come to break the power of death, the instrument of God's adversary, by declaring the divine pardon upon sinful men, must now go down in defeat with them? Is this the moment when the whole mission is undone? Yet the cry must be interpreted in the light of the persecution psalms of Judaism where the suffering of the pious man is the occasion for a supplication for strength from Heaven and the reassurance that God defends his own.

> For Thou hast not abandoned me in
> the distress of my soul
> and hast heard my cry in the bitterness
> of my soul
> and hast heeded the voice of my misery
> in my groaning.
>
> . . . .
>
> Thou [hast] not [abandoned] the soul
> of Thy servant.
>
> [1QH v.12f., 15]

Matthew, loyal as always to his primary source, has carried over the so-called cry of dereliction, revising it to its original Hebrew form. But Luke and John find themselves unable to repeat it. Luke replaces the insinuated doubt with a burst of confidence, "Father, into thy hands I commit my spirit!" (Luke 23:46).[59] John's interpretive word, "It is finished" (John 19:30), conveys a subtle *double entendre.* In the context it has the obvious meaning that the end has come, "I die"; but the Evangelist finds a deeper significance for the expression in the mission of Jesus and the whole history of redemption of which he is the soul and center. "It is accomplished"; that is, the Father's final and decisive act of redemption on behalf of the imprisoned is completed in this act.

The very gloom of the heavily clouded day accentuated the darkness that seemed to engulf Jesus in this bitter hour, as his followers later recalled the scene.[60] Later Christians were to see in Amos' doleful words a prophecy of this strange darkness at noon.

---

59 Based on Ps. 30:6. The authenticity of the well-known prayer for forgiveness from the cross that Luke records remains uncertain (Luke 23:34). The testimony of the oldest manuscripts is divided, some of the most important omitting it (including P^{75}). Whether they are words actually spoken from the cross or an interpretation of Jesus' attitude by Luke or another, they are eloquent testimony to the whole character of Jesus' ministry.

60 There is no need to dismiss this detail as an imaginative symbolic detail, for an oppressive atmospheric condition of the day might have suggested a miracle of judgment to credulous witnesses. See experiences of modern travelers reported by Goguel, *The Life of Jesus,* p. 542, and E. F. F. Bishop, *Jesus of Palestine* (London: Lutterworth Press, 1955), p. 250. On the other hand, darkness was a familiar symbol for the passing of outstanding men. See Virgil, *Geo.* I.463ff.

"And on that day," says the Lord God,
"I will make the sun go down at noon,
and darken the earth in broad daylight."
[Amos 8:9[61]]

The end came suddenly after several hours. Mark says simply, "Jesus uttered a loud cry, and breathed his last" (Mark 15:37). We have already suggested that this is probably the earliest tradition behind the interpretive words of 15:34. It had been understood often as a scream of pain in the throes of death or even as a final cry of despair before expiration. But the Evangelist surely intended another meaning in keeping with his emphasis upon the spiritual torment and triumph that constituted the victory over the realm of Satan won in this eventful moment. This was a victor's shout, such a cry as could split the darkness and tear the veil of the temple. Perhaps the Psalmist's words were in the writer's mind, "God has gone up with a shout, the Lord with the sound of a trumpet" (Ps. 47:5). It is with a "loud voice" that the praises of God are sung by those who know him to be the true Lord.[62] To Paul the reappearance of the triumphant Lord at the end of history would be heralded by a "cry of command" (I Thess. 4:16). The authoritative voice of the exalted Son of Man raises the dead from their sleep to stand before the last tribunal (John 5:25; cf. Rev. 1:10). As they told the Passion Story later, his devoted companions were convinced that he met the end, not with a lamentation that God had deserted him, but with a shout of praise.

The Burial

It was a common Roman custom to leave the bodies of crucified men hanging on their crosses to putrefy and become the prey of carrion birds, a grisly warning to all those who would trifle with the law of the Roman state. No provision was made for any decent burial, but permission was sometimes granted to friends or relatives to take the body away for burial. The oldest tradition in the Gospels informs us that Joseph of Arimathea, who requested the body, had not been associated with Jesus in his work. Rather he was an influential, wealthy

---

61 Cf. Isa. 60:2; Jer. 15:9; Iren., *Adv. Haer.* IV.33.12. Luke may have understood it as an eclipse (Luke 23:45), though this is a manifest impossibility at the vernal equinox. Probably he interpreted the tradition as a prophecy of the final debacle now set in motion by Jesus' death.

62 Luke 17:15; Rev. 5:12, 6:10, 7:12, etc. Cf. the testimony of the second-century Christian leader, Ignatius of Antioch: "I spoke with a great voice, with God's own voice," *Phil.* 7:1.

man who was either a senator in the Great Sanhedrin or else held a comparable position in one of the local councils. Joseph was a native of a Judean town called Ramathaim whose precise location is no longer known. No reason is given for the bold act of this official, who is simply described by Mark as a devout Jew who looked for the fulfillment of the messianic hope of Israel.

The story could be explained as a transfer into historical occurrence of the Servant prediction that "They made his grave with the wicked and with a rich man in his death" (Isa. 53:9). Otherwise we are left to conjecture either that Joseph was drawn in sympathy to this courageous Galilean or that he was moved by a concern that the corpse should not be allowed to defile the land during the holy festival season. The Evangelists are agreed that it was only a few hours before the beginning of the Sabbath. After confirming the surprising fact that the Jew was already dead, Pilate granted Joseph's request. The body was wrapped in a hastily obtained linen winding sheet and placed in a nearby rock chamber owned by Joseph, and the entrance was shut with a flat closing-stone against which a large stone block was rolled or pushed.[63] Haste was necessary lest the men defile themselves before the approaching Seder meal. The Sanhedrin had guarded the people against the danger of apostasy. Roman justice had settled the matter, or so it seemed.

---

63 Dalman, *Sacred Sites and Ways*, pp. 374f. The elaborate details Matthew reports of the sealing of the grave and the posting of a Roman guard at the request of the Sanhedrin (27:62–66) testify to the rapid growth of a defense against Jewish criticism. Its developed form can be read in the apocryphal *Gospel of Peter* 8:29–11:49.

CHAPTER XII

THE EASTER GOSPEL

It is not worth while to remember *that* past which cannot become a present.*

It is the resurrection that is the point of departure for the interpretation of all the rest of the history of the Christian community.†

Easter Faith and the Resurrection Stories

Our study of the historical figure of Jesus began with the faith-understanding of the earliest community of his followers after his lifetime. They hailed him as Messiah and Lord, declaring that through him there was forgiveness of sins, a righteousness beyond human achievement, and the life which God had promised men in the New Age. In and through the historical events that comprised his ministry among the men of his day, they testified that God himself had been acting decisively, confronting men with the issues of life and death, restoring the fallen, and tripping the sure-footed.

One of the earliest summary statements of their faith, we saw, found expression in the baptismal confession of a living and reigning deity, "Jesus is Lord!" (Rom. 10:9; I Cor. 12:3; Phil. 2:11). "If Christ has not been raised, your faith is futile and you are still in your sins," Paul bluntly advises some in Corinth who are undecided about the resurrection hope (I Cor. 15:17). "Christ died for our sins in accordance with the scriptures, he was buried, he was raised on the

---

* Søren Kierkegaard, *Fear and Trembling* (New York: Doubleday and Company, Inc., 1954), p. 41.

† Richard R. Niebuhr, *Resurrection and Historical Reason* (New York: Charles Scribner's Sons, 1957), p. 162.

third day in accordance with the scriptures," is his précis of the gospel that he first received and now preached. To Peter, the lively hope of final salvation is anchored in the reality of the resurrection (I Pet. 1:3). So it goes everywhere in these writings.

The conviction that Christ is the living Lord now present with his people and extending his sovereign rule over the world constitutes the new community of the Church. Without this experience of his lordship and their allegiance to him, their life together, their evangelical ardor, their observance of the first day of the week as a distinctive holy day, their joyful celebrations of the Lord's Supper—all these would be inexplicable. To say "Jesus is Lord" is to confess the resurrection. It is to assert that one who is now known as Lord is none other than the crucified leader who had been raised from the dead. The earthly ministry of Jesus is never recited as a biographical survey of a mission brought to a violent end by death. It is remembered and repeated as an integral part of a total event that began before Bethlehem and came to climax in the crucifixion, resurrection, and continuing reign of Christ.

Out of these astonishing convictions about him, the activities and addresses of his ministry were reviewed and interpreted. For the early Church, the resurrection was the key to the true significance of Jesus' whole mission and the meaning of its new existence. "Post-Easter faith is no more than the correct understanding of the pre-Easter Jesus."[1] That the memories of what Jesus of Nazareth said and did were preserved certainly cannot be understood as the expression of the antiquarian interests of primitive historical societies. The community lived out of a past that had become contemporized with the present. What Jesus once said to his Galilean disciples was understood to be what he now was saying to those united with him in the new life, supplemented by fresh words of counsel, admonishment, and commission. The tradition was made present and living by the risen Christ who spoke through it to the urgent, imperative Now of Evangelist and Church. That is why even the words of the risen Christ are reported in the same direct speech that marked his earthly talk.

The Limitations of Historical Study

It is this surprising and lively persuasion which we are now to set out and to make inquiry about what evoked it. But first we must recognize the limitation imposed upon a purely historical investigation

---

1 Heinz Zahrnt, *The Historical Jesus,* trans. J. S. Bowden (New York: Harper & Row, Publishers, 1963), p. 138.

of the resurrection phenomenon. The outer limit of the historian's task is reached when he records the fact that the earliest communities of believers were convinced that Jesus was not dead but alive and participating in God's sovereign activity in the world. Thus many studies of the mission of Jesus conclude with the record of the death and burial of the Galilean prophet. They refuse to consider as part of the historical story the faith interpretation the Church placed upon these events and their aftermath.

For the researcher's task, the claim that Jesus was received by God to continued life is no more capable of verification (or rejection) than that he was actually the Messiah or that he really healed the sick by the power of God. In the case of the resurrection appearances on which the salvation claims of early preaching are based, just as with the belief in the incarnation and the atonement, we are not dealing with ordinary sensory evidence available to believer and nonbeliever alike for appraisal and decision. According to the Gospels, Jesus made himself known only to those who were in a position to recognize him, those who had a relationship to him in the past and for whom that past was otherwise available only through the powers of recollection. It stands nowhere recorded that foes or critics were met by him and remained unconvinced. He does not appear to a Sadducee or to Herod Antipas or to Caiaphas. These are not strictly external events, "objects in the empirical world," as R. Bultmann puts it. The Christian testimony to the survival of Jesus over the destructive power of death and his enstatement as Messiah and Lord are inaccessible to the probings of historical and textual science.

The alternative, however, is not to suspend the work of historical research and give free reign to psychological, occult, or metahistorical interpretations of the resurrection, though this has often been done. Here we are helped by the modern concern with the problem of history and the search for a new and more adequate historical method that conceives the stuff of history as something more than objective, reportable occurrences and refuses to regard historical reason and historical faith as enemies to the death. R. R. Niebuhr reminds us that we may be plagued by an overly positivistic view of what we mean by a historical event and historical causality. There is about any single historical happening an independence, novelty, and spontaneity that cannot be wholly accounted for by general "laws" of nature and history. "The resurrection shares in the arbitrariness, irrationality, and independence which characterize all events to some degree; and like them, it is problematic."[2] But like them it must be dealt with in itself rather than fitted into some preconceived system. There are "facts" of history that stand out in lonely isolation from anything that has gone before and cannot be duplicated in what follows, and which are not therefore to be accounted for logically by what has preceded or even followed them. Instead they become the means whereby other events can be understood.

Thus any attempt to understand the life and work of the early Christian community apart from the "inner history" that centers in their experiences of the risen Christ is to revert to positivistic views which cannot penetrate into that extraordinary and dynamic group life. We must accept seriously the apostolic testimony that these are real encounters, not just rearranged viewpoints or dawning insights without other ground than subjective reflection.

The Appearances

The First Witnesses

The Evangelists and their predecessor Paul offer various identifications of those who experienced the first Christophanies and the place of the meetings. Paul, whose account of the resurrection appearances is several decades earlier than the records of Matthew, Luke, and John, tells of a sequence that begins with Peter and includes self-disclosures to a group of more than five hundred brethren, to James the brother of Jesus, and finally to Paul himself (I Cor. 15:5–8). He is silent about the women who are mentioned by the Evangelists as the first to become convinced that the crucified rabbi was alive.

Matthew understands that on the day following the Sabbath, the risen Jesus confronted two women returning in haste from the empty tomb: Mary Magdalene and the "other Mary," presumably Mary the mother of James the Less, mentioned by Mark (Matt. 28:9f.). In John's Gospel it is Mary Magdalene alone who first makes the discovery that the body of Jesus is not in the tomb and who is subsequently met by the risen Rabbi whom she first mistakes for the gardener (John 20:1–18). The tradition about the women at the

[2] Richard R. Niebuhr, *Resurrection and Historical Reason* (New York: Charles Scribner's Sons, 1957), p. 171.

tomb is known likewise to Luke who speaks of a larger group including Mary Magdalene, Mary the mother of James, and a certain Joanna (Luke 24:10). These women discover the vacant crypt, but Luke like Mark is silent about any resurrection encounter. Instead it is to Simon Peter that the Lord is said to have made himself known (Luke 24:34), in fulfillment of the prophecy of Jesus at the Last Supper, "I have prayed for you that your faith may not fail; and when you have turned again, strengthen your brethren" (Luke 22:32).[3]

There is an old tradition recorded by Luke that tells of a meeting with two disciples on the Emmaus road (Luke 24:13–35). The risen Lord appears also to the eleven and then to a larger group of disciples (Luke 24:33, 36–49; cf. John 20:19–23), to the eleven with Thomas (John 20:26–29), to seven disciples in Galilee (John 21), to Paul (I Cor. 15:8), and to Stephen (Acts 7:55).[4]

The Place of Meeting

The tradition speaks with no common voice about the scene of the first resurrection encounters. Luke certainly understands these experiences of Simon and the other disciples to have occurred in Jerusalem. In the second volume of his kerygmatic history, he makes explicit his understanding that Jesus was raised on the third day after his execution and that the definitive resurrection appearances occurred during the next forty days. He adds that the disciples were solemnly charged "not to depart from Jerusalem, but to wait for the promise of the Father," that is, the gift of the Holy Spirit (Acts 1:4; cf. Luke 24:49). The implication of the prophecies in Mark 14:28 and 16:7 is that the risen Lord will manifest himself to his disciples in Galilee.[5] Matthew similarly anticipates that the scene of the Christophanies will be Galilee (Matt. 26:32, 28:10), although he relates an appearance to the women in Jerusalem (28:9f.). In his interpretation of the

---

3 In its present form, this saying reflects the actual fact of Peter's leadership in the early Church, stated also by Matt. 16:18 and John 21:15ff.

4 Whether or not Mark's Gospel originally contained an account of resurrection appearances (apart from Mark 8:27–30, 9:2–8) remains a debatable point among scholars.

5 On the problem of the reference of these texts to the resurrection or to the Parousia of Christ, see W. G. Kümmel, *Promise and Fulfilment*, trans. Dorothea M. Barton (Naperville, Ill.: Alec R. Allenson, Inc., 1957), pp. 77–79. The third-century fragment of Mark's Gospel in the Rainer papyri found in Fayyum in Egypt omits vs. 28, perhaps because of its conflict with the later and dominant Jerusalem tradition. The texts most likely are Marcan editorial comments reflecting an old tradition of resurrection appearances in Galilee.

Synoptic tradition and a special "outside" tradition, John reports *both* Jerusalem and Galilean appearances of the risen Jesus. Besides the experience of Mary Magdalene in Joseph's garden outside Jerusalem, the appendix to this Gospel tells of a fishing scene in Galilee when an unrecognized stranger hailed a group of seven disciples. In the ensuing conversation the Beloved Disciple discovered the true identity of the stranger in their midst (John 21:1–14).[6]

It is quite impossible to fit all these details, including the testimony of I Corinthians, chapter 15, into a single unified scheme. But there is a common emphasis on the apostolic authority for the kerygma of the resurrection.[7] That the disciples, individually and in groups, were brought from a situation of mixed memories to a recognition of Jesus' living presence in their midst is the unanimous verdict of these narratives. It is furthermore clear that they experienced his presence at a time of confusion and despair over the unexpected denouement of their expectations. They are said to have received the evidence of his reality with mixed feelings, fearful and reluctant to believe that this could be true.[8] They do not act like men and women who are gullible to any suggestion that they had not been deceived after all and that their crucified leader was in very fact God's Messiah.

Variant Traditions

We may summarize the earliest resurrection appearances in three groups. There are, first of all, the meetings with Peter and the other disciples that may have taken place in Galilee, where the disciples went shortly after the crucifixion of Jesus. To the communities represented in the New Testament these events signified the authorita-

---

6 The story is probably a derivative form of a fishing story that Luke puts early in Jesus' Galilean work. It may be a historicized resurrection appearance (Luke 5:1–11). The Johannine account, although spoken of as the third appearance (21:14), may have been thought of as a first appearance in the source from which it was taken.

7 Applying a form-critical analysis to the Gospel narratives, C. H. Dodd distinguishes the very earliest traditional material in Matt. 28:8–10, the appearance to the women; Matt. 28:16–20, the commission; and John 20:19–21, the appearance to the disciples. More developed forms of the kerygma's statement may be seen in Mark 16:14–15; Luke 24:36–49; John 20:11–17, 26–29. All of these accounts, however, demonstrate the same concern to establish the resurrection appearances on apostolic authority. See C. H. Dodd, "The Appearances of the Risen Christ: An Essay in Form-Criticism of the Gospels," in *Studies in the Gospels,* ed. D. E. Nineham (Oxford: Basil Blackwell, 1955), pp. 9–35.

8 Matt. 28:17; Luke 24:16, 19–24, 37; John 20:25, 21:4.

tive leadership of Peter and the twelve in the Church and the authenticity of the gospel they proclaimed. A second group of witnesses is less clearly defined but probably represents the immediate family of Jesus. At any rate James is specifically mentioned by Paul (I Cor. 15:7).[9] Luke notes that after the final resurrection appearance on the Mount of Olives, the disciples who gathered in a private house in Jerusalem for prayer and planning included also some unnamed women and "Mary the mother of Jesus, and his brothers" (Acts 1:14). We know from the writings of a second-century Jewish-Christian historian named Hegesippus that members of the Lord's family were still influential in the Palestinian Church in his day.[10] The warrant for this authoritative leadership would likely be traced to definitive resurrection appearances of the Lord.[11]

Finally, there are the appearances to the Galilean women who were a part of the corps of associates with Jesus during his work in Galilee and who had accompanied him to Jerusalem.[12] The part these women played in the burial of Jesus' body and in the discovery of the empty tomb has about it the marks of a very early tradition in the Church. To Luke they represent the nucleus of the earliest congregation of Jesus' followers who remained in Jerusalem after his death and received confirmation of his resurrection. It may be that these variant stories reflect in a shadowy way some of the differences of viewpoint within the earliest Jewish-Christian communities involving the primacy of the Galilean or the Judean congregations, the nuclei of the groups, and the leadership of Peter or James, the Lord's brother.[13]

The Nature of the Appearances

Although there is no disagreement at all over the *fact* of the Easter experiences, there is a vagueness and ambivalence in the records about the *form* in which the reality of Christ's presence was made known.

---

9 Cf. the *Gospel According to the Hebrews* (*Gospel Parallels*, 2nd ed. [New York: Thomas Nelson & Sons, 1957], p. 190).

10 Euseb., *Hist.* III.32.6.

11 Martin Albertz has speculated that the Mary of John 20:11ff. is actually the mother of Jesus, confirming the story the Evangelist tells of Mary's attendance of her dying son at the cross. Early Christian tradition identified the Cleopas mentioned as one of the two disciples on the Emmaus road as a brother of Jesus' father, Joseph (Hegesippus, quoted in Euseb., *Hist.* IV.22.4). This would heighten the importance of the Nazareth family in the early Church.

12 Luke 8:1–3; Mark 15:41 par.

13 This is more likely than considering these geographical notices as references to the scene of the expected second coming, with Lohmeyer, Michaelis, Elliott-Binns, Schmauch, and others.

At times the narratives emphasize the human form of Christ's body. He is said to accompany two disciples from Jerusalem to the little village of Emmaus, some seven and a half miles distant, although his appearance is such that they take him for a total stranger until his true identity is recognized, whereupon they sit down to supper together (Luke 24:13–35). Jesus eats bread and broiled fish to convince them that he is not an apparition as they fear but a substantial person (Luke 24:42f.; John 21:13).[14] He invites the doubting Thomas to examine his wounded hands and feet.

Taken alone, these passages might suggest a bodily form indistinguishable from ordinary finite existence. But this is clearly no ordinary corporeal form. Jesus is said to pass through closed doors to confront his frightened followers who are huddled together in an upper room. He engages them in conversation and then suddenly vanishes into thin air. Those like Mary or the two disciples or John, who have been his constant companions for many months and should know him instantly by outward appearance, do not immediately recognize him when he stands before them.

When we turn to the earlier testimony of Paul, we find a flat contradiction of Luke's word that the risen Messiah had a body of flesh and bones. Paul declares that flesh and blood cannot inherit the Kingdom of God (I Cor. 15:49). The form of Jesus' appearance to the apostles, including Paul himself, was truly corporeal, but of a sort that Paul can describe somewhat vaguely as "spiritual." He envisions a complete metamorphosis ultimately for all the followers of the risen Lord. As heavenly life is imparted to men's mortal bodies, they begin to assume a glorified condition, informed by and plastic to the power of God's creative spirit (I Cor. 3:18).

Paul's interpretation remains for us the most perceptive and persuasive. It is apparent that the earliest witnesses to the resurrection are not describing a confrontation with either a reanimated corpse, such as the daughter of Jairus or the son of the widow of Nain, or a

---

14 These elements were used in the early Christian Eucharists as catacomb art verifies. Cf. B. Gärtner, *John 6 and the Jewish Passover* (*Coniectanea Neotestamentica*, Lund: C. W. K. Gleerup, 1959), p. 49; Erwin R. Goodenough, *Fish, Bread, and Wine, Jewish Symbols in the Greco-Roman Period,* Vol. V (New York: Pantheon Books, Inc., 1956), Chaps. ii, iii. The self-disclosure of the risen Lord on these occasions of shared food points to the significance of the Lord's Supper in the early Church as the moment in the community's life when they were singularly aware of Christ's presence among them.

séance with a friend "from the other side."[15] Emphasis upon the material form of the resurrection appearances is identified for the most part with the later layers of gospel tradition associated with the Jerusalem scene. Some scholars see this as a refutation of Gnostic tendencies to believe that the historical Jesus had been a kind of demigod possessing a light substance alien to any of the forms of sensate life in this world. This may be so. But it is just as likely that no specific heresy is undergoing attack here.

Recognition and Identification

A closer study of the passages in the Gospels, the sermons in Acts, and the accounts of Paul's conversion, together with the references in Paul's letters to his own apostolic commission, shows that the emphasis falls not on any organic continuity between the earthly Jesus and the resurrected Christ but rather on a *personal identity.* The one who meets the disciples is not a stranger who bears an unknown name. He is neither an angelic visitant from the heavenly court who comes to comfort and console these downhearted and miserable men nor a second Lazarus whose inevitable rendezvous with death was temporarily put off.

> The outstanding feature of these passages is not their emphasis on the corporeal as such, but on identification and recognition, and hence on the flesh insofar as it is the medium of recognition.[16]

He could not be the risen Jesus for them unless he bore the identifiable marks of his own history that had been involved with theirs in Galilee and Jerusalem.

All recognition requires an appeal to previous experience and a correlation of the present moment with a past held alive through the power of memory. Behind the dramatic accounts of the resurrection meetings is the astonished realization by these Galileans that their *cognition* of the heavenly Lord whom they have never met turns out to be a *recognition* of the rabbi-prophet whom they knew and yet did not really know. In the order of their apprehension, therefore, they were first aware of another presence vis-à-vis themselves before they

---

15 For a recent, level-headed survey of the bearing of psychical research on an understanding of the Easter narratives, with a complete bibliography, see M. C. Perry, *The Easter Enigma* (London: Faber and Faber, Ltd., 1959). He concludes that the view of these Easter appearances as apparitional experiences would lead at most to the conviction that Jesus had survived death; nothing more.

16 Niebuhr, *Resurrection and Historical Reason,* p. 173.

were prepared to declare that this was none other than their beloved Master. To conclude this was to admit that he had been raised from death to life. Thus the declaration of his resurrection was the necessary inference drawn from the indisputable reality of his person and presence in their midst.

It is the recognition and identification of Jesus in these Easter encounters that is the basis of the resurrection stories. The apprehension of his present lordship drives them to the realization that this lordship is grounded in the God who redeemed his life from destruction and saves those who call upon his name. Every psychologizing reconstruction of the Easter event founders on the fact that the cult of Jesus had its origin, not in the inspiration of souvenirs of a former companionship, but in the present experiences of interpersonal encounters. Behind the tendentious and apologetic formulations of these appearance stories are the primary Easter experiences of the recognition of a crucified rabbi who meets them now as their glorified Lord.

The Empty Tomb

Mark believes that the women came to the tomb at Sunday dawn to perform the office of anointing the body. But it is more likely that John is correct in believing that these funerary rites had been performed, however hastily, at the time of his burial. The women came now to view the grave and to wail their dirges.[17] From early time, the tradition associated the resurrection with the third day following the crucifixion, as Paul's summary of the message first preached to the Corinthians shows. "He died. . . he was buried. . . he was raised on the third day in accordance with the scriptures" (I Cor. 15:3f.).[18] A more primitive tradition was less precise, speaking of the resurrec-

---

17 John 20:1; Matt. 28:1. On Jewish practices of anointing the dead, see *Shabbath* 23.5 (Herbert Danby, trans., *The Mishnah* [London: Oxford University Press, 1958], p. 120).

18 Cf. Mark 14:58 par., 15:29 par.; Matt. 16:21 = Luke 9:22; Matt. 17:23, 20:19 = Luke 18:33; Luke 24:7, 46; Acts 10:40. It is usually thought that Hosea 6:2 is the passage the early preachers had in mind, though an interval of 3½ units for a period of time is common in apocalyptic writings. The rabbis interpreted Hosea 6:2 to mean that the general resurrection of the dead would occur on the third day after the end of the world. Hermann L. Strack and Paul Billerbeck, *Kommentar zum Neuen Testament,* I (München: C. H. Beck'sche Verlagsbuchhandlung, 1922), 747, 760.

tion *after* three days, a common Jewish idiom for a short period of time.[19]

The Accounts

Arriving at the sepulchre, the two women are dismayed to find that the entrance is no longer sealed with the flat closing-stone Joseph had pushed into place earlier. Entering the aperture into the anteroom and peering into the tomb chamber, they discover that the body of Jesus is missing. They are greeted by an angelic figure (Luke speaks of two) who chides them for searching for the living among the dead. He reminds them of Jesus' earlier words about his fate and, according to a Marcan note, advises them that the risen Lord will manifest himself to the disciples in Galilee. Whereupon the terrified women flee from the scene. It is of some significance to notice that in the earliest account they seal their lips about what has happened. "They said nothing to anyone, for they were afraid" (Mark 16:8), in contradiction to the angelic command to tell the disciples.[20]

Despite the legendary features, it is doubtful that the story of the empty tomb can be dismissed as a later tradition designed to establish Jesus' survival beyond death and to afford an answer about the form of the resurrection body of Christians in the afterlife.[21] Indeed it appears to be a presupposition of the oldest kerygmatic tradition; for this is the implication of the triadic form: "dead, buried, raised" (I Cor. 15:3f.) and the two-fold form "killed and raised" (Acts 2:23f., 3:15).

The first witnesses to the resurrection were able to preach their faith—that Jesus was the promised one who had been resuscitated by God's act and established in heavenly sovereignty—with no fear that their Jewish opponents would suddenly prove their claim false by

---

[19] Mark 8:31, 9:31, 10:34; cf. Matt. 27:63. A strict interpretation of the Jonah text quoted in Matt. 12:40 would understand the period of sepulture as three days and nights, in disagreement with the Friday to Sunday tradition. N. Walker proposes to make the reference point the Sanhedrin condemnation on *Wednesday* morning, following the new Passion chronology ("After Three Days," *Novum Testamentum,* IV [1960], 261f.).

[20] Luke, however, has them relate their news to the incredulous disciples to whom their hysterical words seemed "an idle tale" (Luke 24:11). John holds that Peter and John were witnesses, with Mary Magdalene, of the vacant rock tomb (John 20:1–10; cf. Luke 24:12).

[21] As, for example, Amos M. Wilder, *Otherworldliness and the New Testament* (New York: Harper & Row, Publishers, 1954), p. 309. By contrast see H. F. Campenhausen, *Der Ablauf der Ostereignisse und das leere Grab,* 2nd ed. (Heidelberg: C. Winter, Universitätsverlag, 1958).

producing the corpse from its grave. That opponents were unable to counteract the apostolic preaching in this way is confirmed by the polemical charges that began to be circulated by the Jewish authorities. It was said that the disciples of Jesus had stolen the body by night from the tomb to deceive the people into believing the nonsensical claim that he had been quickened again to life and then had ascended into heaven.[22]

Hints of these charges are already found in the Gospel tradition. Matthew asserts that the chief priests bribed Roman guards to declare that Jesus' disciples stole his body while they were asleep (Matt. 28:11–15). Behind John's report that Mary Magdalene at first supposed that the gardener had secretly removed the body from its place, there is intimation of the rumors that soon began to circulate (John 20:15). It is of striking importance that Jewish antagonists never denied the claim that the tomb was empty. Instead they struck out against the apostolic claim that the body had been raised to life by charging that Galilean ghouls had desecrated and robbed the grave. John's detail of the spear thrust at the time of the crucifixion (19:34) may also be a refutation of Jewish gossip that Jesus had only swooned on the cross and later revived and gave himself out to be resurrected.[23] Whatever explanation may be given of the disappearance of the body from the tomb, the story is an inherent part of the testimony of the women who were numbered among the Galilean disciples.

The Evidential Value

What was the significance of the story of the empty tomb with its visionary details about angelic apparitions? Contrary to popular understanding, it was never considered to be the foundation of the Easter event nor the source of the Easter faith of the disciples. In and of itself the opened grave signified only one thing: the body of the crucified man had disappeared under mysterious circumstances—no more. Either the grave had been robbed or the whole thing was a case of mistaken identity. The Gospel records offer testimony that the immediate reaction of the women was not exuberant joy in the conviction that Jesus was actually alive, but rather trembling and astonishment. According to Mark they dared tell no one about the deserted

---

22 These rebuttals are reported by Justin Martyr (*Dial.* 108), Eusebius (*Comm. on Isaiah* 18:1), and Tertullian (*Spect.* 30). The medieval Jewish writing *Toledoth Jeshu* makes the same bitter allegation.

23 Cf. Origen, *Contra Celsum* II.55ff.

place. And with all Luke's disposition to recognize the position of women in the ministry of Jesus, he must still confess that the disciples gave no credence whatever to the story the women finally did confide (24:11).

Not upon any second-hand reports tendered by hysterical women, but only on the basis of the apostles' own experiences with the risen Lord, was the Easter gospel verified and declared. Only after the actual events of meeting was the empty tomb recognized as a *confirmation* of their conviction that he had been raised from the dead. It was the risen Christ who explained the empty sepulchre, not an empty sepulchre which explained the risen Christ.[24]

The Easter Revelation and the First Christians

Thus far, the comprehensive significance of the Easter experiences has only been partially reviewed. The inherent limitation of all discussions concerning the form of the appearances of Jesus to his disciples and friends is that at most they can only yield the conclusion that Jesus survived death and was believed to be alive. It is no different with support drawn from research in parapsychology. But the witness of the Easter gospel was not that Jesus' existence had been miraculously extended beyond the catastrophe of death. Early Christians did not talk of the risen Jesus as the return of a man from the dead in the way they spoke of Lazarus or John the Baptist. The testimony was rather that he had *overcome* death. The real meaning of the Easter faith for the early Church never was the self-centered intimation of immortality that it has so often been made out to be, nor the sentimental assurance that we live forever in the hearts of those whose lives we touch. First and foremost it was a theological statement about the true identity and the status of Jesus of Nazareth. The proper corollary of that was the resultant situation this posed for the man who so recognized him, a new situation shaped by forgiveness of sins, righteousness, and the promise of a wholly new life.

The Easter Faith

1. Let us begin with a rehearsal of what Easter signified for these first believers concerning their interpretation of the real identity of

[24] Michael Ramsey, *The Resurrection of Christ* (London: Geoffrey Bles, 1946), pp. 42–44, 71–73. For an alternate view of the story of the women and the empty tomb as an apologetic legend, see Rudolf Bultmann, *History of the Synoptic Tradition,* trans. John Marsh (New York: Harper & Row, Publishers, 1963), pp. 285, 290.

Jesus and the meaning of his mission. In what may be an early creedal summary to which Paul refers in the introduction to his Roman letter, we hear the candidate declare his faith. "[I believe] in the gospel concerning his Son, who was descended from David according to the flesh, and designated Son of God in power according to the Spirit of holiness by his resurrection from the dead" (Rom. 1:3f.). The one whom the nation had rejected as an apostate Jew and a bogus messiah was now hailed as the truly Elect One of God whose credentials were certified by these very events of death and resurrection.

In the earliest tradition no temporal or qualitative distinction was drawn between the resurrection and the exaltation. Asserting that Jesus had not remained subject to death but had received his life anew from God as the first of many brethren, these preachers declared in colorful mythological language that he had been "exalted to the right hand of the Father."[25] Demythologizing what C. S. Lewis describes as "the vertical ascent like a balloon, the local Heaven, the decorated chair to the right of the Father's throne,"[26] this is a declaration of his sovereignty over the whole world. "He must reign until he has put all his enemies under his feet" (I Cor. 15:25).

The uncertainty about Jesus' true identity and hence about the authority of his message was brought to an end for the disciples by the Easter event. He became for them the sign of God's reality in the world. He was certified as God's anointed, and the Kingdom kerygma that constituted his program was established thereby to be wholly authentic, "words of life" in the Johannine language. Now it became certain to them that unmeasured love, a forgiveness surpassing normal calculations, and a willingness above all else to search out and to do the Father's will constituted the conditions for entrance into the realm of God's rule. W. Grundmann summarizes this belief as follows:

> Since Jesus in the face of death continues to be one who receives life, since he continues in his death to be the poor man, the little man, the merciful man, the man hungering after righteousness, the man returning

---

[25] Luke 24:26; Acts 2:32f., 3:13; Eph. 1:20, 4:9f.; Phil. 2:8f.; I Tim. 3:16; I Pet. 3:21f.; *Gospel of Peter* 5, 13; *Barn.* 15:9. Probably Paul in Gal. 3:13 interprets the cross by Deut. 21:23 as a double reference to hanging and elevation (*talah*); H. J. Schoeps, *Paul,* trans. Harold Knight (Philadelphia: The Westminster Press, 1961), pp. 179f. A. M. Wilder finds in Acts 2:23f., 27; 3:13, a primitive conception of Christ "passing immediately from the Cross into his transcendent glory" ("Variant Traditions of the Resurrection in Acts," *Journal of Biblical Literature,* LXII [1943], 313).

[26] Clive Staples Lewis, *Miracles* (New York: The Macmillan Company, 1947), p. 177.

> a blessing for a curse, the man who loses his life, since this is the way he meets death, he fulfills his own preaching. To him belongs God's Kingdom; he is satisfied and obtains mercy and is named the Son of God. He gains life, and he is given authority to awaken this life now in others.[27]

2. If through this resurrection and exaltation Jesus had entered upon the functions of the Messiah, then this must mean that the messianic Kingdom had already begun. This is precisely the implicit theme of the earliest preaching. There is no Messiah who does not exercise a rule, and there is no ruling apart from a realm. The power of the Holy Spirit manifest in the early community, giving boldness to their witness, enabling the believers to stand before hostile authorities, creating and sustaining their community relationships—this divine Spirit is understood to be the authentic sign that the New Order had now commenced. The resurrection-exaltation had placed the believers in a new situation. The character of this new life—an indomitable joy, a newly found ability to return cursing with blessing, the satisfactions of an insatiable hunger for righteousness, the reconciling of enemies and the restoring of the fallen—was ascribed to the activity of the Spirit in their midst. This was the fulfillment of the prophetic promise that in the last time God would pour out his Spirit upon all flesh (Joel 2:28; Acts 2:16f.). And this Spirit was nothing other than the presence and continuing work of the risen and the reigning Lord, viewed subjectively. These early believers, secure in a hope of glory already experienced, were convinced that they were living in the first days of the "Kingdom of God's beloved Son" (Col. 1:13). Upon them the end of the ages had come, and a new age had begun.

It was, to be sure, marked by a continuation of the same life-and-death struggle between God's vicar and the powers of darkness in which Jesus had been engaged in his earthly ministry. Obviously it continued to be genuine historical existence despite what had happened in the resurrection. Life outwardly remained the same. Caiaphas still ruled the Great Court, the peasantry continued to be exploited, and Pilate had quickly forgotten the Galilean provincial he had ordered to death for subversive activity. Yet because of what had happened it was for the early Christians a history already invaded by that sovereign power that would ultimately purge it of its sinful character and make

---

27 Walter Grundmann, *Die Geschichte Jesu Christi* (Berlin: Evangelische Verlaganstalt, 1961), p. 356.

it new. Because of the decisive event of the resurrection it was a new kind of existence. They found that a blessedness could be wrung out of suffering, that health could replace illness and disease, and that men could actually find true life in self-denying service to other people.

3. Reflecting on the significance of the resurrection in relationship to this new God-filled and God-directed life, early Christians found evidence that the God who had raised Jesus from the dead had thereby dealt a decisive blow against the powers of sin and death. At any rate, sources of moral power had become available to meet the day's trials and temptations. Even death, that ancient threat to man's existence, had lost its power to chill his heart and paralyze his hand (I Cor. 15:54ff.; Heb. 2:14f.). The Destroyer himself had been rendered powerless.

"The last enemy to be destroyed is death," is Paul's own statement of a deep conviction of Jewish theology that regarded death as the consequence of man's betrayal of his true calling. On the deepest level, this death was a symbol of the futility of an existence estranged from its pristine destiny and antagonistic to the divine will. It was that negative existence which marked man as a "fallen" creature. Physical death, to which all human flesh is heir, was really external evidence of that inner threat to true existence that plagues all man's life in history. This is the basic conviction behind the association of sin and death in biblical thinking.

When Easter preaching declared that Christ was the victor over the enslaving powers of sin and death, it was to say that by submitting himself to the destructive power by which men try to kill the life from God, Jesus received again a new life from God, stronger than the spurious life from this world. He had despoiled that self-willed, prideful kind of existence that men in their ignorance call life, though it is actually a self-inflicted death. He showed that the only true life is that which comes from and moves toward God. The resurrection confirmed what had been conclusively demonstrated throughout the mission of Jesus. Jesus had never tried to manufacture his own life nor make it contingent upon the world of which he was a part, as though men were simply reflex actions of their environment. Rather he understood himself as one sent into the world at the behest of another, the *Abba*-God, and the strength and direction of all his living were received as gifts from him. The temptations that assailed him to secure political control, and the last and greatest temptation to refuse death and so escape the curse of destruction that angry men wanted to inflict upon him, were insidious invitations to succumb to the death-ridden life of this world.

To the Easter congregation, Christ, by submitting to the powers of sin and death and entering into that total negation of existence called death, had robbed them both of their tyranny over men. Change and disintegration were an established part of life in this world, but they were not fixed by an inexorable divine decree. The word of the resurrection was the glad word that God's ultimate intention was rather change and integration. God would "raise them up," as he had raised Christ, completely renewing their selfhood and accepting them into an indestructible relationship with him.

4. These restatements of the significance the Easter experience held for the way the disciples now understood Jesus and his mission already have pointed to their new self-understanding. They were simultaneously confessions about their own mission in the light of his. It had become clear to them that the fellowship broken before Jesus' execution by their own flight for safety before the arresting officers had been re-established through God's forgiveness. The broken community was now remade, and they made bold to describe themselves in daring terms like God's own people, a royal priesthood, the Body of Christ, the Church. They were God's gathering in Christ.

The group life they had already experienced as a part of the coterie of disciples which had been called together by the Galilean rabbi provided the model for this new community. Perhaps they were influenced in part by such groups as the *Haburoth,* or Pharisaic societies; perhaps, too, by the monastic community at Qumran. To have been a witness to the resurrection and to live now in responsive relationship to the risen Lord was to be drawn into a fellowship of believers who were God's own people of the New Age.

5. No form of Easter faith was sufficient, though, that did not sound a call to action and provoke a response. One is bound to notice that every one of the Gospels' stories of Easter include a summons to "Go, tell" in one form or another. He who was authorized by his own passage through death into life to awaken that new life in them had commissioned them to be his messengers to all men. As they had been forgiven and gathered together by the *Abba*-God, they were called to announce that same forgiveness to all who would listen. Matthew's concluding word of the risen Christ is the most familiar form of a missionary commission found in each of the accounts: "Go therefore

and make disciples of all nations" (28:19a; cf. Luke 24:44–49; John 20:19–23).

They now are to proclaim to men everywhere, Gentile and Jew, that man's true destiny can be realized only in preparing to enter the Kingdom of God to which they are called. The coming of the Gentiles, they believed with Jesus, would distinguish a new and final phase in the operation of the divine plan of redemption within the world. As that mission was carried out and the Gentiles turned in repentance to receive new life from God, the fulfillment of God's decision to effect a new creation would take place. The final consummation was near. Easter signified to them the divine command to continue and complete the mission, for they were the human agents whereby God was gathering the people of the world into one universal realm under his rule.[28] To the early Church the practical significance of Easter was both new life on a personal level and a mission of service to mankind, experienced as a single reality.

Toward a Restatement of the Easter Message

No aspect of the portrayal of Jesus in the Gospels occasions more incredulity, disagreement, or dissent among readers than the amazing claim of the early Christian community that God had raised Jesus from the dead. Explanations from both the debunkers and the credulous abound. What shall be concluded about the relevance of the Easter gospel to man's existence in this modern world? The answer to that question must necessarily implicate the single totality of Jesus' existence: birth, life, suffering, death, resurrection, and reign. The Easter event, we have suggested, is inseparable from and interpretive of the whole mission of Jesus.

The Problem of Language

We must consider anew the whole semantic problem. How is language to be understood, particularly religious language? Contemporary science assumes the necessity of devising patterns and building models as accurate symbolic representations of a real world to which they refer. Any language that comprehends and articulates man's basic understanding of who he is, where he has come from, and what is his destiny must of necessity be a language of parable. In these

---

28 On the universal mission see *supra*, Chapter VIII, pp. 197ff.

metaphors and mythologies there can be enshrined understandings about man, God, and the world, communicable in no other way.

Thus the task of the interpreter is not to eliminate the language of parable and symbol but to choose new mythic forms to express the biblical language and thought forms in ways that speak meaningfully to modern man.[29] If John is to be believed, it is a critical requirement that the parabolic forms become no end in themselves but the vehicle of hearing the authentic word of God spoken through them (John 5:24, 20:29). The resurrection story, no less than the entire mission of Jesus, is thus recognized to be a word spoken about God and about man, expressed in vivid pictorial language and directed to the crucial point of man's understanding of the real truth about who he is and what are the options presented to him for what he will be.

The Resurrection, a Statement About God

The Easter message is a word about God, a grand *Te Deum* that joyfully declares God is still master in his own household. It is of a piece with the Christmas kerygma that Jesus of Nazareth is the eschatological act of God taking place amidst human frailty and under the form of servant obedience. The fact of Jesus of Nazareth was the fact of the Father himself stepping out of his privacy into the public world of men and matter to identify himself and to make delinquent children into dutiful sons. The Easter gospel is the announcement that Jesus is the Father's own word spoken to men, that he is the Father's own deed performed for men. It amounts to this: the grand Lord of Heaven and earth is one who rules in intimate love and goodness, who proposes to bring about a full family relationship among his children, and who meets them in their barricaded isolation and draws them into companionship. It is to say that the God disclosed in this astonishing human life of Jesus is the God who reigns; on that account let the earth be glad. His kingship is not autocratic nor arbitrary power, but responsible care for the health and safety of his creation.

---

[29] On the problem of theological language see Amos M. Wilder, *The Language of the Gospel* (New York: Harper & Row, Publishers, 1964); William Hordern, *Speaking of God* (New York: The Macmillan Company, 1964); Samuel Laeuchli, *The Language of Faith* (New York: Abingdon Press, 1962); T. R. Miles, *Religion and the Scientific Outlook* (London: George Allen & Unwin, 1959); and the debate on demythologizing the New Testament message in the two volumes edited by H. W. Bartsch, *Kerygma and Myth,* trans. Reginald H. Fuller (London: SPCK, 1953, 1962).

The Resurrection, a Statement About Man

The word spoken about God, however, is at the same time a word spoken about man. For these early preachers, Easter was never a purely historical event to be contemplated in detachment, nor was it simply a theological persuasion. It represented something that was happening to them, something that was opening up for them a totally new life. To believe that Christ was raised from death to real life was to testify that men are also raised with him out of death into a life of durative value beyond this present ephemeral existence.

The biblical categories of body, mind, life, and death embrace a conception of man as a total unitary being who either lives out of the emptiness of false existence or the fullness of true existence. The intolerant claim of the New Testament is that there is no authentic living that is not life in relationship to the One acknowledged to be the Maker and Master of his being. To live with God now is to move out of graceless subsistence into graceful existence. The cheerful sadness that pervades much human living is interpreted by Jesus to be the condition of man in his tragic isolation from the Father-God. It is death, both self-chosen and inescapable, that holds dominion over his life, however much he boasts of his freedom to enjoy *la dolce vita.* "Would that even today you knew the things that make for peace! But now they are hid from your eyes" (Luke 19:42).

It is the word of the crucifixion-resurrection to that man that life lived from the world is death; life lived from God alone is genuine life. No one reasonably denies the multifarious maladjustments of man's life in this world. He is the victim of disease and suffering, of inner conflict between the drive to self-affirmation and the acceptance of his own creatureliness. At the end the rubber stamp of death writes Void upon his existence. Despite all this, Easter faith asserts the possibility of a new kind of living wherein men, without escaping from the world, are saved from being destroyed by it.

Here, then, are the claims that the New Testament writers believe to be endemic to the history of Jesus of Nazareth. The most our research into the lifework of Jesus can essay is to set out with reasonable accuracy his essential understandings of the God-man-world relationship and to illuminate the faith of his earliest followers by tracing the impact he made upon them. It remains to be said, however, that the New Testament writers unite with one voice to declare that the coming of God in this life is addressed to the deepest problems of human living; hence they urge that the decision the reader makes to this eschatological message is of the greatest possible moment and urgency. They ask, as faith continues to ask, whether *we* believe that he is the very Son of God who died for us and rose from the dead to arouse in us a lively hope. With that forthright question our task is done and the reader's is begun, for this is now a challenge addressed to the conscience of the hearer. But it is a fair observation that only when the word he speaks is heard as the word of truth about the God whose coming he celebrates that we shall ever really know who he is and what his mission means.

SUBJECT INDEX

INDEX OF PRINCIPAL REFERENCES

New Testament

Gospel of Thomas

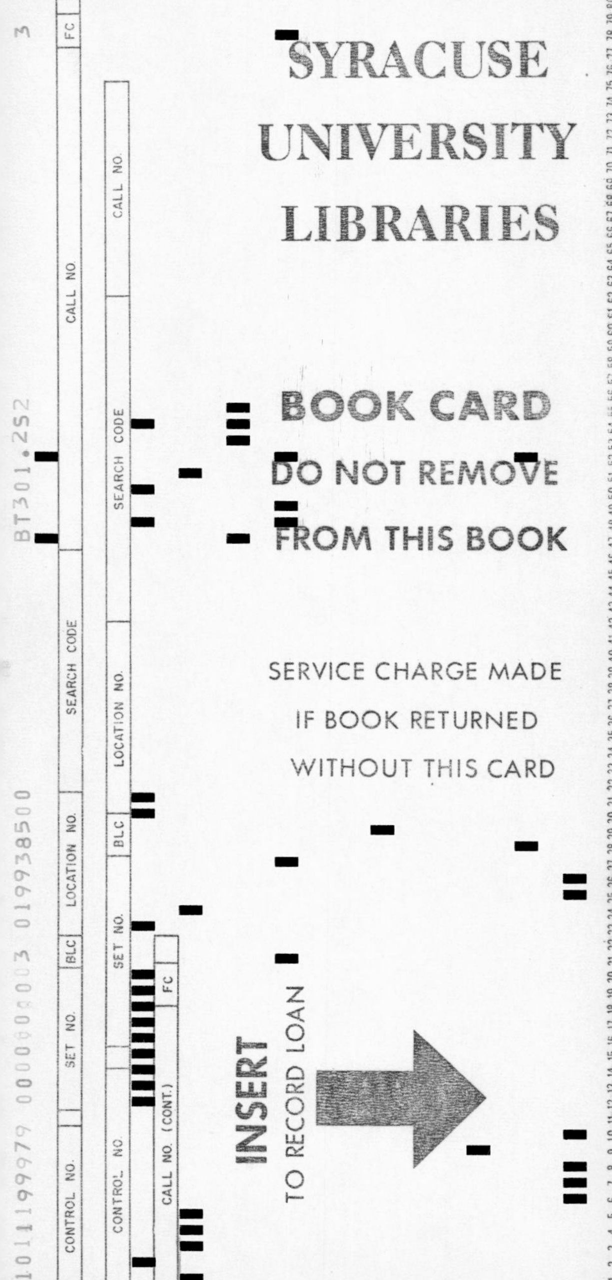
SYRACUSE
UNIVERSITY
LIBRARIES
BOOK CARD
DO NOT REMOVE
FROM THIS BOOK
SERVICE CHARGE MADE
IF BOOK RETURNED
WITHOUT THIS CARD
INSERT
TO RECORD LOAN
CONTROL NO.
SET NO.
BLC
LOCATION NO.
SEARCH CODE
CALL NO.
FC
CALL NO. (CONT.)
1011199979 0000000003 019938500
BT301.2S2
3

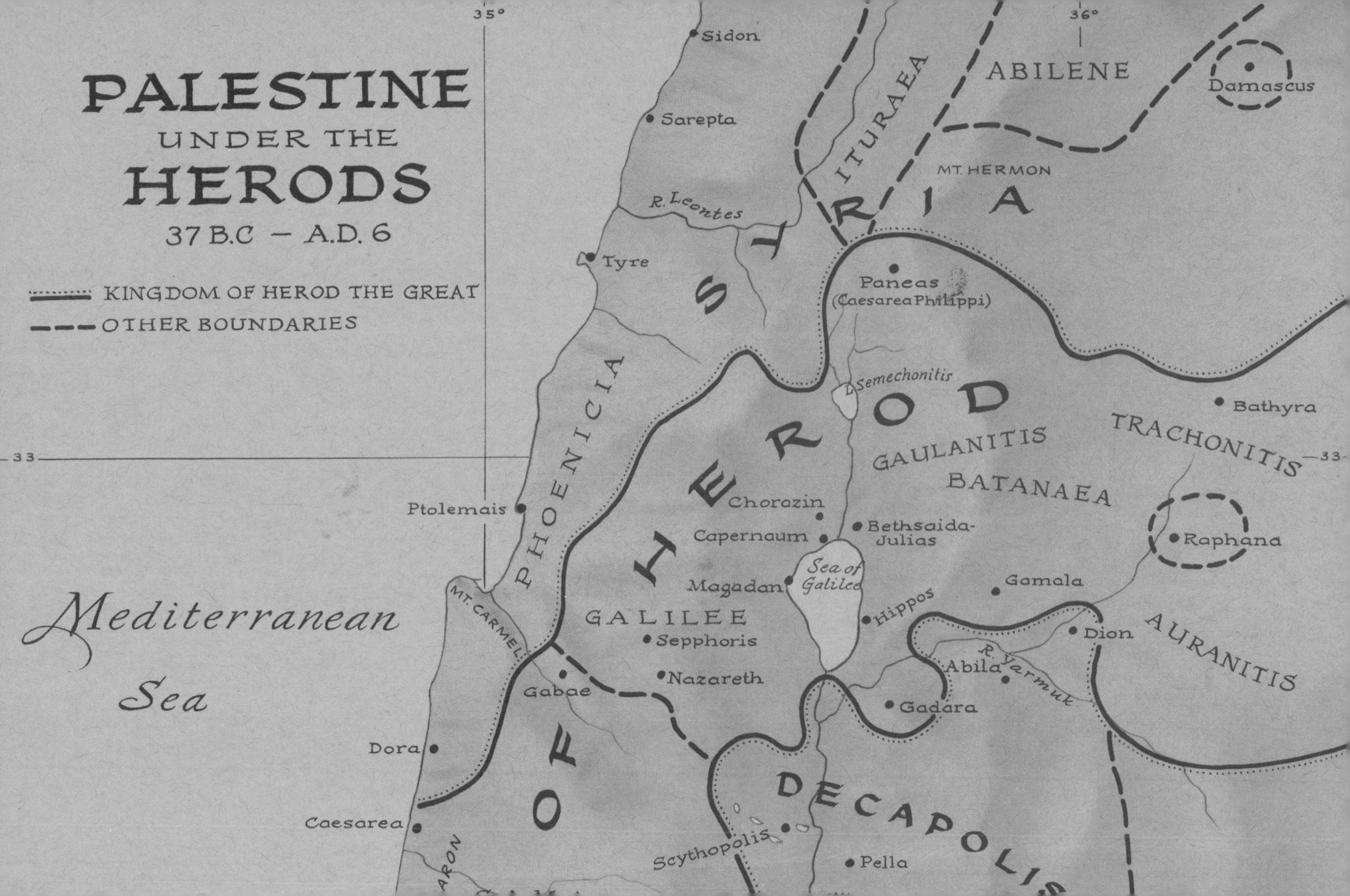
PALESTINE
UNDER THE
HERODS
37 B.C – A.D. 6
KINGDOM OF HEROD THE GREAT
OTHER BOUNDARIES
Mediterranean
Sea
35°
36°
33
33
Sidon
Sarepta
R. Leontes
Tyre
ITURAEA
ABILENE
Damascus
MT. HERMON
SYRIA
Paneas
(Caesarea Philippi)
L. Semechonitis
HEROD
PHOENICIA
Ptolemais
MT. CARMEL
GALILEE
Chorazin
Capernaum
Magadan
Sea of Galilee
Sepphoris
Nazareth
Gabae
Dora
Caesarea
OF
GAULANITIS
BATANAEA
Bethsaida-Julias
Gamala
Hippos
Bathyra
TRACHONITIS
Raphana
AURANITIS
Dion
Abila
R. Yarmuk
Gadara
DECAPOLIS
Scythopolis
Pella